LIFE HISTORIES
OF NORTH AMERICAN
DIVING BIRDS

by Arthur Cleveland Bent

DOVER PUBLICATIONS, INC.
NEW YORK

Published in Canada by General Publishing Company, Ltd., 30 Lesmill Road, Don Mills, Toronto, Ontario.
Published in the United Kingdom by Constable and Company, Ltd., 10 Orange Street, London WC2H 7EG.

This Dover edition, first published in 1986, is a republication of the 1963 Dover edition, an unabridged and unaltered republication of the work first published by the United States Government Printing Office in 1919 as Smithsonian Institution United States National Museum *Bulletin 107*.
Plates 44 through 55, which were reproduced in color in the 1919 edition, are reproduced in black and white in this edition.

Manufactured in the United States of America
Dover Publications, Inc., 31 East 2nd Street, Mineola, N.Y. 11501

Library of Congress Cataloging in Publication Data

Bent, Arthur Cleveland, 1866–1954.
Life histories of North American diving birds.

Reprint. Originally published: Washington : G.P.O., 1919 (Bulletin / United States National Museum ; 107)
Bibliography: p.
Includes index.
1. Divers (Birds)—North America. 2. Birds—North America.
I. Title.
QL681.B517   1986   598'.33097   85-31546
ISBN 0-486-25095-4 (pbk.)

ADVERTISEMENT.

The scientific publications of the United States National Museum consist of two series, the *Proceedings* and the *Bulletins*.

The *Proceedings*, the first volume of which was issued in 1878, are intended primarily as a medium for the publication of original, and usually brief, papers based on the collections of the National Museum. presenting newly-acquired facts in zoology, geology, and anthropology, including descriptions of new forms of animals, and revisions of limited groups. One or two volumes are issued annually and distributed to libraries and scientific organizations.. A limited number of copies of each paper, in pamphlet form, is distributed to specialists and others interested in the different subjects as soon as printed. The date of publication is recorded in the tables of contents of the volumes.

The *Bulletins*, the first of which was issued in 1875, consist of a series of separate publications comprising chiefly monographs of large zoological groups and other general systematic treatises (occasionally in several volumes), faunal works, reports of expeditions, and catalogues of type-specimens, special collections, etc. The majority of the volumes are octavos, but a quarto size has been adopted in a few instances in which large plates were regarded as indispensable.

Since 1902 a series of octavo volumes containing papers relating to the botanical collections of the Museum, and known as the *Contributions from the National Herbarium*, has been published as bulletins.

The present work forms No. 107 of the *Bulletin* series.

WILLIAM deC. RAVENEL,
Administrative Assistant to the Secretary,
In charge of the United States National Museum.

WASHINGTON, D. C.

INTRODUCTION.

The monumental work undertaken and so ably begun by Maj. Charles E. Bendire has remained unfinished, and no additional volumes have been published since his death. In 1910 the author undertook to continue the work and began to gather material for it with the cooperation of American ornithologists. The following well-known ornithologists offered to help in gathering material from their several sections of the country: Harold H. Bailey, Walter B. Barrows, Allan Brooks, Earle A. Brooks, William L. Finley, Benjamin T. Gault, A Brazier Howell, Lynds Jones, Elmer T. Judd, Charles R. Keyes, Arthur H. Norton, Putnam B. Peabody, T. Gilbert Pearson, Charles J. Pennock, Walter W. Perrett, Samuel F. Rathbun, Thomas S. Roberts, Aretas A. Saunders, William E. Saunders, Witmer Stone, Myron H. Swenk, Charles W. Townsend, Edward R. Warren, and Arthur T. Wayne.

The Biological Survey of the Department of Agriculture, at Washington, very kindly placed at my disposal its matchless bibliographical index to published material on North American birds, and a mass of references were carefully copied by Mr. Edward A. Preble. With this and the author's private index as guides nearly every publication of importance relating to North American birds has been consulted.

While the scope of the work was originally intended to cover substantially the same ground covered by Maj. Bendire's work and in practically the same manner, it has since seemed best to somewhat enlarge its scope and to cover more ground, with the different phases of the life histories arranged in a more definite and uniform sequence, so that the reader may more readily find the parts in which he is interested.

The classification and nomenclature adopted by the American Ornithologists' Union in its Check List have been strictly followed, regardless of the author's views on the status of certain species and subspecies; as this is not a work on systematic ornithology, it has seemed best to merely refer to these views briefly in the text and not attempt to discuss them fully.

The main breeding and winter ranges are as accurately outlined as limited space will permit; the normal migrations are given in sufficient detail to indicate the usual movements of each species; it is obviously impossible to give, in a general work of such large scope, all records of occurrence and all dates and no pretense at perfection in this direction is claimed. Many published records, impossible to either verify or disprove, have been accepted if they are apparently within the known limits of ranges.

The nesting dates are the condensed results of a mass of records accumulated from the data in over 60 of the largest egg collections in the country, as well as from contributed field notes and from many published sources. They indicate the dates on which eggs have been actually found in one or more portions of the breeding range of the species, showing the earliest and latest dates and the limits between which at least half of the dates fall. The names of colors, when in quotation marks, are taken from Ridgway's Color Standards and Nomenclature (1912 edition) and the terms used to designate the shapes of eggs, when in quotation marks, are taken from Ridgway's Nomenclature of Colors (1886 edition). The heavy-faced type in the measurements of eggs indicate the four extremes of measurement.

After a few introductory remarks where these seem desirable, the life history of each species is written in substantially the following sequence: Spring migration, courtship, nesting habits, eggs, young, sequence of plumages to maturity, seasonal molts, feeding habits, flight, swimming and diving habits, vocal powers, behavior, enemies, fall migration, and winter habits. An attempt has been made to avoid repetition in dealing with subspecies.

Although preference has been given to original unpublished material, so little of this has been received that it has seemed best to quote freely from published material whenever the life history could be improved by so doing. The author does not guarantee the correctness of any statements quoted, but has selected only such as seem to be reliable. Quotations from or references to published matter are indicated by a date in parentheses after the author's name and the reference may be found by turning to the bibliographical index at the end of each part.

Acknowledgments are due to many who have helped to make the work a success, by contributions and by sympathetic encouragement. Dr. Louis B. Bishop has contributed many hours of careful work in collecting from published material and other sources a mass of data needed for the distributional part of this work and has helped to tabulate and arrange it. He has also been very helpful to the author in his studies of plumages and has helped and encouraged him in many ways. Dr. Charles W. Townsend has furnished a lot of original contributions, has read over and corrected much of the manuscript and has written the entire life histories of the puffin and the great auk, in this part, and a number of others to be published in subsequent parts. Rev. F. C. R. Jourdain has sent us a valuable lot of egg measurements collected from eggs in the British Museum and in other foreign collections. Mr. J. H. Fleming has carefully revised and made valuable additions to the distributional part of the work. Miss Marie H. Manseau rendered much valuable assistance in the preliminary work of reading and indexing published matter and in copying manuscript.

The following American collectors have sent measurements of eggs in their collections: G. A. Abbott, R. M. Barnes, J. L. Childs, W. L. Dawson, C. S. Day, D. R. Dickey, C. E. Doe, J. H. Flanagan, F. S. Hersey, A. B. Howell, A. M. Ingersoll, Lieut. G. R. Meyer, J. P. Norris, jr., L. G. Peyton, J. H. Riley, R. P. Sharples, J. E. Thayer, and F. C. Willard.

A great mass of nesting data has been contributed by practically all of those in the foregoing list and the following: E. Arnold; Egbert Bagg; L. B. Bishop; B. S. Bowdish; J. H. Bowles; W. C. Bradbury; A. W. Brockway; D. E. Brown; F. L. Burns; E. A. Butler; V. Burtch; J. P. Callender; H. W. Carriger; W. L. Chambers; D. A. Cohen; F. M. Dille; H. F. Duprey; O. Durfee; E. R. Ford; N. A. Francis; B. T. Gault; Geological Survey of Canada; I. C. Hall; H. S. Hathaway; R. G. Hazard; L. M. Huey; H. K. Job; E. M. Kenworthy; C. R. Keyes; J. and J. W. Mailliard; T. E. Mc-Mullen; Museum of History, Science, and Art, Los Angeles, California; A. H. Norton; T. D. Perry; P. B. Philipp; E. F. Pope; A. E. Price; A. G. Prill; Provincial Museum, Victoria, British Columbia; J. B. Purdy; S. F. Rathbun; M. S. Ray; R. B. Rockwell; G. R. Rossignol, jr.; D. I. Shepardson; W. E. Snyder; F. Stephens; C. F. Stone; W. S. Strode; C. S. Thompson; A. O. Treganza; J. G. Tyler; University of California; A. Walker; E. R. Warren; A. T. Wayne; B. G. Willard; W. C. Wood; A. D. Dubois; I. E. Hess; A. R. Hoare; A. W. Honywill, jr.; L. B. Potter; H. J. Rust; S. S. S. Stansell; and J. Williams.

Contributions of notes on habits or distribution have been received from the following: F. H. Allen, R. M. Anderson, B. W. Arnold, R. M. Barnes, W. S. Brooks, E. S. Cameron, Frank S. Daggett, W. L. Dawson, Elizabeth Dickens, A. C. Dyke, C. W. G. Eifrig, W. O. Emerson, J. D. Figgins, W. L. Finley, G. L. Fordyce, C. A. Gianini, Jos. Grinnell, R. C. Harlow, W. F. Henninger, A. B. Howell, L. M. Huey, Lynds Jones, L. S. Kohler, H. Lacey, W. deW. Miller, P. B. Peabody, C. H. Pease, E. F. Pope, R. B. Rockwell, A. A. Saunders, Mary C. Schanck, F. A. Shaw, F. Stephens, Cecile Swale, M. H. Swenk, P. A. Taverner, W. E. C. Todd, C. W. Townsend, M. B. Townsend, J. G. Tyler, W. L. Underwood, E. R. Warren, and L. E. Wyman.

The following have contributed photographs: American Museum of Natural History, R. M. Anderson, Bird-Lore, W. S. Brooks, E. S. Cameron, The Condor, W. L. Dawson, D. R. Dickey, W. E. Ekblaw, W. L. Finley, Francis Harper, H. K. Job, Lynds Jones, F. E. Kleinschmidt, D. B. MacMillan, C. F. Stone, J. E. Thayer, C. H. Townsend, and Alex. Walker. All such photographs which have been used have been marked with the name of the photographer.

In the study of molts and plumages free access has been given to the collections of the American Museum of Natural History, the Biological Survey, the California Academy of Sciences, the Museum of Comparative Zoology, the United States National Museum, the University of California, and the private collections of Louis B. Bishop, William Brewster, Jonathan Dwight, and John E. Thayer. Specimens for study have also been loaned by Louis B. Bishop, William L. Finley, the Geological Survey of Canada, F. Seymour Hersey, Lawrence M. Huey, and P. A. Taverner. The conclusions arrived at regarding molts and plumages are based on a careful study of all this material, but even that great mass of material proved lamentably insufficient in many cases to arrive at entirely satisfactory conclusions.

Mr. Charles E. Doe has kindly loaned us an egg of the whiskered auklet, and Col. John E. Thayer an egg of the Kittlitz's murrelet for use in making the illustrations.

We are also indebted to the officials of the following institutions for a mass of data, taken from specimens in their collections, which has been useful in working out distributions and migrations: Biological Survey, California Academy of Sciences, Carnegie Museum, Colorado Museum of Natural History, Geological Survey of Canada, United States National Museum, and University of California.

With the consent of the American Museum of Natural History and Mr. Donald B. MacMillan, Mr. W. Elmer Ekblaw has sent us a full report of the ornithological results of the Crocker Land expedition. This generous contribution has enabled us to publish much new and interesting information regarding arctic bird life in advance of their own plans for future publication. For this exceptional courtesy my readers and I are very grateful. Furthermore, the American Museum of Natural History has kindly placed at our disposal the entire collection of bird photographs made by members of this expedition, from which we have selected what we wanted to use. I am therefore indebted to them for the use of all photographs taken by Mr. MacMillan and Mr. Ekblaw.

Much of the merit in the work is due to the untiring efforts of the author's valued assistant, Mr. F. Seymour Hersey, who has spent many months in the field, often in remote localities, gathering specimens, photographs, and notes for use in this work. The distributional part of the work was practically all done by him, with what assistance Doctor Bishop and the author could give him. No one who has not done work of this kind can appreciate the mass of detail to be handled and the expert knowledge necessary to handle it properly.

Finally, thanks are due to the author's devoted wife, Madeleine V. Bent, for many weary hours of painstaking work in typewriting, reading, and correcting manuscript and in proof reading.

No one is so well aware of the many shortcomings and omissions in this work as the author. Allowance must be made for the magnitude of the undertaking. If the reader fails to find mentioned in these pages some things which he knows about the birds, he can blame himself for not having sent them to

THE AUTHOR.

TABLE OF CONTENTS.

CONTENTS.

LIFE HISTORIES OF NORTH AMERICAN DIVING BIRDS, ORDER PYGOPODES.

By ARTHUR CLEVELAND BENT,
of Taunton, Massachusetts.

Family COLYMBIDÆ. Grebes.

ÆCHMOPHORUS OCCIDENTALIS (Lawrence).

WESTERN GREBE.

HABITS.

Where the sweet waters of Bear Creek empty into Crane Lake the bare shores of a somewhat alkaline lake are transformed into a verdant slough of tall waving bulrushes surrounding a small grassy island overgrown with scattering patches of wild rose bushes, a green oasis of luxuriant vegetation in the waste of bare rolling plains of southwestern Saskatchewan. Here is the gem of all that wonderful bird country, the center of abundance of breeding wildfowl; at least such was the case in 1905 when we found 25 species of water birds nesting in great profusion within an area less than a mile square, as if all had been crowded together in the most favorable locality. On the island we found 61 ducks' nests in a few hours' search, representing 8 species; and in the slough surrounding it canvasbacks, redheads, and ruddy ducks were nesting among the bulrushes and cattails. Numerous noisy shore birds were flying about, avocets, killdeers, long-billed curlews, and marbled godwits. Overhead were floating the characteristic gulls of the region, California and ringbilled gulls, common terns, and the beautiful rosy breasted Franklin's gulls. But it was in the slough itself, amid the constant din of countless yellow-headed blackbirds, that we found the subject of this sketch with a few of its lesser brethren, the eared and the horned grebes, seeking seclusion in the winding aisles of water among the tallest bulrushes and cat-tails. I shall never forget the picture, as I stood in water more than waist deep, of one of these beautiful " swan grebes " sailing out from a dense wall of cat-tails, causing scarcely a ripple as it glided along, the body submerged, the long white neck

1

sharply outlined against the green background, the glossy black crown, the fiery red eyes, and the javelin-like beak. Who could help admiring such a picture of aquatic grace, such specialized mastery of its native element? Its delicately poised head was ever alert, its keen red eyes were watching every motion and, as I moved one step nearer, the graceful neck was arched, the javelin beak plunged downward, and the slim body followed in a curve below the surface, leaving scarcely any wake behind it. The water was clear and I was near enough to follow its course as it sped away beneath the surface a long slender pointed craft, propelled by two powerful paddles and with wings tightly closed. The western grebe is certainly a water nymph of the first class, built for speed and action, the most highly specialized of all our diving birds.

Courtship.—The western grebes reach their breeding grounds in the inland lakes during May, early in the month in North Dakota, about May 8 to 12 in southern Canada, and before the end of the month farther north. I have never witnessed their nuptial performances, but Mr. William L. Finley has sent me the following notes on the subject:

The first action, which I have often noticed during the nesting season of the grebe, is when the two birds swim side by side. They throw the head and neck back which gives one the impression at a distance that the birds are preening their plumage. When I saw the action near at hand, I noticed that each bird arched its neck continually, the bill turned straight down and the black crest spread. At the same time, both birds curved and swayed their necks back in a rythmical manner, touching them against their bodies. It was like a backward bow.

A second performance, the water glide of the grebe, was not as common as the antics just mentioned. However, it seemed to be a climax to the performance above. As the two birds swam side by side both suddenly stood upright as if walking on the top of the water and rushed along, splashing the surface for 20 or 30 feet, with wings tight to the body. Then they dropped to their breasts in a graceful glide that carried them along for about 15 feet farther.

The third performance might well be termed purely a wedding dance. I saw it three times within close range, and each time it was exactly the same. As two birds were swimming together, both dove. They rose to the top of the water a few moments later, each holding a piece of moss or weed in the bill. Instantly they faced each other and rose, treading water, with bodies half above the surface and necks stretched straight up. They treaded around, breast to breast, until they made three or four circles, and then dropped down to a normal attitude, at the same time flirting the moss out of their mouths and swimming off in an unconcerned manner.

The first two performances are typical mating or courting antics, while the last is the most significant wedding dance I have ever seen in bird life.

Nesting.—The Crane Lake colony, referred to above, was a typical, large colony of the plains or prairie region. I visited this colony two years in succession and made several trips into the slough each season. It was almost impossible to count or even to estimate the number of western grebes in this colony, for the nests were scattered over a wide area among the reeds or bulrushes (*Scirpus lacustris*), and many of them were beyond our reach in water too deep to wade; there were certainly hundreds, and perhaps over a thousand of them. The nests were floating in water 2 feet deep or more and consisted of compact masses of rubbish, dead and rotten reeds, mixed with a few green flags, and plastered with soft slimy vegetable substances. They were generally anchored to growing bulrushes in plain sight, but some were well concealed from view in thick clumps. They were built up from 3 to 5 inches above the water and measured from 18 to 25 inches in diameter, the inner cavity being from 7 to 9 inches in diameter. We were surprised to find the bodies of a large number of these grebes lying dead on or near their nests, during both seasons, and were unable to account for it; sometimes two bodies were found at one nest. Muskrats were quite common in this slough, and a pair of minks had a den on the island; perhaps the latter may have indulged in a midnight massacre. In another deep-water slough, near Crane Lake, we found a small colony of 12 or 15 pairs of western grebes nesting among the cat-tail flags (*Typha latifolia*), where the nests were often well concealed in thick clumps.

Although they were not so shy and retiring about their breeding grounds as the other grebes, I was never able to surprise a western grebe on its nest until one cold, rainy day when I waded into the slough and saw the birds sliding off their nests all around me, swimming away almost under my feet and bobbing up unexpectedly near me; the sun came out soon afterwards and I longed for my camera; I tried to repeat the experience later but never succeeded. Apparently they sit more closely in wet weather, but under favorable circumstances do not find it necessary. Evidently both sexes assist in incubation. They seldom, if ever, cover the eggs with the nesting material as other grebes do. I once flushed a female ruddy duck from a clump of bulrushes, but a careful search revealed nothing but grebes' nests and later I took from a grebe's nest two eggs of the western grebe and an egg of the ruddy duck. The smaller grebes also occasionally lay an egg in a western grebe's nest.

In North Dakota the western grebes breed abundantly in some of the sweet-water lakes, generally in deep water and often among the tall canes and wild rice which grows 8 or 10 feet high. The extensive marshes of tall canes (*Phragmites communis*) bordering the Waterhen River in Manitoba form a safe and almost inaccessible breeding resort for this species where large numbers find a congenial summer home. The water in these marshes is too deep to wade and the canes are so thick that it is almost impossible to push a canoe through them. The few nests that we found were near the edges of small ponds or channels and well concealed in the thick growth; the nests were large and well-made structures of dry, dead canes, 2 or 3 feet in diameter and built up 6 or 7 inches above the water.

The large grebe colonies of the Klamath Lake region in southern Oregon and northern California have been described by several well-known writers. The lakes in this region contain probably the largest western grebe colonies in this country where thousands of them breed in harmony with Caspian and Forster's terns, white pelicans, and other water birds. This region has long been famous as a profitable field for plume hunters, where they have reaped a rich harvest, making $20 or $30 a day and during the height of the breeding season killing several thousand birds a week. The breasts of the western and other grebes were in great demand for the millinery trade; for the paltry sum of 20 cents apiece they were stripped off, dried, and shipped to New York. Such slaughter could not have continued much longer without disastrous results. Through the activities of the Audubon Societies, the attention of President Roosevelt was called to the need of protection, and on August 8, 1908, he set apart the Klamath Lake Reservation, and on August 18, 1908, the Lake Malheur Reservation, thus saving from destruction the largest and most interesting wild-fowl nurseries on the Pacific coast. Mr. W. L. Finley (1907a) has enjoyed good opportunities for studying the western grebes in these colonies and writes thus interestingly of their habits:

Lower Klamath Lake is a body of water about 25 miles long by 10 or 12 miles wide. About its sides are great marshes of tules. The whole border is a veritable jungle, extending out for several miles from the main shore is an almost endless area of floating tule islands, between which is a network of channels. Here, where we found the nesting colony of western grebes, we had good chances to study the habits of these birds.

About one of these islands we found the floating grebe nests every few feet apart, and counted over 60 in a short distance. We rowed up to one end and landed and then waded along just inside the thick growth of tules that grew along the edge. From this place partly concealed as we were, we could look through the tules and see the grebes swimming and diving near their nests. Across the channel along the edge of the opposite island were many more grebe nests, and some of the birds were sitting on their eggs.

The nests of the western grebes were, as a rule, built up of dry reeds higher out of the water than those of the eared grebe. I never saw a case where this bird covered its eggs with reeds before leaving them. Many times we saw them sitting on their eggs during the day. In other cases, they seemed to leave the eggs to be hatched out partly by the sun. The usual number of eggs we found in a set were 3 and 4, although we often found 6 and 7. In several cases, we found places among the dry tules where an extra large set of eggs had been laid. We saw 16 eggs in one set, but there had been no attempt at a nest, and the eggs had never been incubated.

Eggs.—The number of eggs to a set seems to vary greatly, though 3 or 4 seems to be the usual number, according to my experience; I have frequently found 5 or even 6, and I have taken one set of 11, but this was probably laid by 2 or 3 birds. Other writers report various numbers from 5 to 10. Apparently there are certain nests in which eggs are dumped indiscriminately by several birds, but never hatched. Other marsh-nesting birds, such as terns, ducks, and coots, occasionally drop their eggs in the grebes' nests.

The eggs of the western grebe are not handsome and not particularly interesting. They vary in color from dull bluish white or cream color to various shades of dirty buff or olive buff. They are unspotted, but the accumulated dirt on the rough shells often gives them a mottled effect, even after being washed. They are generally more or less nest-stained and are often plastered with mud or covered with bits of nesting material. The shell surface is always dull and lusterless and sometimes lumpy. In shape they vary from " elliptical ovate " to "cylindrical ovate." The measurements of 53 eggs in the United States National Museum average 58 by 37.5 millimeters; the eggs showing the four extremes measures **65** by 37.5, 61.5 by **40,** and **50** by **34** millimeters.

Young.—The period of incubation is about 23 days. In Saskatchewan I have found downy young, recently hatched, as early as June 8, but the majority of eggs do not hatch until the last of June or early in July of that region. The young are graceful little fellows with long necks and small heads; they are quite precocious and they can swim and dive soon after they are hatched. Mr. Finley (1907*a*) writes in regard to them:

On two or three different occasions, we watched one of the little western grebes cut his way out of the shell and liberate himself. The wall of his prison is quite thick for a chick to penetrate, but after he gets his bill though in one place, he goes at the task like clockwork and it only takes him about half an hour after he has smelled the fresh air to liberate himself. After the first hole, he turns himself a little and begins hammering in a new place and he keeps this up till he has made a complete revolution in his shell, and the end or cap of the egg, cut clear around, drops off, and the youngster soon kicks himself out into the sunshine. It does not take his coat long to dry; in fact, he often does not give it a chance, for his first impulse seems to be to take to water and ride on his mother's or father's back. The grebe chick never stays in the nest longer than a few hours. A chick that is just hatched is clothed in the most delicate coat of soft gray fur, lighter below and darker on top.

The first day, as I lay hidden in the tules waiting for a picture, I saw a pair of grebes swimming along only 20 feet distant. I could catch glimpses of them as they passed just beyond their nest. One of the birds carried a chick on its back. The grebes have a way of taking their young with them, for the little fellows lie on the back just under the wing coverts with only their heads sticking out. At the slightest alarm the mother raises the feathers a trifle and covers the chick completely. One can readily tell when a grebe has a chick on her back even if it is not visible, because she generally swims higher in the water.

As I was lying low in the reeds, another pair of grebes swam past. The back of the one bird was high out of the water. She was carrying two young, but at the time neither was visible. But soon one of the youngsters got anxious to crawl out on the hurricane deck, as it were. Each time his head appeared, the mother would reach back and cover him up. Finally one of the little fellows crawled clear out in full view and she let him sit there for a moment. But I could see this was not the customary way of riding, for she soon raised her wing and covered him. Occasionally she picked up bits of something from the surface and reaching back fed her babies. A little later, while the father was swimming near by, I saw one chick slip off the mother's back and go paddling toward him. He seemed to lower his body slightly in the water and the youngster floated aboard.

The old grebes dive and swim readily under water with the young on their backs, but occasionally when they are frightened they lose their chicks. Several times while we were rowing about the lake we came unexpectedly upon old grebes carrying young. At such times, when the old birds are scared, it seems very difficult for them to hold the chicks in place when they dive. In most cases the young birds come to the top of the water after the mother dives. When we approached the little fellows they tried to dive, but could not stay under long or go very deep, so they were easily caught.

Plumages.—The downy young of the western grebe is entirely different from the young of any other American grebe; its plain, unspotted coat suggests a closer relationship with the loons than with the other grebes. It is covered with short, thick down, as soft and smooth as silk velvet. The upper parts are " light mouse gray " in color, darkest on the back, lighter on the crown and shading off to " pallid mouse gray " on the neck and sides and almost to pure white on the belly; there is a triangular naked spot on the crown. The young grebe retains its soft downy covering as it increases in size, and it is nearly fully grown before its first real plumage is assumed. There is no distinctive juvenal plumage, and the first winter plumage is not strikingly different from that of the adult. The young bird in the fall is dark gray or dusky instead of black on the crown and hind neck; the line of demarcation is not so sharply drawn between the dark crown and the white throat, and the feathers of the back are edged with grayish white. A partial prenuptial molt in the spring produces the black crown of the nuptial plumage and the light edgings on the back disappear by wear. In this first nuptial plumage adults and young are practically indistinguishable.

The seasonal changes of the adult are not conspicuous, for the fall plumage is much like the nuptial plumage; the black of the crown is duller and less clearly defined in the fall. There is a complete postnuptial molt in July and August, during which the wing quills are all shed simultaneously and the bird becomes incapable of flight. A partial prenuptial molt, involving mainly the head and neck, produces the nuptial plumage.

Food.—Very little seems to be known about the food of the western grebe, but it probably lives largely on fish and other aquatic animals. Prof. John Macoun (1909) mentions a specimen "that had an amphibian (*Amblystoma navortium*) 10½ inches long in its stomach." It has been known to feed on aquatic grasses, and on the seacoast it pursues the schools of small herring. It has a peculiar habit, which has never been satisfactorily explained, of filling its stomach with great wads of its own body feathers. Dr. Frank M. Chapman (1908) says on this subject:

Possibly the adults may swallow the feathers secured through their frequent preening, but I am at loss to understand why chicks not more than 3 days old should have their stomachs tightly stuffed with a ball of their parents feathers. In the stomach of one I found a compact wad of 238 feathers, and in another there were no less than 331.

Behavior.—This grebe, like others of its family, experiences considerable difficulty in rising from the water, but when once under way it is a strong and rapid flyer. It is a curious looking bird in flight, with its long neck and slender body stretched out in a straight line, with big feet dragging behind and small wings vibrating at high speed. It could not be mistaken for anything else, for it is in a class by itself. Col. N. S. Goss (1889) writes:

The birds ride the water lightly, and their silky plumage, slender build, long-waving necks, and graceful carriage can but attract the attention of the most indifferent of observers. Like all of the race they are expert swimmers and divers, and can quietly sink out of sight in the water without an apparent motion, but their ordinary manner of diving is to spring forward with a stroke of their feet, almost clearing the water and disappearing about 3 feet from the starting point. They are at home on the waves, and it is almost impossible to force the birds to take wing, but when in the air they fly with great rapidity, with neck and feet stretched out to their full extent, and in alighting, often do not attempt to slacken their speed, but strike the water with partially closed wings with a force that carries them on the surface from 20 to 40 feet.

It has always been difficult for me to separate the notes of the western grebe from the grand chorus of sounds in a thickly populated slough, teeming with yellow-headed blackbirds, coots, and other water birds, but as nearly as I could learn, it has two distinct notes, a shrill piping whistle, suggesting the whistling alarm note of the osprey, and a short, rolling croak in a subdued tone. Doctor Chapman (1908) says:

The swan grebe's voice is a loud, double-toned, whistled *c-r-r-ee-er-r-r-ee*, which can be heard distinctly when the bird is beyond reach of the eye in the open waters of the lake, and even a poor imitation of this far-reaching call brings the lakes of the prairie or plain more clearly before me than the memory of the note of any other of their bird inhabitants.

Mr. W. L. Dawson (1909) describes it as " a voice, high and broken, like nothing else perhaps so much as the creak of a neglected pulley block." He says that the notes of the two sexes are different.

Winter.—During the latter part of September the western grebes migrate to the Pacific coast, where they spend the winter in large numbers, from Puget Sound to Lower California and Mexico, both on the seacoast and in the larger lakes. They often gather into large flocks, sometimes numbering several thousands, and wander about, following the movements of the fish on which they feed and which they are expert in catching.

DISTRIBUTION.

Breeding range.—Western North America, particularly the prairie regions. East to central Manitoba (Lake Winnipegosis, Lake Manitoba, and Shoal Lake), east central North Dakota (Devil's Lake region), central eastern South Dakota (Hamlin County), and Nebraska (Garden County). South to northern Wyoming (Lake De Swet), central Utah (Utah Lake), and southern California (Mystic Lake, Riverside County). West to central western California (Lake Merced, San Francisco County), central Oregon (Klamath Lakes), and central western British Columbia. North to central British Columbia (Stuart Lake, Cariboo district), northern Alberta (near Edmonton), and north central Saskatchewan (Quill Lake). Noted in summer, but not found breeding, in Arizona (near Yuma) and southern California (Santa Barbara and San Diego).

Winter range.—West and south of the Rocky Mountains, mainly on the Pacific coast. East to central British Columbia (Okanagan Lake), western Washington (Olympia), western Nevada (Pyramid Lake), southwestern Arizona (Gila River), and northern Mexico (Chihuahua). South to southern Mexico (Pueblo and Jalisco). West to the Pacific coast of Mexico and the United States. North to southern British Columbia (Vancouver Island) and northern Washington (Puget Sound region).

Spring migration.—Northward along the Pacific coast starting in April. Lower California: Colnett Bay, April 7–8. California: Santa Cruz Island, April 24 to May 2; Salton Sea, April 19. Washington, Steilacoom, April 21; Lake Chelan, May 11; Columbia River, May 19. British Columbia: Elko, Bayne Lake, May 2; Stuart Lake, May 6; Vancouver Island, April 24 to May 6.

Northeastward across the Rocky Mountains early in May. Nevada: Washoe Lake, May. Montana: Great Falls, May 9. Alberta: Banff, May 8. Saskatchewan: Indian head, May 12 to 30.

Fall migration.—Southwestward across the Rocky Mountains. Wyoming: Douglas, October 13. Colorado: Vicinity of Denver, October 25 to November 28. Arizona: Gila River, November.

Southward along the Pacific coast: British Columbia: Vancouver Island, September 28; Sumas, November 2. Washington: Cape Disappointment, September; Puget Sound, October 10 to 12. Oregon: Near Corvallis, October 24. California: Mono Lake, September 2 to 21; Monterey, arrives September 25. Mexico: Jalisco, La Barca, October 2.

Casual records.—Kansas: Lawrence, November 3. Minnesota: May. Iowa: Blackhawk County, spring. Wisconsin: Lake Koshkonong, January 4. Indiana: Indianapalis, September. Ohio: Near Youngstown, October 28 to 30. Ontario: Lake Huron at Sarnia. Other Ontario and Quebec records are *holboelli.* Alaska: Near Dixon Entrance, May 28. Yukon Territory: Teslin Lake. October 21.

Egg dates.—North Dakota: 46 records, May 18 to July 9; 23 records, May 28 to June 10. Manitoba and Saskatchewan: 13 records, June 7 to 26; 7 records, June 8 to 16. Oregon and Washington: 11 records, May 20 to July 2; six records, May 30 to June 12. Utah: 8 records, May 20 to June 15; 4 records, May 22 to 25. California: 6 records, May 20 to June 23; 3 records, June 1 to 8.

COLYMBUS HOLBŒLLI (Reinhardt).

HOLBŒLL'S GREBE.

HABITS.

The extensive, deep-water marshes about the southern end of Lake Winnipegosis, intersected by numerous sluggish streams or dotted with many small, shallow ponds, all of which are full of fish or other forms of aquatic life, furnish ideal breeding grounds for this and other water fowl. The banks of the Waterhen River, which flows northward from Lake Winnipegosis into Waterhen Lake, are broadly lined with many miles of tall golden canes swarming with bird life of various kinds; countless yellow-beaded blackbirds are busy with their nesting in the densest canes or clinging to the tops of the swaying stalks and pouring out their ceaseless chatter; Franklin's gulls or black terns are flying overhead with gentle notes of protest; various species of ducks are swimming in the creeks and pond holes; and the graceful western grebes glide in and out among the canes where their nests are hidden. Here the shy Holboell's grebe breeds in abundance, probably more abundantly than anywhere else throughout its extensive range; though it is so seldom seen that one does not realize how common it is until a systematic search is made for nests. Waterhen River and the lake into which it flows are said to have been so named on account of the abundance there of this species, although the name "waterhen," or "poule d'eau," is applied to any of the grebes or coots.

Nesting.—Throughout the month of June, 1913, we found a great many nests of this grebe in various localities in this region. Although it frequented the vicinity of the same swamps, in which the western grebes and horned grebes were breeding, we did not find any nests of Holbœll's grebe actually in the canes (*Phragmites communis*). All of the nests we found were in more open situations and were more or less widely scattered. On June 7 we found, what might almost be called a colony, seven nests, in an extensive tract of short, dead, broken-down flags and reeds which extended out into the lake for a hundred yards or more near the entrance to the river. As the water was 3 or 4 feet deep, I had to work from a canoe and experienced some difficulty in photographing the nests; for, with the tripod standing in the water, the camera was but little above the surface. Even in such an open situation the nests were surprisingly inconspicuous and it required the practised eye of my guide to locate most of them. They were generally placed where the broken-down reeds (*Scirpus lacustris*) were thickest and often where they were so matted together that it was difficult to push a canoe through them. They were low, flat, carelessly built structures, raised but slightly above the surface, in which the eggs were wet and almost awash, and were made of dead and rotten reeds and flags, water mosses, algae and other drift rubbish. The eggs were usually wholly or partially covered with the nesting material. During several visits to this locality I saw but one Holbœll's grebe near its nest and only occasionally in the distance; though I lay in wait for them for a long time at some little distance in the canes.

It is certainly one of the shyest of the water birds. Its hearing must be very acute; for only rarely could I surprise one in the marshes, when it would disappear instantly. What few birds I saw were generally swimming at a distance, singly or in pairs, often far out on the lake, where they always dove long before I could get within gunshot range. Only once did I succeed in surprising one on its nest and get a fleeting glimpse. Mr. Herbert K. Job had located a nest in a little cove on a nearby pond; we approached it cautiously, paddling silently around a little point and into the cove; we were just in time to see the grebe stand up in the nest, hastily attempt to cover the eggs, glide off into the water, and disappear in the reeds so quickly that we could hardly realize what had happened. This was a larger, better built, and probably a more typical nest than those described above; it was floating in water about 3 feet deep and anchored near the edge of growing flags (*Typha latifolia*) and reeds (*Scirpus lacustris*); it measured 24 inches in diameter, the inner cavity was 6 inches across and slightly hollowed, and the rim was built up 2 or 3 inches above the water; it was made principally of dead reeds and flags, with a few green stems of the same, matted together with a mass of algae and water mosses; it was lined with well-rotted flags.

Throughout the greater portion of its breeding range the Holboell's grebe is a widely scattered, solitary species. It breeds to some extent in the sloughs and marshes of the northern plains and prairie regions, but is more universally common in the marshy lakes and ponds in the timbered regions of northern Canada, where one or two pairs only are usually found in each of the smaller lakes.

Dr. Joseph Grinnell (1900) found this grebe breeding quite commonly in the delta of the Kowak River, Alaska, in June, 1899, where nearly every pond or lake was the home of a single pair. He describes what might be considered its courtship performance as follows:

We had just moored our steamer to the river bank and I was pushing my way among the willows back toward a strip of spruces when I was startled by a series of most lugubrious cries from directly in front of us.

After a moment's hesitation I concluded it must be some species of loon, although I had never heard such a note before. Advancing as quietly as possible I came upon a small lake which was almost surrounded by spruces and margined on my side with willows. I could see nothing on the surface for some minutes. A loon would surely have shown himself during that time. Suddenly the curious cries broke forth again, and there within 20 yards of me, in a thin patch of grass growing near the shore, were two grebes resting on the water. They both took part in the "song," though the voice of one was notably weaker than that of the other. One of the birds would start with a long wail and then the other would chime in with a similar note, both winding up with a series of quavering cries very much like the repeated whinnies of a horse. During these vocal demonstrations the neck would be thrown forward and the head and bill tilted upward at an angle of 45°. During the performance the birds were nearly facing each other, but at the conclusion one, presumably the male, would slowly swim around the other. A slight movement on my part spoiled this interesting scene, for both birds instantly disappeared beneath the water, leaving scarcely a ripple. Finally I barely discerned the head and neck of one near a snag in the dark reflection of the opposite shore.

He says of its nest:

The nest consisted of a floating mass of sodden marsh grass, a foot in diameter. It was anchored among standing grass in about 2 feet of water. It was 20 feet from the shore on one side and about the same distance from the edge of the ice, which still existed in a large floe in the center of the lake. The top of this raft of dead grass presented a saucer-shaped depression, which was 2 inches above the surface of the surrounding water. The eggs lay wholly uncovered and could be plainly seen from shore.

Mr. P. M. Silloway (1902) found a small colony of Holboell's grebes in Swan Lake, Montana, where he located five pairs of the birds and collected seven sets of eggs on dates ranging from June 4 to 20, 1902. The nests were located in an extensive growth of buck brush and reeds which lined the margin of the lake and covered a marshy area of about a square mile. Most of the nests were placed among the reeds and made of the usual materials. Two of the nests were among the back brush, where the water was over 2 feet deep; in one " the material was piled upon coarse twigs of buck brush, apparently brought up from the bottom "; the other " was made on depressed branches of the bushes, a large, strong mass of decayed reeds with some new material intermingled in the top."

Mr. Edmonde S. Currier (1904) refers to a colony of from 6 to 10 pairs which he found breeding in Leech Lake, Minnesota, in 1902 and 1903.

One nest was high and dry on a muskrat house—a hollow in the side of the house, and about 10 inches above the water. The muskrat house was in a patch of tall canes, growing in deep, open water, forming a small island. The other nests were similar in situation, style of architecture, and material used. They varied only in size, and this depended upon the time the birds had been laying. Nests containing only one egg were simply irregular piles or rafts of floating flags soft and rotting, with the egg often awash and covered with foam. In more advanced sets the nests formed quite a mass of material, with a deep cup above water line. No birds were seen on the nests, or leaving them, but in 1902 I saw one swimming away from a patch of canes in open water that contained a nest.

Eggs.—The Holbœll's grebe raises only one brood during the season, but if the nest is robbed a second set of eggs is promptly laid. The set generally consists of four or five eggs; sometimes three are considered enough; six eggs are occasionally laid and rarely seven or even eight. The eggs resemble closely those of other grebes in general appearance and vary greatly in size, so that it is not always easy to identify them. In shape they vary from nearly " ovate " to "elliptical oval," " elongate ovate " or to nearly " fusiform."

The color of the clean, freshly-laid egg varies from pale bluish white to " cartridge buff," but the color, which is never quite pure, soon becomes partly or wholly obscured by muddy, dirty, nest-stains and the egg is often plastered over with mud and bits of nest material, giving it a dark mottled appearance. Much of this can be washed off, but the stains seem to be indelible.

The measurements of 60 eggs, in the United States National Museum, average 53.7 by 34.5 millimeters; the eggs showing the four extremes measure **64.5** by **37.5, 49** by 33, and 50.5 by **30** millimeters.

Young.—The period of incubation proved to be 22 or 23 days for eggs of this species which we hatched out in our incubators.

The young are very precocious and can dive and swim instinctively soon after they have hatched. As soon as they are able to feed and to swim about they may be seen riding in safety on their mother's back as she swims about the lake, clinging to her plumage when she dives and coming to the surface with her, as if nothing had happened. It is said that the mother bird turns her head and feeds the young

while riding on her back. Then soon learn to dive and to feed themselves on small fish, insects, aquatic worms, and vegetable matter.

Plumages.—The downy young show considerable variation in
color patterns, but in a general way they may be described as practically black above when first hatched, fading to blackish brown or
seal brown as the chick increases in size; this color includes the sides
and crissum, leaving only the belly pure white; the head and neck
are broadly and clearly striped, longitudinally, with black and
white; the chin and throat are often spotted with black but are sometimes clear white. There is usually a distinct white V on the top of
the head, starting on the forehead, above a superciliary black stripe
which usually includes the eyes, and terminating in broad white
stripes in the sides of the neck; there is also a median white stripe
or spot on the crown and the back is, more or less distinctly, marked
with four long stripes of dull white or grayish. The lighter
stripes, especially on the head and neck are often tinged with buffy
pink. This downy covering is worn until the young bird is more
than two-thirds grown, the colors becoming duller above and grayer
below. The first real plumage is acquired early in September, dark
above and white below, as in the adult, but signs of youth are retained in the head and neck, both of which are more or less striped
with black and white on the sides; the neck is also more or less
rufous. I have a specimen in this plumage taken November 15, but
I have other specimens taken in November and December, apparently young birds, which have lost all traces of the stripes and the
rufous neck. The stripes always disappear during the fall or early
winter, but the reddish neck is often retained until the young bird
acquires its first nuptial plumage. This closely resembles the adult
nuptial plumage but the colors are duller and not so pure; the chin
and throat are whiter, the red of the neck is mottled with dusky, the
crown is browner, fading gradually into the mottled cheeks; the
sharply defined color pattern of the head, so conspicuous in the
adult, is very much obscured in the young birds. At the first postnuptial moult, when the bird is a little more than a year old, I
think that old and young birds become indistinguishable, although
I am not sure that another year is not required to accomplish this.
The postnuptial or summer moult is complete and is prolonged
through August and September. The adult fall plumage is characterized mainly by the absence of red which entirely disappears from
the neck and breast and is replaced by a white breast and a dusky
neck; the pale gray of the chin, throat, and cheeks is sharply defined
against the dusky neck, as it is against the red neck in the spring;
young birds have no such sharp line of demarcation; the crown is also
darker than in young birds. I have seen one specimen, No. 15994

in the collection of Dr. Jonathan Dwight, in nearly full nuptial plumage, collected November 25, but I can only regard this as an exceptional case of retarded or suspended moult. A partial prenuptial moult occurs early in the spring involving mainly the plumage of the head and neck and producing the clearly defined black crown, gray cheeks, chin and throat and the brilliant red neck and breast of the nuptial plumage. I have seen specimens in which this moult was complete before the end of February and others in full winter plumage in March; I think the moult usually occurs in April.

Food.—Holbœll's grebe feeds to some extent on small fish or minnows which it obtains by diving, but its food consists largely of other things and it can live perfectly well in lakes where there are no fish at all. In the lakes of Manitoba it lives largely on crawfish, amblystomae, and aquatic insects; its bill of fare also includes various aquatic worms, insects, and their larvæ, small crustaceans, fresh water mollusks, tadpoles, and some vegetable substances. An adult bird caught on the ice near my home was fed on small live shiners which it ate readily. Mr. Robert J. Sim (1904), who made a careful study of a captive Holbœll's grebe, gives the following account of its feeding habits:

On the second day I placed a 4-inch wild fish (shiner?) in a dish filled with water. This was set on the floor in front of the bird. He gave the fish a slight poke whereupon it swam around violently. Making a quick thrust he caught it, grasping it crosswise with the bill—not impaling it. The fish then went through a course of pinching from head to tail, being hitched along from side to side in the bill. It was then turned about and gulped down head first. Later in the day three out of four strips of raw whitefish were eaten, each about the size of a man's finger. These the grebe bruised and shook until small fragments flew several feet around. At this time of the year live food was scarce, but we succeeded in finding a few small aquatic animals. By the 27th of February the grebe had eaten—all voluntarily—the following: 10 live goldfish (2 to 5 inches long), 2 pieces raw steak (taken from water), 1 4-inch wild fish, 2 large tadpoles, and 7 medium sized dragon-fly larvæ.

In swallowing the large goldfishes the bird's jaws seemed to be distended laterally, and he gulped so violently that the back of his head struck his back with a hollow " tunking " sound. This operation apparently jarred the fish past the sticking point. When very hungry the grebe swallowed the fishes alive. Of the crawfishes offered him only the small or soft ones were eaten, and no great relish was shown. Earthworms, when their season came, were eaten with avidity, but raw beefsteak (lean) was the principal article of diet with the bird during his stay with us.

The stomach of this bird is sometimes wholly or partially filled with feathers.

Behavior.—In flight Holbœll's grebe is easily recognized in any plumage; its size is distinctive, being halfway between a loon and one of the smaller grebes; in the full nuptial plumage the red neck and gray cheeks are conspicuous if the bird is near enough to see them, or at a greater distance the pure white under parts and white wing patches show up in marked contrast to the black upper parts; young birds in the autumn can be recognized by their size, shape, and white wing patches, as the horned grebes are much smaller and the loons have no white in the wings. Its general appearance is decidedly loonlike, with its long neck stretched out in front and its large feet held together straight out behind to serve as a rudder for a tailless bird. It can not rise off the ground or ice at all and is frequently caught in consequence. It can rise readily from the water, like a duck, but not without considerable pattering along the surface, beating it with wings and feet. When well under way its flight is swift, strong, direct, and well sustained. When migrating along the Atlantic coast I have always seen it flying singly and not more than a few feet above the water.

It is a strong and rapid swimmer and like all of its tribe a splendid diver. It usually prefers to escape by swimming rapidly away if the enemy is not too near, but, in the latter case, it dives like a flash, so quickly that it is useless to try to shoot one if it is watching. When undisturbed and not hurried it makes a graceful curving plunge, leaving the water entirely and going straight down with its wings closed; probably it can dive to a greater depth in this way than in any other. It can also sink gradually downward until only its head is above water or go swimming off among the reeds with only its bill and eyes showing. When really alarmed it goes under water with astonishing rapidity, so quickly that we can not see how it is done, but it is probably accomplished by a sudden kick and forward dive.

Mr. Aretas A. Saunders writes me that he watched a pair of these birds—

diving and evidently feeding under water. I timed them to see how long they stayed under, and, after several observations of both birds, found the time to be almost uniformly 55 seconds in every case. The time was so exact that I could tell when a bird dove just when to expect it to reappear.

Mr. Sim (1904), in describing the habits of his captive bird, says:

In ordinary swimming the feet struck out alternately. The tarsi extended downward and outward. In diving the bird was not observed to spring forward in the common grebe manner, but rather let himself down very quickly as though drawing his head back through a hole. When it was below the surface I could scarcely realize that the creature before me was a bird, so slender was he and so swiftly did he dart about and shoot through the tangle of aquatic vegetation. It was amazing. The wings were entirely covered by the feathers and the feet struck out simultaneously at the sides, far astern. Their movements could scarcely be followed.

Mr. Alvin R. Cahn (1912), who had an excellent opportunity to study this species at close range through an opening in the ice of Cayuga Lake, describes its movements under water as follows:

The water was clear, and the bird could be seen plainly, shooting and zigzagging about, midway between the surface and the bottom. While swimming under water, the neck is extended to its utmost, and both legs and wings are used. With neck outstretched, the bird offers the least possible resistance to the water, there being a smooth and gradual transition from the tip of the slender bill to the middle of the back, the widest part of the body. The speed which is developed under water is marvelous, at times it being almost impossible to follow its movements, which were so rapid that the bird appeared more like a large, gray fish darting about. When coming to the surface the bill and head appeared slowly, when a glimpse of the observer caused it to dive again. In diving, even though the body was under water, the bill went down first, so that it really dove instead of sinking quietly.

On its breeding grounds Holbœll's grebe is often seen swimming about in pairs in marshy ponds or on the lakes. When undisturbed it swims quite buoyantly with its head drawn down on its folded neck, much as a duck swims, occasionally rolling over on its side to wash and preen its plumage or pointing its bill up in the air to give its loud weird call. But on the slightest scent of danger it sinks until its tail is below the surface, its back is awash, and its head is stretched up to watch and listen as it swims rapidly away. Should a human being approach within a hundred yards of the shy creature, it is gone for good; if on a large lake, it swims quickly away under water and appears again only in the dim distance; if near a marsh, it seeks shelter in the reeds and does not show itself again. Human intimacy is not encouraged by this vanishing water sprite.

One beautiful moonlight night in June, as we lay at anchor near some Manitoba marshes, I had a good chance to study the love song of this interesting bird. The night was calm and the mosquitoes made sleep impossible, as we lay rolled in our blankets on the deck of our little boat, listening to the varied voices of the marsh. The activities of life in the marshes do not wholly cease at sundown; birds are very active and noisy during the hours of twilight or all night long when there is bright moonlight; even on dark nights hardly an hour passes without some vocal signs of life. This night seemed particularly favorable, quiet and cool after a long hot day. The Franklin's gulls and black terns which were feeding over the marshes in the cool of the evening kept up their restless beating long after it seemed possible for them to see their insect prey. The chattering of bronzed grackles and Brewer's and red-winged blackbirds, as well as the rhythmic chants of the yellowheads quieted down at dusk; but their notes were frequently heard all through the night as the birds awoke to change their positions on their insecure roosts in the reeds. The long rolling diminuendo call of the sora rails and

the horse gutteral croaks and grunts of the coots, with many variations, furnished the necessary accompaniment to the chorus. But
the real striking features of the concert, the solo parts, were the
weird cries of the Holbœll's grebes, heard only at infrequent intervals. The performance begins with a series of loonlike wailing
cries, loud and piercing at first, and then runs off into a series of
short, plaintive, vibrating wails, " *ah-ooo, ah-ooo, ah-ooo, ah-ah-ah-
ah-ah;*" sometimes it ends in a more staccato, chattering trill and
might be indicated thus: " *whaaa, whaaa, whaaa, whaaa, whaaa,
chitter-r-r-r-r-r.*" There is considerable variation in the length
and form of the song in different individuals. The love song of the
Holbœll's grebe may be heard at any time during the day or night,
but it is indulged in more freely in the early morning and toward
the dusk of evening.

Mrs. Lizzie T. Burt described the notes of an adult bird, which
was captured on the ice near my home on February 14, 1913, as loud
trumpetings, suggesting the cries of the loon and resembling the
sound made by what is known as a Gabriel's horn on an automobile.
This grebe has several other notes, one of which is aptly described by
Mr. Silloway (1902), as follows:

It is a coarse, prolonged nasal *quonk*, the nasal quality being most pronounced, the intonation being very suggestive of the braying of a donkey.
Indeed, the natives call this grebe the " jack driver," and anyone familiar
with the nasal volume of tone produced by *C. holboelli* will readily admit the
appropriateness of the popular name.

Mr. W. L. Dawson (1909) refers to its notes as follows:

Owing to the furtive habits of the various swamp dwellers, it is often difficult to distinguish notes, but I have attributed a harshly raucous *cawack,
awwack caawwrrack* heard in June upon the Pend d'Oreille River to this
species. It is generally similar to the yark of the horned grebe but has several
times the volume.

Mr. Allan Brooks (1903) says that in British Columbia, where
both species are abundant, the Holbœll's grebe " wages incessant
war upon" the horned grebe, "the large birds diving and coming
up beneath the smaller ones time and again to the terror of the poor
little fellows, who often desert their nests in consequence." It must
be a formidable foe with such a sharp and powerful beak. When
once it has passed the downy young stage it must be well able to
defend itself and escape from its enemies.

Fall.—During the migrations I have always found this grebe to
be a solitary species, but, according to others, it seems to be more
or less gregarious at times. Mr. John Macoun (1909) speaks of
" large flocks seen on Prince Edward Island, August 7, 1888." On
the Pacific coast it more often congregates in flocks on the migrations and during the winter, though I doubt if it actually flies in

flocks. In its winter quarters on the coast of Washington Mr. W. L. Dawson (1909) associates this species with the "characteristic bird population which stretches along at just a little more than gunshot range from shore," when he finds it "almost invariably numbered with this shifting, distrustful company of sea fowl, pigeon guillemots, buffleheads, mergansers, and scoters."

Winter.—All through the fall, winter, and spring these grebes are fairly common on the New England coast, where they may be seen riding the waves just off shore, feeding in the shoals just beyond the breakers, in company with loons, horned grebes, golden-eyes, scoters, and red-breasted mergansers. It is interesting to watch them with a powerful glass as they dive through the breakers, where their movements can sometimes be plainly seen through the face of an incoming wave.

As Holbœll's grebe is inclined to winter somewhat in large inland lakes, it is sometimes caught by the freezing of lakes which are usually open. Mr. Alvin R. Cahn (1912) has published the following acount of his experience with it on Cayuga Lake, New York, in February, 1912:

The freezing of Cayuga Lake offered a rare opportunity for a study of this most interesting and apparently little known bird. Until the present time, the Holboell's grebe has been considered only a rare visitant at the southern end of the lake, one or two being recorded almost every winter. It has proved, however, to be the predominant grebe during this winter, 28 individuals having been taken. The reason of its unprecedented abundance here is undoubtedly to be found in the six weeks of extremely cold weather, and the consequent closure of waters in other regions. The sudden closing of the lake's surface in one night left these birds in an absolutely helpless condition, since open water is a necessity for taking flight in this group of birds, Holbœll's grebe being no exception to the rule. As a result, 11 beautiful specimens were picked up alive from the ice in perfectly good physical condition. If approached while sitting on the ice, these birds made no attempt to escape. They would strike at the outstretched hand, and would emit calls very loonlike in general quality. Once the bird alights upon the ice, it is unable to take flight, and must await starvation or other tragic end. At best, all it can do is to flap its wings and possibly scrape along over the ice a few feet. The position of the legs, together with the smooth surface of the ice, rendered these efforts at locomotion entirely futile.

A bird (referred to above) was caught on the ice near Taunton, Massachusetts, on February 14, 1913; it would undoubtedly have starved to death, as it was unable to rise off the ice. On December 27, 1909, a bird was brought to me which was caught in a yard in the city of Taunton, having been bewildered by a thick snowstorm and become exhausted. There are numerous other similar records.

DISTRIBUTION.

Breeding range.—Northern North America and northeastern Asia. East to northern Ungava and Hudson Strait. South to southern Labrador, southwestern New Brunswick (St. Croix River and St. Andrews), probably parts of Quebec and Ontario, central western Minnesota (Grant County) and North Dakota (Turtle Mountains and Sweetwater Lake). West to northwestern Montana (Swan Lake), central northern Washington (Okanagan and Chelan Counties) and northwestern Alaska (Selawik Lake, coast of Norton Sound and Yukon River). North to northeastern Siberia (Saghalin Island and Marcova and Gichiga, Anadyr District), Yukon Territory (Forty Mile) and northern Mackenzie (Fort Anderson, Nahanni River, and Peel River).

Occasional in summer south of its breeding range. New Jersey (Englewood, June), New Hampshire (Kingston and Newton, birds seen from May 15 to August 5, with young July 2 to August 1) and Washington (Bellingham Bay). Maine breeding records are considered erroneous and Labrador nestings are open to doubt.

Winter range.—Mainly on the Atlantic and Pacific coasts. From eastern Maine (Washington County) and west central New York (Cayuga Lake) south to North Carolina; casually to Georgia (St. Marys) and Tennessee (Reelfoot Lake). From southern British Columbia (Okanagan Lake and Vancouver Island, Victoria) and western Washington (Puget Sound region) south to southern California (Santa Barbara). Also on the Great Lakes: Lake Ontario (Toronto), Lake Erie (Near Ashtabula, Ohio), Niagara Falls and Lake Michigan (near Chicago, Illinois). Wintering records from the interior are few and unsatisfactory. Recorded in winter from the Pribilof Islands (St. Paul), Aleutian Islands (Unalaska), Kodiak Island, and Japan.

Spring migration.—Along the Atlantic slope the birds start northward in April. Pennsylvania: Warren, April 18. New York: April 21 to May 30. Connecticut: Long Island Sound, May 3 (latest). Rhode Island: May 2 (latest). Massachusetts: May 24 (latest). Maine: April 24. Hudson Strait: June 20 (arriving).

On the Pacific coast and through the interior late in April or early in May. British Columbia: Douglass, April 20 to May 10. Southeastern Alaska: Forrester Island, May 3 to 10; Kuiu Island, April 25 to May 6; Admiralty Island, May 7; Heceta Island, May 24. Western Alaska: Bristol Bay, May 30. Indiana: Park Side, April 29. Michigan: Greenville, March 12. Ontario: Toronto, April 24 to May 1; Lake Nipissing, May 10. Alberta: Edmonton, May 10; Lily Lake, May 13 and 14. Mackenzie: Fort Providence, May 25.

Fall migration.—Southward along both coasts and through the interior. Mackenzie: Blackwater River, October 8. Northwestern Alaska: St. Michael, September 22 to October; Kuskokwim River, October 10; Nushagak, October 12. Commander Islands: Novem-

ber 24.   Central Alaska: Fairbanks, October 7.   Southeastern
Alaska: Silver Bay, September 21; Sitka, October.   Yukon Terri-
tory: Teslin Lake, September 28.   British Columbia: Yellowhead
Lake, August 28 to September 2; Sumas, October 12.   California:
Lake Tahoe, September 6.   Alberta: Athabaska Landing, Septem-
ber 15; Edmonton, October 16.   Maine: Umbagog, October 24.
Ontario: Ottawa River, October 16 to November 25; Toronto, Octo-
ber 21 to 31.   Montana: Lubec, September 25 to 27; Gallatin County,
October 17.

Casual records.—The type was taken in Greenland, where the
species occurs casually.

Egg dates.—North Dakota and Minnesota: 23 records, May 23 to
July 16; 12 records, May 31 to June 13.   Manitoba: 17 records, May
27 to August 1; 8 records, June 2 to 11.   British Columbia and
Washington: 9 records, May 13 to July 1; 5 records, May 29 to
June 13.   Alberta: 8 records, May 24 to June 21; 4 records, June
3 to 17.

COLYMBUS AURITUS (Linnaeus.)

HORNED GREBE.

HABITS.

A long drive over the prairies of North Dakota brought us to the
home of our host and guide, Mr. Alfred Eastgate, in a picturesque
spot by the side of a little pond surrounded by trees and shrubbery.
It had been an eventful day, May 30, 1901, my introduction to the
fascinating bird life of the western prairies. Everything was new,
strange, and interesting, possessing that peculiar charm which a
naturalist experiences only on his first day in an entirely new region.
We had stopped several times to explore the timber belts, teeming
with small birds, and to examine nests of goldeneyes and ferruginous
roughlegs. I had made the acquaintance of at least a dozen new
birds and had learned to see other familiar species in a new light
as I met them in their summer homes on the prairies and in the
sloughs. In the little pond by the house were a pair of beautiful
horned grebes, resplendent with their full nuptial plumage and their
great fluffy heads; with them were two pairs of blue-winged teal, a
pair of shovelers, and several lesser scaup ducks; a noisy pair of
killdeers were running along the shore and several ring-billed gulls
and black terns were flying overhead. The grebes had recently arrived on their breeding grounds and were busy with their courtships
and preparations for nest building; their weird and striking notes
were heard frequently all through the evening and it was a fitting
ending to such a delightful day to be lulled to sleep by the love song
of the horned grebe.

Nesting.—This pair built their nest in this little pond, but we
went away before the eggs were laid and we did not find any more

nests of this species that season, although they are not uncommon in that region. The horned grebe is nowhere abundant, but it is widely and evenly distributed all through the northern prairie regions. In Saskatchewan I recorded it as uncommon in 1905 and rare in 1906, though we found a few nests each season. I found two nests on June 7, 1905, in the Crane Lake slough within a short distance of the western grebe colony. The first nest was well concealed in the middle of a clump of tall reeds (*Scirpus lacustris*) and was floating in water about knee-deep. It was made of wet rotten reeds and rubbish and measured 10 inches in diameter outside and 7 inches inside; it contained five eggs, which were only about 2 inches above the water. The second nest was in a more open situation but was similarly constructed; it contained nine eggs and was somewhat larger than the first nest, measuring 13 by 12 inches in outside diameter.

In the Magdalen Islands, in 1904, we found a few pairs of horned grebes nesting in the small ponds near East Point, where, even as late as June 22, the sets were incomplete or perfectly fresh. A nest, found wth one egg in it on the 18th, now held three fresh eggs; probably more would have been laid as the eggs were covered and the bird was not incubating; this would seem to indicate that an egg is laid every other day. The nest was a floating mass of dead and green flags, mostly the latter, mixed with soft aquatic mosses and algae; I could pass my hands completely under it and lift it without materially disturbing its floating capacity; it was partially secured from drifting by being anchored to the dead stalks of a scanty, open growth of flags (*Typha latifolia*), in water about 18 inches deep. It was in perfectly plain sight, and even conspicuous at a long distance, as were all of the nests of this species in that locality, for the broken-down flags of last year's growth, offered little concealment; later in the season the new growth of flags would probably have hidden it. This nest measured 14 inches in outside diameter, but the inner cavity was only about 4 inches in diameter. The grebes were very tame and swam slowly away, watching us intently within gunshot range. I have always found this species very bold and conspicuous, in marked contrast to the pied-billed grebe, which is very seldom seen near its nest. I was much impressed with the striking beauty of a handsome male that we shot; it had the most beautiful eye that I have ever seen in any bird, brilliant scarlet, finely veined and penciled, with an irregular ring of yellow around the pupil, gleaming like fire in its setting of soft velvety plumage.

The nests are made of whatever soft vegetable substances are easily available, mixed with mud, and are usually more conspicuous than those of the pied-billed grebe. The grebes themselves are generally much more in evidence than the dabchicks, making identification much easier. The horned grebe covers its eggs when it leaves them, but incubates regularly; it is not particularly shy and has been photographed on its nest; it is not easily driven from the vicinity of its nest, and will soon return to it if given a good chance.

Eggs.—The eggs of the horned grebe are absolutely indistinguishable from those of either the eared or the pied-billed grebes. In shape they vary from " elliptical ovate " to " elliptical oval." The shell is fairly smooth with very little luster. The ground color is dull bluish white or pale olive white, which is generally more or less, and often wholly, concealed by a deposit of mud and dirt or by nest stains which will not disappear with washing. The set usually consists of 4 or 5 eggs, but sometimes 3 eggs are incubated and sometimes as many as 9 or 10 are found in a nest; perhaps these large sets are laid by more than one bird. If only one brood is raised in a season, there is a great variation in the dates, but Dr. P. L. Hatch (1892) has suggested that as the young "have been seen swimming with the parent as early as the first week in May, and at the tenderest age as late as the 3d of August," there may be two broods raised occasionally. The measurements of 45 eggs, in the United States National Museum and the author's collections, average 44 by 30 millimeters; the eggs showing the four extremes measure **47.5** by 29.5, 46 by **31.5, 40** by 29 and 43 by **28** millimeters.

Plumages.—The downy young is almost black above, striped and spotted with grayish white; there is a median white stripe on the occiput and a white **V** on the forehead, extending down the sides of the neck in broad irregular stripes; the sides of the head, neck, and throat are white tinged with " salmon buff " and spotted with dusky; the under parts are white and the sides dusky. The young can swim and dive like experts soon after they are hatched. They develop rapidly and soon acquire the juvenal or first plumage, which is worn through the late summer and into the fall; it is similar to the first winter plumage, but is characterized by the dusky stripes and spots on the sides of the head and throat. These dusky markings disappear during the fall and the young birds become similar to the adults. Young birds in the first winter can be distinguished by the light edgings of the feathers of the backs, by the lighter and browner plumage in the crowns, and by the smaller or lighter colored bills; adults have clear black crowns, the cheeks are usually purer white, the plumage of the heads is more fluffy, and the bills are larger and blacker. The prenuptial molt apparently includes the entire head and body plumage, and young birds are indistinguishable from adults after the first spring. The spring molt usually occurs in April, sometimes a little earlier or later, but it is usually completed before the middle of May. Birds in full nuptial plumage have been taken as far south as South Carolina and they are not uncommon on the Massachusetts coast; but even here most of the birds migrate north before the molt is complete. The complete postnuptial molt occurs in the later summer and early fall, but is often not completed before October or later.

Food.—One of the horned grebe's favorite articles of food is small fish, which it is quite expert at chasing and catching, as it darts about swiftly and skillfully under water, catching them unawares and pursuing them at full speed. While living on the coast in winter it feeds on shrimps, minute crustaceans, and salt water minnows. On inland waters it eats a large proportion of animal food, such as small frogs, tadpoles, aquatic lizards, leeches, beetles, and other insects. It also feeds to some extent on grasses and other vegetable matter. Audubon (1840) speaks of having found large quantities of grass seeds in the stomach of this grebe. Mr. W. L. McAtee (1912) has made an exhaustive report on the food of this species, as follows:

The most remarkable point about the food habits of grebes is that the stomachs almost invariably contain a considerable mass of feathers. Feathers are fed to the young, and there is no question that they play some essential though unknown part in the digestive economy. As they are finely ground in the gizzards it is probable that finally they are digested and the available nutriment assimilated. Feathers constituted practically 66 per cent of the contents of the 57 horned grebe stomachs examined. However, it is not likely that they furnish a very large percentage of the nourishment needed by the birds. As the nutritive value of the feathers is unknown, this part of the stomach contents is ignored. The other items of food are assigned 100 per cent, and the percentages are given on that basis. Various beetles, chiefly aquatic, compose 23.3 per cent of the food; other insects (including aquatic bugs, caddis and chironomid larvae, dragon-fly nymphs, etc.), nearly 12 per cent; fishes, 27.8 per cent; crawfish, 20.7 per cent; and other crustacea, 13.8 per cent. A little other animal matter is taken, including snails and spiders, and a small quantity of vegetable food was found in two stomachs.

Behavior.—The flight of the horned grebe is strong, direct, and well-sustained; it looks, when on the wing, much like a miniature loon. Its neck and its legs are stretched out to their full extent, fore and aft, and its wings vibrate very rapidly. In winter it is difficult to distinguish from the eared grebe, but it can be easily distinguished from the pied-billed grebe by the absence of brown in its plumage and by its white secondaries, which are very conspicuous in flight. Its wings are small in proportion to its weight, so that it experiences some difficulty in rising from the water or from the ground; in rising it has to run along the surface for a long distance, beating the water with both wings and feet; but, when well under way, it attains very good speed. When migrating it usually travels singly or in small scattered flocks. Along the New England coast we frequently see horned grebes migrating, with the scoters in October, a mile or two offshore; often several are in sight at one time, but I have never seen them in anything approaching a flock. Throughout the interior, where they are more numerous, they seem to fly in flocks. Audubon (1840) mentions a flock of 30 which alighted near him in a pond, and states that they migrate in flocks, flying high in the air and following the courses of streams.

The horned grebe swims buoyantly and rapidly, using its feet alternately; it also has the power of sinking below the surface and swimming with its body partially or wholly submerged and with only its bill protruding. Coues (1877) and some other observers seem to think that this is accomplished by so regulating its respiratory processes that its body is increased or decreased in bulk; he cites the following instance to illustrate it:

Once holding a wounded grebe in my hand, I observed its whole body to swell with a labored inspiration. As the air permeated the interior, a sort of ripple or wave passed gradually along, puffing out the belly and raising the plumage as it advanced. With the expiration the reverse change occurred from the opposite direction, and the bird visibly shrunk in dimensions, the skin fitting tightly and the feathers lying close.

I have always supposed that grebes and some other water birds had the power of regulating their displacement, and consequently their floating and sinking ability, by their control of their plumage, compressing the feathers of the body to reduce the displacement and expanding them to increase it; the above incident, cited by Coues, seems to be open to this interpretation as well as any other.

This grebe is just as good a diver as the rest of its tribe. Mr. E. Howard Eaton (1910) says:

I have often seen it remain under water for three minutes and cover a distance of at least 30 rods at one drive.

Dr. Charles W. Townsend (1905) has well described its diving power, as follows:

The diving of this grebe is often a beautiful piece of work. The bird springs vigorously upward and forward, the bill cleaves the water on the downward curve just as the feet leave it, while the whole body describes an arc. The wings are closely applied to the sides, and do not flop out as in the Alcidae, where they are used for flight under water. In the grebes the feet are the propelling power in the forceful initial spring and in the movements below the water. That the wings are kept close to the sides under water I have been able to observe when the grebes were borne up in the advancing rollers on Ipswich Beach. The clear water before the waves broke revealed the diving birds. The full beginning of the dive, as described above, is often curtailed in all degrees, so that the head is below water before the feet emerge, or the jump is lost entirely, and the bird disappears suddenly with a vigorous kick, or mysteriously and quietly sinks in the water. The duration under water depends somewhat on its depth as well as on the abundance of food there. Thus a grebe close to the rocks stayed under from 30 to 35 seconds, while the same bird a short distance out was under water from 45 to 50 seconds each time. They often remain below the surface longer than this.

The love song of the horned grebe is a wonderful combination of weird, loud, striking notes, difficult to describe, but, when once heard, it will never be forgotten; it consists of a series of croaking and chattering notes, followed by several prolonged piercing shrieks; it seems remarkable that such a volume of sound can come from so small a bird. At other times it is usually silent. Prof. Lynds Jones (1909) says:

When the numbers are so great that large companies are found there is a perpetual conversational undertone decidedly pleasing in quality, accompanied by a sort of play among the birds.

Mr. W. Leon Dawson (1909) says that—

they raise a curious far-sounding note of complaint, *keogh keogh*, with a nasal twang or more sharply, *keark keark*, or even *yark yark*.

Winter.—In its winter haunts on our coasts the horned grebe is commonly seen singly, or in small flocks, just outside the breakers along the beaches or near the rocky shores, diving for its food, playing about in the waves, or riding buoyantly over them; occasionally one is seen asleep with its bill tucked under its scapulars. Often it is more gregarious, particularly on inland lakes, where sometimes as many as 150 to 200 are seen in a flock. When alarmed the whole flock suddenly disappears, all diving in unison. They are said to hunt in flocks, at times, after the manner of mergansers, chasing schools of small fry which are more easily caught in this way. Individuals which linger too far north are sometimes caught by the freezing of lakes and perish for lack of food.

DISTRIBUTION.

Breeding range.—Northern parts of the northern hemisphere. In North America east to southwestern Ungava, eastern Quebec (Magdalen Islands), southwestern New Brunswick (Milltown) and eastern Maine (Washington County). South to southern Ontario (St. Clair Flats formerly), southern Wisconsin (Lake Koshkonong) and northern Nebraska (Cherry County). West to southern British Columbia (Ashcroft, Okanagan and Kamloops) and northwestern Alaska (lower Yukon and Norton Sound). North to central Alaska (Yukon River at Nulato and Fort Yukon), Yukon Territory (near Herschel Island) and northern Mackenzie (60 miles southeast of Fort Anderson and Athabaska-Mackenzie region, north nearly to border of forest) and Keewatin (Fort Churchill). Recorded during summer south of the normal breeding range in Massachusetts, Connecticut (Melrose, July 26; Litchfield County, supposed to have bred in 1906) and Indiana (Sheffield). Michigan breeding records doubtful. In the Old World the species breeds in Iceland, northern Scotland, northern Europe (south to Denmark and Gottland Island in the Baltic Sea) and throughout Siberia.

Winter range.—In North America mainly within the United States and principally on the seacoast. From central New York (Tioga County) and coast of Maine, south to Florida (Lake Wimlico and Amelia Island). West along the Gulf coast to Louisiana. From southern British Columbia (Okanagan Lake and Vancouver Island) and northwestern Washington (Bellingham Bay) to southern California (along the coast and casually inland). Has been recorded as wintering in the Pribilof and Aleutian Islands (Unalaska) and southeastern Alaska (Sitka). In the interior winter records are mostly from the region of the great Lakes; Ohio, northern Indiana, Illinois (Lake Michigan), southern Ontario (Lake Ontario) and Michigan.

Outside of North America the species winters in central and southern Europe south to the northern coast of Africa and the Azores. In Asia south on the coast of China and Japan to the Tropic of Cancer.

Spring migration.—Northward along the Atlantic slope, during April and early May. South Carolina: Second week in April. District of Columbia: Washington, April 17. New Jersey: April 14 to 23 (latest May 3). New York: Arriving March 20 to April 10, departing middle of May. Connecticut: Long Island Sound, May 3 (latest). Massachusetts: May 6 (latest). Maine: Leave late in April.

Northward along the Pacific coast and through the Rocky Mountain region. California: Santa Cruz Island, April. Oregon; Netarts Bay, March 9 to 21. British Columbia: Elk River, April 22. Wyoming: May 15. Alberta: Lily Lake, May 13; Athabaska Landing, May 12. Athabaska River: Fort McMurray, May 14. Yukon Territory: Fort Reliance, May 14; Forty Mile, May 20.· Southern Alaska: Kuiu Island, April 28 (arriving); Prince of Wales Island, May 10–14. Alaska: Lower Yukon at Nulato, last of May.

Northward through the interior. Kansas: April 15 to 30. Iowa: April 19. Illinois: Chicago, April 12 to 27. Ohio: Cedar Point, March 25 to April 21; Waverly, April 20 to 28. Michigan: April 12 to 23. Minnesota: April 23.

Fall migration.—Southward along both coasts and through the interior. Ungava: Koksoak River, September 15. Maine: Arrive September. Massachusetts: October 1 (earliest). Connecticut: September 12 (earliest). New York: Arrive October 10. New Jersey: October to November. Virginia: Dismal Swamp, October 9. South Carolina: October 25 (earliest). Florida: Hillsboro County, October 28. Ohio: Waverly, September 17 to October 24; Oberlin, arrives October 1 to 15, departs November 25. Iowa: November 11 (latest). Kansas: September. Northern Alaska: Norton Sound, leave the middle of October. Southeastern Alaska: Valdez Narrows, September 18; Admiralty Island, September 24. Mackenzie: Mackenzie River, October 8. Yukon Territory: Forty Mile, September 20; Teslin Lake, October 17. Washington: Blaine, October. Oregon: Netarts Bay, September 9. Idaho: Saw-tooth Lake, September 25 to October 4. California: Mono Lake, September 2 to 21; San Benito County, October 14.

Casual records.—Has been recorded from Greenland, Herschel Island River, Yukon Territory, the Bermuda Islands, and the Commander Islands.

Egg dates.—North Dakota: 14 records, April 6 to July 7; 8 records, June 4 to 25. Manitoba and Saskatchewan: 11 records, May 31 to July 7; 6 records, June 3 to 10. Alberta and British Columbia: 9 records, May 20 to July 7; 5 records, June 4 to 17. Ontario and Quebec: 9 records, May 28 to June 27; 5 records, June 4 to 21. Nebraska: 2 records, June 29 and August 12.

COLYMBUS NIGRICOLLIS CALIFORNICUS (Heermann).

AMERICAN EARED GREBE.

HABITS.

The little eared grebe is widely and evenly distributed throughout western North America; from the Great Plains west to the Pacific coast and in most of the inland marshy lakes it is an abundant species. It seems to me that the name American should be retained, as our bird is well established as, at least subspecifically, distinct from the European eared grebe.

Courtship.—During the spring migration in May the birds are busy with their courtships. Mr. Aretas A. Saunders writes to me that all the birds he saw on the spring migration in Montana were in pairs and that they are evidently mated when they arrive on their breeding grounds. Mr. W. L. Dawson (1909) has gracefully described their activity at this season as follows:

It has been a blazing day, for June, even in the Big Bend country, but now the sun has sunk behind the Cascades and the earth has already begun to exhale the fresh odors of recovering darkness. Most birds have properly tucked head under wing, and even the nighthawks are less feverish in their exertions; but not so with the eared grebes. It is the magic hour of courtship, and near and far from the open water or its weedy margins sounds the mellow *poo-eep poo-eep* of these idyllic swains. The sound is given deliberately with a gently rising inflection, but seems to vanish into silence at the end with a sort of saber-like flourish. Now and again some Romeo, more ardent than his mates, bursts into an excited *hicko rick up, hicko rick up, hicko rick up.* The birds spread freely all over the lake irrespective of their nesting haunts, and so numerous are they that at times they maintain a chorus of the volume and persistency of that furnished by a first-class frog pond in March.

Nesting.—In the shallow, marshy lakes of the western plains the eared grebe breeds in extensive colonies, populous thickly settled communities, which my companion, Mr. Herbert K. Job, used to call "cities of the submerged tenth." None of the other small grebes breeds in such large or such densely populated colonies, in which it is often impossible to pole a canoe, or even to wade, without over-turning the nests. Often times there are only narrow lanes of water, through which the inhabitants may come and go to their respective domiciles; yet they never seem to quarrel in the narrow streets or experience any difficulty in finding their own homes. When disturbed, by human intrusion, they slip off their nests into the water, often without diving and swim out into the lake, where they gather in a large flock and quietly watch proceedings. They are always in evidence about their nesting colonies and are not nearly as shy as the pied-billed grebes. The pied-billed grebe nests in small scattered colonies and the horned grebe usually singly or in widely separated nesting sites. Neither of them ever nests, so far as I know, in dense colonies like the eared grebe. Moreover the nests of the eared grebe are almost always in open situations, whereas the nests of the other two species are usually more or less concealed in some kind of vegetation. The nests of the eared grebe are also smaller and less elaborately built than those of the pied-billed or the horned grebes. Mr. B. F. Goss (1883) gives us a very good illustration of this, as follows:

The eared grebe breeds in communities. The first colony that I found was in a small lake in northern Dakota. The nests were built on floating débris about 15 rods from shore, where the water was perhaps 3 feet deep. Old flag leaves, rushes, reeds, etc., had been driven by the wind into the point of a bay, forming a mass 2 or 3 inches deep and several square rods in extent. This mass was firm enough to hold up the birds in most places, but was full of holes where they could dive through. There were at at least 25 nests on an area of 10 by 20 feet. They were made of partly decayed moss and reeds brought up from the bottom, and were small, not more than a handful of material to a nest.

Mr. A. W. Anthony (1896) describes a colony in southern California as follows:

Halfway down the lake the marsh grass was found to extend in a broad band entirely across from shore to shore, and the water was of a uniform depth of about 18 inches. Forcing the boat into the grass, which reached a foot or more above the water, we found a number of small circular openings 100 feet or more in diameter, each fairly covered with nests of the eared grebe. As we came upon the first colony, dozens of grebes, all in beautiful nesting plumage, were seen on their rafts of floating grass, each frantically endeavoring to reach enough moss to cover her eggs before diving out of sight to appear again out in the open water. And numerous chicks just from the egg dove hastily out of sight and escaped in the thick grass. So close together were the nests that often three or four sets could be taken without moving the boat. Most of the eggs were so far advanced in incubation that they were not taken, but by selecting the cleanest sets and testing them by putting them in the water we secured about 75 sets, about 60 of which were saved in fair condition.

The sets ranged from 1 to 5 (mostly 3) while those found at the other end of the lake were from 6 to 10. The nests exhibited surprising regularity and not a little ability on the part of the architects. The rafts all consisted of a number of stems of the long marsh grass, laid in the form of a triangle, with the ends crossed to keep them from floating apart. A second triangle was laid across the first so as to make a six, or often a five, pointed star, between the points of which several stems of grass were left growing acting as a mooring, and so preventing the nest from floating away. In the center an open space was left, in and over which was built the nest itself, which was a mass of mud and moss brought up from the bottom (apparently). A hollow in the center which contained the eggs usually also contained an inch of water, as the nests were almost submerged.

Mr. Robert B. Rockwell (1910) says of the nesting habits of the eared grebe in Colorado:

The eared grebes' nests were easily distinguishable by the flimsy and apparently careless manner in which they were constructed, being very slight, straggling platforms of large, rank, green dock stems, cat-tails stalks, rushes, weeds, and grass, usually floating in comparatively open water, or in very sparse growths of cat-tails, with no apparent attempt at concealment. The nests were very flat, the nest cavity often being actually below water level, and the eggs in most cases being wet. How these eggs with damp shells retained enough heat either from the parent or from the sun's rays to hatch them, is a problem which I have been unable to solve. And as a matter of fact quite a perceptible per cent of old nests examined contained addled eggs.

On June 12, 1905, while exploring an extensive breeding colony of Franklin's gulls in a marshy lake, near Crane Lake, Saskatchewan, I found a large number of eared grebes scattered about among the gulls' nests and well concealed in the thick growth of bulrushes (*Scirpus lacustris*) with which that end of the lake was thickly overgrown. The nests were the usual small floating masses of rotten reeds, water mosses and other vegetable rubbish, with which some of the eggs were wholly or partially covered; the nests measured from 12 to 14 inches in diameter externally and 5 to 6 inches internally; the eggs were not more than 2 to 3 inches above the water, usually less.

Dr. T. S. Roberts (1900) relates a similar experience:

This colony of Franklin's gulls has as associates and intimate neighbors many coots, pied-billed grebes, black terns, a few Forster's terns, and, most notable of all, because so unexpected in this place, a colony of American eared grebes (*Colymbus nigricollis californicus*). There were a hundred or more of these latter birds and they had established themselves in the very midst of the gull colony. Their nests, which were the very poorest structures that could be called by such a name, were disposed in two or three principal groups, were close together, and were intimately mingled with the gulls' nests. Perhaps because they had drifted, some of them rested directly against gulls' nests, but they had not been abandoned. The nests were partially submerged platforms of green vegetation pulled up from the bottom and were without even as much form and stability as is usually possessed by the rude structure of the pied-billed. The eggs were half under water, and it seemed a marvel how they stayed on the loose platforms at all. They were only imperfectly covered. These grebes, unlike their pied-billed relatives, stayed close by their nests and for the most part on them. When driven off they all swam rapidly away in a body and circled around at a safe distance, only to return immediately as soon as the coast was clear. In clambering up onto these frail nests they tipped and nearly sank the whole affair, but it nevertheless afforded sufficient support for them to lie for hours basking in the sun, often on one side, with the head held awkwardly up, and one leg waving clear of the water—a curious attitude, which it took us some little time to make out in detail with the aid of our glasses.

Eggs.—The American eared grebe lays from 3 to 9 eggs and raises but one brood in a season; the usual set consists of 4 or 5 eggs and the larger numbers are proportionately rare or perhaps the work of more than one bird. The eggs are absolutely indistinguishable from those of either the horned grebe or the pied-billed grebe; there is no constant difference in size, shape, or color. The shape is usually "ovate" or "elliptical ovate," but some eggs are more elongated to "elongate ovate" or nearly "fusiform." The ground color, when first laid, is bluish or greenish white, but it soon becomes permanently stained, from contact with the nest, until the eggs show a variety of shades of buff or brown colors, which will not wash off. The eggs are often more or less covered with mud or bits of vegetable matter, which can be removed by washing. The measurements of 55 eggs, in the United States National Museum, average 43.5 by 30 millimeters; the eggs showing the four extremes measures **47** by 30.5 45.5 by **32, 39** by 29, and 43 by **27.5** millimeters.

Morris (1903) gives the period of incubation as about three weeks for the European bird and Yarrell (1871) says that both sexes incubate; probably either of these statements would apply equally well to the American bird. Much discussion has arisen over the question whether grebes incubate their eggs or leave them to hatch from the heat generated by decaying vegetation in the nest or by the warmth of the sun's rays. It seems hardly likely that sufficient heat could come from the decaying vegetation in the nest, as the nests are always wet and the water in which they are built is usually cold during the nesting season; I have never been able to detect any appreciable warmth in the nesting material and have often noticed that the eggs were warm on top, as if they had recently been left by a sitting bird, and cold on the under side where they came in contact with the wet nest; the reverse would be true, if the nest supplied the heat. Grebes, particularly of this species, have frequently been seen incubating by many observers. I believe that they all incubate regularly, particularly at night and during inclement weather. The eggs are covered with the nesting material purely for concealment. I have no doubt that on bright, warm days the eggs are frequently left for long periods, when the heat of the sun helps to continue the hatching process; perhaps on very hot days the covering of wet rubbish may protect the eggs against too intense heat. There are numerous cases on record where eggs have been killed by too much heat, during a protracted hot spell. Mr. William G. Smith reported, in his notes sent to Major Bendire, two such cases in Colorado, where the thermometer registered 108 in the shade during the nesting season; the nests which were in open situations suffered most severely; he said that during the heat of the day the birds did not seem to be able to sit on their nests in the hot sun and practically all of the eggs were destroyed.

Young.—Mr. Robert B. Rockwell (1910) gives us the following good account of the behavior of young grebes:

A baby grebe half the size of a chick can swim as fast as a man can wade through the water comfortably, and the distance they can swim under water at this tender age is surprising. They hide very effectively by diving and coming up to the surface under tiny bits of floating moss or rubbish, where they lie perfectly still with only the tips of their tiny bills exposed above the water. Their feet are abnormally large, which probably accounts for their remarkable swimming ability, and when quiet in the water the feet and head float on the surface, the rest of the body being submerged. The only note of the young grebe is very similar to the " cheep " of the domestic chick, first heard when the egg is pipt—very weak and tiny at first, but growing in strength and power as the bird becomes larger, until by the time the young are three-fourths grown the note is quite loud and clear.

The young birds have a peculiar habit of riding on the back of the parent birds. This is apparently done for the purpose of imaginary protection to the young, as we only observed it when broods of young were surprised close to the shore, and were seeking safety in the middle of the lakes. At such times the parent would swim close alongside the young bird and by raising the fore part of the body out of the water would submerge the posterior portion, upon which the youngsters would scramble with alacrity. The wings of the parent were then raised something after the fashion of a brooding hen, and often several babies would be cuddled comfortably beneath them. It was quite comical to see a well-laden parent bird attempt to take on an additional chick, as this often precipitated the entire brood into the water, and this was always the signal for a wild scramble back on " board ship," during which rather strenuous performance the doting parent was the victim of an animated mauling. This additional weight on the parent's back did not seem to affect their swimming powers, and the speed with which a mother grebe carrying a half a dozen babies could leave danger behind was surprising.

Plumages.—The downy young is glossy black on the back with a few brownish or grayish longitudinal stripes anteriorly; the head is dusky, more or less striped or spotted with whitish; the under parts are white, becoming dusky on the sides and tinged with pinkish buff on the breast and throat. The young birds are nearly fully grown before the first winter plumage is acquired, which appears first on the breast and last on the neck and rump. Young birds in the fall look very much like the horned grebe in corresponding plumage, but they are somewhat smaller, with smaller and slenderer heads and necks, and the shape of the bills is different and characteristic of the species. The first winter plumage of the eared grebe, dark above and white below, is similar to the adult winter plumage, but the black of the back is browner and the colors of the head are duller and less distinctly outlined; the bill is also smaller and not so clearly defined in shape. A first prenuptial molt takes place in April and May, which involves nearly all, if not all, the contour feathers and produces a plumage closely resembling that of the adult. At the first post-nuptial molt, the following summer, the plumage is completely renewed and young birds become indistinguishable from adults at an age of 14 and 15 months.

Adults have two molts, a partial prenuptial molt, involving the head and neck and, at least part, if not all of the body plumage, which begins in December, and a complete post-nuptial molt in August and September. Thus it will be seen that the winter plumage, or perhaps it should be called the fall plumage, is worn but three or four months in the fall. Individuals vary greatly in the times at which this plumage is acquired and replaced. Adults in the fall have white throats, have less brown in the sides and have only traces of the yellowish brown ear tufts; but they can be recognized by the size and shape of the bills and by the darker backs and heads; many birds also have more or less black in the throats during the fall. The prenuptial molt into the adult spring plumage is sometimes prolonged into May but is usually completed by May 1.

Food.—The food of the eared grebe consists principally of water insects and their larvae, beetles, tadpoles, very small frogs and shrimps, all of which it obtains by diving; it also feeds to some extent on various water plants; and feathers, presumably from its own body are often found in its stomach. Dr. T. S. Roberts (1900) says:

The stomachs and gullets of several birds collected by the writer and kindly examined by Professor Beal, of the Biological Survey at Washington, contained a mass of insect débris to the exclusion of all else. One stomach alone furnished some 15 different species, among them several varieties injurious to the interests of man. The chief part of the food, however, during the time of our visit to the colony, and that on which the young were largely fed, was the nymphs of dragon flies which were then to be found in immense numbers in the meadows near by. The writer counted no less than 327 of these insects in a single stomach.

Behavior.—The eared grebe is seldom seen in flight, except on migrations, for the bird seems reluctant to leave the water and prefers to escape by diving or merely swimming away at a moderate speed, for it is not a shy species. It can, however, rise from the water readily and fly quite swiftly. It swims easily and glides through the water very smoothly, with scarcely a ripple. It can wholly or partially submerge its body while swimming or it can dive like a flash. When diving in deep water it often leaps into the air and plunges straight down, as if to gain impetus in this way. It dives with its wings closed and probably swims under water with only its feet in use. It is less inclined to remain under water or skulk in the reeds than the other small grebes, but prefers to come to the surface and watch proceedings from a distance. In its spring plumage it can easily be recognized by the slender shape of its head and neck, held straight up, and by the long pointed crest, which is usually erected; the effect is entirely different from that produced by the round, fluffy head of the horned grebe or the smooth head of the pied-billed grebe. Young birds in the fall might be recognized by the small slender heads and necks, but this is not a very conspicuous character.

In addition to the love notes, mentioned under the courtship performances, the eared grebe frequently indulges in a series of rasping, shrill calls and piercing cries. Yarrell (1871) says of the European bird:

The note of this species is a soft whistling *bib*, *bib*, and during the breeding season like *bide wide wide wide wide* uttered quickly.

Mr. Aretas A. Saunders writes to me in regard to its vocal powers:

I have had a considerable acquaintance with this species in the past year but have seldom heard a sound from it. Once, however, I observed a large flock of fall migrants of this species on Rock Creek Lake, Powell County, Montana, and these birds kept up a continual noise all the time. The note from a single bird is a short, harsh, high-pitched call that sounds like *wa-a-a*. The sound produced by the entire flock somewhat resembled the honking of a flock of snow geese. This flock numbered about 175 birds. They kept in a body in the middle of the lake and were not feeding. Why they kept up the continual clatter was a mystery to me, and rather remarkable because the species is usually so silent.

This species, as well as the western grebe, has suffered seriously from market hunting for the millinery trade, notably in the lake regions of Oregon and California, where thousands were shot every week during the breeding season; they were tame and easily killed. The breasts were stripped off, dried, and shipped to New York, where they were much in demand for ladies' hats, capes, and muffs. The hunters realized about 20 cents for each skin, which brought them in a handsome income. Fortunately this practice has been stopped, in that locality at least, by the establishment of protected reservations. There have been times in the past when the eggs of the eared grebe were used largely for food. Its habit of nesting in large, densely populated colonies made it an easy matter to gather the eggs in large quantities, which were salted down in barrels of brine for future use, but this custom does not seem to prevail to any extent to-day. These two destructive agencies undoubtedly reduced the abundance of the species considerably, but it is probably holding its own again now or perhaps even increasing where it is protected.

Fall.—The fall migration starts late in August and proceeds slowly. Throughout the northern portion of their breeding range the birds linger until driven out of the lakes by freezing; but from the southern portions of its breeding range the species never wholly disappears, although the individuals seen in winter were probably not bred in that vicinity. There is a coastwise movement as well as a southward migration in the fall; the species winters abundantly along the southern half of the California coast, as well as farther south, and in the lakes of the interior.

DISTRIBUTION.

Breeding range.—Western North America. East to central Manitoba (Shoal Lake and Red River), southwestern Minnesota (Heron Lake), northern Iowa (Eagle Lake, Hancock County, and Clear Lake, Cerro Cordo County), and eastern Nebraska (West Point and Omaha). South to southern Texas (Lavaca and Bexar Counties), northern New Mexico (San Miguel and Rio Arriba Counties), northern Arizona (Stoneman's and Mormon Lakes and near Flagstaff), and southern California (Escondido, San Diego County). West to the Sierras of California (also Bear Lake, San Bernardino Mountains, and Elizabeth Lake, Los Angeles County), probably eastern Oregon and eastern Washington (east of Cascade Mountains) and south central British Columbia (Kamloops). North to southern Mackenzie (Great Slave Lake).

Winter range.—Southward mainly west of the Rocky Mountains, particularly along the Pacific coast. East to Nevada (Carson City) and Texas (San Antonio). South to Guatemala (Lake Duenas). West to the Pacific coast; western Mexico (Guaymas), Lower California (off La Paz and Magdalena Bay) and California (entire coast). North to Washington (Nisqually Flats).

Spring migration.—Northeastward starting in April. Lower California: Colnett Bay, April 8; San Quentin Bay, May 9. Colorado: Barr Lake, April 14. Wyoming: Lake Como, May 4. Nebraska: End of April. Kansas: Last of April to middle of May. Missouri: April 9 to May 3 (formerly). Montana: Teton County, May 1.

Fall migration.—Southwestward across the Rocky Mountains. Montana: Custer and Davenport Counties, October 2. Idaho: Coeur d'Alene Lakes, October 9. Colorado: El Paso County,

October 27. Wyoming: November 10. Missouri: September 22 to November 2 (formerly). Kansas: September to November. Northern Arizona: September. Oregon: Fort Klamath, November 7. Lower California: San Jose del Cabo, October 18. Jalisco: Ocotlan, September 28.

Casual records.—Indiana: May 19 and November 5. Wisconsin: Several spring specimens. Illinois: Lake Michigan, winter (?). Michigan records are discredited.

Egg dates.—North Dakota and South Dakota: 41 records, April 29 to July 23; 21 records, June 4 to 27. Colorado: 19 records, May 10 to July 20; 10 records, May 28 to July 6. California: 14 records, April 22 to August 2; 7 records, June 8 to 19. Saskatchewan: 9 records, June 10 to 26; 5 records, June 13 to 22. Oregon and Washington: 9 records, May 3 to July 5; 5 records, June 1 to 12. Utah: 3 records, April 22, June 20 and July 2.

COLUMBUS DOMINICUS BRACHYPTERUS Chapman.

MEXICAN GREBE.

HABITS.

As this little tropical species, the smallest of the grebes, is the only one of the North American grebes that I am not familiar with in life, I must draw wholly from the observations of others for an account of its life history. Unfortunately, published notes on its habits are very scanty, so the story will be short and incomplete. Prior to 1899 the San Domingo grebe (*Colymbus dominicus*) stood on our Check List, as found in the West Indies, southern Texas, Mexico, and Lower California, as well as in tropical South America. But Frank M. Chapman (1899b) discovered certain geographical varieties of the species worthy of recognition in nomenclature and separated it into three subspecies. His description separates the Mexican form, which also ranges into Texas and Lower California, from the West Indian bird under the name of *brachypterus*, having a much shorter wing and a smaller bill. This seems to be a well-marked subspecies in which the characters are constant.

Mr. Vernon Bailey (1902) observes:

These tiny grebes are as common in the ponds of southern Texas as the dabchick in the North. In open water they bob on the little waves, and in quiet pools where the willows overhang the banks swim and dive among the sedges and pink water lilies. When not seeking food below the surface of the water they usually keep close to some cover, and in the middle of the day if not hidden in the sedges are found sitting close under the shore grass or in the shade of a bush or low-hanging tree.

Nesting.—Mr. Frank B. Armstrong, who has collected many sets of eggs of this grebe near Brownsville, Texas, wrote to Major Bendire in 1891 about its nesting habits. The nests are placed in the middle of a secluded pond, floating in three feet of water and exposed to the full rays of the sun. He says that the birds cover the eggs when they leave the nest to protect them from the excessive heat of the sun, and states that both sexes help in the incubation. I have two sets of Mexican grebe's eggs in my collection taken by Mr. Armstrong near Brownsville, Texas; one set of three fresh eggs was collected on April 8, 1898, from a nest in a creek; and one of four fresh eggs was taken on April 23, 1900, from a nest in a pond; the nests were made of rushes, trash, and dead vegetable matter.

Although the bird found in the West Indies is now considered subspecifically distinct, its habits are probably similar, and, as we have so litle to draw from on this species, I shall quote from what Mr. Philip H. Gosse (1847) has to say about it in Jamaica. He writes of its nesting habits:

Early in August I found near the edge of Mount Edgecombe pond a nest of this grebe—a round heap of pond weed and rotten leaves, flattened at the top, and slightly hollowed; it was about 15 inches wide and 6 or 8 inches thick. The top was damp, but not wet, and very warm from exposure to the sun's rays. We drew it on shore, for it was entangled among the branches of a fallen tree, but not attached to them, and presently found on the matted weed just below the surface, in the place where we had dragged it, a large white egg, excessively begrimed with dirt, doubtless from lying on the decaying leaves. On being cleansed I found it covered with a chalky coat, easily scratched off.

A few weeks after I again visited this pond. On approaching before sunrise (for I had traveled by the brilliant starlight of the tropical heavens) I saw a grebe sitting on a new nest, in the same spot as I had found the former one. This nest was composed of similar materials and contained four eggs. Early in December we found another nest with the young just peeping from the egg. It is probable, therefore, that several broods are reared in a season."

The Mexican grebe has recently been found breeding in Bexar County, Texas, by Messrs. Roy W. Quillin and Ridley Holleman (1916), who say:

About 10 miles south of San Antonio there is a large marshy lake which covers something like a thousand or twelve hundred acres. Being the only body of water of this size in this part of Texas, and having exceptional surroundings, it is the mecca of the water birds of this county. Practically the entire lake is surrounded by a barrier of cat-tail reeds, tules, and marsh grass, which in some portions is one hundred or more yards in width.

While searching for nests of the American eared grebe in a secluded inlet of this lake we located our first nest with eggs of the San Domingo grebe (*Colymbus dominicus brachypterus*). Both cat-tails and tules were growing at this point, but not so thickly as they are generally found. In one of the small patches of open water which break the monotony of these reed jungles the nest was anchored. In general appearance the nests examined by us average somewhat smaller than nests of the American eared grebe, this being especially true of the hollow in which the eggs are deposited. The nests were composed of decayed reeds of every description, heaped into a cone-shaped mass measuring from

4 to 6 inches in height and from 14 to 24 inches in diameter at the base, tapering to 6 or 8 inches at the top, and they were liberally plastered with mud, especially the depression which held the eggs. The area of this depression, the depth of which is about 1 inch, is determined by the number of eggs in the clutch, as they fit snugly into it.

Of five nests located from June 25 to July 9 two contained 4 eggs and three 3 eggs. All these sets were from slight to heavily incubated. The eggs were badly stained, and the majority retained a rich brown cast even after the most vigorous scrubbing. In all cases the eggs were covered by a thin layer of damp, decayed reeds.

We were unable to flush the bird from any of these nests and were able to identify them only by patient and lengthy waiting. These grebes are very hard to see on this lake, as they keep close to the reeds, and if found a short distance from them they immediately slip under the water and disappear. However, they were seen feeding in the company of American eared grebes, Florida gallinules, and American coots.

Eggs.—The breeding season for the Mexican grebe is so prolonged, from April to December, that it seems likely that two or three broods may be raised in a season. This habit is decidedly exceptional among water birds, although there is some evidence to indicate that the pied-billed grebe may raise two broods in a season. The Mexican grebe lays from three to six eggs, usually four or five. In shape the eggs vary from " elliptical oval " to " oval," with a tendency to become " fusiform " or more or less bluntly pointed at both ends. The shell is fairly smooth and quite glossy. The color is said to be bluish white or dull buffy white, but all that I have seen are so badly nest stained that the original color is no longer visible. The eggs in my collection vary from " cinnamon buff " to " cream buff," with numerous darker stains and specks of dirt. The measurements of 49 eggs in the United States National Museum and the author's collections average 33.9 by 23.4 millimeters; the eggs showing the four extremes measure 38 by 24, 35 by 25, 30 by 22.5, and 32.5 by 22 millimeters.

Plumages.—The downy young when first hatched is "blackish brown " above, which fades to "olive brown " in older birds; there are three narrow, broken, longitudinal white stripes on each side of the back, which disappear in older birds; the head and neck are broadly and irregularly striped with black and white; the crown is mostly black with a triangular or V-shaped rufous patch in the center; the belly is white. This downy covering is not replaced by the first real plumage until the young bird is fully grown, when the first winter plumage is acquired. Young birds can then be distinguished by their smaller bills; the head is leaden gray, with a darker crown and a whitish throat; the neck and chest are brownish or dusky and the sides are dusky. During the following spring, when the young bird is nearly a year old, it assumes a plumage which is practically adult. I have seen young birds undergoing this molt in May.

The adult nuptial plumage, characterized by the slate-gray head and neck, with the clear black crown and throat, is often worn until October; and the time of the postnuptial molt varies greatly in different individuals. This molt is probably complete, though I have not been able to trace it fully. Sooner or later a winter plumage is acquired, which is not very different from the nuptial plumage, except that the lower parts are purer white and there is more or less white in the chin and throat; perhaps these are sometimes wholly white, but more often the black predominates. This adult winter plumage, which is very different from the first winter, is apparently worn from October to March, when a limited prenuptial molt produces the spring plumage.

Food.—Nothing seems to have been published on the food of this species except the following unsatisfactory note by Mr. Gosse (1847):

> The gizzards of all that I obtained were filled with a finely comminuted substance, rather dry, of an unctuous appearance, and mingled with short silky filaments. A close examination with a lens failed to determine its nature; but I believe it to have been principally vegetable.

Behavior.—The same writer tells of their behavior:

> The ponds of the cattle pens are the favorite resorts of this little grebe. I have been most familiar with it at the pond of Mount Edgecumbe, which, though not more than an acre or two in extent, used to be speckled with a good number of these miniature ducks, their little black heads and the tops of their backs alone being visible above the surface. On the slightest alarm they dive with the quickness of thought, and so vigilant is their eye and so rapid their motion that, ordinarily, the fowling piece is discharged at them in vain. It is commonly said of some birds that they dive at the flash of the pan; but though I always used percussion locks I could never succeed in hitting one until I formed a screen of bushes, behind which I might fire in concealment. I then found no difficulty. Hence, I infer that their quick eye detects and takes alarm at the small but sudden motion of the falling hammer. They remain long and swim far under water, coming up where quite unlooked for. Some that I have had an opportunity of observing when swimming a little beneath the surface shot along with expanded wings, almost with the celerity of a fish. They do not always dive, however, when frightened; sometimes they sink deeper than before, and swim away almost submerged. When not alarmed they call and answer each other, with a loud clang, like the note of a trumpet.

Winter.—The Mexican grebe seems to be a resident throughout the year in the regions which it inhabits. Its short wings hardly enable it to rise above the surface of the ponds in which it lives, so that it is incapable of, or poorly equipped for, long migratory flights. It seems to be perfectly content to spend its life in the waters of its birth, where it is perfectly at home. Its plumage is so thoroughly impregnated with oil and its breathing apparatus is so specialized that it moves about in the bottom of the pond as freely as on land, living an amphibious life of ease and comfort and interested only in its watery surroundings.

DISTRIBUTION.

Breeding range.—Mexico and Central America from Panama north to the Rio Grande region of southern Texas. Occurs in the cape region of Lower California and has been attributed (probably erroneously) to the "Valley of the Colorado." Apparently resident and breeding throughout its range. Eggs have recently been taken in Bexar County, Texas (10 miles south of San Antonio). Replaced by closely allied forms in South America and the Greater Antilles.

Egg dates.—Texas: 39 records, March 3 to September 6; 20 records, June 3 to August 5.

PODILYMBUS PODICEPS (Linnæus).

PIED-BILLED GREBE.

HABITS.

This widely distributed and well-known bird, the little "dabchick," is practically resident, or nearly so, throughout the southern portion of its range, though probably there is a general movement southward in winter and the summer residents are therefore not the same individuals that are seen in that region in winter. The dates given below show that this grebe is an early migrant, pushing northward soon after the ice has left our northern ponds and streams. Its favorite haunts when migrating are small sheltered ponds and sluggish streams where it can paddle about in comfort and seek shelter, when danger threatens, among the bushes, reeds or grasses which line the shores or where it may hide under the protecting vegetation of overhanging banks. In such situations it seems to vanish mysteriously, skulking in some sheltered nook, with only its bill above water, well deserving its common name of "water witch."

Courtship.—Audubon's (1840) spirited drawing of the "pied-billed dabchick," as he calls it, shows this bird in the midst of active courtship, which is a lively performance; the ardent suitor rushes about in the most excited manner, splashing along over the surface of the water or repeatedly diving below it and coming up again near his intended mate and voicing his admiration in a variety of soft cooing notes.

Nesting.—As soon as their love affairs are settled the grebes begin to search for a suitable nesting site. This is generally well chosen and the nest more successfully concealed than is the case with the other grebes. The nature of the nesting site varies considerably in different localities.

Mr. William Brewster (1906) describes a former nesting site of the pied-billed grebe in Massachusetts as follows:

On June 13, 1891, Mr. Walter Faxon found a number of pied-billed grebes breeding at Great Meadow. There can be little doubt that they had been established there for sometime previous to this, for the shallow brush-grown reservoir which they inhabited had then been in existence for nearly 20 years. On the occasion just mentioned, Mr. Faxon saw or heard at least six or eight different birds, one of which was accompanied by chicks only a few days old, and on April 27, 1892, he discovered a nest containing five fresh eggs.

During the following eight years Great Meadow was frequently visited by our local ornithologists, and the manners and customs of the grebes were closely studied. One or two birds often appeared in the pond as soon as it was free from ice—this sometimes happening before the close of March—and by the middle of April the full colony was usually reestablished. It was difficult to judge as to how many members it contained, for they were given to haunting the flooded thickets, and we seldom saw more than three or four of them on any one occasion; but at times, especially in the early morning and late afternoon when the weather was clear and calm their loud cuckoo-like calls and odd whinnying outcries would come in quick succession from so many different parts of the pond that one might have thought there were scores of birds. Probably the total number of pairs did not ever exceed a dozen, while during some seasons there were apparently not more than five or six. They built their interesting floating nests in water a foot or more in depth, anchoring them to the stems of the sweet gale and button bushes, and laying from five to eight eggs, which usually were covered by the bird whenever she left them. Although a few sets of eggs were taken by collectors, the grebes reared a fair number of young every season, and without doubt they would have continued to resort to Great Meadow for an indefinite period had not the reservoir been abandoned, and its waters almost completely drained in the autumn of 1901; since then the bids have ceased, of course, to frequent the place.

The pied-billed grebe is not easily driven from its favorite nesting haunts by the encroachments of civilization and is occasionally found nesting in suitable localities in thickly settled regions or near our large cities. A striking instance of this is shown in Mr. Clinton G. Abbott's (1907) account of the nesting of this species in the Hackensack Meadows, near New York City, in 1906, where an extensive cat-tail swamp offered a congenial home for grebes and gallinules.

Mr. Arthur T. Wayne (1910) says of its breeding habits in South Carolina:

This is an abundant permanent resident, breeding in fresh-water ponds or large rice-field reservoirs, where the water is generally from 4 to 10 feet deep. The birds are mated by the last of February, and the nests, which are commenced about the middle of March, are composed of decayed vegetable matter anchored to buttonwood bushes or reeds.

In the North Dakota sloughs, in 1901, we found the pied-billed grebe nesting abundantly, in company with canvasbacks, redheads, ruddy ducks, and coots, and examined a large number of nests, which may be considered as fairly typical of its normal nesting habits throughout the greater portion of its breeding range. The depth of water in which the nest is located varies greatly, but most of the nests are placed in water not over 3 feet deep. The nests are usually anchored to, or built up around or among, dead or growing reeds or rushes. Sometimes they are well concealed in thick clumps of reeds, but usually they can be easily seen, although not so conspicuous as those of the horned or eared grebes. The nests are generally scattered and only a few pairs of birds were found in each slough. When located in deep water the nest is strictly a floating affair, but otherwise it is more often partially connected with the bottom. A large amount of material is collected and piled up into bulky mass, mostly below the surface of the water, often large enough to fill a bushel basket; on top of this, above the water, a smaller and neater nest is built. The material consists of whatever the bird can conveniently find in the vicinity in the way of decayed vegetable matter, dead reeds, flags, rushes, or grasses; sometimes fresh, green flags are mixed in with the rubbish and often the whole structure is plastered together with a quantity of the soft, green vegetable scum which grows in stagnant water. This wet and slimy structure is built up but a few inches above the water, usually from 2 to 4 inches, and measures about a foot in diameter; the nest cavity is but slightly hollowed and the eggs are partially buried in the soft material.

Eggs.—The pied-billed grebe lays from 3 to 10 eggs, but the extremes are rare and the set usually consists of from 5 to 7 eggs. In shape the eggs are " elliptical ovate " or " elliptical oval," sometimes almost " fusiform." The shell is generally smooth, with a slight luster, but sometimes dotted with small excrescences or lumps. The color of the clean, freshly laid egg is dull bluish white or pale olive white, but it soon becomes stained or clouded with various buffy shades; some sets are uniformly stained as dark as " wood-brown " or " Isabella color;" generally more or less mud and bits of nesting material sticks to the egg, giving it a mottled appearance. The measurements of 48 eggs in the United States National Museum collection average 43.4 by 30 millimeters; the eggs showing the four extremes measure **47** by 30, 44 by **32, 39** by 29.5, and 44 by **28** millimeters.

Mr. C. H. Pease made some interesting observations on the nesting operations of this species at Canaan, Connecticut, during May and June, 1913. He sent the results of his observations to Dr. Louis B. Bishop, who has given them to me. On May 22 he found the nest completed and the first egg laid; on May 28 the eighth and last egg was laid, one having been laid each day. The first two eggs hatched on June 15, one in the forenoon and one in the afternoon; and the last egg hatched at 9.15 in the morning of June 21; the record shows that the period of incubation, in this case, was from 23 to 24 days. On June 22, the day after the last egg hatched, only one young bird was left in the nest. On July 3 he saw the whole family of eight, " half grown in less than two weeks."

Both sexes incubate. So far as I know, only one brood is raised in a season; but there are some very early and very late dates for nesting which may indicate two broods. The question of whether this grebe regularly incubates its eggs or leaves them to be hatched by the warmth of decaying vegetation has provoked considerable discussion. Like all the smaller grebes, it frequently covers its eggs, with the soft material of which the nest is composed, when it leaves its nest; but this is not always done and often, when the bird is surprised and forced to leave in a hurry, it does not have time to do so. The pied-billed grebe is seldom seen sitting on its nest. I have examined a great many nests and have attempted to approach cautiously enough to catch a glimpse of the incubating bird, but have never been able to see one on its nest; some other observers have been more fortunate. I believe that it incubates regularly during the greater part of the time. It is one of the shyest of the grebes; it slips away from its nest on the slightest alarm and keeps out of sight. I have watched for an hour or more within sight of half a dozen nests and not caught a glimpse of a single grebe, although they were undoubtedly watching me all the time.

Young.—The young are very precocious and leave the nest soon after they are hatched; usually some of the young are swimming about before the last of the eggs have hatched. They are expert swimmers and divers, by instinct, though they can not remain under water more than a few seconds. I have taken recently hatched chicks out of a nest, which were too young to have been taught by their parents, and seen them dive and swim away or hide among the reeds with only their little bills protruding above the surface. Sometimes the parent bird carries them on her back where they cling tenaciously while she dives and brings them up again, none the worse for their ducking. They are truly little " water witches " by inheritance. Rev. Manley B. Townsend writes me that, on June 24, 1910, he saw an adult, with young, chasing a muskrat on the surface of a slough in Nebraska, and raises the question whether these animals, which are generally considered to be strictly vegetarian in their habits, kill young grebes. Undoubtedly many are killed by pickerel or other large fishes and by snapping turtles or large frogs.

Dr. Arthur A. Allen (1914) has written a very interesting account of his studies into the family affairs of the pied-billed grebe, illustrating it with some remarkable photographs of this shy bird. It is well worth reading or quoting in full, but space will permit only the following extract:

I was first directed to the spot by a friend who said that " coots " were nesting there. I was not a little surprised, therefore, when, after wading for a short distance along the edge of the pond, my attention was attracted by a splash in the water ahead, accompanied by a startled note like the syllable *keck*, and a few seconds later a grebe bobbed into sight. Instead of immediately sinking again, as one learns to expect of a grebe, it rose up on its legs and began beating upon the water with its wings. Such behavior bespoke something very unusual happening in the near-by nest. I looked just in time to see the last of the striped young scramble from it and disappear beneath the water. Then ensued a series of maneuvers on the part of the bird which were evidently intended to distract my attention. The customary silence, ease, and grace of diving were entirely abandoned. Each appearance above the water was announced by a shake of the body, followed by a beating of the wings on the surface, and a flip of the fete as it again dove, which sometimes sprayed water for more than a yard. This performance took place within 10 or 15 feet of me, and sometimes the bird swam in even closer. At such times it rested rather high on the water, holding its tail, if we may speak of it as such, erect, and nervously flashing the light areas on the flanks, as do the gallinules.

Meanwhile the young birds had made their way toward the center of the pond. The largest could not have been more than a few days old, and yet, when I tried to catch them, they showed all the ingenuity of the old birds, diving, doubling, swimming with just the bill showing, or lying concealed in a bunch of water weeds, with only the nostrils above the surface. Had the water been less clear I probably should have been unable to catch any of them; but, as it was, I could follow them as they escaped in various directions. They were even conspicuous when attempting to hide. I was reminded of the old story of the ostrich which buried its head in the sand to escape detection; for, in spite of the fact that only the bill was exposed above the water, the entire body was nearly as conspicuous as though floating on the surface. In diving, as in floating, the wings of the young projected nearly at right angles from their bodies, even more so than in other precocial birds.

The largest of the young had already reached the open water beyond my depth, and when I returned to the shore the old grebe swam toward it, changing her alarm not of *keck, keck* to a softer *cup, cup*, as though calling to it. Swimming beyond it, she turned her tail toward it and slightly raised her wings. This was the signal for the young one to crawl upon her back, which it repeatedly attempted to do until its mother, disgusted with such clumsiness, clapped her wing on its neck and started off at a great rate for the other end of the pond. When far enough away she checked her speed and gave it another chance. Then with her wobbly passenger she continued to the end of the pond, where she was joined by her mate. Here they sported about for some time, the young bird plunging from the back of one and swimming across to the other, all seemingly forgetful of the rest of the family. Finally they disappeared into the rushes, and I continued my course around the pond.

Plumages.—The downy young is prettily and quite strikingly marked with black and white; it is mainly glossy black above, with longitudinal stripes of grayish white on the neck and back; the crown is black, more or less variegated with " walnut brown " or " burnt umber," sometimes in the form of a central patch, and with two broad superciliary stripes of white meeting on the forehead and two white stripes above them; the sides of the neck and throat are variegated with black and white and the sides of the body are more or less washed with dusky; the under parts are grayish white, lightest on the belly. The bird is fully half grown before the real plumage appears, which shows first on the breast and then in the wings; it is nearly full-grown before the down entirely disappears. The large series of specimens in the United States National Museum collection seems to indicate that the full adult plumage is acquired during the first year. Many young birds retain the black and white stripes on the head until late in October, though some have completely changed before that time into the brown plumage of the first winter, in which the bright russet color of the neck, breast, and flanks is conspicuous. The black throat of the adult and the black band on the bill are acquired just prior to the breeding season. Some adults show traces of the black throat in the fall or have it well developed, but partially concealed by the whitish tips of the feathers.

Food.—The pied-billed grebe feeds largely on animal matter such as small fish, snails, small frogs, tadpoles, aquatic worms, leeches and water insects; it also eats the seeds and soft parts of aquatic plants to some extent. Balls of its own feathers often occur in its stomach. Although this grebe is more essentially a fresh water bird than the other species, Audubon (1840) states that when its favorite ponds and streams are frozen over, it may occasionally be seen in bays and estuaries searching for shrimps and fry.

Behavior.—This species is less often seen in flight than the other grebes, for it seems to prefer to escape by diving or skulking, but it is well capable of rapid flight, when necessary, in spite of its small wings. When rising from the water it runs along the surface for a long distance, beating the water with its broad paddles until it can rise into the air, when it flies swiftly away in a straight line, moving its wings very quickly and with its neck and feet outstretched. When migrating it often flies high in the air. It seems to be incapable of rising from the ground and its movements on dry land are so awkward that it spends very little time out of the water; although it sometimes crawls out onto lily pads or marshy shores to sun itself or preen its feathers. The water is its natural element, where it is completely at home. I can remember distinctly how much ammunition I wasted in my old muzzle-loading gun, when I was a boy, in vain attempts to bag the elusive "hell-diver," as we used to call it. My attempts were seldom successful and I used to think that it dove at the flash of the gun; with a modern gun and nitro powder the results might have been different. Anything which even looked like a duck was considered legitimate game in those days and the silky grebes' breasts were proudly presented to my girl friends. The pied-billed grebe is no less expert than others of its tribe in diving; ordinarily, in a hurried dive, it plunges forward and disappears like a flash, swimming away for a long distance under water, to appear suddenly at some unexpected spot or perhaps to vanish and keep out of sight; it also has the power so to contract its displacement that it can swim along with only its head and neck above water, or it can gradually sink down backward, like a disappearing frog, without making a ripple. I have always supposed that the grebes do not use their wings under water, but Audubon (1840) had a good chance to study them in captivity and says:

We placed them in a large tub of water, where we could see all their sub-aqueous movements. They swam round the sides of the tub in the manner of the puffin, moving their wings in accordance with their feet, and continued so a much longer time than one could suppose it possible for them to remain under water, coming up to breathe, and plunging again with astonishing celerity.

Except during the breeding season this grebe does not associate much with other species; it is usually seen singly, in pairs, or in very small parties. Dr. Frank M. Chapman's (1912) experience shows that it is not always so solitary; he says:

On Heron Lake, Minnesota, in early October, I have seen pied-billed grebes, in close-massed flocks, containing a hundred or more birds, cruising about in open water.

Prof. Lynds Jones writes me that:

On small bodies of water they mix somewhat with the other water birds, more from necessity than from choice. Threatened danger will almost always result in the separation of the grebes from the ducks with which they may be associated.

Rev. W. F. Henninger reports that he has seen them associated with blue-winged teal and black duck and playfully chasing around with them.

The vocal powers of the pied-billed grebe are limited to a few notes, heard mainly in the breeding season, for at other times it is generally a silent bird. Dr. Chapman (1908) describes its love notes as follows:

Its notes, as I have heard them in the Montezuma marshes, are very loud and sonorous with a cuckoo-like quality, and may be written *cow-cow-cow-cow-cow-cow-cow-cow-cow-cow-uh*, *cow-uh*, *cow-uh-cow-uh*. These notes vary in number, and are sometimes followed by prolonged wailing *cows* or *uhs*, almost human in their expressiveness of pain and fear. This is apparently the love song of the male, in which his mate sometimes joins with a *cuk-cuk-cuk*, followed by a slower *ugh, ugh, ugh*.

Mr. W. L. Dawson (1909) designates the notes as "an odd bubbling giggle, *keggy, keggy, keggy, keggy, keggy, keggy, keggy*, etc., rendered with great rapidity"; he also refers to a single excited *aow*, uttered from time to time. Mr. E. E. Thompson (1890) describes a peculiar call note "*pr-r-r-r-r- tow tow tow tow tow*" which he ascribed to this species in Manitoba.

The pied-billed grebe may be distinguished in the field from other grebes by the absence of white in the wings, by the general brownish tinge, and by the short, thick, henlike bill.

Rev. C. W. G. Eifrig has sent me the following account of an incident, which well illustrates the ability of this species to conceal itself:

It had been very dry for a long time. The sloughs were dry or nearly so. While walking through one, I saw a grebe in the fringe between the plant growth of the center and the outer shore where there was hardly enough cover for a grasshopper to hide. Nor could it find cover in the center, for that is where I came from. It could not dive, because the water was only 3 or 4 inches deep. So being forced to adopt desperate means, it threw itself over a tussock in the shallow water, where at once it became invisible at a distance of 10 to 15 feet. And the tussock was only as large as 2 or 3 hands. Its neck was lying across, the body pressed against the side as closely as posible and so its colors harmonized exactly with the blackish brown of the tussock.

Two somewhat similar incidents are related by **Mr. Delos E. Culver** (1914) which show that these and similar hiding poses are probably frequently used by pied-billed grebes.

Fall.—On the fall migration these grebes proceed slowly through September and October, lingering on the inland ponds and small streams in family parties, in pairs or even singly, sojourning regularly in certain favorite spots, but working gradually coastwise. They show a decided preference for fresh water at all seasons, but as the ponds and streams become frozen, they are forced to resort to the open tidal creeks and estuaries. In such places they spend the winter on our southern Atlantic and Gulf coasts and as far north as Washington on the Pacific coast. They also winter to some extent in the rivers and open lakes of the interior, particularly in the Southern States and Mexico.

DISTRIBUTION.

Breeding range.—Nearly entire North and South America in suitable localities. In North America east to Quebec, New Brunswick, and the Atlantic Coast States. South to Gulf States and Mexico. West to the Pacific coast. North to Vancouver Island, central British Columbia (Cariboo district), southern Mackenzie (Great Slave Lake and valley of the Mackenzie River), and Ontario (Sudbury, Parry Sound district, and Ottawa).

Actual nesting records for Central and South America are not numerous, but the species is resident south to Argentine Republic and Chile. The bird breeding in the West Indies has been separated as *Podilymbus podiceps antillarum* Bangs, but its validity has been questioned.

Winter range.—Birds breeding in the northern United States and southern Canada winter in the southern United States and Mexico. From New York and New Jersey (occasionally), Virginia (Ashland, Hanover County), and District of Columbia (Potomac River) southward and from the Gulf States west to Texas (McLennan County) and Arizona (Colorado River). On the Pacific coast from Vancouver Island (Barkley Sound) southward. The species is largely resident south of the United States.

Spring migration.—Northward beginning in March. New Jersey: March 15 to April 20. New York: March 23 to April 15. Massachusetts: March 1 (earliest). Maine: April to May 19. Missouri: During March. Ohio: April 1 to 10, earliest March 16. Illinois: March 23 to April 15. Wisconsin: April 13. Michigan: March 12 to 28. Nebraska: Middle of April. Colorado: Boulder County, April 7. Wyoming: May 5. Montana: May 23.

Fall migration.—Southward starting in September. Nova Scotia: Halifax County, November 5 (latest). Ontario: Ottawa, November 7 (latest). Maine: September 1 to November 13. Massachusetts: December 10 (latest). New York: September 15 to November 1. Michigan: October to November. Wisconsin: October 20. Ohio: September 1 to October 25, latest November 4. Saskatchewan: Dirt Hills, October. Colorado, Boulder County, October 16.

Casual records.—Recorded from Cape Horn and Straits of Magellan, Hudson Bay (York Factory), and Bermuda (perhaps regular in winter).

Egg dates.—Michigan and Wisconsin: 33 records, May 14 to August 10; 17 records, May 30 to June 9. Illinois: 27 records, May 10 to July 8; 14 records, May 26 to June 10. California: 26 records, April 23 to August 6; 13 records, May 22 to June 15. North Dakota: 18 records, May 19 to June 23; 9 records, May 29 to June 8. Colorado: 12 records, May 10 to July 6; 6 records, May 18 to June 9. British Columbia and Washington: 11 records, April 4 to June 3; 6 records, April 13 to May 27. New York and New Jersey: 8 records, May 15 to August 8; 4 records, June 3 to 17. Texas: 4 records, June 2 and 28; August 23 and 25. South Carolina: 4 records, April 11, 18, and 30, and May 1.

Family GAVIIDÆ. Loons.

GAVIA IMMER (Brünnich).

LOON.

HABITS.

Among the picturesque lakes of the wilder, wooded portions of the Northern States and Canada—where dark firs and spruces mingled with graceful white birches, cast their reflections in the still, clear waters—sportsmen and appreciative nature lovers have found attractive summer resorts. Here, far from the cares of the busy world, one finds true recreation in his pursuit of speckled trout, real rest in his camp among the fragrant balsams, and genuine joy in his communion with nature in her wildest solitudes. The woodland lakes would be solitudes, indeed, did they lack the finishing touch to make the picture complete, the tinge of wildness which adds color to the scene, the weird and mournful cry of the loon, as he calls to his mate or greets some new arrival. Who has ever paddled a canoe, or cast a fly, or pitched a tent in the north woods and has not stopped to listen to this wail of the wilderness? And what would the wilderness be without it?

Spring.—Loons love solitude and return each year to their chosen lake soon after the ice goes out in the spring. This usually occurs late in April in Maine and correspondingly later farther north. We saw them migrating in large numbers along the south coast of Labrador between May 23 and June 3, 1909; they were in loose detached flocks in which the individuals were widely scattered. The spring flight on the Massachusetts coast is prolonged through April and May, the heaviest flight occurring about the middle of May. The migration is mainly along the coast, a short distance off the shore, though they fly across Cape Cod at its narrowest part, from Buzzards Bay into Cape Cod Bay.

The loons are apparently paired when they arrive on their breeding grounds and I believe they are usually mated for life. They show strong attachment to their old home and return year after year to the same spot to nest, even if they have been repeatedly disturbed. Apparently they do not desert a locality until one or both of the pair are killed. Loons are nowhere really abundant, but they are evenly distributed over a wide breeding range, are universally known, and are so conspicuous that they seem to be commoner than they actually are. Nearly every suitable lake within the breeding range of the species has its pair of loons, or has had it, and many large lakes support two or more pairs. The breeding range of this species is becoming more and more restricted as the country becomes cleared and settled; the loons are being gradually killed off or driven away. A pair of loons nested in Quittacus Pond, Lakeville, Massachusetts, about 14 miles from my home, in 1872, but the eggs were taken and both birds were shot; none have nested in this section of the State since. The same story is true of many another New England lake where the insatiable desire to kill has forever extirpated an exceedingly interesting bird.

Nesting.—The description of three nests which I have examined will serve to illustrate the ordinary nesting habits of this loon. The first nest was found on June 16, 1899, near Brooksville, Maine; it was located in the water near the marshy and reedy shores of a secluded little cove on a large pond. The loon was incubating and we saw her slide off into the water with a big splash, going directly under and swimming away almost under our boat, the ripples on the surface and a row of bubbles marking her course; when she reached the entrance to the cove, about 15 yards past us, she came to the surface and flapped along, rapidly disappearing around a point and leaving a foaming wake behind her. The nest was a large circular mass of wet, soggy, half-rotten reeds and other vegetable matter heaped up in the shallow water near the edge of the growing reeds; it measured about 2 feet in diameter, was only slightly hollowed in the center, and was built up about 6 inches above the water. It contained two nearly fresh eggs, which were lying parallel to each other and about 2 inches apart.

The second nest, found on June 6, 1900, was on a little rocky islet, only about 10 yards long, in Cathance Lake, Washington County, Maine. The nest was only about 2 feet from the water, with a well-worn pathway down which the bird could slide into the water. It was well concealed under some alders, little maples, and other underbrush, and was a wet mass of green mosses, mixed with a few twigs, built on the rocks with one small rock left bare near the middle of the nest. It measured about 25 inches in outside and 16 inches in inside diameter. The inner cavity was about 3 inches deep and the outer rim was built up about 4 inches, so that the moss was only about an inch thick in the center of the nest. The two fresh eggs were lying in the center of the nest about an inch apart. We did not see the loon leave the nest, but we saw the pair swimming about in the lake and heard their weird cry.

The third nest was found, on June 23, 1912, on the shore of a heavily wooded island in Sandy Lake, Newfoundland. It was placed just above an open sandy beach, among some small scattered underbrush, 30 feet from the shore. The lake had been very much higher a few weeks previously and probably, at the time the nest was built, it was near the edge of the water. Another nest, in the same general region, was similarly located, probably for the same reason. The birds in both cases had worn a pathway to the water, where the prints of their feet were plainly visible in the sand. The nest was merely a slight hollow in the bare ground with a wide rim of dry grass, bits of sticks and rubbish around it. This loon did not leave the nest until I was within 50 feet of it; but she made good speed, scrambling down to the lake, half running, half flying, and flapping away over the surface until she reached water deep enough for diving. The two eggs in the nest were heavily incubated; one of them was nearly ready to hatch and the other was addled, as is often the case.

Loons are reported by many observers as nesting on muskrat houses. I have never seen such a nest, but suppose they must select the old, abandoned houses or else build up piles of rubbish themselves which look like muskrat houses. I believe that they prefer to occupy the same nest every year and they probably add to it a little each year.

Eggs.—This loon lays normally two eggs, one of which is often infertile; sometimes only one egg is laid and occasionally three are found in a nest. Audubon was quite confident that three eggs was the usual number and many other writers have referred to it. I have never found a set of three eggs and believe that they are very rarely seen. The eggs vary but little in shape from "elliptical ovate" to "elongate ovate." The shell is thick, smoothly granular, and has a dull luster. The ground color varies from dark to light olive brown or from dark to light olive green with various intermediate shades. They are rather sparingly marked with small spots of "clove brown" or "bister," and occasionally with lighter spots of drab; the markings are usually much scattered. I have seen it stated in print that a set usually contains one brown and one green egg, but I have not found it to be so in the nests that I have examined. The measurements of 41 eggs in various collections average 88.9 by 56.2 millimeters; the eggs showing the four extremes measure **96.5** by **61** and **82** by **52** millimeters.

Only one brood is raised in a season, but if the first set of eggs is taken, another set is laid within three or four weeks; sometimes even a third set is laid if the first two have been disturbed, but this would not be likely to happen unless the first set was laid very early. Mr. Ora W. Knight (1918) gives the period of incubation as "very close to 29 days." The pair keep together during the incubating period and probably both take part in it, though this is difficult to determine, as the sexes look so much alike. Incubation is practically continuous; the eggs are never allowed to become too cool, though they will stand considerable chilling, and they are never covered with rubbish. While incubating, the loon sits very low and is spread out quite flat; she is not so conspicuous as her striking colors would indicate.

Young.—Mr. C. William Beebe (1907) made a study of two young loons, which were hatched from eggs brought to the New York Zoological Park, from which he drew the following conclusions:

It is probable that young loons are, from the first, fed on whole, not on macerated or regurgitated fish. The actions of swimming and preening are instinctive. The method of swimming is usually by alternate strokes. These become simultaneous when a sudden spurt or great speed is desired. The arc of the swimming stroke, in the young chick, is much more lateral than in the adult bird. Loon chicks can progress more easily and rapidly over the ground than can the adults, in spite of the preceding conclusion. Progression, however, is never by walking, but by frog-like leaps. Diving, catching fish or swallowing them head first are almost congenital instincts, much improved by practice within the first week. There is no instinctive fear in these young birds. It is probable that the young loons instinctively recognize the usual rolling, laughter-like call of the parents, judging from their reaction to the notes of the giant kingfisher.

Mr. F. A. Shaw, writing to me of the habits of loons at Sebago Lake, Maine, says:

When the loon family is approached by boat, the parent bird retires to a safe distance and by loud cries and by flapping the wings on the water endeavors to draw attention from the little ones to herself. If closely pursued the young, even in their downy first plumage, will dive and swim under water for several feet. I have seen them dive and swim under clear, calm water, and bright bubbles would stand on their little backs. On returning to the surface, they would shake themselves and their downy covering would be perfectly dry.

Audubon (1840) says, of the food and development of the young:

The young of the loon are covered at birth with a kind of black stiff down and in a day or two after are led to the water by their mother. They swim and dive extremely well even at this early stage of their existence, and after being fed by regurgitation for about a fortnight, receive portions of fish, aquatic insects, and small reptiles, until they are able to maintain themselves. During this period, gray feathers appear among the down of the back and belly, and the black quill feathers of the wings and tail gradually elongate. They are generally very fat, and so clumsy as to be easily caught on land; if their retreat to the water is cut off. But should you miss your opportunity and the birds succeed in gaining the liquid element, into which they drop like so many terrapins, you will be astonished to see them as it were run over the water with extreme celerity, leaving behind them a distinct furrow. When the young are well able to fly, the mother entices them to remove from the pond or lake on which they have been bred, and leads them on the wing to the nearest part of the sea, after which she leaves them to shift for themselves. Now and then, after this period, the end of August or beginning of September, I have still seen the young of a brood, two or three in number continuing together until they were induced to travel southward, when they generally set out singly.

Mr. Cecil Swale writes, in a letter to Mr. W. E. Saunders:

When a pair of young ones can fly, the parents appear to call in another pair to celebrate and they certainly do it; for several years we have noticed that on one particular day, and only one that summer, six loons will be seen in the air at once making a lot of noise; four of the birds seem equally strong and make wide circles round the other two. It is generally August before this happens.

August seems rather early for young loons to be flying, as they are usually not strong on the wing until the middle or last of September.

Plumages.—The young loon, when first hatched is completely covered with soft, thick, short down; the entire upper parts including the head, neck, chest, and sides are dark colored, " fuscous black " on crown and back, " fuscous " on throat and sides; only the central belly portion is white, tinged laterally with grayish. I have not been able to find any specimens showing the change from the downy stage into the first winter plumage. The latter, however, is well represented in collections and is well marked; it is chiefly characterized by the well-rounded feathers of the back and scapulars which are broadly edged with gray or whitish; the top of the head, hind neck, and rump are blackish or sooty, grading off gradually on the sides of the neck into the fine dusky mottling of the throat; the chin, sometimes the throat and the underparts are white. This plumage is worn for nearly a year without much modification, the light edgings above bleaching out to white or wearing away and the throat becoming whiter toward spring. The bill is horn colored in the fall, becoming darker in the spring, but never black. Probably there is an incomplete prenuptial molt. The postnuptial molt is complete and produces early in the next fall the second winter plumage, which is similar to the first winter plumage except that the dark crown is more clearly defined, the throat is pure white and the feathers of the back, which still have broad light edgings, are less rounded and more *nearly square* at their tips. This plumage is worn for only a short time in some individuals which begin to show signs of molt into the second nuptial plumage as early as November or December, by the growth of a few of the jet-black feathers with white spots on the back, wings, rump, and flanks; usually this molt is not much in evidence until February; from that time on the prenuptial molt advances to the head and neck and by April or May the second nuptial plumage is completed. This is similar to the adult nuptial plumage, but is duller, more dingy, and often incomplete, with more or less white in the chin and throat. Specimens in this plumage have been found to have the sexual organs somewhat enlarged, indicating that the birds probably breed when about 2 years old. The bill is now black and never again becomes as light colored as in young birds. At the next postnuptial molt the young bird becomes fully adult, when a little over 2 years old.

The adult winter plumage, assumed during the third fall, is characterized by the black bill and by the *square* tipped feathers of the back and scapulars, which have no light edgings but have a faint suggestion, a ghost as it were, of the white spot of the nuptial plumage in a shade of gray only slightly lighter than the rest of the feather. This plumage is worn for only a short time, as in the second-year bird; specimens in this plumage are very scarce in collections and it is difficult to find one that is not either molting into it or out of it; the postnuptial molt into it begins sometimes by the last of August, but sometimes not until October; and the prenuptial molt out of it may begin in November or later in the winter and may not be completed until spring. Apparently some individuals, perhaps very old birds, do not assume this winter plumage at all, for I have seen birds in fully adult breeding plumage in September, October, and November.

Food.—This loon feeds largely on fish, which it pursues beneath the surface with wonderful power and speed. The subaqueous rush of this formidable monster must cause great consternation among the finny tribes. Even a party of fish-hunting mergansers is promptly scattered before the onslaught of such a powerful rival; they recognize his superior strength and speed, as he plunges in among them, and must stand aside until his wants are satisfied. Even the lively trout, noted for its quickness of movement, can not escape the loon and large numbers of these desirable fish are destroyed to satisfy its hunger. Some sportsmen have advocated placing a bounty on loons on this account, but as both loon and trout have always flourished together until the advent of the sportsmen, it is hardly fair to blame this bird, which is such an attractive feature of the wilds, for the scarcity of the trout. We are too apt to condemn a bird for what little damage it does in this way, without giving it credit for the right to live.

Mr. Hersey's notes state that a loon killed at Chatham, Massachusetts, in February had in its gullet 15 flounders averaging about 4 inches in length, but several of which were 6 inches long; in addition to this hearty meal its stomach was completely filled with a mass of partly digested fish.

Audubon (1840) says of its food habits:

Unlike the cormorant, the loon usually swallows its food under the water, unless it happens to bring up a shellfish or a crustaceous animal, which it munches for awhile before it swallows it. Fishes of numerous kinds, aquatic insects, water lizards, frogs, and leeches, have been found by me in its stomach, in which there is generally much coarse gravel, and sometimes the roots of fresh-water plants.

Dr. B. H. Warren (1890) says:

The stomach contents of seven loons, captured during the winter months in Chester, Delaware, Clinton, and Lehigh Counties, Pennsylvania, consisted entirely of fish bones and scales; two other specimens, purchased in the winter of 1881 from a game dealer in Philadelphia, were found to have fed on small seeds and portions of plants, apparently roots.

A loon which was kept for a while at the New York Aquarium, in a pool with skates and sculpins, was very aggressive, according to Mr. C. H. Townsend (1908); although "supplied with an abundance of live killifishes, its activity led it to strike frequently at the large fishes and it succeeded in swallowing one of the sculpins with a head larger than its own."

Dr. P. L. Hatch (1892) says:

Though fish and frogs are preferably their food, they do nicely without them when supplied with aquatic vegetation. If undisturbed by being fired at, they will visit the same localities daily during the season for their food.

Mr. W. F. Ganong (1890) gives a full account of an instance where a young loon attempted to eat a fresh-water clam, by inserting its bill into the open shell of the mollusk, which was about 2 inches long; the young loon found the clam too strong for it and lost part of its bill in consequence.

Mr. Cecil Swale writes that the loons " catch their fish across the bill and then with a quick toss bring the fish's head into the throat, stretch the head and neck straight up and the fish seems to work its own way down."

Behavior.—Dr. Bell says, according to Mr. Thomas McIlwraith (1894) :

The loon, in common with some other waterfowl, has a curious habit, when its curiosity is excited by anything it does not understand, of pointing its bill straight upward, and turning its head rapidly round in every direction as if trying to solve the mystery under consideration. Once when in my shooting skiff, behind the rushes, drifting down the bay before a light wind, I came upon a pair of these birds feeding about 20 yards apart. They did not take much notice of what must have seemed to them a clump of floating rushes, and being close enough to one of them I thought to secure it, but the cap snapped. The birds hearing the noise, and still seeing nothing living, rushed together, and got their bills up, as described, for consultation.

These birds are said to spear the fish with the bill closed, and to bring them to the surface so that they may turn them endways for the purpose of swallowing. The gulls, hovering overhead, and seeing what is going on down in the clear water, watch for the moment the fish is raised to the surface, when they swoop down and carry it off. When many hungry gulls are present, this process is repeated till the patience of the loon is quite exhausted.

The loon navigates the air as a high powered cruiser plows the sea under forced draft. Perfection of design, with ample power effectively applied, produce the desired result. The lines are perfect; the strong neck and breast, terminating in the long sharp bill, are outstretched to pierce the air like the keenest spear; the heavy body, tapering fore and aft, glides through the air with the least possible resistance; and the big feet, held close together and straight out behind, form an effective rudder. The power is applied by wings— which seem too small—driven at high speed by large and powerful muscles. Its weight gives it stability and great momentum. It can not rise off the land at all and before it can rise from the water it must patter along the surface, half running and half flying, beating the water with both feet and wings, for a long distance; even then it experiences considerable difficulty unless facing a strong wind. But when once under way its flight is strong, direct, rapid, and long sustained. While coot shooting off the coast we used to estimate the speed of a passing loon by noting the time required to fly from our line of boats a known distance to the next line of boats, where a puff of smoke would announce its arrival; we were convinced that, under favorable circumstances, the loon often attains a speed of 60 miles an hour. Its momentum is so great that when shot, high up in the air, it will strike the water in falling at a surprisingly long distance, plowing up the surface or bounding along over it. I have been told of serious damage being done to a gunner's dory where one of these heavy birds had fallen into it. A 15-pound bird flying at the rate of a mile a minute might be expected to cause some trouble under the circumstances. The flight of a loon is decidedly distinctive; such a rakish craft, long and pointed at both ends, could not be mistaken for anything else. The great northern diver can be distinguished from the red-throated loon by its heavier build, and, if near enough, the adult bird can be recognized by its black head and neck.

I have never seen a loon fly, except when alighting, with anything but perfectly steady and rapid wing beats, but the Hon. R. Magoon Barnes (1897) relates an experience which is an exception to this rule. On the Illinois River, during the spring migration, he saw a loon "making great circles in the air, flapping its wings and then sailing." It "circled round and round and round, very much after the fashion of a bald eagle; rising spirally higher and higher, continuing the flapping of its wings, and the sailing movements until it reached a great altitude. Finally, after it had raised in the air until it appeared but little larger than a blackbird, it straightened out its wings, and pointing its long neck toward the North Pole sailed with great rapidity." With wings set "it seemed to coast or slide down hill, as it were, toward the north." He watched the bird as far as he could trace it, but "could see no movement of the wings," though it "seemed to be traveling at a tremendous rate."

A loon requires nearly as much space to alight in the water as to rise from it, and creates quite as much commotion at the finish of its flight as at the beginning; its small wings are unable to check the momentum of its heavy body; it circles lower and lower until it can stand the shock of sliding into the water, striking it with a tremendous splash, plowing a long furrow and sending the spray flying. It is not a graceful performance, but it is full of force and power.

The loon is a rapid swimmer and a wonderful diver. It is much more at home in the water than elsewhere. Its plunge beneath the surface is exceedingly quick and graceful, causing little disturbance; with wings closely folded, it is propelled by its powerful paddles alone, which usually work alternately, driving it at a high speed. The loon can swim for a long distance under water and always prefers to escape in this way. While endeavoring to escape in this way it often swims with only its bill protruding, which is nearly invisible and after a brief breathing spell it is fortified for another

long swim below the surface. When wishing to indulge in an unusual burst of speed, it uses both wings and feet with marvelous
effect, but ordinarily I believe that the wings are not used. It is
certainly capable of catching fish without making this extra effort.
Its diving ability in dodging at the flash of a gun is well known. I
once saw a remarkable exhibition of this power by a loon which
was surrounded by gunners in a small cove on the Taunton River.
There wer six or eight men, armed with breechloading guns on both
sides of the cove and on a railroad bridge across it, all within short
range. I should not dare to say for how long a time the loon succeeded in dodging their well-directed shots, or how many cart-
ridges were wasted before the poor bird succumbed from sheer exhaustion; but it was an almost incredible record.

The behavior of loons under certain circumstances shows peculiar
traits of character; playfulness and curiosity are both highly developed. Rev. M. B. Townsend contributes the following sketch of their
sunrise greeting:

A beautiful sight was that of three loons facing the rising sun, standing almost
erect on the water, their great wings vigorously flapping, the sun shining
full upon their pure white breasts. It seemed almost like an act of religious
devotion in honor of old Phoebus.

Dr. P. L. Hatch (1892) relates the following account of another
early morning performance:

It has been my privilege to witness some scenes of their matutinal jollifica-
tions, which have always occurred at the earliest dawn, and have terminated
with the advent of the sun. The night is spent in proximity to each other
on the water, somewhat removed from the land. And in the earliest morning,
notes of the parent male soon call out a response from the other members of
the family, when they all draw near, and after cavorting around each other
after the manner of graceful skaters for a brief time, they fall into line, side by
side, and lifting their wings simultaneously, they start off in a footrace on the
water like a line of school children, running with incredible speed a full quarter
of a mile without lowering their wings or pausing an instant, wheel around
in a short circle (in which some of them get a little behind) and retrace their
course to the place of starting. This race, after but a moment's pause, is
repeated over and over again, with unabated zest, until by some undiscoverable
signal it ceases as suddenly as it began. Its termination is characterized by a
subsequent general congratulation manifested by the medley of loon notes. This
walking, or rather running, upon the face of the quiet lake waters is a marvel
of pedal performance, so swiftly do the thin, sharp, legs move in the race, the
wings being continuously held at about half extent. Soon after this is over,
the male parent takes to wing to seek his food in some distant part of the
same or some other lake, which is soon followed by the departure of the
female in another direction, while the young swim away in various directions
to seek their supplies nearer the place of nightly rendezvous.

Curiosity has cost many a loon his life, for it is an easy matter to
tole one within gunshot range by remaining hidden, and waving some
suspicious object. The loon can not resist the impulse to investigate,

unless it is an old bird which has learned by experience. A man partially concealed in grass or underbrush near the shore of a lake will sometimes serve to arouse the curiosity of some old loon who will call up a number of his companions to talk it over. They will then swim around in circles, gradually working in nearer. A sudden movement will cause them to dive like a flash or go scudding away; but they will swim up again, alternately advancing or retreating, until a shot from the man satisfies their curiosity.

I must let some abler pen than mine describe the vocal performances of this species, for it has a wonderful variety of notes, each of which probably has its special significance, and I feel wholly unable to do justice to the subject. Mr. Francis H. Allen writes to me:

The commonest notes, which are heard both by day and by night, are a weird maniacal laughter and a prolonged yodeling note which is much higher pitched in the middle than at the beginning or the end. This latter note is very loud and can be heard at a great distance.

Mr. William Lyman Underwood, who is an expert in imitating the notes of this loon, says that he recognizes four distinct calls: First, a short, cooing note, often heard when there are several loons together; second, a long drawn-out note, known among the guides as the night call; third, the laughing call, which is familiar to everybody who has ever been in a loon country; and fourth, another call which is not often heard, known among the guides as the storm call. This last is a very peculiar and weird performance which the guides regard as a sure sign of a coming storm. The notes of the loon can be closely imitated by the human voice, after a little practice—so closely that loons can be made to answer or can be called up; but the notes can be almost exactly reproduced on a little musical instrument known as an ocarina, or more commonly as a " sweet potato." Mr. Underwood says that these instruments are made in different keys and that the proper one for the loon call is D $5\frac{1}{2}$.

Mr. E. Howard Eaton (1910) gives the following good description of two of the loon's commonest notes:

The scream of the loon, uttered at evening, or on the approach of a storm, has to my ear, an unearthly and mournful tone resembling somewhat the distant howl of a wolf. It is a penetrating note, loud and weird, delivered with a prolonged rising inflection, dropping at the end, resembling the syllables A–ooó–OO, or as is often written Ó–Ō–ōōh. Its laughter, however, is of a more pleasing quality, like the syllables hŏŏ, hŏŏ, hŏŏ, hŏŏ, hŏŏ, uttered in a peculiarly vibrating tremolo.

This loon also has a peculiar warning cry as a signal of danger to its young, which they promptly obey, also a different warning cry to its incubating mate.

Fall.—On the fall migration the young birds precede the adults by about three weeks, and they go much farther south. The principal flight is along the coast, where they are, at times, very common, flying with the scoters and generally crossing headlands or long capes. They usually fly high in the air, singly, or in small groups widely scattered, but I have often seen a large number in sight at one time. While anchored off the coast coot shooting on foggy mornings in October, I have listened with interest to the laughing calls of migrating loons, which were probably keeping in touch with each other and with the coast line by this method of signaling in the fog. Sometimes they stop to rest and congregate in large numbers in the water, several miles off shore, in what we call " conventions," where we could hear, on a still morning, the constant murmur of their voices in soft conversational tones. It is a constant temptation to all gunners to shoot at passing loons, for they are swift, strong fliers and are very hard to stop; it is particularly exciting on a foggy morning when so many are heard and only an occasional fleeting glimpse is seen. There is no good excuse, however, for shooting them, as they are practically never used for food. They are exceedingly hard to kill, and it is well-nigh useless to chase a wounded loon. On the coast of Labrador loons are shot for food, and I can testify from experience that they are not bad eating, though I should not consider them to be in the game-bird class.

Winter.—Loons spend the winter on inland lakes and streams to some extent throughout their winter range, which extends as far north as they can find plenty of open water. As they require a large open space in which to rise from the water they are sometimes caught by the freezing of ponds, where they are either shot or starve to death. By far the greater number of them spend the winter on the seacoast, where they are usually seen singly or in small parties, but occasionally in large gatherings, which can hardly be called flocks, numbering from 40 to 100 birds, sometimes far out at sea. They are common on the coast of New England, swimming just outside the breakers off our beaches, where they are always conspicuous, standing up at full height to flap their wings or rolling over on their sides to preen their plumage, their white breasts glistening in the sunlight, as they swim around in a circle with one foot up in the air. In stormy or foggy weather they are often noisy. I believe that they usually sleep on the water, but when it is safe to do so they often come ashore to sleep. I have several times surprised one well up on a sandy beach, where it had been spending the night or had gone ashore to dry and sand its plumage. Its attempts to regain the water were more precipitous than graceful, as it scrambled or stumbled down the beach, falling on its breast at every few yards, darting its head and neck about, humping its back and straining every muscle to make speed, at which it was surprisingly successful.

DISTRIBUTION.

Breeding range.—Northern parts of the Northern Hemisphere, chiefly North American. East to eastern Greenland (north to Scoresby Sound), northern Iceland (Isle of Grimsey), Labrador, Newfoundland, Nova Scotia, and New England. South to Maine, New Hampshire, and Vermont (regularly), Massachusetts (rarely), Connecticut (casually), northern New York (Adirondack Mountains), central eastern Pennsylvania (Monroe County, casual), northern Ohio (formerly), northeastern Indiana (Steuben, Lagrange, and Noble counties), northeastern Illinois (Deer Lake, Lake County, casual), northern Iowa (Winnebago, Cerro Gordo, and Hancock counties), and northeastern California (Eagle Lake and near Mount Lassen). West to western Washington (Pierce County and Bellingham Bay), British Columbia (Okanagan Lake, Vancouver Island, and Queen Charlotte Islands), southern Alaska, and the Aleutian Islands (Kyska Island and probably others of the chain). North to northwestern Alaska (Norton Sound and Kotzebue Sound), Mackenzie (throughout the region), Banks Land (Mercy Bay), Barrow Strait, Cumberland Sound Region, and Greenland (north to Upernivik district).

Recorded in summer, but not breeding: California (Los Angeles County), Mississippi (Bay St. Louis), South Carolina (near Charleston), New York (Long Island), and Massachusetts (off the coast). Also from the Outer Hebrides and Shetland Islands and the coast of Norway.

Winter range.—Mainly within the United States (particularly along both coasts) and western Europe. East to northern New England (Maine) and the Atlantic Coast States. South to Florida (Caloosahatchee region) and the Gulf Coast (Louisiana and Texas). West to the Pacific coast (Lower California to British Columbia). North to the northern United States and the Great Lakes. Has been recorded from Nova Scotia in winter. In Europe from the British Isles south to the Azores, Madeiras, the Mediterranean and Black Seas.

Spring migration.—Northward mainly in April and May. South Carolina: Leave March 28. North Carolina: Raleigh, April 13 (latest). New Jersey: April 14 to May 9. New York: Long Island, May 24–28 (latest June 1). Rhode Island: May 28 (latest). Quebec: April 12 (arrival). Labrador: April 14 (earliest). Greenland: Ivigtut, May 15 (earliest). Kansas: last of March to end of April. Ohio: April 20 to May 21. Michigan: April 1. Manitoba: May 1 to 4 (arrival). Mackenzie: Athabaska River, May 20; Fort Simpson, May 23. Yukon Territory: Forty Mile, May 28. California: San Diego, April 4 to May 9; Santa Barbara, April 28 to

May 4. Southern Alaska: Kuiu Island, April 25 to May 6; Admiralty Island, May 16; Bocadequadra, May 28. Northern Alaska: Norton Sound, May 15 to 25 (arrival).

Fall migration.—Southward mainly in September and October. Greenland: Ivigtut, November 18 (latest). Labrador: Davis Inlet, October 2; Battle Harbor, October 12. Rhode Island, September 15. North Carolina: Fort Macon, arrives in September. South Carolina: Arrives October 17 to 27. Yukon Territory: Forty Mile, September 25. Mackenzie River: Near Nahanni River, leaves October 15. Alberta: Lily Lake, September 24; Edmonton, October 30. Idaho: September 25 to October 4. Nebraska: September and October. Missouri: October 20 to November 20. Alaska: Norton Sound, leave October 1; Wrangell Island, November 5; Shumagin Islands, September 2. Southern California: Pacific slope, arrives October 15.

Egg dates.—Maine and New Hampshire: 28 records, June 2 to August 10; 14 records, June 14 to 27. Ontario and Quebec: 12 records, May 21 to July 12; 6 records, June 15 to 23. British Columbia and Washington: 11 records, April 29 to May 29; 6 records, May 3 to 19. Michigan and Wisconsin: 11 records, May 7 to June 26; 6 records, May 20 to 28. Iceland and southern Greenland: 8 records, May 29 to July 12; 4 records, June 4 to 19. Anderson River: 2 records, June 25 and July 3.

GAVIA ADAMSI (Gray).

YELLOW-BILLED LOON.

HABITS.

This large and handsome diver is essentially a bird of the Arctic coast. Few naturalists have ever seen it and very little is known of its habits. It is one of the rare species about which I have hoped to learn something new, but I regret to say that I have been unable to add much to its life history beyond what has already been published and that is meager enough. It seems to be fairly common, or even abundant, along the Arctic coasts of northwestern North America and eastern Siberia.

Spring.—Mr. John Murdoch (1885) says of its appearance at Point Barrow:

They are first to be seen about the end of May, or early in June, at the " lead " of open water and flying inland to their breeding grounds. As the sea opens along the shore and open holes are found in the lagoons they are to be looked for in such places, gradually going out to sea as the season advances. Fully fledged young were seen August 7, 1883. The breeding grounds are probably around the swamps and lakes some distance inland.

Mr. John Koren, in his notes published by Thayer and Bangs (1914), says:

The yellow-billed loon is common along the Arctic coast of east Siberia. It seems to prefer drift ice, and was very numerous between the mouth of the

Kolyma River and Chaun Bay, swimming among the ice. It was observed once only in a lake—July 20, 1912. A skin, however, was seen in the possession of a native at Shornoy Myss, a point about 300 miles up the Kolyma River. No nests, or young birds, were found during the trip, and no specimens were taken.

Nesting.—Mr. Roderick MacFarlane (1908), the veteran naturalist who has done more than any other one man to add to our knowledge of the nesting habits of northern birds, was equally unfortunate in hunting for the nest of this rare bird. He writes:

Although this species was very numerous on the polar shores of Liverpool and Franklin Bays, where it no doubt breeds, yet we never succeeded in finding even one well authenticated set of its eggs, while it is possible that the two *Adamsii* eggs referred to on page 452 of volume 2, of the Water Birds of North America, by Baird, Brewer, and Ridgway, may have belonged to the great northern diver.

There is a set of eggs in the collection of Col. John E. Thayer, taken by Capt. J. Smythe on June 21, 1898. The nest is described as made of twigs and grasses, situated 6 feet from the water, on an island in the Mackenzie River, near its mouth. These eggs are not distinguishable from ordinary eggs of the common loon; the ground color is "Dresden brown" or halfway between that color and "sepia"; and the markings are in no way distinctive.

Eggs.—Mr. R. M. Barnes writes me that he has received an egg of this species taken by the Rev. A. R. Hoare near Point Hope, Alaska, in June 12, 1916.' The nest is described as a bare tussock or hummock surrounded by water in a small lake on the tundra. Mr. Hoare adds: "Could not shoot male or female, though both remained near and were identified by myself." Mr. Hoare also sent me a set of two eggs, with the parent bird, taken the same season in the same locality, in wet grass on a small island. The eggs are "elliptical ovate" in shape; the color of one is "Saccardo's umber" and of the other "snuff brown;" the first is sparingly and the second rather profusely spotted with "bone brown."

I received another set of two eggs, with the parent bird, taken the same season by Mr. T. L. Richardson near Point Barrow, Alaska. No data came with this set. The eggs are "elongate ovate" in shape, slightly lighter than "bister" in color and sparingly spotted with "bone brown." I am inclined to think that the yellow-billed loon habitually nests in or around the tundra pools at considerable distances back from the coast which are so difficult of access during the breeding season that very few nests have been found. The measurements of 17 eggs in various collections, said to be of this species, average 89 by 56.9 millimeters; the eggs showing the four extremes measure **95** by 60, 92 by **66,** 80 by 56, and 85 by **53.5** millimeters.

Plumages.—The downy young of this species is very light colored, varying from "natal brown" on the back and rump to "wood brown " on the head, neck, and sides, and to " tilleul buff," or nearly white, on the belly. The molts and plumages seem to be similar to those of the common loon. Prof. R. Collett (1894) has made an extensive study of the plumages of the yellow-billed loon in Norway, and the following items are taken from his excellent paper on the subject:

The young of the year are barely full grown the first autumn. One from the neighborhood of Tromsö has still a shortish and undeveloped bill. During the first autumn the winter plumage is recognizable by the light, somewhat sharply defined margins of the feathers of the back. In shape these feathers are rounded or almost pointed. The 1-year-old bird (South Varanger, June 23, 1891) still bears its worn first winter plumage. The light margins of the upper surface have become bleached, almost whitish, and partly worn, from which the feathers begin to assume the more square-cut edge, which at once distinguishes the back of the adult bird from those of younger ones.

In the autumn and winter of the second year the birds still retain a gray plumage, which is, however, easily distinguishable from that of the young ones by the color and shape of the back feathers. The light margins on the upper parts have been thrown off, and the back, on the whole, has become darker; most of the feathers have a lighter grayish-brown patch where the large white summer spots will subsequently appear. But these patches are often weakly margined and party indistinct. In shape these feathers are somewhat square cut, as in all old individuals. The bill has attained its full length and shape, and its color is about the same as in individuals in their nuptial plumage. The lower neck bar is more or less indicated by the dusky terminal rays on the feathers, which are here more dense and darker than on the throat.

I am inclined to think that the plumage just described is identical with, or indistinguishable from, the adult winter plumage; at all events, he does not seem to have pointed out any differences which might not be accounted for by individual variation.

He says, further:

The nuptial plumage is assumed when the individual is at least 2 years old.

If we may reason by inference from what we know of the molts and plumages of the common loon, I should say that young birds might be expected to begin assuming the adult nuptial plumage at any time during their second winter, from December to February, or when 18 or 20 months old, the time varying greatly in different individuals.

The seasonal molts and plumages of the adult are, evidently, practically the same as in the common loon. Professor Collett (1894) has considerable to say about the transformation of feathers, implying a color change without molt or combined with it; but I am inclined to think that no changes take place except by wear or by molt. He hardly seems to have proven his case and his following statement seems to contradict his claim:

The recoloration takes place rapidly, probably in the course of a few hours in each individual feather, and it is quite exceptional to find feathers in the course of transformation.

The molt into the winter plumage is very irregular and much prolonged, and the plumage is worn for only a short time. He refers to a specimen taken on September 22 in which the molt had begun, others taken in October and November in transitional stages, and one taken on October 5 in which the summer plumage was almost entirely retained. A specimen taken on January 11 " still retains a number of white-spotted summer feathers on its back and shoulders," and one taken at the beginning of May shows molt into the summer plumage. The two molts are so prolonged and so irregular that they may almost be said to overlap.

Dr. Witmer Stone (1900) describes an adult winter bird as follows:

One adult specimen, September 29, has just completed the molt, and the new wings are only half grown; above glossy black with a tinge of green appearing " scaly " in certain lights, top of head and back of neck black, feathers on sides of neck slightly tipped with black. The flight feathers in the loons are evidently lost all at once, as in the ducks.

Behavior.—Professor Collett (1894) says of the habits of the yellow-billed loon: " But little information has been obtained on the Norwegian coasts. Some of the specimens were caught in nets in which they had been entangled when diving." One " was taken on a hook which was laid at a depth of about 15 fathoms." In the specimens that he dissected the stomachs were " filled with the remains of fishes, and had a quantity of gravel in " them. " The last specimen received contained an example of *Cottus scorpius* [total length 270 mm., a full grown female with roe]."

Mr. Joseph Dixon (1916) refers to the flight of this species as follows:

The flight of the yellow-billed loon in migration was one of the most impressive sights of our Arctic trip. A dim speck low over the frozen tundra or glaring ice fields suddenly develops wings which beat rapidly with the rhythm and energy of a steam engine. The huge bill and neck seem to be extended slightly upward and the bird glides swiftly forward in a straight line with none of the undulating movements of the brant and eider ducks. The rapid " swish, swish," of the huge wings dies away in the Arctic silence, and the next moment one is gazing in the distance where a rapidly diminishing dark object seems to be boring a hole in the low clouds in the east. There was no variation in speed or direction, and the birds traveled at least 40 miles an hour over a measured distance.

Mr. Murdoch (1885) writes:

They are generally to be seen alone or in pairs, seldom more than three or four together, and are silent birds compared with *C. torquatus.* I only heard this bird " laugh " once during the whole of my stay. The " laugh " appeared to be harsher than that of *torquatus.*

Mr. F. Seymour Hersey, in his field notes, describes the call of this species as " a wild, ringing laugh, similar in many respects to that of the common loon, but louder."

Macfarlane (1908) says:

An Eskimo of our bird and egg gathering party observed a male *Somateria V. nigra* struck and killed on the wing by an attacking bird of the species under review.

Fall.—When the Arctic Ocean is closed with ice these loons are forced to leave their summer homes, but where they go is one of the many unsolved problems in American ornithology. They have been frequently taken on migrations in the lakes and rivers of northern Canada, but even these are frozen in winter. A few have been taken or seen in the vicinity of the Aleutian and Commander Islands and even on the coast of Alaska south of the peninsular.

Winter.—Professor Collett (1894) says that the yellow-billed loon "visits the coasts of Norway annually, especially during the autumn and winter, in some years even in considerable numbers," which suggests the possibility that its main migration route may be westward, along the Arctic coasts of Asia and Europe, to its principal winter home in the vicinity of Norway. He says:

The winter visitors usually appear in October, and most of the specimens hitherto examined have been obtained during the period from October to December. During their visits to the Norwegian coasts these birds, on some occasions, penetrate to the interior of the southernmost fjords (for instance, the Christiania Fjord); but most of them appear to stop on the northern shores. They disappear, as a rule, during the spring and summer, although it is not improbable that stray individuals pass the summer without breeding on the shores of Norway.

DISTRIBUTION.

Breeding range.—Authentic eggs (accompanied by parent) have been taken at Point Hope, Point Barrow, and Salmon River, Alaska, and at the delta of the Mackenzie River. Dresser records a nest on the River Omolai, Siberia.

It has been reported in summer from northwestern Alaska (Norton Sound, Kotzebue Sound, and Selawik Lake north to Point Barrow), east along the Arctic coast to Liverpool and Franklin Bays and from the lakes in the interior of northern Mackenzie; also from northeastern Siberia west to the Yenisei River and the Taimur Peninsula. It is supposed to breed more or less commonly throughout this region, but authentic eggs are very rare in collections and there is considerable evidence that many of the birds found in summer are not breeding. Dixon found no signs of breeding in 14 specimens shot between June 3 and July 16 at Humphrey Point, Arctic Alaska. It has been found very numerous in De Salis Bay, Banks Land, and its main breeding grounds may prove to be the islands north of the Arctic coast. Ross took three birds at the Boothia Peninsula and it has occurred accidentally in Greenland.

Winter range.—Largely unknown. Has been reported from China and Japan in small numbers and on the northwest coast of Norway from Tromsö southward (common). Also taken or otherwise recorded in winter from the Commander Islands, Great Britain (6 examples), Upper Austria, and Italy.

Spring migration.—Birds leave the coast of Norway early in spring, although single individuals have been taken from May to the end of July. They reached Point Barrow May 15, 1882, and May 25, 1883; Colville River, June 6, 1909; and Point Humphrey, Alaska, June 3, 1914. At this time they are also common in the Mackenzie region (Mackenzie River above Fort Simpson, May 20, 1905; Hay River, Great Slave Lake, May), but it is unknown by what route they reach this section. Specimens have been taken in spring and summer in southeastern Alaska (Admiralty Island, May 25, 1911) and seen about June 1, 1911, at Admiralty Island; June 5, 1911, south end of Lynn Canal, and June 17, 1911, east shore of Lynn Canal. The record from Loveland, Colorado, May 25, 1885, is erroneous.

Fall migration.—Route unknown. They have been noted in the Mackenzie region: Fort Enterprise, September 26; Mackenzie River near mouth of Nahanni River, October 15; Franklin Bay, migrating west, September 6. Arctic Sound, between Cherre Islands and Kater Point, Northwest Territory; last seen, September 16. Alaska: Point Barrow, September 29; St. Michael, October 14; St. Paul Island, Bering Sea, one taken in August; near Nushagak, September 21. Gulf of Anadyr, Siberia, September 1. In southeastern Alaska one was taken August 17, 1911, at Dixon Harbor and one seen in November, 1910, at Gastineau Channel. One was taken at Kodiak, November 1, 1868. The species usually arrives on the coast of Norway in October (earliest September 22).

Egg dates.—Alaska: 4 records, June 6, 7, 10, and 17. Mackenzie: 2 records, June 20 and 21.

GAVIA ARCTICA (Linnaeus).
BLACK-THROATED LOON.
HABITS.

The status of the European form of the black-throated loon, as an American bird, can not be clearly demonstrated without some study of the systematic status of this group of loons. From the study of a large number of specimens, from various portions of the circumpolar range of the black-throated loon, it becomes apparent that there is probably but one species, which may be divided into four subspecies, all of which intergrade in all of the characters which separate them and all of which show so much individual variation that averages alone will identify them. Size is the most satisfactory character, but even in this there is some overlapping.

Mr. N. A. Sarudny (1912), who described the Asiatic bird under the name *Urinator arcticus suschkini*, claims that the Asiatic bird is smaller and has a shorter bill than the European. Perhaps, if we had more material for study, we might be able to confirm his views; moreover, we should naturally expect to find the Asiatic bird intermediate in all characters between the European and the American birds; but, strangely enough, the largest bird we have seen, with a bill measuring 2.87 and a wing measuring 13 inches, was taken at St. Michael, Alaska; it is referable to a new Asiatic form, *Gavia viridigularis* Dwight, and was probably a straggler from Siberia.

The color characters are equally unsatisfactory, or more so. Mr. Sarudny (1912) separates his Asiatic bird from the European bird on several color characters, which are very variable and which, at best, make this bird only intermediate between the European and American birds. With what scanty material we have in this country to study, it would be unwise to express an opinion, at this time, on the validity of the two Asiatic subspecies. The Asiatic bird, *viridigularis*, apparently, sometimes wanders to northwestern Alaska on migrations; it may occasionally breed in the vicinity of Norton Sound. So, if we are to recognize this bird as distinct from the European, it is apparently the former and not the latter which belongs on the American list.

The European bird, *Gavia arctica arctica* (Linnaeus) seems to have no standing as an American bird. I have been unable to find an American specimen which I could identify as *arctica;* all the specimens which I have been able to locate, taken in eastern North America, are either typical *pacifica* or are nearer that than anything else. Numerous records are based on erroneous identifications of immature common loons, *Gavia immer.* For further information regarding all the American records that we could trace, I would refer the reader to a recent paper on the subject by my assistant, Mr. F. Seymour Hersey (1917).

I have therefore no reason for including the life history of the European bird in this work. So little is known about the distribution and habits of the Asiatic bird that I shall not attempt to write a fragmentary story, which probably would not differ materially from what I have written about the Pacific loon.

DISTRIBUTION.

Breeding range.—Northern parts of the Northern Hemisphere, chiefly (if not entirely) confined to Europe and Asia. East to northeastern Siberia (Chaun Bay; Cape Bolohaja, Baranov; and Gichiga and Marcova, Anadyr district). Southern limits poorly defined. Probably south to Japan and eastern Prussia. West to the British Isles (northern Scotland, the Outer Hebrides, Orkney and Shetland Islands). North to the Faroe Islands, Iceland, and the Arctic coast and outlying islands (Kolguev, Nova Zembla?). North American breeding records are very doubtful. Apparently there is not a single North American taken set of eggs accompanied by parent birds to establish the breeding of this species in the Western Hemisphere. Siberian birds have been described as a distinct subspecies (see text), but its range is not well known.

Winter range.—Birds have been recorded in winter from near the northern limit of its breeding range, Lapland (Varanger Fiord). It also winters from the British Isles, Heligoland, and Prussia south to Spain, Portugal, the Mediterranean, Black and Caspian Seas, and along the coast of eastern Siberia to Japan.

Casual records.—Some Alaska records probably refer to the Siberian subspecies. All other American records seem to refer to something else.

Egg dates.—Lapland: 12 records, May 28 to June 23; 6 records, June 6 to 12. Finland: 8 records, June 6 to 17; 4 records, June 10 to 14. Sweden: 7 records, May 25 to June 20; 4 records, June 7 to 11.

GAVIA PACIFICA (Lawrence).

PACIFIC LOON.

HABITS.

Spring.—The Pacific loon is well named, for, except during the breeding season, it is an abundant species along the Pacific coast of this continent. The spring migration is well marked, as the following observation, sent me by Mr. A. B. Howell, will illustrate:

April 12, 1910, detached parties were migrating northward past Ensenada Bay, Mexico, so frequently as to be almost one continuous flock. There were thousands. May 2, 1913, I witnessed a similar flight near Santa Barbara, California.

Mr. Bernard J. Bretherton (1896) says that it arrives at Kodiak Island

about the middle of May. On account of its large size, and a habit it has of flying round before it finally alights, makes the arrival of this bird very noticeable. These birds approach the island from the east, flying very high and in pairs, seeming at once to give their attention to selecting a suitable place to nest. They fly from one lake to another, describing large circles in the air, and giving forth their harsh cry, which gives rise to their native name of "Googara." They were never noticed to arrive in the night, as many migrants do.

Mr. John Murdoch (1885) says that, at Point Barrow—

they arrive early in June, and before the ponds are open are generally flying eastward as if they had come up along the open water at sea and were striking across to the mouths of the rivers at the east. As the ponds open they make themselves at home there, and evidently breed in abundance, though we were unable to find the nest. One of their breeding grounds was evidently a swampy lagoon some five or six miles inland, but the nests are inaccessible.

Nesting.—Mr. W. Sprague Brooks has sent me the following notes on a nest which he found at Demarcation Point, Arctic Alaska, on July 4, 1914:

The nest was on the edge of a shallow slough on the tundra about 200 yards from the shore of the Arctic Ocean. This slough was about 3 acres in area, but another nest was found in one of about half an acre. Enough room to take wing seems to be all that is required. The nest itself was in the aquatic vegetation along the edge and was merely a soaking wet mass of roots, stems, and the accompanying mud, of this same plant torn from the bottom. In the three nests of this species that I found the bird on being disturbed did not show any particular concern, merely swimming off to the other side of the slough and keeping an eye on my activities.

Macfarlane (1908) refers to a nest of this species found near Stuart's Lake, British Columbia, on May 29, 1889, and two nests found early in June, 1890, north of Cumberland House, showing that the Pacific loon breeds far inland. In his notes on the birds of the lower Mackenzie and Anderson Rivers, Macfarlane (1891) says:

This is the most abundant of all the divers in the region under investigation. Nests were discovered in the wooded country, in the Barren Grounds, and on the shores and islands of the Arctic coast. In situation and composition they resemble those of *U. imber*. In all about 165 nests, most of which contained two eggs, were secured in course of the five seasons, from 1862 to 1866, inclusive.

Eggs.—The eggs of the Pacific loon are much like other loon's eggs, but they average smaller than those of the black-throated loon and larger than those of the red-throated loon. In shape they are " elliptical ovate " or " cylindrical ovate," usually the former and very rarely nearly " ovate." The ground color is " Prouts' brown," " Saccardo's umber," " cinnamon brown," " dark olive buff," or " Isabella color," very rarely " pale olive buff." The egg is usually sparsely covered with small spots, but often there are a few scattering larger spots, of the darkest shades of brown or nearly black; some eggs show underlying spots or pale shades of lavender or drab. The measurements of 41 eggs, in the United States National Museum, average 75.5 by 47 millimeters; the eggs showing the four extremes measure 87 by 45, 80 by 51, 68.5 by 46, and 70.5 by 44 millimeters.

Young.—Nelson (1887) gives the following account of the behavior and food of the young:

When the young can follow their parents all pass to the coast, and during calm, pleasant weather, the last of July and in August, they are very common in all the shallow bays along shore. On one occasion downy young, not over one-fourth grown, were found on August 30. They were in a pond over 2 miles from any place where fish could be found, so that the parents must have flown 4 miles at least for each fish taken to them. One of the young birds had a half digested tomcod about 6 inches long in its gullet, and one of the parents was seen coming in from the seacoast 5 or 6 miles away with a fish of the same size crosswise in its beak.

Plumages.—The downy young is plainly colored; the short thick down, with which it is covered, is " light seal brown " on the back, " clove brown " on the sides, head, and neck, and " light drab " on the breast and belly. A specimen in the American Museum, in New York, collected in northeastern Siberia on September 16, 1901, shows the change from the downy stage into the first winter plumage. This is similar to the corresponding plumage of the common loon, but this species can be recognized by its smaller size. In the first winter plumage the under parts are pure white, the throat and sides of the head are largely white, more or less streaked or mottled with dusky, and the upper parts are dark blackish brown; the characteristic feature of this plumage is that the feathers of the back are broadly margined with light gray, giving it a scaly appearance. This plumage is worn during the winter and part of the following spring; when the bird is nearly a year old it begins to show progress toward maturity by a partial molt. Macgillivray (1852) quotes Temminck's description of this stage in the European bird, as follows:

The young, when a year old, have the head and hind neck pale gray; the throat and fore part of the neck white; but on the throat and sometimes on the fore part of the neck, there appear some violet-black feathers mixed with white feathers; the longitudinal streaked band of the sides of the neck begins to form; the streaks of the lower part of the neck equally appear, and some black feathers without spots, appear on the back, rump, and sides.

A complete, first, postnuptial molt takes place in the latter part of the summer, producing a second winter plumage which is similar to and probably indistinguishable from the adult winter plumage. During the winter and spring further progress toward maturity is made, producing a second nuptial plumage, of which Macgillivray (1852) gives Temminck's description, as follows:

At the age of 2 years the gray of the head and nape become deeper, and assume a blackish tint, but only on the forehead; the violet black of the throat and forepart of the neck appear, but are variegated with some white feathers; the longitudinal bands are formed; the feathers of the sides and of the upper part of the back, the scapulars, and wing coverts assume the white bands and spots; the upper mandible becomes blackish, but its base, as well as a portion of the lower mandible, are still of a gray color.

Perhaps some individuals may require another year to reach the full maturity of plumage, but probably most birds may be considered adult and acquire their full plumage at an age of 2 years. Certainly during the third autumn, and probably during the second, the adult winter plumage is assumed. This differs from the first winter plumage in being uniformly dark blackish brown above, without any lighter margins on the feathers of the back; the throat and lower half of the head are also purer white, without any dusky markings. The prenuptial molt involes practically all of the contour feathers and the postnuptial molt is complete.

Food.—I find nothing published on the food of the Pacific loon except an occasional reference to one being seen flying inland with a fish in its bill, presumably for its young. Small fish probably constitute the principal part of its food.

Behavior.—Coues (1877) gives an interesting account of the habits of this species on the coast of southern California; he writes:

They were very plentiful about the Bay of San Pedro. The first thing that attracted my attention was their remarkable familiarity; they were tamer than any other waterfowl I have seen. They showed no concern at the near approach of a boat, scarcely availed themselves of the powers of diving, in which the whole family excels, and I had no trouble in shooting as many as I wanted. They even came up to the wharves, and played about as unconcerned as domestic ducks; they constantly swam around the vessels lying at anchor in the harbor, and all their motions, both on and under the clear water, could be studied to as much advantage as if the birds had been placed in artificial tanks for the purpose. Now two or three would ride lightly over the surface, with the neck gracefully curved, propelled with idle strokes of their broad paddles to this side and that, one leg after the other stretched at ease almost horizontally backward, while their flashing eyes, first directed upward with curious sidelong glance, then peering into the depths below, sought for some attractive morsel. In an instant, with the peculiar motion, impossible to describe, they would disappear beneath the surface, leaving a little foam and bubbles to mark where they went down and I could follow their course under water; see them shoot with marvelous swiftness through the limpid element, as, urged by powerful strokes of the webbed feet and beats of the half-opened wings, they flew rather than swam; see them dart out the arrow-like bill, transfix an unlucky fish, and lightly rise to the surface again. While under water, the bubbles of air carried down with them cling to the feathers, and they seem bespangled with glittering jewels, borrowed for the time from their native element, and lightly parted with as they leave it, when they arrange their feathers with a slight shiver, shaking off the last sparkling drop. The feathers look as dry as if the bird had never been under water; the fish is swallowed head first, with a curious jerking motion, and the bird again swims at ease, with the same graceful curve of the neck.

Mr. Wilfred H. Osgood (1904) says of its behavior in Alaska:

It was exceedingly abundant along the Chulitna River, where from 8 to 15 individuals were seen almost daily. These were generally seen going up and down the river, flying singly, or more often in pairs, about 100 yards above the water and religiously following the course of the stream. They were quite wary and we seldom approached one on the water nearer than 150 yards, even when we were slipping noiselessly downstream. The adult birds, sitting on the water at a little distance, appear as if their heads were entirely white, particularly if a ray of sunlight bears on them. The rapidity with which they swim under water is amazing, as we repeatedly observed when one would dive at a point about 150 yards in front of our canoe and in a few moments appear at about the same distance astern.

Macfarlane (1891) says that—

The Pacific loon is noted for its peculiarly loud, weird, and prolonged shrill scream during the season of nidification.

Murdoch (1885) refers to the vocal powers of this species as follows:

Their peculiar harsh cry, "kok, kok, kok," from which they get their name, "Kaksau," is to be heard all summer, and the birds were seen nearly every day, flying backward and forward and inland from the sea. During the breeding season these smaller loons have a habit of getting off alone in some small pond and howling like a fiend for upward of half an hour at a time. It is a most bloodcurdling, weird, and uncanny sort of a scream, and the amount of noise they make is something wonderful. They can be heard for miles.

Fall.—The same writer says of their movements in the fall:

After the breeding season they are frequently to be seen in the open pools along the shore, especially when the lagoons have broken out. They are always very wild and difficult to secure. They are plenty through August and the greater part of September along the shore, and occasional stragglers remain around open holes well into October. Some appeared to be feeding young as late as the middle of September, 1882, as they were seen going inland from the sea carrying small fish.

The fall migration route seems to be straight south down the Pacific coast of North America. The winter range extends from British Columbia southward to Lower California, but the species is apparently most abundant in winter in the southern portion of this range, for it occurs more abundantly on the California coast as a migrant than as a winter resident. Mr. A. B. Howell writes me that—

During migration they often gather in flocks of 50 or more just beyond the surf during the heat of the day. While some sleep with their heads beneath their wings, others play, chasing their companions or paddling around on their sides with one foot in the air. They seem to be fond of fishing in company with the cormorants.

DISTRIBUTION.

Breeding range.—Northern portions of North America. East to the Melville Peninsula (Winter Island), Southampton Island, Hudson Bay, western Ungava (Long Island, north of Cape Jones), and northwestern Greenland (Carey Islands). South to central Keewatin (York Factory), southern Mackenzie (Great Slave Lake), central British Columbia (Stuarts Lake) and southwestern Alaska (Kodiak Island and Alaska Peninsula). West to Bering Sea. North to northwestern Alaska (Point Barrow), Banks Land, and the entire Arctic coast of Alaska and Mackenzie. Also northeastern Siberia west to the Indigirka River.

Turner records them as present throughout the year in the Aleutian Islands and breeding on the Near Islands (Semichi). Recorded in summer and may occasionally breed in Queen Charlotte Islands (Skidegate, several July 9), southern Alaska (Sitkan district, few pairs; Admiralty Island, few pairs remain), Herald Island (two

taken in June), Kuril Islands (Simushir) and Japan (near Hakodadi July 13). May occasionally reach northern Labrador and
southern Greenland.

Winter range.—South mainly along the Pacific coast. From
southern British Columbia (Puget Sound region) to Lower California (at least, to San Quentin Bay, perhaps farther south). Some
Alaskan birds may winter on the Asiatic coast (Japan, Tojiri, one
taken March 14) and in the Aleutian Islands; and it is possible that
individuals from the interior may pass the winter in the southern
part of James Bay.

Spring migration.—Northward in April and May. Lower Cali-
fornia: San Quentin Bay, April 12; Coronados Islands, May 15.
California: Santa Cruz Island, April 12 to 15; Santa Barbara, April
28 to May 4; Monterey, occasionally to June 10.   Southeastern
Alaska: Forrester Island, May 1 to 25; Admiralty Island, May 5.
Northwestern Alaska: Yukon mouth, May 15 to 25; Kotzebue Sound,
May 26 (earliest); Point Barrow, June 4, 1882, and June 13, 1883.
Arctic coast: Demarcation Point, June 3. Dates for the Mackenzie
region are late, July 2 being the earliest at Fort MacPherson. Yukon
Territory: Forty Mile, May 28. Melville Peninsula, June 28.

Fall migration.—Southward in September. Last seen at Hudson
Bay: Cape Churchill, August 24. Mackenzie: Great Bear Lake, September 9; mouth of Coppermine River, taken in October. Northwestern Alaska: Point Barrow, September 28 (and later); St.
Michael, September 16. Southeastern Alaska: Valdez Narrows,
September 18. They arrive on the coast of California during September; the single Arizona bird was taken September 20 and a Colorado (Breckenridge) bird November 15.

Casual records.—Guadaloupe Island (one found dead in 1875),
Arizona (Fort Verde), New Mexico (near Clayton), Iowa (near
Sabula), and New York (Long Island, April 29). The Long Island
and Iowa birds have been erroneously recorded as *arctica.*

Egg dates.—Mackenzie: 57 records, June 10 to July 23; 30 records,
June 23 to July 4. Northern Alaska: 8 records, June 15 to July 6;
4 records, June 17 to 30. Hudson Bay: 3 records, June 8, July
1 and 14.

GAVIA STELLATA (Pontoppidan).

RED-THROATED LOON.

HABITS.

The rugged coast of Labrador, with its chain of rocky islands, ice-
bound for nine months of the year and enveloped in fog or swept
with chilling blasts from drifting icebergs during most of the other
three, seems bleak and forbidding enough as we pick our way
through the narrow channels back of the outer islands. But in the

interior it is different. Though the summer is short, the sun is high in the heavens and the days are long; the abundant moisture in the air stimulates the growth of vegetation; the snow disappears rapidly and the verdure of spring follows quickly in the wake of retreating winter. Within a few feet of a vanishing snowbank I have seen the dwarfed willows, recently uncovered, already budded and bursting into leaf and a few yards farther away fully leaved out or even blossoming. Back from the rocky coast only a short distance the rolling hills are softly carpeted with deep mosses, covered with fresh verdure and dotted with blooming wild flowers in great variety and profusion. Here among the thousands of small lakes and ponds in the sheltered hollows, fed with the water from melting snow and studded with little islands, the red-throated loons find a congenial summer home and hither they come as soon as the fetters of winter are unlocked. We saw them everywhere along both the south and north coasts almost daily, flying inland to the lakes or even about the little ponds on the islands.

Courtship.—Audubon's (1840) graphic pen thus describes their courtship:

High over these waters, the produce of the melted snows, the red-throated diver is seen gamboling by the side of his mate. The males emit their love notes, and, with necks gracefully curved downward, speed by the females, saluting them with mellow tones as they pass. In broad circles they wheel their giddy flight, and now, with fantastic glidings and curves, they dive toward the spot of their choice. Alighted on the water, how gracefully they swim, how sportively they beat it with their strong pinions, how quickly they plunge and rise again, and how joyously do they manifest to each other the depth and intensity of their affection. Now with erected neck and body deeply immersed they swim side by side. Reynard they perceive cunningly advancing at a distance; but they are too vigilant for him, and down like a flash they go, nor rise again until far beyond his reach. Methinks I see them curiously concealed among the rank weeds under the bank of their own islet, their bills alone raised above the water, and there will they remain for an hour, rather than show themselves to their insidious enemy, who, disappointed, leaves them to pursue their avocations.

Many of the birds are paired before they start on their northward migration, as they are often seen migrating in pairs, traveling high in the air, their long necks pointing northward and their white breasts glistening in the sunlight. Perhaps they are mated for life, as the common loon is supposed to be. They often arrive on their breeding grounds while the lakes are still frozen, when they frequent the mouths of rivers or the open sea until the melting snows produce the first pools of water in the interior and their summer homes become habitable. After that they return to the sea only to feed.

Throughout northern Alaska the red-throated loon is the most abundant and most widely distributed species, a characteristic fea-

ture of the Arctic tundra, where it can be seen at any time flying up
or down the rivers or to and from the tundra pools. The harsh,
goose-like, honking calls or the weird, shrill cries of this species may
be heard at all hours of the day, or even during the short Arctic
night, the most characteristic sounds of these northern solitudes.

Nelson (1887) says:

At St. Michaels and the Yukon they arrive with the first open water
from May 12 to 20, and by the end of this month are present in large numbers.
Their arrival is at once announced by the hoarse, grating cries, which the
birds utter as they fly from place to place or float upon the water. When
the ponds are open on the marshes the red-throated loons take possession,
and are extremely noisy all through the first part of summer.

Nesting.—The nesting habits of this species are in no wise different
from those of the other loons. Mr. Lucien M. Turner, in his unpublished notes, gives the following good description of a typical
nest:

A nest of dry grass stalks and blades, together with weeds and sticks, was
found on one of the small islets off the mouth of Whale River, Ungava, July
1, 1884. The interior of the nest was of fine grass and few feathers which
from the dampness of the situation or material used in construction of the nest
had become discolored beyond recognition. Three eggs, of the dark pattern of
coloration, were in this nest. They were quite fresh, the last egg had probably
been just deposited. The bird fluttered into the pool, on the margin of which
the nest was placed, and then floundered through the weeds and grass beyond from which she took to rapid flight and either she or her mate returned
after awhile and hovered around in circles uttering an occasional *ka–ka–ka;*
and, at times only a growling, single syllable of the note.

Mr. M. Abbott Frazar (1887) took seven sets of eggs of this species
in southern Labrador and says that it

breeds on the edges of the smaller ponds (often mere pools of surface water
only a few rods square), on the larger islands they make no nest, but simply
lay their eggs in a slight hollow on the bare ground, usually on a slight rise not
over 1 foot from the water's edge. The space about the egg is perfectly bare,
the grass or other vegetation being trampled flat. Hence the spot is easily discovered, and the bird if sitting can be seen for a considerable distance.

Audubon (1840) says:

The nest was placed within a few feet of the water, and well-beaten tracks,
such as are made by otters, led to it. Whenever the birds went to this spot
they walked nearly erect in an awkward manner, but when they sat in their
nest they laid themselves flat on the eggs, in the manner of a goose or duck.
In no instance did they alight on the islands, but always on the water, at some
distance, when, after examining all around them for awhile, they crawled
silently out, and moved to the spot which contained their treasure.

In northern Alaska, Nelson (1887) noted that the eggs "are laid
directly upon the ground, and the spot chosen is frequently wet and
muddy. One nest was found on frozen ground, and ice was floating
in the pond."

Dr. Joseph Grinnell (1909) describes a nest found at Glacier Bay, Alaska, on July 16, 1907, as follows:

This was in the rank grass at the edge of a pond a few yards back from the shore of one of the small islands on the east side of the bay. The parent was seen to swim away from the nesting place, and by her peculiar actions indicated its proximity. There were two eggs on the point of hatching. Instead of the usual floating structure, the eggs in this case rested on the bare, wet mud, 2 feet back from the water's edge, there being no nesting material whatever.

Eggs.—The red-throated loon, like others of this genus, regularly lays two eggs. Most writers agree that this is the invariable number, but Audubon and some others have stated that three eggs are often laid. Sets of three must be exceptional, and occasionally one egg may be all that a nest contains. Frequently only one young bird is hatched, but in such cases the other egg is infertile.

The egg is " elliptical ovate " or " cylindrical ovate " in shape, with occasionally a tendency toward " ovate " or toward " fusiform." The shell is smooth and somewhat glossy. The ground color is " bister " or " sepia " in the darkest eggs, " auburn," " Brussels brown," " brownish olive," " light brownish olive," or " Saccardo's umber " in others, and " Isabella color " or " deep olive buff " in the palest eggs. Some eggs are nearly spotless, but usually they are sparingly and irregularly spotted with small spots or with scattering larger spots, rarely with irregular blotches, of the darkest shades of brown, such as " clove brown " and " blackish brown "; some eggs also have underlying spots of various shades of drab and very rarely these are the only markings. The measurements of 58 eggs, in the United States National Museum, average 72.5 by 45; the eggs showing the four extremes measure **80** by 47, 79.5 by **48, 62.5** by 41.5, and 68 by **40.5** millimeters.

The period of incubation seems to be unknown; it is probably somewhat less than that of the common loon, as it is a smaller species. Both Yarrell (1871) and Macgillivray (1852) state that both sexes assist in the incubation. Certainly the pairs remain together all through the breeding season, to guard the nesting site and to care for the young jointly. Macgillivray (1852) says:

The female continues to sit, crouching over her eggs, until a person comes very near, when she starts forward, plunges into the water, and on emerging usually takes to wing, but sometimes swims about with great anxiety, as does the male, should he happen to be present. On being deprived of their eggs, they may be heard for several evenings lamenting their loss with loud melancholy cries.

Young.—Both parents are very solicitous in the care of the young. When danger threatens the old bird sinks her body below the surface, with only the head and neck stretched up above it, the young bird climbs upon her back and she swims away with him to safety.

The young are experts at swimming and diving; they are soon taught to hide among the vegetation while their parents draw attention to themselves by flying excitedly over the pond or swimming in circles a short distance from the shore. Mr. Edward A. Preble (1908) noted that—

> When the nesting pond was approached, the male usually flew away, but the female invariably refused to leave her offspring, and if absent soon appeared and alighted beside them, diving, swimming about, and encouraging them in their efforts to escape, and endeavoring to attract the attention of the intruder to herself. The old birds fished in the lake near by and were often seen carrying small fishes to the young.

Nelson (1887) says:

> The young are led to the streams, large lakes, or sea-coast as soon as they are able to follow the parents, and they fall easy victims to the hunter until, with the growth of the quill feathers, they attain some of the wisdom of their parents. The end of August sees all upon the wing, except now and then a late bird, and from September 15 to 30 they gradually become more and more scarce, until only a very few can be found the first of October.

Plumages.—The young loon when first hatched is completely covered with short, thick, dark brown down, " seal brown " above, shading gradually to " drab " below. As it increases in size these colors become paler, particularly on the under parts, which fade out to "light drab" or "ecru drab" on the belly and to dark "walnut brown" above. A series of young red-throated loons, collected by Turner in Ungava, shows that their development is very slow. A young bird, collected July 30, was evidently hatched very early, but it is still wholly downy, although nearly half grown, and the wing quills are only just started. Another, collected September 19, is in the juvenal plumage and fully grown, but there is still some down on the flanks and hind neck. Turner states in his notes that this bird " would not have been able to sustain flight for fully another month." Evidently, as in the ducks, the body plumage is fully acquired and the last of the down has disappeared from the flanks long before the primaries are grown and the flight stage is reached.

In the juvenal plumage the head and neck are mottled with "mouse gray" and dirty white, the gray predominating on the crown and throat; the upper parts are dusky, mottled on the back and wings with "drab-gray" spots or V-shaped markings; these markings are much larger and more decidedly V shaped on the scapulars, becoming smaller and more broken up into rounded spots on the back. This plumage is worn without any very decided change throughout the winter; there is considerable individual variation in the size, shape and arrangement of the markings; but as a rule the gray mottling gradually disappears from the throat and the markings on the upper parts become whiter, smaller and more rounded, as the season advances. The V-shaped markings, however, are characteristic of the first winter plumage and never disappear entirely during the winter; they are never seen in any subsequent winter plumage and may consequently be regarded as sure signs of immaturity.

At the first prenuptial molt, which is only partial, the head and neck acquire a plumage resembling that of the adult, but dull and incomplete; the red throat patch is dull yellowish red and much restricted; the white markings of the back have largely disappeared by wear. At the next complete molt, the first postnuptial, when a little over a year old, the young bird assumes the adult winter plumage. This is similar to the first winter plumage except that the throat is immaculate white, or nearly so, and is sharply separated from the crown which is mottled with dusky gray and white; the back is mottled with round white spots.

The adult has two annual molts; a partial prenuptial molt, involving at least all of the feathers on the forepart of the body, produces the handsome head and neck of the nuptial plumage and quite an extensive growth of dark, new, glossy feathers on the back and scapulars. I have seen the beginning of this molt as early as December 28, but usually it is accomplished during March and April; and a complete postnuptial molt, during the latter part of the summer, produces the adult winter plumage, described above. The adult winter plumage is often not complete until late in the season. I have seen birds in very much worn plumage and only partially molted in December; this plumage is worn for a comparatively short time and the molt into it is often incomplete and sometimes not accomplished at all. I have seen a bird in full spring plumage in October and another, in the same month, in regular winter plumage with the full, rich, red throat of the nuptial plumage. Fall adults are scarce in collections and, if we had them in large series, we might be surprised to know to what extent old birds retain part or all of their spring plumage during the fall.

Food.—The food of the red-throated loon consists principally of small fishes which it obtains by diving and chasing them under water. On the coast of Labrador the little capelin is its principal prey, which it flies to salt water to seek. Mr. W. L. Dawson writes to me that—

It was a pretty sight to see a straightaway race between this bird and a herring. The fish rose to the surface with the bird in hot pursuit, and it took 20 feet, after the bird came near enough to the surface to be seen, to catch the sprat. Once at the surface and overtaken, the fish tried twisting and turning, but the bird was better at it and soon had the fish down. I took pains to notice that the diver did not spear, but seized the fish.

In addition to fish it eats a variety of animal food, when available; frogs, fish spawn, crustaceans, mollusks, shrimps, leeches, and aquatic insects have been reported by various writers; it has even been suggested that it occasionally eats portions of aquatic plants.

Behavior.—The flight of this loon is swift, strong and exceedingly direct; it is capable of long sustained flight and it generally flies in a straight line at a great height. The neck is outstretched to its fullest extent, the bill points straight forward and the large feet are extended backward, held close together, to serve as a rudder in place of its useless little tail. A long, slender figure, pointed at both ends, with small wings vibrating rapidly, can generally be recognized as a loon at even a long distance, but the various species can not be distinguished with certainty even at a short range except in full nuptial plumage; I know of no field mark by which the young birds may be recognized. The red-throated loon rises more easily from the water than the other species and gets under way more quickly; when alighting on the water it drops in heavily, striking at an angle, making a great splash and plowing up a furrow as it slides along the surface. It swims rapidly on the surface or with its body submerged. In diving it can sink quietly out of sight or dive like a flash, causing scarcely a ripple; but when not hurried or when intending to make a deep dive the neck is arched and the body thrown forward in a downward plunge with the wings closely pressed to the sides. Under water it makes astonishing speed, faster than a man can run along the shore, and it is useless to pursue one in a boat or a canoe; it can even outdistance an ordinary power boat. I believe that it ordinarily swims under water by using its feet alone, working them alternately; but when an extra burst of speed is desired the wings are also brought into play and the result is marvelous. Dr. George Suckley (1860) noted this habit, as follows:

Another individual which I obtained at New Dungeness, Straits of Fuca, I had an excellent opportunity of examining at a time it was attempting to escape from a shallow lagoon to the open water of the straits by swimming through the narrow outlet. Although slightly wounded, it moved so rapidly that I was obliged to run as fast as I could to keep up with it. At the same time, as the water was clear and shallow, I was able to watch its motions distinctly. It had the head and neck extended nearly perfectly straight, the bill acting as a " cut water," and, in addition to the ordinary propulsion by the feet, used the wings exactly as if flying. Indeed, the bird was flying through water instead of air.

The ordinary call note of the red-throated loon, which is a very noisy bird on its breeding grounds, is a goose-like, honking cry, which Nelson (1887) has described very well as follows:

The harsh *gr-r-ga gr-r, gr-r-ga, ga, gr-r*, rising everywhere from the marshes during the entire 24 hours, renders this note one of the most characteristic that greets the ear in spring in these northern wilds. The red-throated loon is one of the very few birds which raised its voice in the quiet of the short Arctic night. In spring, with cranes, they foretell an approaching storm by the increased repetition and vehemence of their cries.

Turner writes in his notes:

The Indian name, at Fort Chimo, for this species is Kashagat, derived from its note. This name is derived from the prolonged cry of the bird, which is the syllable *ka* repeated many times, slowly at first and finally blended, as it flies to or from a feeding place high in the air to command observation, and with accelerated flight to whirl and slowly descend with motionless pinions to the water, where a splash from the momentum of the bird conceals it as it sinks to slowly rise to reconnoiter the surroundings for danger.

It indulges also in a variety of weird, loud cries, similar to those of the common loon, which are the notes most frequently heard on migrations, especially when calling to each other at long distances on the water or when separated in a fog. Mr. William Brewster (1883) has described these notes very well as follows:

On calm mornings the male sometimes indulges in a prolonged outburst of harsh, discordant cries, which are uttered with such volubility and variety of intonation that one might imagine a dozen birds to be engaged. This perform-ance reminded me of the clamor of a flock of geese. It was evidently the loon's masterpiece, for during its production he would sail proudly about on the water with erect head and swelling plumage. It was so loud that it could be heard at a distance of a mile or more.

Fall.—As soon as the young birds are able to fly and the molting season of the adults is practically over, sometime in September, they begin to leave their breeding grounds and by the first of October are all on the way south. The migration along the New England coast is mainly in October accompanying the main flight of the scoters. After leaving the fresh-water lakes of their summer homes they resort to the seacoast for migration and seem to prefer to spend the fall and winter on salt water. When traveling they fly at a great height and in a direct course along the shore, a mile or two out from the land; they usually fly singly, although often several are in sight at one time, widely scattered. There is, however, some feeling of sociability among them, most noticeable on foggy days, when they manage to keep in touch with each other by frequent interchange of call notes, as if helping each other to maintain the same general line of flight. They are even somewhat gregarious at times, gathering in small parties on the water to rest and calling to their passing com-panions; these gatherings are sometimes quite noisy and are well known to gunners as "loon caucuses." They are shy and difficult to approach on the water at such times, but when migrating they pay but little attention to the gunner's boat, swiftly passing over it in a direct course; they are often shot at, but seldom killed, for their densely feathered breasts are almost impervious to shot and they are very tenacious of life; if wounded, it is useless to pursue one, for it is more than a match for its enemies when in the water.

Mr. W. L. Dawson tells me the following interesting story of how one of these loons helped another out of a difficulty. He came upon a red-throated loon wrestling with some crude oil under its wing, within a few feet of the water on a California beach. He writes:

The bird awaited my approach warily, as if realizing the disadvantage of his position, but as I pressed too close with focussed camera, he sprang to wing, provoking me to a futile snap, plumped into the water almost immediately and struck out for deeper water. A mate, I will not say the mate for there were two red-throated loons in sight, saw his comrade's plight and hurried forward so eagerly that he took wing in his anxiety to succor, and did the "shoot-the-chutes" act with a fine display of wing and splash of water. After this the newcomer pressed forward toward me, as though to cover his comrade's retreat and paraded up and down at close quarters while the other bird was pulling away. It was difficult to believe that either parental instinct or sex gallantry took a part here. It was more likely a bit of fraternal altruism.

The inland migration route includes the Great Lakes and follows the valleys of the large rivers, but it is eventually coastwise. It winters occasionally in the interior, where it can find large bodies of open water and is sometimes caught by a sudden freeze when it perishes on the ice or snow for lack of food. The principal winter home of the species, however, is at sea and it extends along practically the whole of both coasts of the United States.

DISTRIBUTION.

Breeding range.—Northern parts of the Northern Hemisphere. In North America east to northern Greenland (Floeberg Beach, latitude 82° 27' N., Bowdoin Bay, and Whale Sound), Labrador, and Newfoundland. South to New Brunswick (Bay of Fundy, formerly), central Quebec (Point de Monts), central Keewatin (Fort Churchill), southern Mackenzie (Great Slave Lake and perhaps somewhat south of that latitude), Queen Charlotte Islands (Graham Island), and southern Alaska (near Sitka; Glacier Bay; Prince William Sound, Cordova; Cooks Inlet, Seldovia). West to the Aleutian and Commander Islands and Bering Sea. North to northern Alaska (Point Barrow and the Arctic coast), Banks Land (Mercy Bay), Melville Island, Ellesmere Land, and Grant Land (82° 30' N.). Stray birds occasionally summer in northern United States and southern Canada. Said to have bred once at Pittston, Pennsylvania.

In the Old World: East to northeastern Siberia (Delta of Kolyma River, Cape Serdze, and Anadyr district) and Bering Sea. South to Saghalin Island and Kuril Islands (Paramushir and Shunishu). Southern limits of breeding range over much of Siberia and Europe very poorly defined. West to British Isles (Ireland, northern Scotland, the Outer Hebrides, Orkney and Shetland Islands). North to Iceland, Scandinavia, the entire Arctic coast of Europe and Asia,

Nova Zembla, Kolguev, Spitzbergen, Franz Joseph Land, and New Siberia Islands.

Winter range.—In North America principally along the seacoast. East to Maine and the Atlantic Coast States. South to Florida (Anclote River). Apparently absent from the rest of the Gulf coast. On the Pacific coast from Puget Sound region of British Columbia and Washington south to California (entire coast and two interior records). It also winters in the Aleutian Islands. Occurs in winter throughout the Great Lakes (New York, Lake Ontario; Indiana; Illinois, near Chicago; Wisconsin and Michigan). Has been taken once in Arizona in winter (near Tucson), and during migration stragglers sometimes occur in Missouri, Iowa, Nebraska, Idaho, and Montana.

Old World birds winter from the British Isles south to Spain and Portugal, the Mediterranean, Black, and Caspian Seas, and from Japan to southeastern China and Formosa.

Spring migration.—Northward along both coasts of North America and in the interior. South Carolina: April 8. New York: Last of March to June 1. Connecticut: April 30 (latest). Rhode Island: April 27 (average departure), May 22 (latest). Southern Greenland: Sukkertoppen, June 2. Northeastern Greenland, Stormkap, June 8 and 11. Indiana: May 4 and 11 (latest). Michigan: March 3 to April 25 (occasionally May). Alberta: Lily Lake, May 2. Mackenzie:Athabaska Lake, June 2 (earliest); Great Slave Lake, June 10 (earliest); Mackenzie River, near Nahanni River, June 3 (earliest). Yukon Territory: Forty Mile, June 15. California: Santa Barbara, April 27. Washington: Lapush, June 11 (latest). British Columbia: Vancouver Island, June 4 (latest). Southeastern Alaska: Forrester Island, May 11; Admiralty Island, May 1. Northwestern Alaska: St. Michael, May 12 to 20 (earliest); Point Hope, May 17 (earliest); Point Barrow, June 5 (earliest); Demarcation Point, June 12. Banks Land: Soon after June 1. Melville Sound: June 16.

Fall migration.—Southward starting in September. The last individuals were noted in northeastern Siberia: Great Liakoff Island, September 9. Alaska: Point Barrow, August 16 and September 17; St. Michael, September 15 to 20. Wellington Channel: August 28. Melville Peninsula: Winter Island, September 14. Northwestern Greenland: Early August to October. Northeastern Greenland: Stormkap, September 4. Yukon Territory: Teslin Lake, October 21. Mackenzie: Fort Franklin, September 22 and 27. Keewatin: Knee Lake, September 9. Birds arrive in Massachusetts: October 1 to 17. New York: September 19 (August 24, earliest). New Jersey: Delaware River, October 20. South Carolina: Mt. Pleasant, October

15. Idaho: Lake Coeur d'Alene, October 6. California coast: Arrives in September.

Egg dates.—Greenland and Iceland: 33 records, May 10 to July 21; 16 records, June 6 to 21. Mackenzie: 15 records, June 10 to July 25; 8 records, July 1 to 6. Northern Alaska and Siberia: 11 records, June 6 to July 15; 6 records, June 26 to July 4. Hudson Bay and Labrador: 8 records, May 30 to July 5; 4 records, June 6 to 19.

Family ALCIDÆ, Auks, Murres, and Puffins.

LUNDA CIRRHATA (Pallas).

TUFTED PUFFIN.

HABITS.

After six long days at sea we were thoroughly tired of tossing about on the turbulent waters of the Pacific Ocean, weary of watching even the graceful evolutions of albatrosses, fulmars, and petrels, and we hailed with delight our first glimpse of the Aleutian Islands, as the rugged peaks of the Krenitzin group, Tigalda, Avatinak, and Ugamak, looked up in the horizon, dimly outlined in the foggy distance. They are the sturdy sentinels of rock that guard the entrance to Bering Sea, shrouded in perpetual mist, their snow-capped summits enveloped in heavy banks of cloud. Such is the gateway to this interesting region and here we were introduced to its wonderful bird life. We had seen a few tufted puffins at sea, migrating toward their summer home, but it was not until we reached the entrance to Unimak Pass that we began to realize the astonishing abundance of this species in that region. The sea was smooth, and scattered over its surface for miles, as far as we could see, were thousands and thousands of tufted puffins. We stood in the bow and watched them in their ludicrous attempts to escape as we passed through them. The wind was very light and was behind us, which made it almost impossible for them to rise from the water; they flopped along the surface in the most helpless manner; they barely managed to avoid being run over, but almost never succeeded in flying and only occasionally did they have sense enough to escape by diving, at which they were very skillful. They had probably only recently arrived and were congregating in the vicinity of their breeding grounds. The tufted puffin is largely pelagic in its habits, during the great part of the year migrating well out at sea, almost out of sight of land, and gradually working in toward shore, as the breeding season approaches. They are usually in pairs when they arrive.

Spring.—The arrival of the "Toporkie," as they are called, is a cause of great rejoicing among the Aleuts, for it heralds the approach of summer and means an abundant supply of good food, for both birds and eggs are a welcome relief from salted and dried seal meat on which they have been living. As soon as the puffins are sufficiently abundant about the islands where they breed the natives organize merry hunting parties to capture them. On certain days they frequent their breeding grounds in immense numbers, flying back and forth in straight lines, crossing and recrossing the small grassed-topped island, just high enough to clear it. The birds are swift fliers and seem unable to change their course quickly. The Aleuts take advantage of this peculiarity and catch them in large, long-handled nets, which are suddenly raised in front of the birds and which they can not dodge. It is a simple process when the birds are flying thickly, and large numbers are taken in this way. The birds are killed by biting the head or breaking the back. Besides furnishing a welcome supply of fresh meat, the birds are skinned and the skins are cured and used for clothing. A parka made of puffin skins is not only a very warm but a very light and serviceable garment. About 45 skins are required to make one parka, which is made like a shirt with a hood and is worn with the feathers on the inside.

Nesting.—Among the Aleutian and Pribilof Islands we found the tufted puffin breeding in a variety of situations. On June 15, 1911, we visited a small rocky island in Nazan Bay, Atka Island, on the rounded top of which enough soil had accumulated to support a rank growth of heavily tufted grass. As we drew near we could see a few quaint white faces, with flowing plumes, peering out from the crevices in the rocks, and many more of them half hidden in the long grass. The comical solemnity of this species and the long snowy locks, slightly tinged with yellow, have suggested the appropriate name by which it is called the "old man of the sea." Long before we landed the puffins had all left the island, flying out to meet us, circling about us several times until their curiosity was satisfied and finally settling down on the water to watch proceedings from a safe distance. The crevices in the rocks were inaccessible, but there were plenty of burrows in the soil among the grass. We dug out several burrows, but found no eggs and concluded that most of the birds had not laid.

On Bogoslof Island, on July 4, 1911, we found a few pairs of tufted puffins breeding in burrows in the sandy bluffs above the beaches and in the sandy and stony slopes about Castle Rocks, among the great murre colonies. Their burrows were rather shallow, and in one I could plainly see the egg without opening the burrow; they were generally profusely lined with feathers and straws. Some of the material must have been stolen from the neighboring gulls' nests or brought from a long distance; for there was no vegetation on the island.

On Walrus Island, on July 7, 1911, we found numerous pairs nesting under the loose rocks in the center of the island among the paroquet, crested, and least auklets, where they made poor attempts at nests of straw and feathers. The grassy uplands were entirely occupied by glaucous and glaucous-winged gulls, but a large open space of bare ground was so honeycombed with burrows of tufted puffins that we could hardly walk without breaking into them. The entrances to occupied holes were decorated with gull feathers and with the broken shells of murres' eggs; the nests at the ends of the shallow burrows were rudely made of gulls' feathers and dry grasses. Very few puffins were seen, as they were busy incubating on their single eggs, but if we dug them out, they went scrambling off toward the water, bounding over the ground in their frantic efforts to fly. Mr. William Palmer (1899) mentions a nest, found on this island " on August 7, which contained a slightly incubated egg. This nest was placed between bowlders, open to the sky, and was made of seaweeds and seaferns. It was quite large, about 15 inches in diameter, scanty in material, and practically bare in the center."

The nesting habits of this puffin in the great bird reservations on the coast of Washington have been well described by Messrs. William Leon Dawson and Lynds Jones. The largest colony on this coast seems to be on Carroll Islet where in 1907 Mr. Dawson (1908) estimated that there were 10,000 tufted puffins nesting. In 1905 Mr. Dawson estimated the puffins on this island at 5,000, showing a decided increase in two years under protection. This island is a " high, rounded mass of sandstone, tree crowned, and with sides chiefly precipitous. The crest is covered also with a dense growth of elderberry, salmon berry, or salal bush, while the upper slopes are covered with luxuriant grasses." Professor Jones (1908) says of the nesting of the tufted puffin here:

The only places where this species was not present and nesting were the rock precipices and the forested area, except, of course, the ledges, which were wholly occupied by murres and cormorants. Even the fringe of dense brush contained many nests. It is well known that the typical nesting habit of these birds is to find or make a burrow, usually among the rocks. The most of such burrows observed seemed to have been cleared of débris by the birds and some of them had clearly been made by the birds without much, if any, natural cavity, to mark the beginning. An occasional burrow was so shallow that the bird or egg could be seen but most of them extended a number of feet into the ground. In walking over a turf-covered, steep slope one needed to be careful not to break through these burrows and take a headlong tumble. In climbing such a steep slope the mouths of the burrows afford a comfortable foothold. In descending such a slope rapidly you are more than likely to have the leg bearing the most strain bumped just behind the knee by a frightened bird as it rushes headlong from its nest. One of our pleasant surprises with these birds was the finding of some nests beneath the thickly matted salal bushes, but without the semblance of a burrow. Clearly the birds considered the bushes a sufficient protection from marauding enemies, and were content to simply arrange their nest material upon the ground.

Mr. Dawson (1909) says:

A 45-degree slope of soil is the characteristic nesting site of the puffin. Here tunnels are driven at random to a depth of 3 or 4 feet, and so close together that once, on Erin, by placing a foot in the entrance of a burrow and fetching a compass, I was able to touch with the hands the entrance of 25 others, apparently occupied. This may have been an unusually populous section, but reckoning at half that rate, an acre of ground would carry 2,700 burrows. Hard or rocky soil is not shunned in prosperous colonies, but many efforts here are baffled outright and " prospects " are at least as numerous as occupied burrows. Elsewhere the top soil on precipitous, clinging ledges may be utilized, or else crannies, crevices, and rock-hewn chambers.

The tufted puffins have always been one of the interesting features of the famous Farallone Islands and their nesting habits there have been described by various writers. Here they seem to prefer to nest in the crevices in the cliffs and in cavities under the bowlders which form natural burrows from 2 to 5 feet in depth. Sometimes crude nests are made of coarse, dry weeds, but more often there is no attempt at nest building.

Eggs.—This puffin lays but one egg, which is usually " ovate " in shape; some specimens are more pointed, with a tendency toward " ovate pyriform." The shell is thick and lusterless. The color is very pale bluish white, or dull, dirty white. Many eggs show a few, and some numerous, spots or scrawls of various shades of gray or pale brown, which sometimes form a ring around the larger end. The measurements of 43 eggs in the United States National Museum and the writer's collections average 72 by 49.2 millimeters; the eggs showing the four extreme measure **78** by 50, 73.5 by **51.5, 65.5** by 49.5, and 68.5 by **45** millimeters.

Young.—Apparently two broods are raised in a season, at least in the southern portion of its breeding range, for eggs are found in the Farallone Islands early in May and fresh eggs are found again early in July. Mr. W. Otto Emerson states positively that two broods are raised and gives the period of incubation as 21 days. Both sexes incubate. Mr. Emerson says that they take turns at the duties of incubation every 12 hours, relieving each other at night and morning. Each bird spends a part of the day or night at sea in search of food, but, when not so occupied, it may be seen standing like a sentinel at the entrance of the burrow, waiting to relieve its incubating mate.

Mr. Emerson says:

The young are fed in the burrow until fully feathered and large enough to take care of themselves in the sea water. The food of the young consists of shellfish, mussels, sea urchins, small smelt, sardines, herring, and perch.

The young puffins are gluttonous feeders and will gorge themselves with food until they can hardly move. They are also very pugnacious, fighting among themselves and biting at anything that comes within reach.

Plumages.—The young when first hatched is completely covered with long, soft, silky down, sooty black above and sooty grayish below. It remains in the nest until it is at least partly fledged; in the juvenal plumage the feathers of the belly are largely white, but ordinarily these white feathers are soon replaced by those of the first winter plumage. In this plumage the upper parts are blackish and the under parts dark brown, but the feathers of the belly are whitish basally; young birds during the first winter can be readily distinguished from adults by their smaller, weaker, bills without the grooves, by their brown irides and by the entire absence of the crests or ear tufts. At the first prenuptial molt, which is only partial, the face becomes partially white, the first ear tufts, which are dull yellowish brown in color, are acquired, the irides become white and the bill is partially developed. At the first postnuptial molt, during the following August and September, the adult winter plumage is assumed by a complete molt.

Adults have an incomplete prenuptial molt, involving at least the head and neck and perhaps much of the contour plumage, and a complete postnuptial molt. At this latter molt the white face and the long, flowing plumes of the nuptial plumage disappear, the cuirass or horny covering at the base of the bill is shed and the white irides become pale blue. In the winter plumage the face is wholly dark brown and the ear tufts or plumes are either entirely lacking or replaced by rudimentary dull yellowish plumes. Winter adults often have many white or gray-tipped feathers on the under parts.

Food.—The food of the tufted puffin consists mainly of fish, such as smelts (sometimes 8 or 10 inches long), sardines, herring, and perch, which it catches by diving and swimming swiftly under water and which it carries crosswise in its bill. It also feeds largely on various mollusks, sea urchins, and other sea food, including algae. Its powerful beak is well designed for crushing the shells of mollusks and sea urchins. Most of its food is obtained at sea, for which it often travels many miles.

According to Prof. Harold Heath (1915) these puffins which are very abundant about Forrester Island, Alaska, make themselves a nuisance to the fishermen in that region; he writes:

For fearlessness, pluck, and dash the tufted puffins have no equal on the island, and the maledictions and gaff hooks hurled at them during the fishing season were probably as numerous as the birds themselves. While their natural food consists almost wholly of sand launces, they are by no means averse to cleaning the bait from the fishermen's hooks. For hours at a time they will follow a rowboat, and rarely indeed is a fisherman able to sink a line below their diving depth, or slip it into the water without detection. Fortunately not all of the puffins are engaged in this thrifty method of gathering food, and the boatman is usually able to cross some other fisherman's path and switch the pest on to his trail.

On one occasion a puffin was stunned by an accurately aimed gaff hook and was hauled aboard. Upon recovering consciousness it was held by the feet and fed herring until the exasperated boatman terminated its career by wringing its neck. This is perhaps an extreme case, but it serves to illustrate the boldness of the species and to furnish a reason for the steady increase in numbers which the natives have observed during the past 20 years.

Behavior.—The tufted puffin, with its heavy body and small wings, experiences considerable difficulty in rising from the water in calm weather or with the wind behind it; I have often seen it make futile attempts to do so, flapping along the surface, dropping into the water and trying again and again. It is equally incapable of rising from the land and generally prefers to launch into the air from a cliff or steep hillside, where it glides downward for several feet before gaining headway enough to fly. But, when once under way its flight is strong, direct, and well sustained. It makes long flights to and from its feeding grounds and on migrations. It usually flies well up in the air, but it can not rise abruptly or change its course suddenly; it usually circles about in long curves, rising gradually.

It is a good diver, swimming below the surface with both wings and feet in use, but it does not like to dive and prefers to escape by some other method, if possible. It often dives directly out of the air into the water or plunges below the surface as soon as it alights, which is a rather clumsy performance. It is quite active on land, walking about in a lively manner or standing erect on its toes. Its attitude is one of ludicrous solemnity, suggestive of its common name, "sea parrot." It is exceedingly tough and hard to kill, carrying off a lot of heavy shot; when wounded, it is useless to pursue it. Its body is so solid and muscular that the means ordinarily used for killing birds hardly proves effective; one particularly tough individual which, for three times in succession, I supposed I had killed, finally escaped.

This puffin, like most sea birds, is a sociable species on its breeding grounds, where it seems to live on good terms with its neighbors. It occasionally borrows a little nesting material from the gulls, but it never disturbs the eggs of other species. Mr. Chester Barlow (1894a) writes of finding a dead Cassins' auklet and its egg in a burrow occupied by an incubating tufted puffin, from which he inferred that the puffin had killed the auklet and taken possession of its home. Mr. Milton S. Ray (1904) cites the following incident:

On one occasion I chased a rabbit to a burrow among the rocks, but the animal had scarcely entered when out it quickly jumped. I looked in, and there, sentinel like, stood the puffin on guard with a bill full of "bunny's" fur.

The young puffins are very quarrelsome among themselves and are particularly aggressive toward human beings, but their weapons are not formidable. The old birds, however, are both vicious and formidable and must be handled with thick gloves, if at all. Their beaks are powerful and sharp, they will bite at anything which comes within reach and often hang on with such bulldog tenacity that their strong jaws must be pried apart. They can inflict severe wounds, biting through the flesh to the bone.

Several writers have referred to the tufted puffin as quarrelsome and noisy on its breeding grounds, where its notes are said to resemble the growling of a bear. I have always found it absolutely silent, and believe that these references to its vocal powers are based on hearsay or on confusion with the notes of auklets or other birds occupying the same breeding grounds.

Winter.—After the breeding season is over and the young are able to take care of themselves they all move away from their summer homes, to roam about on the open seas, where very little seems to be known about their winter habits. I have seen this species farther from land, by several hundred miles, than any of the other Alcidae and suppose that they are widely scattered during the winter over the north Pacific Ocean.

DISTRIBUTION.

Breeding range.—Coasts and islands of the North Pacific and Bering Sea and portions of the Arctic Ocean. From California (Santa Barbara Islands, rarely San Nicholas) and from Japan (north end of Yezo) and the Kuril Islands north to northwestern Alaska (Cape Lisburne) and northeastern Siberia (Koliutschin Island).

Winter range.—In most of its range a permanent resident, but northerly breeding birds winter somewhat south of their summer home. Recorded in winter north to the Aleutian Islands.

Spring migration.—Migration consists principally of returning to its nesting grounds from the near-by open sea. Birds arrive at the Pribilof Islands about May 10 (occasionally as early as March 5), St. Michael June 8, Kotzebue Sound June 25 (or later), and Gichiga River, Anadyr district, Siberia, May 1 to 15.

Fall migration.—Birds remain in northeastern Siberia, Anadyr district, until October 15 (a few even later), and a specimen was taken at St. Michael, Alaska, as late as October 12, Walrus Island, October 2, and St. Paul Island, December 8.

Casual records.—Reinhardt records a specimen taken in Greenland and Audubon obtained and figured a bird from the mouth of the Kennebec River, Maine. Records from the Bay of Fundy are erroneous.

Egg dates.—Farallone Islands: 81 records, April 30 to July 8; 41 records, May 27 to June 17. Washington: 12 records, May 30 to July 23; 6 records, June 19 to 27. Southern Alaska and Aleutian Islands: 11 records, June 17 to July 18; 6 records, June 29 to July 7.

FRATERCULA ARCTICA ARCTICA (Linnaeus).

PUFFIN.

HABITS.

Contributed by Charles Wendell Townsend.

The puffin is a curious mixture of the solemn and the comical. Its short stocky form and abbreviated neck, ornamented with a black collar, its serious owl-like face and extraordinarily large and brilliantly colored bill, suggestive of the false nose of a masquerader, its vivid orange red feet and legs all combine to produce such a grotesque effect that one is brought almost to laughter on seeing these birds walking about near at hand. The parrotlike appearance of the bill has earned the name of " parroquet," or " sea parrot," by which it is known in Labrador and Newfoundland. Besides being grotesque it is singularly confiding or stupid, and it is this, it seems to me, that is leading rapidly but surely to its downfall and final extinction, unless refuges are created and respected where it can breed undisturbed. At the present time the most southerly breeding station is Matinicus Rock off the middle coast of Maine. Here only two pairs are left. The only other breeding place left on the coast of the United States is at Machias Seal Island. Here in 1904, according to Dutcher (1904), there was a colony of 300 of these birds. It is probable that the coast of Maine was formerly the resort of large numbers of this species. According to Knight (1908) a few pairs probably bred on Seal Island not far from Matinicus as recently as 1888. Audubon (1840), who visited the Bay of Fundy in 1833, says it bred commonly on the islands in the bay " although not one perhaps now for a hundred that bred there 20 years ago." Now, they are nearly if not entirely extirpated. Macoun (1909) gives only one breeding locality for Nova Scotia, namely, Seal Island, Yarmouth County; but it is probable that a century ago the coast swarmed with these interesting birds. Along the Newfoundland coast the puffin is still to be found breeding, but in much diminished numbers. At Bryon Island in the Magdalen group and at Bird Rock puffins still breed, as well as at Wreck Bay, Anticosti, and elsewhere on this island. On the Labrador coast their numbers are rapidly diminishing. The westernmost of the Mingan Islands where auks, murres, gannets, and puffins formerly bred in great numbers, and which bear the name of the Parroquet Islands, are now almost devoid of bird life. The gannets have ceased to nest there and the puffins are almost wiped out. In 1906 we saw no puffins near these islands, and in 1909 only two were to be seen. Near the eastern end of the Mingan group of islands is Bald Island. Here in 1906 we found about 150 pairs of puffins. At Wolf Island, near Cape Whittle, in

1884 Frazer found a colony of about a thousand puffins. Still farther to the east is the famous Parroquet Island near Bradore. Audubon (1840) visited this island in 1833. He says:

> As we rowed toward it, although we found the water literally covered with thousands of these birds, the number that flew over and around the green island seemed much greater, insomuch that one might have imagined half the puffins in the world had assembled there.

In 1906 Townsend and Allen (1907) passed near this island and say of these puffins:

> There were at least 500 of them, perhaps many more.

In 1860 Coues (1861) thus describes the island at the mouth of Hamilton Inlet on the eastern Labrador coast:

> The Parrakeet Islands are three in number, lying along the western shore of Esquimau Bay, just at its mouth. The one I visited is the innermost, as well as the largest, though the others are equally crammed with birds. It is about a mile in circumference. As we rounded the island close to the shore they came tumbling out of their holes by hundreds and, with the thousands we disturbed from the surface of the water, soon made a perfect cloud above and around us, no longer flying in flocks, but forming one dense continuous mass.

He also records them in numbers in the bay near Rigolet. Forty-six years later, in 1906, Townsend and Allen saw only 13 puffins on a steamer trip from Battle Harbor to Nain, stopping at Rigolet, and only 43 on the return trip. Six years later, in 1912, Bent (1913) " did not see a single puffin north of the Straits." He spent nearly two months between Battle Harbor and Cape Mugford. When shot at on their breeding grounds the survivors continue to fly by close at hand, offering the gunner tempting shots. Both Audubon and Coues seem to have yielded to this temptation and shot great numbers of puffins. What can be expected of the ignorant and ruthless? The story is everywhere the same—a rapid diminution in the numbers of this picturesque and interesting bird.

Courtship.—I have watched groups of these birds off the southern coast of Labrador during the courtship season. They swim together in closely crowded ranks, rarely diving, for their thoughts are not on food. At frequent intervals individuals rise up in the water and flap their wings as if from nervousness. Again two males fight vigorously, flapping their wings meanwhile and making the water foam about them. Again two, possibly a pair, hold each other by the bills and move their heads and necks like billing doves. Now several are seen to throw their heads back with a jerk until the bill points up, and this is repeated a number of times. Edmund Selous (1905), who has watched this action near at hand in the puffins of the Shetlands, says the bill is opened wide but no sound is uttered. The brilliant lining of the mouth is therefore the result of sexual selection and it evidently forms a part of the courtship display.

Nesting.—The puffin is a social bird and nests in colonies. One of the largest breeding colonies remaining at the present time is on Parroquet Island off the southern coast of Labrador near Bradore. Here the birds burrow into the friable soil and utilize crannies among the rocks for their nests. Of a similar, but smaller, colony at Bald Island off the middle of the southern coast of Labrador, I have made a more intimate study. Here in June, 1909, we found about 150 pairs breeding. The island is formed of limestone with a flat surface of several acres of loose, dark soil on which stood and lay a forest of dead stalks of the cow parsnip (*Heracleum lanatum*). The new leaves were just beginning to push up from the ground at the time of our visit on the 8th and 9th of June. In this loose soil, but chiefly under the large fragments of rocks that were partly embedded in the surface, were the nesting burrows of the puffins. Most of these nests in the burrows under the large rocks were just beyond the reach of the arm, extended to full length in the hole, but a few were accessible, as their length was little more than 2 feet. The holes in the loose soil were generally about 30 inches long, often curved and descending at a slight angle to a few inches or a foot below the surface. Frazar (1887) says of the burrows at Wolf Island, southern Labrador, that:

They are seldom over 4 feet deep and generally take an abrupt curve near the opening and run along usually near the surface of the ground. Several that I opened curved in such a way that the nest, which is an enlarged cavity at the end of the burrow, with a little straw laid on the bottom, was exactly under the entrance and only a thin crust of soil between the two.

Sometimes several burrows communicate and a single one may have two openings. In walking over a field filled with the burrows of this bird, one is in constant danger of breaking through into the numerous tunnels. At the end of the burrow is the nest, a loose mass of dead grass, sometimes with a few feathers, in which rests the single egg. In exploring the holes with outstretched arm, we found that gloves were very necessary, as the enraged parent bird was capable of inflicting considerable damage to the unprotected fingers with her keen-edged and powerful bill, and, when seized, she could scratch vigorously with her sharp nails. The work of digging the holes falls chiefly on the male, and he is at times so intent upon this work as to suffer himself to be taken by the hand. The inner toenail on each foot is well adapted for the digging process, as it is strong, curved, and sharp, and the other toenails are but little inferior.

Eggs.—Only one egg is laid, as a rule. Frazar (1887) found, in a colony of a thousand pairs at Cape Whittle, 12 burrows, each containing two eggs. The egg is rounded ovate in shape, and generally a dull white when first laid, but it soon becomes soiled. A few eggs are spotted with concealed chocolate markings, while some have distinct spots and blotches. The measurements of 41 eggs, in the United States National Museum collection, average 63 by 44.2 millimeters; the eggs showing the four extremes measure **67** by **47, 58** by 43, and 63 by **41.5** millimeters.

Young.—Both sexes incubate, although the greater part of this work falls upon the females. Baird, Brewer, and Ridgway (1884) state that the period of incubation is 1 month. Audubon (1840) says it is probably from 25 to 28 days. Only one brood is raised in a season. When the young are 4 or 5 weeks old they are able to leave their burrows and follow their mothers to the sea. A large nesting colony such as that at Parroquet Island, near Bradore, Labrador, is a place of intense interest early in August, when the parents are busily engaged in filling the wants of the hungry young. The water all about the place is dotted with puffins; there are weird looking groups of the birds on the rocks and the air is filled with the birds returning with food and those going farther afield in quest of more. The returning birds all have capelin—often several—or other small fish hanging from their bills by the heads, and in the swift flight of the birds the fish trail out parallel to the bill. The young birds wait at the mouth of the burrow for the feast and are always clamorous for more. Fish appears to be the chief of their diet, although shrimps and other crustacea and mollusca may be added.

Plumages.—[Author's note: The young puffin is hatched in a coat of long, soft, thick down which covers the whole body; the central belly portion is white, sometimes tinged with yellowish or light gray; the remainder of the down, covering the upper parts, the throat and the crissum, is light "seal brown" with "drab" shadings; in some specimens the upper parts are "Prout's brown" or "Vandyke brown." The plumage appears first on the wings and then on the back and the last of the natal down disappears on the neck, rump, and flanks. This first winter plumage is somewhat like the winter plumage of the adult, glossy brownish black above and pure white below; but the loral and orbital regions are more extensively dusky than in the adult, and the bill is very small, weak, undeveloped and pointed. This plumage is worn all winter and apparently through the first spring, until the young bird becomes indistinguishable from the adult after the first postnuptial molt, a gradual development of the bill taking place during the spring and summer. The adult has only a limited prenuptial molt in the spring and a complete postnuptial molt in the late summer and fall. In the adult winter plumage the face, or the whole lower portion of the head above the black collar, is much darker gray than in the spring; whether the light gray, almost whitish, face of the nuptial plumage is produced by molting or only by fading I can not say. The most conspicuous seasonal change in the puffin is in the bill.]

The bill of the puffin is in truth a mask, for it is large and brilliant only during the season of courtship, and is mostly cast off to be replaced by a smaller, duller one for common use the rest of the year. The bill is the same in the two sexes, and, at the height of the breeding season, is a brilliant scarlet with triangular patches of steel blue at the bases of both mandibles; about the middle of the upper mandible, on either side, is a narrow band of white. The commissure, bare of feathers, is a brilliant orange. The whole inside of the mouth and tongue is a light yellow. Nor is this all, for the eyes during the courtship season are provided with a narrow horizontal horny line below, and one running diagonally back above while the edge of the eyelids is a vivid vermillion. The eyes themselves are small and blue-black, and sparkle in the wonderful setting.

After the breeding season the puffin puts aside its mask by shedding the following pieces, according to Coues (1903):

1, Basal rim or collar; 2, nasal case or saddle; 3, mandibular case or shoe; 4, 5, strips at base of mandible, one on each side; 6, 7, subnasal strips, one on each side; 8, 9, prenasal strips one on each side.

The horny appendages of the eyelids are also shed. The horny molt by which the whole bill becomes smaller takes place at the same time with the feather molt in August and September. The orange skin at the commissure becomes pale and shrunken and the feet change from brilliant orange red to yellow.

Food.—The food of the puffin is almost exclusively fish and on the Labrador coast the capelin seems to be their favorite. Crustacean and other forms of marine life are doubtless also eaten.

Behavior.—Puffins are as a rule unsuspicious and generally allow a close approach. As one approaches in a steamer or other boat, the swimming bird shows its anxiety by nervously dipping its head into the water from time to time. Then it is apt to show the greatest indecision as to which action to adopt—flight below the water or above. Both actions—aerial as well as subaqueous—can be described as flight, for the wings, although held somewhat differently, are as vigorously used below the water as in the air. In the former as in the latter case the feet are not used but trail behind. One can easily observe the beginning of the subaqueous flight, for the wings are flapped out for their first stroke as the bird enters the water. Unless the wind be strong against them, they have great difficulty in rising from the water, and often splash along the surface for some distance before they can rise above it. Many a time they give up the attempt and rest before trying again, but often continue the flight by dipping below the surface, without a pause in the process. I have often seen them emerge from a wave, fly across the trough and enter the next wave without apparent change in their method of propulsion. Again I have seen them come out of the water flying, only to plunge down into the water and continue the flight below the surface. On the surface they paddle along skilfully like little apoplectic short necked ducks and their small orange red legs are plainly visible. Their diminutive tails are sometimes cocked up at an angle. The tails are spread as they dive.

On the land puffins walk with great dignity without resting the tarsus on the ground, although this at times is done. Although the tarsus is vertical, the body of the bird is sometimes as horizontal as a duck's body, but at other times, as when anxious about the intentions of a human intruder, the neck and body are both stretched up.

The aerial flight of the puffin is rapid with swift beatings of the little wings, and with frequent swaying or turning from side to side, as is the case in all the Alcidae. Flocks wheel and turn together with the regularity of shore birds, now showing their black backs, now flashing out their white breasts and bellies. The similarity in these habits between these two groups is doubtless explained by their close relationship. Brewster (1883) thus describes the manner of the descent of the puffin from the high cliffs of Byron Island:

Launching into the air with head depressed and winds held stiffly at a sharp angle above their backs they would shoot down like meteors, checking their speed by an upward turn just before reaching the water.

In a strong wind puffins sometimes poise in the up currents on the edge of a hill or cliff as motionless as a hawk under similar circumstances. As they alight in the water their feet are spread out on either side with the toes wide apart, so that in the breeding season the orange red webs make a brilliant display. They alight with a splash and as a rule bend the head foreward so that it momentarily goes below the surface, but soon regain their balance and ride the water lightly like ducks.

The note of these birds as I have heard it in flight near its nesting place is a low purring note, a *purr-la-la-la*. When struggling in the hand they utter harsh croaks. Boraston (1905) says:

As the bird flies, especially if returning to its burrow with fish, it utters a peculiar sound—a deep-throated, mirthless laughter, as it were, which may be imitated by laughing in the throat with the lips closed.

Edmund Selous (1905) says:

The note of the puffin is very peculiar—sepulchrally deep, and full of the deepest feeling. Another note is much more commonly heard, viz, a long, deep, slowly rising *Awe*, uttered in something of a tone of solemn expostulation, as though the bird were in the pulpit.

Audubon (1840) compares the cries of the young to the " wailing of young whelps." Chapman speaks of a captive bird with a ' hoarse voice, half grunt, half groan," and some of the birds that Audubon kept on board his vessel on the Labrador were " fed freely and were agreeable pets only that they emitted an unpleasant grunting noise, and ran about incessantly during the night, when each footstep could be counted."

Their relations with other species are at times playful or warlike, depending on the point of view. Thus I once watched a puffin chase three black guillemots by repeatedly diving and swimming under water toward them while they followed the same tactics in eluding the pursuit. At last all four came to the surface near together, the ardor of the chase evaporated, and they all seemed unconscious of each other's presence.

Winter.—The full migration of the puffin along the New England coast takes place in October or later. During the winter they frequent by preference the waters off rocky headlands, like Cape Ann or Marblehead, and may best be observed at such places, or in winter steamboat trips along the coast. Their food habits at this season are much the same as in more northern waters already described.

DISTRIBUTION.

Breeding range.—Coasts and islands of the North Atlantic. Formerly from Maine and the Bay of Fundy, Newfoundland, the Gulf of St. Lawrence, and Labrador north to southern Greenland. Now restricted on the coast of Maine to Matinicus Rock and Machias Seal Island; and in the Gulf of St. Lawrence to Bryon Island, Bird Rock, Anticosti, Bald Island, and Bradore. Probably extirpated from the remainder of the above range south of northern Labrador. Some Greenland records probably refer to *F. a. naumanni* but *arctica* has been taken at Holsteinborg (and elsewhere?).

In Europe breeds from Berlenga Islands, off Portugal, north to Norway, the British Isles (mainland of Great Britain, Ireland, Scilly Islands, Outer Hebrides, Orkney, and Shetland Islands), the Faroes and Iceland.

Winter range.—Birds probably winter as far north as they find open water, but there is little definite information on this point. They occur along the coast of Maine south to Massachusetts, rarely to Long Island, New York, and casually to the Delaware River (near Chester, Pennsylvania). Audubon recorded it from the mouth of Savannah River.

They also winter about the coast of Great Britain and south to the western Mediterranean Sea (Spain, east coast, Italy, Sicily, Malta, and the coast of Morocco), casually to the Azores and Canary Islands.

Spring migration.—Migration dates are almost wholly lacking. A bird was taken on Long Island, New York, March 30 (one found April 30 was badly decayed and may have died weeks previously).

Massachusetts, leave sometime in March. They arrive on their breeding grounds in the British Isles from the last of March to early May somewhat earlier than they do in North America.

Fall migration.—Migration along the New England coast takes place in October (Massachusetts, October 16). A bird has been recorded from the Ottawa River in October, and a specimen was taken at Davis Inlet, Labrador, as late as October 4.

Egg dates.—Gulf of St. Lawrence: 34 records, June 6 to July 10; 17 records, June 15 to 26. Great Britain: 9 records, May 27 to June 30; 5 records, June 4 to 8. Iceland: 8 records, May 22 to July 16; 4 records, June 11 to 24. Newfoundland and eastern Labrador: 5 records, June 8 to July 7; 3 records, July 1 to 3. Maine: 3 records, June 19 and July 27.

FRATERCULA ARCTICA NAUMANNI Norton.

LARGE-BILLED PUFFIN.

HABITS.

The puffin of the coasts and islands of the Arctic Ocean from Greenland to Nova Zembla has been separated from the common Atlantic Puffin as a large subspecies. The difference in size had long been known and was recognized in nomenclature by Naumann under the specific name *Mormon glacialis* of Leach.

Mr. W. Elmer Ekblaw writes to me in regard to this puffin:

According to the Eskimo, the puffin is constantly increasing in numbers on the northwest coast of Greenland, the increase having become most marked within the last 10 years. The older Eskimo state that to see the puffin was formerly a rare occurrence, and that some years the people living near the usual nesting sites of this bird saw none throughout the season, whereas now they never fail to observe it rather commonly.

The puffin occurs nowhere very abundantly in comparison with the murres and dovekies, but at some places it is rather common. According to the Eskimo it nests toward the west end of the Crimson Cliffs, at Cape Parker Snow and Cape Dudley Digges, at Cape Alexander on Saunders Island, on Northumberland Island, and on Hakluyt Island, the greatest number being found toward the west end of the Crimson Cliffs, and on Hakluyt Island.

Nesting.—Its nesting sites are the cliffs and steeper slopes of the outermost capes and the islands along the outer coast. It nests in flocks, nearly always in the same locality as the murres. The nest is placed in burrows in grass, in moss-covered talus slopes, or in turfy places on the cliffs. The eggs are found in June or early July.

Eggs.—Very few eggs have found their way into collections; what eggs are available seem to be exactly like those of the common puffin, but average slightly longer. The measurements of 7 eggs, in various collections, average 63.8 by 43.8 millimeters; the eggs showing the four extremes measure **67** by 45, 66 by **46, 59** by 42.5, and 62 by **42** millimeters.

Food.—Mr. Ekblaw says:

It feeds upon the same kind of food as does the murre—fish, crustacea, etc., especially upon a species which, from the Eskimo description, Fabricius translates as " Pulex maris alti rostro serrato."

Behavior.—The Eskimo say that the puffin is not at all shy. It does not dive, when out on the sea, until it is approached very near. It generally feeds in pairs on the water. It flies about as fast as a murre. In season, the Eskimo women frequently catch it in their nets, when they are out on the cliffs primarily for murres.

This puffin seems to be in part a migrant; but not much is known concerning its times, route, or extent of migration. Certainly it is found even in winter in Greenland waters. It comes to the Cape York district at the same time as the murres, generally in company with them, about the 10th of May, It leaves about the same time as the murres, in late August. It lives mostly out on the open sea.

It is rather strange that so little is known about the migrations and winter home of this subspecies. There seem to be no satisfactory records for North America, outside of Greenland, and I could never understand why Greenland should be considered as faunally a part of our Continent.

DISTRIBUTION.

Breeding range.—Coasts and islands of the Arctic Ocean from central western Greenland (Baffin Bay; Disco Bay, north to Smith Sound) east to Spitzbergen and Nova Zembla. Some Greenland records of *F. a. arctica* undoubtedly apply to this form, while records of *naumanni* from northern Labrador are doubtful. Audubon's record from Grand Manan with little doubt refers to *arctica*.

Winter range.—Unknown. Probably not far from its breeding grounds if open water occurs.

Egg dates.—Greenland: 16 records, June 1 to July 16; 9 records, June 19 to 20.

FRATERCULA CORNICULATA (Naumann).

HORNED PUFFIN.

HABITS.

This name seems somewhat misleading and not particularly appropriate, for the so-called horn over the eye is not horny at all, but merely a soft epidermal papilla full of living tissue, which the bird can raise or lower at will; moreover a similar, but smaller, excrescence is found in the Atlantic puffin. The horned puffin is essentially an Alaskan and a Bering Sea bird, being found breeding throughout the whole length of the Alaskan coast, from Cape Lisburne, north of the Arctic Circle, south nearly to British Columbia; it also breeds westward throughout the Aleutian Islands and on all the coasts and islands of Bering Sea. It would seem as if the name

Alaskan or Pacific puffin would be far more appropriate. This is only one of many misnomers in our nomenclature of North American birds.

Spring.—Mr. E. W. Nelson (1887) says.

At the Fur Seal Islands these birds arrive about the 10th of May, in pairs, but near St. Michaels I have never seen them before the 10th of June and rarely before the 20th of that month. At the latter place and at other northern points their arrival is governed by the date when the ice leaves the coast for the summer.

Nesting.—The northernmost colony on which I have any notes is on Puffin Island, a small, precipitous rocky islet near Chamisso Island, in Kotzebue Sound, which is now a reservation. Dr. Joseph Grinnell (1900) visited this colony and made the following report:

On July 9, 1899, I spent the afternoon and night on Chamisso Island. On this island and a smaller detached one bearing northwest from it, the horned puffins were breeding in immense numbers. Their nest burrows were dug in the earth on top of the islands, principally on the verge of the bluffs. These burrows were from 1 to 3 feet in length, with an enlarged nest cavity at the end. The eggs generally lay on the bare ground, but there was often a slight collection of grasses between it and the earth. The parent bird was frequently found on the nest and would sometimes offer courageous resistance to being dragged forth, inflicting severe nips with its powerful mandibles. Where there were rock slides on the side of the island, natural crevices and holes among the fallen bowlders were taken advantage of for nesting sites. In such places eggs were to be found from the surf to the top of the island, and by crawling amongst the bowlders many eggs were discovered, but often in such narrow crevices that they could not be reached. The birds usually flushed from their nesting places before the collector reached them, being probably warned by the vibration of footsteps on the rocks which I noticed to be quite perceptible when one was in a narrow chasm. The eggs laid in these rocky niches were usually provided with a scanty bed of dry grasses. All the eggs secured were fresh and proved more palatable for the table than the murre's eggs.

Mr. Hersey visited this colony on August 2, 1914, when probably most of the young were hatched, although he found a few eggs. His notes state that he frequently saw a bird leave the host of circling puffins, fly up to the entrance to a burrow, flutter a moment, and then fly off. A minute later a bird would fly out from the nest and soon after the other would fly in to take its place on the nest. Once he saw two birds emerge from one burrow.

We found the horned puffin widely distributed among the Aleutian Islands. There was a small breeding colony on a precipitous rocky headland near the entrance to Chernofsky Harbor, but we could not reach it and had to be content with shooting a few birds as they circled out over us. At Atka Island, on June 15, 1911, we found a small breeding colony on a steep rocky island in Nazan Bay where we saw the birds flying in and out of inaccessible crevices in the cliffs; we were too busy with other more important things to devote much time to them.   There were also a few pairs of horned puffins circling with a cloud of tufted puffins about another small island in this bay, where a large number of the latter species were breeding.   Mr. L. M. Turner (1886) says of the nesting habits of this species among the Aleutian Islands:

Their nests are placed on the ledges of the highest cliffs of those islands where foxes are found, and on islands where foxes are not found these birds breed generally at the bases of bluffs, under the large rocks which have become detached and fallen down.   Their nest is composed of just whatever happens to be there, be it sticks, stones, or earth.   A few feathers may be dropped from the bird, but not for an evident purpose of nest construction.   A single egg of clear white color is laid on the bare gravel or earth.   The egg is very large for the size of the bird, and when cooked is tolerable eating.   The bird sits long at a time on the egg, and does not leave it until hunger compels her to seek food.

Mr. H. W. Elliott (1880) says:

This mormon, in common with one other species, *M. cirrhata*, comes up from the sea in the south to the cliffs of the islands about the 10th of May, always in pairs, never coming singly to, or going away from, the Pribylovs in flocks. It makes a nest of dried sea-ferns, grass, and moss, slovenly laid together, far back in some deep or rocky crevice, where, when the egg is laid, it is ninety-nine times out of a hundred cases inaccessible; nothing but blasting powder would open a passage to it for man.   It has this peculiarity: It is the only bird on these islands which seems to quarrel for ever and ever with its mate.   The hollow reverberations of its anger, scolding, and vituperation from the nuptial chamber, are the most characteristic sounds, and indeed the only ones that come from the recesses of the rocks.   No sympathy need be expended on the female.   She is just as big and just as violent as her lord and master.

Mr. B. J. Bretherton (1896) gives an unique account of the nesting habits of this species on Kodiak Island; he writes:

On first arriving, these birds do a great deal of flying; they gather in bands, and sit perched on the rocky face of some high bluff, and keep up a continuous whistling call, at irregular intervals the whole band will leave the bluff and fly a short distance out to sea and return.

The eggs of this species are laid in a tunnel, or burrow, dug in the ground by the bird, and a few handfuls of dry grass and feathers constitute the nest.

The construction of the tunnel is unique; it always has an opening at both ends.   The nesting site is some high rocky bluff overhanging the sea, and near the top where the soil lies on the rock, the bird commences its excavations, first constructing a sort of runway for a few feet along the face of the bluff, then going directly inward, sometimes in a straight line, while others are crooked.   In the same way, the length of the tunnel is very variable, and the nest may be at most any distance from 2 to 10 feet from the face of the bluff. From the nest, the tunnel passes on inland, making a sharp upward turn to the surface of the ground.

The same burrows are used year after year, but whether by the same birds or not was not ascertained.   Some burrows have by long usage become as large as rabbit holes, while newly made ones are only just large enough to admit the birds.   Both entrances are used indiscriminately by the bird, and it is surprising to see with what accuracy they can fly directly into the holes in the ground.

The southernmost breeding colony of horned puffins, so far as I know, is on Forrester Island in southern Alaska, where Prof. Harold Heath (1915) estimated that "not over two or three thousand made their homes" in the summer of 1913. According to his notes, "they form small colonies in the face of a cliff some distance from human habitation and at all times appear to be at peace with their more numerous relatives," the tufted puffins. They apparently nest here in burrows in the soil, in essentially the same manner as the tufted puffins.

Eggs.—The horned puffin lays a single egg, which is large for the size of the bird and "ovate" in shape with a tendency toward "ovate pyriform"; the shell is thick, roughly granulated and lusterless. The ground color is dull white, dirty white, or creamy white. There are seldom any very conspicuous spots, but nearly all eggs show more or less evident shell markings, spots or scrawls, of "pale lavender gray," or pale olive or buff; some eggs appear quite spotless but even these, on close examination, have very faint markings. The variation in size is considerable, but the average size is only slightly less than in the eggs of the tufted puffin. The eggs of the two species can not be distinguished with certainty. The measurements of 38 eggs showing the four extremes measure **74** by 50, 73 by **50.5, 58** by 43.5, and 61.5 by **41** millimeters.

Young.—Both sexes assist in the process of incubation and in the care of the young. The period of incubation is unknown. Mr. Nelson (1887) says of the development and behavior of the young:

The young take wing in August at the Seal Islands, but north of that point they are rarely fledged before some time in September.

On September 9, 1879, I visited a small islet a few miles from St. Michaels, where the puffins were breeding in great numbers. The islet arose about 25 feet above the sea and was a mass of rugged basaltic bowlders. Among the crevices hundreds of the puffins were breeding. Both species were here, but the tufted species was in very small numbers compared with the host of the other kind. The young were mostly about half grown, but many only just from the shell and some not even yet hatched were found. The young could be easily located under the stones by the thin metallic piping note they kept uttering during the parents' absence. As we walked about the old birds could be heard scuttling about below, uttering a hoarse, snuffling, rattling note, which sounded at a short distance like a low growling noise. With a slipping noose on the end of a ramrod it was an easy matter to capture any number of them by simply walking about and peering down into the crevices, and when a bird was seen pass the noose over the bird's bill and drag the captive out. They would scratch and bite viciously and utter their usual note in a loud hoarse key.

During our stay the air was full of birds circling about, and often passing within a few feet of us. The young were easily captured by removing the stones, and they also fought when taken. The loose rocks were surrounded by a network of passages, and if it had not been for the birds stupidity they could have easily avoided capture. As we began removing the stones overhead, young or old would scramble forward and thrust their great beaks into the first crevice which offered, although not an inch wide, and then they would push and struggle desperately to force their way through until taken in hand. Even when they managed to escape after being dragged out they would frequently scramble back to the same place again. It was a common occurrence for them to strike among the rocks with a thud as they tumbled off their perches toward the water, and then scramble over the rocks with laughable haste and finally plunge under water and make off, or go flapping desperately along the surface until exhausted. Overhead circled hundreds of the birds, nearly all of which carried fishes in their beaks for their young. These fishes were sticklebacks and sand lances. Some of the birds carried from three to five small fishes at once; the latter were all placed side by side crosswise in the bird's bill.

Mr. Turner (1886) gives us another chapter in the story, as follows:

The young leave the nest before being able to fly. The parent assists them to the water; and, should they have been reared on the face of a high bluff, the old bird catches the young one by the wing and they flutter at a long angle to the water. The old bird endeavors to keep under the young one. I have seen them drop their young accidentally and cause great consternation of the parent, which could not check her flight immediately, but returned and showed great solicitude by turning the young one over and over in the water to see if it was injured. During severe storms the young are taken to the lee of some reef or islet until the waves become quiet.

Plumages.—The downy young of the horned puffin is practically indistinguishable from that of the common puffin; the central belly portion is white, sometimes tinged with yellowish or light gray; the upper parts, the throat and the crissum are light "seal brown" with "drab" shadings; in some specimens the upper parts are "Prout's brown" or "Vandyke brown." The progress of the molts and plumages is the same as in the eastern species except that in the first winter plumage, which follows the natal down, the loral and orbital dusky space is darker than in *arctica* and nearly as dark as the crown; the black throat of *corniculata* is also acquired with the first plumage. Young birds can be distinguished from adults during the first year by the much smaller and slenderer bill, which does not reach its full development until the second spring. After the first postnuptial molt, when the young bird is about 13 or 14 months old, it assumes the adult winter plumage.

The adult has a complete postnuptial molt in August or September and probably a partial prenuptial molt in the spring. The dark face is characteristic of the winter plumage, but the most striking change is in the bill, which molts as in the common puffin. Mr. Nelson (1887) describes this molt, which takes place in September, as follows:

At this time the bill molt was just commencing. The first evidence of this process is shown by the wearing away of the lower mandible on the under surface at the angle. This wearing appears to be brought about by the friction of this point on the rocks, as the birds use the projecting angle as a hook to aid them in climbing—as I frequently saw them do. The wearing of the lower edge of this mandible leaves a horny scalelike plate on each side of the mandible, with its lower edge free and easily scaled away in small fragments. The inclosed angle of the mandible is now a soft cartilaginous projection, which shrivels and reduces the size of the beak at that point. Next the horny, beadlike rim along the base of the upper mandible gradually loosens at each end below, and at the same time becomes freed from its attachment to the mandible, leaving a deep sulcus between, exactly as if done by a skillful cut with a scalpel. This beadlike rim now forms a part of the skin of the head and moves as such, perfectly independent of the beak. Then the narrow piece of sheath between the nares and the cutting edge of bill loosens and scales off. The entire base of the mandible is now in an exfoliating state and scales away, working toward the point of the beak. The narrow piece along the frontal line is pitted—each pit marking the position of a feather, as is shown in many cases where minute feathers are present. When this horny cover is removed a callous membrane bearing feathers is exposed, and these feathers extend up and pierce the fallen scale. The basal angle of the lower mandible becomes pliable before the horny cover breaks, and a dark suffusion shows as though a watery fluid had exuded between the horny sheath and the cartilage.

Food.—Early in the morning many of the puffins, nearly all of those that are not incubating, leave their breeding grounds and fly out to sea in search of food; they may be seen going and coming more or less during the day, with their bills full of small fish for their mates or for the young; at night they all return. Their food consists mainly of small fishes, such as sand lances, sticklebacks, and smelt. Mr. Turner (1886) says:

Their food is composed of mollusks of various kinds, a few shreds of certain seaweed fronds, and larvae, which are abundant on some of these seaweeds.

Behavior.—Puffins play the part of the clown among birds; their appearance is comical in any attitude, and their movements are ludicrous enough as they walk about on their toes, in a semierect position, with a droll dignity peculiarly their own, or stand peering out of their nesting burrows, with an air of stupid inquiry. They are certainly fantastic combinations of the solemn and the burlesque. They are much at home on the rocks, where they are very active on their feet, walking or running with ease. When launching into the air off the rocks they glide swiftly downward with feet widely spread, sweeping in a wide circle out over the water and returning soon again to fly past or over the point from which they started. They seem to be impelled by curiosity or by their attachment to their homes to repeat this flight maneuver over and over again, flying in a large circle or in an ellipse, out over the ocean and back again past the cliffs. Hunters take advantage of this habit to lie in wait for them and shoot them, but if too much molested they become more wary. They are very hard to kill, however, as they are very tenacious of life. Their flight is not particularly swift, but quite steady, strong, and protracted; the wings are moved very rapidly and constantly;

the body and head are held in compact form and the feet are carried straight backward to help in steering. They swim buoyantly and are expert divers. In diving the body is often raised clear of the water, and a curving downward plunge is made. Under water they use both wings and feet, flying rapidly through the water in pursuit of their finny prey.

Horned puffins are sometimes quite noisy when quarreling in their burrows, but at other times they are usually silent except for a variety of low growling or grunting sounds, frequently heard on their breeding grounds, which are probably love notes or friendly communications.

Winter.—During the latter part of September, or as soon as the young birds are able to fly, they leave their breeding grounds in northern Bering Sea for their winter quarters. Many winter in the open waters about the Aleutian Islands and farther south along the Alaskan coast; many probably spend the winter wandering over the open ocean. Probably the birds which breed south of the Alaska Peninsular do not migrate far from their summer haunts.

DISTRIBUTION.

Breeding range.—Coasts and Islands of the North Pacific, Behring Sea, and the Arctic Ocean. From southern Alaska (Forrester Island, St. Lazaria Island, and Prince William Sound) west throughout the Aleutian Islands. North along the Alaskan coast (St. Michael, Kotzebue Sound, and Cape Lisburne), and on the Pribilof Islands, St. Matthew, St. Lawrence, and the Diomede Islands. Also from the Commander Islands north along the Siberian coast to Bering Strait (East Cape) and Koliutschin Island. As Nelson saw a bird at Herald Island, it may breed there also. Probably breeds in the Kurile Islands.

Winter range.—Southern Bering Sea and the North Pacific Ocean. From the Aleutian and Commander Islands south along the Alaskan coast to the Queen Charlotte Islands, and along the Asiatic coast to the Kurile Islands. Taken once in California (Pacific Grove, Monterey County).

Spring migration.—Taken at Nushagak, Alaska, May 9. They arrive at the Pribilof Islands, May 10; at St. Michael, June 10 to 20; and at Chamisso Island, Kotzebue Sound, June 25.

Fall migration.—Taken at St. Matthew Island, September 22. They depart from their breeding grounds near St. Michael, September 20, and at the Pribilof Islands, September 10; but individuals probably remain on the open sea at no great distance much later.

Egg dates.—Alaska, north of peninsula: 24 records, June 24 to September 1; 12 records, June 27 to July 9. Alaska, south of peninsula: 13 records, June 6 to July 11; 7 records, June 17 to July 5.

CERORHINCA MONOCERATA (Pallas).

RHINOCEROS AUKLET.

HABITS.

This curious auklet, the largest of its group, is a bird of our more northern Pacific coast; it is not so well known, as its abundance at certain points should justify, because of its nocturnal habits on its breeding grounds; like the petrels it is seldom seen by daylight except when unearthed in its nesting burrow. It is essentially a bird of the open sea, seldom entering the straits and inside passages and never coming onto the land except to breed, coming and going during the hours of darkness.

Nesting.—One of the principal breeding resorts of this species is Destruction Island, off the coast of Washington, which Mr. W. Leon Dawson (1908a) has described as—

a flat-topped island with sharply sloping or nearly perpendicular sides, rising 60 feet above tide. Covered by dense growth of vegetation, chiefly salmonberry and salal thickets growing to height of a man's head, or higher on top; same with grass and bushes of other sorts on sides. Composed of deep loam (guano?), clay, gravel (incipient conglomerate of Pleistocene age) in descending series, resting unconformably upon the upturned edges of Miocene sandstone. Extensive area of sandstone reefs exposed on all sides of island at low tide, including ribs and ridges of sculptured rock unreached by water save in time of storm.

He estimated that about 10,000 rhinoceros auklets were nesting on this island.

Mr. Dawson (1909) has given us the following attractive account of the arrival of these auklets on the island:

Late in April the auklets, stirred by a common impulse, muster from the wide seas and move upon Destruction by night. If there has been any scouting or premature development work, it has been carried on by night only and has escaped observation. In fact, it is a point of honor among the auklets never to appear in the vicinity of the great rookery—or aukery—by day. At the tribal home-coming, the keepers tell us, there is a great hubbub. If the location be a brushy hillside, the birds upon arrival crash into the bushes like meteors and take chances of a braining. Upon the ground, they first argue with old neighbors about boundaries. If growls and barks and parrot-like shrieks mean anything, there are some differences of opinion discovered. Perhaps also the details of matrimony have not all been arranged, and there is much screaming avowal.

Gradually, however, order emerges from chaos, and the birds set to work with a will renovating the old home or driving new tunnels in the loam, sand, clay, or even hardpan. The burrows are usually 5 to 8 feet in length and about 5 inches in diameter, terminating in a dome-shaped chamber a foot or more across and 7 or 8 inches high. Each tunnel has a spur or blind alley which, presumably, is occupied by the male during the honeymoon. For lining, the nuptial chamber boasts nothing more pretentious than a few dead salal leaves and a handful of dried grasses. The amount of labor involved in this home-delving is very considerable. My guide once took an egg from a tunnel driven 10 feet straight into a clay bank; and I followed another through sand to a depth of 15 feet, only to find it empty. This last, I take it, was the work of a jilted suitor, venting his feelings by showing the coquette what a fine house she might have had.

Prof. Lynds Jones (1908) also says of their burrows:

The birds burrow into the perpendicular banks which face the ocean in many places, or into the turf-covered banks which are only a little less steep. The burrows may lead almost straight into the bank for a dozen to 15 feet, or more nearly parallel the surface, apparently depending somewhat upon the character of the soil. The few attempts to burrow into coarse gravelly material were soon abandoned in favor of the sandy soil. A very few nest burrows were made within a foot of the surface of the turf and could be uncovered from above. Every burrow examined was forked, the shorter and unused branch invariably being the one nearer the face of the bank, while the used branch continued some distance into the bank, ending in a nest of grassy material mixed with feathers where the hole was enlarged for more room.

Prof. Harold Heath (1915) found the rhinoceros auklet breeding still more abundantly on Forrester Island, southern Alaska, during the summer of 1913. He writes:

Generally speaking, the rhinoceros auklet occupies burrows in the sloping sides of the island from the shore line to a height of from 400 to 500 feet, their number and distribution depending upon the nature of the soil and the character of the surrounding vegetation. The most favorable nesting sites appear to be the dense spruce woods where the shadows are of such depth that ferns and underbrush find but scanty foothold, and the soil is soft and friable. In such localities over 400 burrows have been counted in an area 600 feet square, but where the salmon and elder berry are abundant, and ferns form a tangled mat, or rock outcrops are plentiful and the soil thin the nests are of less frequent occurrence or are absent altogether. While no complete and accurate count is possible it is safe to say that not less than 15,000 pairs of these birds found a home on Forrester Island during the past season.

Judging from this year's observations, the breeding season commences in the latter half of May. At this time the old burrows, which have caved in during the winter or have become clogged with débris brought in by mice, are given a thoroughgoing cleaning, and the accumulation of spruce needles and cones, decayed grass, moss, leaves, stems, and earth scraped to the front of the entrance forms a conspicuous mound in many instances. In some cases the tunnels have already been cleared to some extent by the Cassin auklet and to a less degree by the ancient murrelet, but the relations of these birds appear to be undisturbed even when two species occupy the same home.

As a general thing the opening of the nest is about the base of stumps or trees or under logs, and only rarely does it occupy open ground away from the forest. As to the burrow, it is a highly variable structure, neglecting the fact that it is at least 8 feet in length. In extreme instances it attains a length of fully 20 feet, and, as indicated in the accompanying diagrams, its configuration is subject to many variations. There is usually one main channel, rarely with two outlets, and from this there are one or more blind offshoots. In one of these the nest is frequently placed, but it is by no means a usual occurrence to find it close to the entrance as some of the Haidah men declare to be the case.

The composition of the nest depends upon the material at hand. Where spruce trees abound the building materials are largely small twigs; where salmonberry, moss, and ferns are in the vicinity these are utilized, and in either case are fashioned into a shallow, saucer-shaped nest. The single egg, white with obscure lavender spots, is laid in June from the 1st to the 15th. Newly hatched young were found as early as the 27th, but the greater number hatch out during the first week in July. The period of incubation lasts about three weeks, as far as can be determined from the data at hand, though it must certainly be somewhat more extended when the burrow is poorly drained, and the nest a soggy mass. On August 6 several burrows were opened and found to be empty, and about the same time the fishermen reported having seen young birds, accompanied by one or both parents, some distance out at sea.

The duty of incubation rests upon both parents, as individuals of either sex have been found in the burrows during the day. During this time the mate is fishing at sea, and returns shortly before dark, or, more accurately, about 10 p. m. The day shift now puts to sea to return in the early morning hours.

Eggs.—The single egg of the rhinoceros auklet much resembles the egg of the horned puffin, both in size and shape. The shape is usually not far from " ovate," and the texture of the shell is fairly smooth but dull in luster. The color is dull white, often spotless, but more often with faint spots of pale lavender, gray, or light brown; some eggs are quite heavily spotted with darker brown. One egg in the United States National Museum has a faint cloudy wreath of pale lavender about the larger end; others have wreaths of lavender spots overlaid with spots or scrawls of " tawny olive " or other light shades of brown; all of these are very pretty eggs. Mr. Dawson (1909) refers to the markings on the egg as " traces of an ancient color pattern, undoubtedly heavy, still persisting in faint lines of umber and in subdued shell markings or undertints of lavender and lilac," which he thinks indicate a former habit of nesting in the open. The measurements of 39 eggs in various collections average 68.5 by 46.2 millimeters; the eggs showing the four extremes measure **73.5** by 47, 70 by **50, 63.7** by 44.6, and 65 by **42.6** millimeters.

Plumages.—The downy young is described by Mr. Ridgway (1887) as " uniform sooty grayish brown, very similar to corresponding stage of *Lunda cirrhata*, but rather lighter in color and with more slender bill." The natal down disappears last from the neck, rump, and flanks, being replaced by the first winter plumage, the dusky feathers of the wings and back appearing first, and then the whitish feathers of the breast.

Young birds in their first autumn may be distinguished from winter adults by their much smaller bills and by the entire absence of the postocular and rictal plumes. This first winter plumage is worn without much modification until late winter or early spring; the dark tips of the breast feathers gradually wear away, and are sometimes gone by December, leaving the bird with pure white under parts; the white plumes on the sides of the head sometimes begin to appear in December, but sometimes not until March. Early in the spring the horn begins to grow on the upper side and the accessory piece on the under side of the bill; the white plumes become quite fully developed, and the young bird in its first nuptial plumage becomes practically indistinguishable from the adult.

The adult has a complete moult during the late summer and early fall, at which the horn and lower accessory piece are shed from the bill and the adult winter plumage is acquired. This is similar to the adult nuptial plumage, except that the white head plumes are shorter and not so fully developed. I believe that these plumes are seldom, if ever, wholly lacking in winter adults. The bill of the adult in winter is much larger than that of the young bird, and there is usually a soft knob indicating where the horn has been.

Food.—From the examination of 10 specimens killed off the California coast in winter, Dr. Joseph Grinnell (1899) found that—

The food consisted entirely of a small yellow crustacean, which filled their gullets. We saw none of these anywhere near the surface of the water, so they must have been caught by diving to a considerable depth.

Mr. C. B. Linton (1908) states that he and Mr. Willet secured several specimens off the California coast in November and December, and that the " craws examined contained freshly caught sardines 3 to 4 inches long." The stomach contents consisted of the " meat and bones of small fish."

Professor Heath (1915) says:

The food of the rhinoceros auklet, whether young or old, consists wholly of sand launces, according to the reports of the natives, and an examination of a few stomachs supports their claim.

He says further, referring to their feeding habits and their long daily flights in search of food:

On rare occasions they were reported by fishermen operating upward of a mile from shore, but in the great majority of cases they sought more open water at some distance from land, such as the channel between Forrester and Dall Island. A marked exception to this rule may be witnessed throughout the summer on the eastern side of Dall Island in Kaigani and Tlivak Straits. Here the tide sets strongly, especially in the region of the narrows of Skookum Chuck at the north end of Dall Island, and with an abundance of floating organisms serving as fish food the conditions are most favorable not only for auklets but for several other water birds, such as gulls, ancient and marbled murrelets, pigeon guillemots, and cormorants. In order to reach this locality the rhinoceros auklet makes a round trip journey of at least 60 miles if it flies directly over Dall Island. This, however, is doubtful, as flocks have been seen at nightfall coming down the straits on the east side of Dall, and after rounding the southern end their course is doubtless a bee line for home. Under such circumstances it requires a completed journey of fully 120 miles to bring them to the feeding grounds and back again. Whatever their route, it is certain that they are most rapid flyers, and in the dim evening and morning light it is a difficult feat to follow their bulletlike flight against the sky. If the day be foggy or dark, the usual early morning departure may be delayed for an hour or so. Under such circumstances they rest in front of their burrows, or wander about the neighborhood, uttering their curious nasal cry of four short notes rapidly repeated.

Behavior.—Doctor Grinnell (1899) gives an interesting account of his efforts to get within gunshot of a rhinoceros auklet swimming on the water, which well illustrates its power of diving and swimming for long distances under water. He also says:

The manner and pose of the rhinoceros auklet, resting or swimming on the water are quite different from those of any other sea bird met with around Catalina. It is short and chunky, with head drawn in close to the body, leaving scarcely any tract that might be called a neck. The water line comes up to about the lower edge of the wings when closed against the body, so that the bird does not rest lightly on the water, like a gull or phalarope. The head is held on the same line as the body, directly out in front, so that the top of the head and back are on the same level. The whole bird at a little distance looks most like a block of wood floating on the water. We did not once see one flying. They all preferred to dive. One which was shot at and probably slightly wounded, attempted to take flight but failed to get clear of the water, and after dragging along the surface for several feet, instantly dove. The great ease and rapidity which is shown in diving and traveling under water is remarkable. We heard no note, and there was never but one in sight at a time. They were mostly seen about a quarter of a mile from shore.

Professor Heath (1915) writes:

In former times the rhinoceros auklet was far more numerous than it is at the present time, according to the reports of the Indians. As late as 50 years ago many of the slopes now untenanted afforded nesting sites for these and other birds, and the hills now occupied had a far greater population than one finds to-day. In those earlier times the sky was literally darkened as they put out to sea, and the sound of their cries was a veritable babel. The diminution might naturally be ascribed to the activity of the natives, who relish this species above all others, but the natives themselves meet such a claim with the evidence of many scores of years when, with a much larger tribe than at present, they gathered eggs and birds in vastly greater numbers without any appreciable decline in the bird colony. Their explanation rests solely upon the belief that the decrease is due entirely to the rank growth of underbrush and ferns which form a tangled mat too dense to permit of ready flight to and from the burrows. In former times, even within the memory of some of the older men of the tribe, the country was much more open; and it is certainly a readily observed fact that this species avoids the thickets and seeks out more open ground. Occasional nests are found in salmonberry patches, but well-worn runways invariably lead into the open.

Mr. Dawson (1909) describes the method used by the Indians for catching the auklets on Destruction Island as follows:

When the female begins to brood her single egg the male spends his days at sea, returning after nightfall to feed his mate and, it may be, exchange places with her. The Indians take advantage of this habit to catch the birds, which they account good eating. Having first selected a populous neighborhood, they thrust grass into a set of contiguous burrows, pressing it in to arm's length for the purpose of detaining the returning bird later in the evening. At 9 o'clock or such a matter they post themselves in the gathering gloom to watch their traps, secreting themselves, if need be, in the bushes. The colony is silent now, but presently there is a sudden whirr of wings, a dark object strikes the bank and disappears. Instantly the watchful native closes the entrance of the burrow and seizes the confused auklet from behind. It is creepy business, and not less so now that the whole scene is lighted up by the accusingly benignant eye of the lighthouse. However, one may be pardoned a strictly psychological study, even in the robbing of a henroost.

Winter.—As soon as the breeding season is over the hosts of auklets leave their underground burrows, their mysterious nocturnal visits cease, and they scatter out over the ocean, where they spend the winter in the pursuit of happiness and the search for food. They are widely scattered at this season and seem to prefer a solitary existence.

DISTRIBUTION.

Breeding range.—Coasts and islands of the North Pacific. From Washington (Destruction Island) north to southern Alaska (Forrester Island, St. Lazaria Island, and Egg Island, 200 miles west of Fort Wrangell) and west to the Aleutian Islands (Atka, Agattu, and Umnak Islands), the Kurile Islands and northern Japan (Yezo). Said to have formerly bred on the Farallones.

Winter range.—The open sea from Washington (Pacific coast, rare in Puget Sound) south to California (Farallones to San Diego) and rarely Lower California (San Geronimo Island and Cerros Island). In Asia winters south to southern Japan.

Spring migration.—Northward in April and May. Birds remain along the coast of California until early May (latest June 2), but the first arrivals on the breeding grounds at Destruction Island, Washington, are often seen during April. Specimens were noted in southeastern Alaska (Kuiu Island) May 18.

Fall migration.—Takes place in September and October. Birds have been noted at Point Pinos, California, September 27, and common by October 14. A bird, evidently a migrant, was taken on Puget Sound (Tacoma) September 21, and specimens were taken at Departure Bay, British Columbia, from September 23 to November 2.

Egg dates.—Southern Alaska: 22 records, May 10 to June 22; 11 records, June 9 to 20. Washington: 10 records, April 21 to June 18; 5 records, April 24 to June 13.

PTYCHORAMPHUS ALEUTICUS (Pallas).

CASSIN'S AUKLET.

HABITS.

Like the preceding species, the Cassin's auklet is nocturnal in its habits on its breeding grounds, as it is distinctly a pelagic species and comes ashore only to breed, coming and going under the cover of darkness. Yet it is decidedly the best known of the auklets, as it has by far the widest breeding range, from the Aleutian Islands to central Lower California, and it is an abundant bird all along our Pacific coast at all seasons of the year.

Nesting.—It is probably migratory to some extent, but, as with most of the Alcidae, its spring and fall migrations consist mainly of a movement onto its breeding resorts in the spring and departure from them to the open sea in the fall. Prof. Harold Heath (1915) says that "the natives state that Cassin auklet arrives on Forrester Island about March 1," as it begins nesting early. In his account of the nesting habits of the species on this island he states that he was unable to distinguish any external mark of identification between the burrows of the Cassin's auklet and the ancient murrelet.

It was accordingly impossible to determine the exact numbers of the two species. It can be said, however, that the Cassin auklet has been found to occupy several sites from the sea level to a height of 500 feet, and the presence of eggshell fragments in many places indicates their general distribution over the island and in small numbers on Lawrie and South Islands. As in the case of the ancient murrelet, the openings of the burrows are located about the roots of trees, or beneath partially buried logs or stones. The tunnel itself ranges from 2 to 4 feet in length, and is usually only sparingly branched. Whether they occupy the same home season after season is not known. It is certain, however, that several of the tunnels have been occupied at one time by mice, as is evidenced by accumulations of gnawed cones in some of the lateral galleries or in the material scraped from the main canal and accumulated about the entrance.

On Forrester Island the duties of nest building are no more onerous than characterizes the species elsewhere. A few twigs of the Sitka spruce, together with old or mouse-eaten cones and occasional fragments of moss, appear to be all that is necessary. The length of the incubation period was not determined, though Captain John (a remarkably keen and accurate naturalist of the Haidah Tribe) says that it lasts "about two weeks." Fully three weeks more are required to bring the fledgling to the time of departure from the nest. During the time of incubation the female occupied the burrow in five cases at least, and the Indians claim that she is fed during the night by the male and never leaves the nest until the young is several days old.

One of the most populous colonies of this species is to be found on the Farallone Islands, of which Mr. W. Leon Dawson (1911) writes:

The Cassin auklets are everywhere. Burrows predominate, but there is not a cleft, nook, crack, cranny, fissure, aperture, retreat, niche, cave, receptacle, or hidey-hole from the water's edge to the summit of the light tower which is not likely to harbor this ubiquitous bird. The interstices of the stone walls contain them to the number of thousands. Every cavity not definitely occupied by puffin, petrel, or rabbit is tenanted by an auklet, and in many cases quarters are shared. If one's imagination is not sufficiently stimulated by regular occurrences, it will be jogged by appearances in unexpected places—an old nest of rock wren or pigeon guillemot, an inner recess of a murre cave, an abandoned spur of puffin burrow, an overturned wheelbarrow or neglected board lying on the ground, driftwood on the beach—anything affording the slightest prospect of protection or cover. A pile of coal, sacked up and awaiting transfer from landing to siren, was found to be full of them. Since this was the rule from center to circumference of this magic isle, we conclude that the Cassin auklet is the commonest bird on the Farallones, and estimates of population anywhere short of one or two hundred thousand do not take account of the facts.

Mr. A. B Howell has sent me the followinig notes on the Cassin's auklet:

There are but few of the islands along the California coast and halfway down the peninsula of Lower California on which this auklet does not breed. Coming in from the sea it selects a suitable spot, usually more than 50 feet above the ocean, and tunnels out a burrow in the loam, which varies from one to several feet in length. These are used year after year until their entrances are big enough to fit a puffin. When available sites of this kind become crowded they readily occupy niches among the rocks and the corners of caves. The odor emanating from the burrows strongly reminds one of a badly kept chicken house. Fresh eggs are found by the middle of March and may be found in numbers until the middle of July, though the nesting season would seem to vary greatly in different years. Of perhaps 50 nests examined by me on Los Coronados Islands the first part of July, 1910, all held eggs in various stages, except three which contained small young. On June 30, 1913, this order was reversed, and out of many nests examined by Messrs Dickey, van Rossem, and myself three eggs were obtained, and the remainder held young in all stages. It is also worthy of note that at the latter time there were not nearly as many birds breeding as at the former. The eggs are deposited on the bare ground or occasionally a few bits of weed.

Mr. Chase Littlejohn sent the following notes to Major Bendire:

This auklet arrives at the island, on which it intends to nest, between 9.30 and 10 in the evening, according as the weather is clear or cloudy—the darker the sky the earlier they come—and immediately drop into the grass and are soon in their holes, where they both take a hand in digging and cleaning out whatever has accumulated since it was last occupied. After this house cleaning is done, or a new hole is dug, the nest is made, the egg deposited, and incubation begins at once, which is taken part in by both parents, and as near as I could determine these duties are exchanged nightly; while one sets the other is away, far at sea, on the feeding grounds. On his or her return to the hole a greeting note is sounded, and immediately the one on the nest answers and comes to within a few inches of the entrance to meet the mate which has just returned. Here the peculiar rasping love note is repeated over and over with hardly an intermission for at least half an hour (I have listened that long), sometimes by one and oftener by both. While this salutation is going on they are constantly bowing to each other, and so absorbed are they in their greeting that the hand can often be placed on them for a short time without attracting their notice, probably each thinking it is the other that is doing this, but when the discovery is made that there is an intruder about they at once scurry into the farthest end of their hole, which is from 2 to 6 feet long, and there remain quiet. At the end of the hole the nest is situated and is composed of a few coarse grass blades, or oftener of the large flower stems of a plant known to the natives as pooch-ki, and which is eaten by them—the natives—the same as we use celery. These stalks are from one-half to 1 inch in diameter and often 18 inches long; they are cut into lengths by the birds using their beaks for that purpose. One remarkable thing about these holes is no matter how close they may be to each other no two ever intersect, although they wind in and out, up and down in every direction. Another peculiar and interesting habit is that each hole is supplied with a short side tunnel a foot or so in length, in which the birds deposit their excrement. The nest is always very clean. The love or greeting note mentioned above can be produced, as near as I could get it, by the syllables *kwee-kew* repeated over and over. In listening to it one could not help thinking of the sound made by a squeaky bucksaw in a splintered log of wood. They also utter a peculiar gnawing, grunting sound which I was unable to put on paper. They are very pugnacious when taken in the hand and will scratch and bite very hard, often drawing blood. For food they are, strange to say, excellent, being the only sea bird with which I am acquainted that is even passable.

Eggs.—The single unmarked egg of Cassin's auklet is between "ovate" and "elliptical ovate" in shape, usually nearer the former and with nearly equally rounded ends, but some eggs are quite pointed at one or even both ends. The shell is smooth, but quite lusterless. The color is dull white, milk white, or creamy white, but the egg shows a decidedly bluish or greenish tinge when held up toward the light. The egg is usually somewhat, and often much, nest stained. The measurements of 60 eggs, in the United States National Museum collection, average 46.9 by 34.3 millimeters; the eggs showing the four extremes measuring **51** by 34.5, 45 by **37, 44** by 34, and 45 by **31.5** millimeters.

Both sexes incubate, relieving each other during the night. The universal rule among sea birds is to raise only one brood during the season, but there is considerable evidence to show that this species is an exception to the rule. The breeding season is much prolonged, from April to November, which means that more than one brood is raised or that the breeding grounds are so overcrowded that different individuals have to breed at different seasons. The former supposition seems to be the more likely. Mr. Walter E. Bryant (1888) says:

Several young are supposed to be raised during the season. Many nests were found occupied by young in down and one adult bird sitting upon a fresh egg; in some nests the egg was kept warm by contact with the young. In no instance were two old birds found in the same nest, and no birds were found at the time search was made without an egg or young, or both. The majority of the adult birds were females, although both sexes were found sitting. If provoked, either young or old will seize a finger and hold on. The old birds are silent when on the nest, but the downy young make a faint peeping when disturbed. When taken from the nest they endeavor to crawl out of sight, and if tossed into the air they descend quickly and hide themselves from the light. They commenced flying this year as early as April 2, and eggs have been found as late as November 20, showing a breeding time extending through eight months.

Mr. A. W. Anthony, in his notes sent to Major Bendire, refers to a nest "containing a nearly fledged young and an adult female incubating a fresh egg; the fledgling was crowded into a branch burrow away from the main nest." Mr. W. Otto Emerson, in his notes, states that two or three broods are raised and that he has found fully grown young in the same hole with the parent bird sitting on the second laying. Possibly in all of these cases the young bird and the egg may have belonged to different parents, but this hardly seems likely, unless the young bird may have been sufficiently frightened by the process of opening the burrow to have run into a compartment occupied by an incubating bird. If this bird is such a prolific breeder as it seems to be this would account for its great abundance over such a wide breeding range.

Young.—Mr. Emerson gives the period of incubation as 21 days and Mr. Littlejohn as 30 days. The chick remains in the nest and is fed by its parents on regurgitated food until it is fully fledged and able to fly. Mr. Emerson says that the young are fed in the same manner that a pigeon feeds its young, the parent throwing up a thick, creamy, chocolate-colored matter, containing what he took to be small marine insects. He says that the young become "rolling fat while in their holes and the old birds are never poor from the cares of incubation." The young remain in the burrows until able to fly.

Plumages.—The downy young is "Blackish brown" or "fuscous black" when first hatched, fading to "fuscous" or "hair brown" when older, on the upper parts; the throat, breast, and flanks are paler; and the belly is "ecru drab," "drab gray," or "drab." According to Mr. Howell's observations, "pin feathers begin to show at the base of the down when the chick is but 2 or 3 days old. They first show through on the underparts, then on the head, and the down gradually is shed from the end of the feathers until a small tuft below the chin is all that remains." The first plumage, which is thus acquired directly from the downy stage, is not strikingly different from that of the adult. The bill is decidedly smaller, however, the throat is whiter and the wings and tails are browner in young birds. The first nuptial plumage shows no very marked change and the young bird closely resembles the adult; birds with smaller bills and slightly whitish throats are probably young birds. Adults have no conspicuous seasonal changes of plumage, except that the fall plumage looks brighter and fresher. The clear, slaty-blue and black plumage of adults in the fall, together with the larger bills, will usually serve to distinguish them from young birds.

There is apparently a complete molt in August and September and probably a partial prenuptial molt during the latter part of winter.

Food.—Cassin's auklets feed well out at sea, where they spend most of their time, singly, in pairs, or in small flocks; some of their food is obtained on or near the surface, but they must dive to considerable depths for some of it. Mr. F. Stephens (1893) found that—

> The stomachs of some examined contained shrimps. For some it simply dipped its head under water, for others it dove a few inches.

Mr. Emerson noted marine insects among its food and Professor Heath (1915) says:

> The food of the young, and of the adults as well, was found to consist of copepods and an undetermined species of shrimp or amphipod.

Probably a great variety of small marine animals are included in its diet.

Behavior.—The flight of Cassin's auklet is swift, steady, and direct; when flying over the water it flies low, just clearing the waves, and even over the land its flight is low. Mr. Bryant (1888) writes that—

> One, attracted by a lantern carried by Mr. Emerson, flew with characteristic swiftness directly at it, but missed and struck against the side of a house, where it was picked up stunned. Auks have struck persons walking without a light, but always below the shoulders.

Referring to the clumsiness of this species, Mr. Dawson (1911) writes:

> The Cassin auklet seems incapable of controlling the force of its flight, and the wonder is that the birds are not every one of them dashed to pieces in a single night. In this respect they remind one of nothing else so much as beetles or moths, which come hurtling into the region of candlelight, crash against the candlestick, and without an instant's pause begin an animated search afoot. This crash-and-crawl method seems not exceptional but characteristic in the auklet. It was especially noticeable in the paved area just outside our work-room door. Crash! announced the arrival of another food-laden messenger from the unknown deeps. The impact of collision with the building invariably stunned the bird so that it fell to the ground, but it immediately began a frantic search, and as likely as not, before you could lay hands on it, disappeared in a crack under the doorstep.

Mr. Stephens (1893) says:

> They dive well, and can stay under water two minutes or more. They swim fast for so small a bird. On being chased with a boat they often preferred diving to flight, and then their speed was greater than when swimming, requiring sharp rowing to get within shooting distance. They often changed their course while under water, and several times baffled me in that way. They are so small that one can not see them very far in rough water. Wounded birds observed at short distances were observed to use their wings in diving, and probably in all cases diving is simply a flight under water.

Although apparently a silent bird at other times, this auklet is a very noisy bird on its breeding grounds at night. Mr. Dawson's (1909) graphic pen describes the evening concert as follows:

The stage setting is perfect, down to the footlights. Now, for the orchestra: " *Petteretteretterell, etteretteretterell* "—it is the tap, tap of the petrel conductor calling the island to attention. Soon ghostly forms steal about in the gathering gloom. Voice answers voice as each moment flies. The flitting shadows become a throng and the chorus a tumult. But in the grand melange there is a new note. A quaint burring croak wells up from the ground, elfish, gruesome, portentous. The Cassin auklets are waking up. Heard alone, the auklet chorus reminds one of a frog pond in full cry. As one gives attention to an individual performer, however, and seeks to locate him in his burrow, the mystery and strangeness of it grows. The vocalist is complaining bitterly of we know not what wrongs. We must be within 3 feet of the noise as we stoop at the burrow's mouth; the volume of it is earfilling; yet its source seems furlongs off. Now it is like the squealing of a pig in a distant slaughter pen. We lift our heads, and the stockyards are reeling with the prayers and cries of a thousand victims. And now the complaint falls into a cadence, " *Let meee out, let meee out, let me out.* " A thousand dolorous voices take up the chorus. The uproar gets upon the nerves. Is this a bird lunatic asylum? Have we stumbled upon an avian madhouse here in the lone Pacific? And are these inmates appealing to the moon, their absent mistress?

Mr. Charles A. Keeler (1892) says:

Their note resembles the creaking of a rusty gate, and may be represented by the syllables *creek a reek, creek a reek, creek a reek.*

Cassin's auklets, especially when fat, make very good eating, and have doubtless been used largely for food by many tribes of Indians or by fishermen. Professor Heath (1915) says:

In ancient times this species figured largely in the natives' bill of fare, and large numbers were annually taken by means of snares or were attracted by bonfires and subsequently knocked down.

Large numbers of Cassin's auklets are occasionally washed up dead on the beaches of our Pacific coast. Mr. J. H. Bowles (1908) discovered that, in one case at least, this mortality was due to an epidemic of intestinal tapeworms. In addition to finding dead birds of this and other species strewn along the beach, he noted that—

The ocean was rather plentifully dotted with sick birds, some of them so close in as to be rolled over and over in the breakers.

The intestines of a shearwater were packed solid with tapeworms.

These worms were about 3 inches long, rather slender, and marked with alternate rings of white and brownish black. There were many hundreds of the disgusting parasites in every bird, making death from starvation an absolute certainty.

Mr. Howell writes me that on the Coronados Islands—

These birds suffer a great deal from the depredations of duck hawks, a pair or two of which are usually found near the auklet colonies. Even though the latter attain an amazing speed when pitching from the top of the islands when released from the hand, the falcons overtake them with the greatest ease and continue to slaughter, after their hunger has been appeased, for the mere fun of it. This is perhaps why the auklets visit the colonies only after nightfall.

Winter.—The fall migration is not well marked, and probably the winter home of this auklet is ot far from its breeding grounds, as it apparently spends the winter at sea throughout most of its summer range.

DISTRIBUTION.

Breeding range.—Pacific coast, from Lower California (Cerros, San Benito, San Geronimo, San Martin, Todos Santos, and Los Coronados Islands) northward to southern Alaska (Forrester Island, Egg Island, 200 miles west of Fort Wrangell and Sanak Islands) and the Aleutian Islands (Atkha Island). North of California it is somewhat local in its distribution.

Winter range.—The open sea in the vicinity of its breeding places at least as far north as Washington (Puget Sound).

Casual records.—It is said that a specimen taken in Kamtschatka is in the Berlin Museum.

Egg dates.—Farallone Islands: 64 records, April 3 to July 20; 32 records, May 29 to June 18. Lower California: 29 records, March 10 to June 8; 15 records, April 6 to May 18. Santa Barbara Islands: 10 records, May 16 to June 29; 5 records, June 4 to 9. Sanak Islands, Alaska: 2 records, June 6; 2 records, June 7; and 1 record, July 3.

PHALERIS PSITTACULA (Pallas).

PAROQUET AUKLET.

HABITS.

The auklets, like the fur seals, of the Pribilof Islands spend the greater part of their lives at sea and return to these lonely fog-bound islands in Bering Sea to rear their young, where they are wholly engrossed with the cares of reproduction. My short visit to these islands in the summer of 1911 served only as an introduction and gave me but a slight glimpse into their life histories. Our introduction to the famous fur-seal islands was characteristic of that dismal climate. We had been sailing by compass all night from Bogoslof Island, and morning found us still groping in the prevailing thick fog, which serves to keep the seals' coats cool and moist, but is a menace to mariners. At last, when we had about concluded that we had missed our reckoning and had passed the islands, we began to see a few of these large white-breasted auklets flying past us to the eastward. Turning, we followed them, and before long we could hear the barking, roaring, and bellowing of the fur seals in their rookeries on St. Paul Island. Feeling our way carefully toward them until we could dimly see the outline of the cliffs, we crept along the shore into Village Cove.

Spring.—The paroquet auklet, or " baillie brushkie," as it is called by the natives, arrives in the Commander Islands about the last of April and in the Pribilofs early in May. It is not nearly as abundant as the least auklet and is much less gregarious. It does not fly about in such enormous flocks or swarms, but is comparatively solitary in its habits, quiet, and unobtrusive. A few were always to be seen sitting in little groups on the low rocky cliffs of St. Paul Island or flying out to circle around us in quiet curiosity. Probably many of them were away at sea on their feeding grounds, and some were calmly dozing on the rocks. Their nests or eggs were safely hidden away in the remote crevices in the cliffs or under large rocks beyond our reach.

Nesting.—On July 7, 1911, I spent one of the most eventful afternoons of my life studying the nesting habits of this and the hosts of other sea birds that make their summer home on the wonderful, little, rocky islet of the Pribilof group, Walrus Island. Here we found the paroquet, crested, and least auklets, together with the tufted puffin, nesting under the loose piles of water-worn bowlders which were piled up in a great ridge in the beachlike center of the island, connecting the higher extremities. By rolling away such of the bowlders as we could move, we succeeded in uncovering some two dozen nests. Compared with the other auklets, which were very lively and noisy, the paroquet auklets were very gentle and tame; they did not seem to be greatly disturbed or alarmed by our rock moving operations; we usually found the female, and occasionally the male, sitting quietly on its single egg, serenely looking at us with its big white eyes. The curious up-turned red bill and the white under parts were easily recognized even in the dark recesses of its nesting caverns. There was only a single egg in each case, which was lying on the bare rock or soil or on a bed of loose pebbles; no nesting material had been brought in.

The paroquet auklet breeds abundantly on the high rocky islands of northern Bering Sea and into Bering Strait. On the precipitous cliffs of St. Matthew Island, 200 feet or more above the sea, we saw a few pairs apparently breeding among the fulmars and puffins, but their eggs were beyond our reach in the inaccessible crevices in the rocks. They were so tame and unsuspicious that I took a snapshot at one as it sat on a lofty pinnacle of rock within a few feet of me, watching the cloud of fulmars sailing below.

Eggs.—The single egg is practically " ovate " in shape, with a slight tendency toward " elliptical ovate " in some specimens. The shell is finely granulated, almost rough and without any luster. The color is usually dull white or bluish white, but some eggs are decidedly bluish, about the color of heron's eggs, but darker than the palest of these. The measurements of 33 eggs, in various collections average 54.3 by 37.3 millimeters; the eggs showing the four extremes measure **58** by 33.5, 57.5 by **40**, **51.5** by 37, and 52.5 by **33** millimeters.

Plumages.—The downy young, when first hatched, is " fuscous black " on the crown, " fuscous," " Benzo brown," or " hair brown " on the back, sides, throat, and breast, and " pale drab gray " on the belly. These colors fade somewhat with age. A specimen, collected September 1, is nearly fully grown, but is still all downy except that the wings are about half grown, the white stripe is visible back of the eye and feathers are visible under the down on the cheeks, breast, back, and scapulars; the bill has also begun to assume the shape characteristic of the species. This bird must have hatched late, for another specimen, taken in July, is farther advanced into the first winter plumage, with traces of the natal down still left on the head, the neck, the center of the breast and the hinder parts of the body. This specimen indicates that the first winter plumage is similar to the adult, the under parts being pure white and the chin and throat mottled. I have never been able to find any fall or winter birds in collections and so can not determine what differences, if any, exist between old and young birds in the fall, or what seasonal changes take place in adults.

Food.—The paroquet auklet flies out to sea for its food every morning and returns to its mate on its breeding grounds at night. Its food consists mainly of amphipods and other small crustaceans, which it finds swimming on or near the surface or obtains by diving down to rocky bottoms at moderate depths. Mr. Nelson (1887) says:

Wherever we found these birds during our cruise they were always observed feeding offshore, and at Plover Bay every one shot had its craw distended with small crustaceans, and, as these latter animals swarm in all the waters of this bird's haunts, it is only reasonable to suppose that they form its usual food. Brandt's idea that the peculiarly shaped bill is used to pry open bivalves is not well founded. The deep water and very abruptly sloping beaches, where these birds are most numerous, render it impossible for them to find a supply of bivalves, and the bird's beak is altogether too weak to be used in the manner indicated. Doctor Dall suggests that the peculiar bill is used for picking crustacea out of crevices in the rocks and from under round stones. The idea that the peculiar recurved bill of this bird must have some unusual office is not unnatural; but my observations of the bird's habit of invariably feeding some distance offshore and rarely in water less than 10 to 20 fathoms deep, render any such use highly improbable, if not impossible.

Behavior.—The flight of the paroquet auklet is very much like that of the smaller auklets—swift, direct, and strong, with frequent turnings from side to side as its course is altered. It can be easily recognized by its large size and white breast; it also usually flies at a higher elevation above the water than the other species. It travels long distances in search of food. It swims buoyantly and rapidly and it is a very good diver.

I have no recollection of ever having heard the paroquet auklet utter a sound; it impressed me as being a particularly silent bird. Mr. Nelson (1887) noted that it has "a low, sonorous, vibrating whistle," and Doctor Stejneger (1885) says that its " voice is a clear, vibrating whistle, somewhat resembling that of *Cepphus grylle* and *columba.*"

Winter.—By the middle or the last of August most of the young are on the wing and are beginning to leave the islands, from which they have practically all disappeared by the 1st of September. They gradually move out to sea and probably spend the winter on the open ocean. They must winter considerably farther south than the other auklets, for while the others have frequently been taken in winter near the Aleutian and Commander Islands, there are no winter records for the paroquet auklet in these regions. Doctor Stejneger (1885) says that he was not able to obtain a single specimen, even during the latter part of the summer, in the Commanders; that it was never "seen or heard of" during the winter, "nor was it ever during that season picked up dead on the beach after heavy gales." On the Asiatic side it wanders as far south as the Kurile Islands. Mr. Rollo H. Beck (1910) has taken a number of specimens in January off Monterey, California; they were several miles offshore, where they are probably more common than is generally supposed.

DISTRIBUTION.

Breeding range.—Coasts and islands of Bering Sea. From Kodiak Island, the Aleutian Islands, Commander Islands, probably the Kurile Islands, and perhaps Kamtschatka northward to Bering Strait (Diomede Islands). Birds seen in July and August in southeastern Alaska were probably nonbreeding individuals or early migrants.

Winter range.—Southward on the North Pacific, rarely taken ashore, and southern limit unknown. Recorded in winter from Oregon (Netarts Bay), and California (San Francisco Bay, Monterey Bay, off Point Pinos and Eureka, Humboldt County). On the Asiatic coast south to Kurile Islands.

Spring migration.—Birds arrive at the Commander Islands late in April and at the Pribilof Islands from April 30 to early May. Migrants were seen at Forrester Island May 4. One was shot at Nushagak May 22. One taken at Sitka June 8 may have been a late migrant.

Fall migration.—Birds have been seen in Prince William Sound July 13 and August 27. The species leaves its nesting grounds in the Pribilof Islands from August 20 to September 1: None are recorded from California before December 17.

Casual records.—Recorded as occurring once in Sweden, but apparently this specimen has been recorded as the crested auklet also, and I have had no way of verifying either identification.

Egg dates.—Northern Bering Sea: 3 records, July 20, August 22 and 26. Pribilof Islands: 3 records, June 8, July 7 and 16.

ÆTHIA CRISTATELLA (Pallas).

CRESTED AUKLET.

HABITS.

Among the thousands of tufted puffins that dotted the surface of the ocean, as we approached Unimak Pass on our way to Bering Sea, and among the great rafts of least auklets that we encountered among the Aleutian Islands, we frequently saw small or large flocks of crested auklets, sometimes containing as many as 40 or 50 birds, which we recognized by their larger size and wholly gray appearance. Its manner of flight, size, color, and crest have suggested the local name of " sea quail," from a fancied resemblance to the California quail.   Mr. H. W. Elliott (1880) refers to this " fantastic bird " as " the plumed knight of the Pribylov Islands." The native Aleut name, " cannooskie," means little captain.

Nesting.—The crested auklet arrives in the Pribilof Islands early in May, where Mr. William Palmer (1899) says that it—

breeds in colonies of some 10 to 20 pairs on the roughest and usually most prominent points on the bluffs, and I think also among the bowlders above high tide, and where the egg is placed in the deepest and most inaccessible recesses.

Mr. Elliott (1880) writes:

So well do these birds succeed in secreting their charge, that although I was constantly upon the ground where several thousand pairs were laying, I was unable successfully to overturn the rocks under which they hide, and get more than four perfect eggs, the sum total of many hundred attempts.

This species is intimately associated on its breeding grounds with the paroquet auklet; it is found everywhere that the latter species is found and its nesting habits are exactly the same. The entrance to Kiska Harbor, in the Aleutian Islands, is protected by a high promontory; at the base of its steep sloping sides great masses of large, loose rocks and bowlders line the shores, forming a rough beach and offering attractive nesting sites for crested and least auklets, pigeon guillemots, Pacific eiders, and perhaps harlequin ducks, all of which we found abundant and apparently breeding here. We saw crested auklets flying out from these rocks and found their feathers and droppings in remote crevices under the rocks, but their eggs were too well hidden to see and were beyond our reach; the rocks were far too large for us to move.

On Walrus Island, in the Pribilof group, we found them nesting with the paroquet and least auklets in exactly similar situations under the loose bowlders which were piled up on the beach. Here we had no trouble in moving the rocks sufficiently to uncover the eggs, but we experienced considerable difficulty in identifying the eggs. Whereas the paroquet auklet usually sat complacently on its egg or crouched near it, the crested auklet usually ran away as soon as we began to move the rocks, and we would soon see it scurrying out from under our feet and flying off to sea. Only occasionally did we succeed in catching one near enough to its egg to identify it. The single egg was laid on the bare rock or ground or on a bed of small loose stones, which could hardly be called a nest. At the time of our visit, July 7, 1911, the eggs of this and the other auklets were in various stages of incubation, but no young were found.

The following account by Mr. C. H. Townsend (1913) would seem to indicate that the center of abundance of the crested auklet lies south of the Alaska Peninsula. He writes:

On the evening of August 1 the *Albatross* came to anchor in Yukon Harbor at Big Koniushi Island, of the Shumagin group. While the ship was working her way into this wild and uninhabited bay everyone noticed the increasing numbers of crested auklets. The farther in we went the more numerous they became, until the captain called me to the bridge to tell him what I could about them.

The birds were nearly all of the crested species and were present in myriads. The surface of the water was covered with them and the air was filled with them. Large, compact flocks launched themselves into the air from the lofty cliffs and careened toward the vessel with great speed and whirring of wings. The crested auklets were here more numerous than were the " choochkies " (least auklets) at St. George, in the Pribilofs, celebrated as the center of abundance for that species.

Twilight did not come until after 9 o'clock, and during the long evening the birds were amazingly active. Flocks of them continued to come in rapid succession from the cliffs, many passing close to the ship at high speed and swinging about the harbor. After the anchor was dropped near the cliffs a loud blast of the whistle made the auklets still more abundant. The bird legions started from the cliffs, until the misty air and the water about the ship was alive with them. It was a memorable ornithological display, and when darkness came the birds were still moving actively.

These birds appeared to be nesting chiefly in crevices in the cliffs, although they could be heard under the bowlders near the beaches.

Eggs.—The single egg of the crested auklet can not always be distinguished with certainty from that of the paroquet auklet, although it is usually slightly longer and more pointed. In shape it varies from " ovate " to pointed ovate, or more rarely to " rounded ovate." The texture of the shell is finely granulated, but hardly rough, and without any luster. The color, in all I have seen, is pure white or dull dirty white with occasional stains. The measurement of 30 eggs, in various collections, average 54.2 by 37.9 millimeters; the eggs showing the four extremes measure 60 by 41, 5, 59 by 42.5, 50 by 38.5, and 55 by 32.5 millimeters.

Young.—Incubation is apparently performed by both sexes, but its duration is not known. Both parents also assist in the feeding and care of the young, which remains hidden in the nesting cavity until it is fully fledged and able to fly, about the last of August, or later.

Plumages.—The color of the downy young varies from " clove brown " to " hair brown " above and from " hair brown " to " light drab " below. When nearly grown the dark plumage begins to appear on the back and wings; the gray breast plumage appears next and the natal down disappears last on the neck, chest, sides, rump, and crissum, when the young bird is fully grown.

The first winter plumage, which succeeds the natal down, is similar to that of the adult, dusky above and gray below; but the crest and auricular plumes are entirely lacking and the bill is very small and simple. This is the plumage which was described by Pallas as *Uria dubia.* This plumage is worn during the winter until the partial prenuptial molt in the spring, when the peculiar adornments of the head are assumed and young birds become practically indistinguishable from adults.

The seasonal molts of the adult consist of a complete postnuptial molt in August and September and a partial prenuptial molt in the late winter or early spring, involving mainly the head and neck. The conspicuous seasonal change is wholly in the head, which is so striking as to have induced Pallas to describe the winter adult, as a distinct species, under the name *Alca tetracula.* Fall adults can be distinguished from young birds by having larger bills; the frontal crests are also present, but are much smaller and less conspicuous than in the spring; and the white auricular plumes are generally more or less in evidence. The most striking seasonal change is in the bill; in the spring and summer this becomes much swollen and very grotesque in shape; its color is a brilliant " orange chrome," yellowish horn-colored at the tip. Doctor Coues (1903) describes the curious combination of parts, which make up the bill, as follows:

A nasal plate, filling nasal fossa, separate from its fellow of opposite side; a subnasal strip prolonged on cutting edge of upper mandible backward from nostrils; a semicircular plate at base of upper mandible over angle of mouth; a large shoe encasing posterior part of under mandible—the latter single, the other three pieces in pairs, making seven in all which are molted.

During the progress of the postnuptial molt, in September, these deciduous horny plates are shed, after which the bill shrinks to its winter proportions, the smaller dark-colored bill giving the bird an entirely different appearance.

Food.—The food of this species is very much the same as that of other auklets, mainly crustaceans and other small sea animals. Doctor Stejneger (1885) found the digestive organs of one " filled with a semifluid violet-red matter, which 'he took' to be the remains of a cephalopod." Mr. C. H. Townsend (1913) says:

We found that a considerable part of the food of this and other kinds of auklets consisted of amphipod crustaceans or " beach fleas," as they are called, when found under bits of seaweed along shore. These small crustaceans, less than a quarter of an inch in length, are amazingly abundant in Alaskan waters and, as a never-failing food supply, account for the surprising abundance of auklets of all kinds.

Behavior.—The flight of the crested auklet is more direct and business like than that of the others. They usually fly in small, dense flocks close to the water. They are active swimmers and can rise easily from the surface. Like the rest of their tribe they are expert at diving and probably obtain much of their food on or near the bottom at moderate depths. In diving, the body is raised and the plunge is made straight downward, but it is all done so quickly that it is hard to see how it is accomplished. Mr. Palmer (1899) speaks of their flight maneuvers as follows:

Unlike the preceding species, they usually fly in small, compact flocks over the land about their breeding places; and during the season this is a common occurrence, especially near the village of St. George where, among the countless thousands of the least auklet, small flocks of this dark-bodied and peculiarly-crested species are conspicuous when they sweep in over the land. At such times they fly over the arc of quite a large circle, returning again far out to sea. They are very wary, but may be readily observed with care. Upon approaching a flock perched upon a rocky shelf they will instantly take flight. One can then conceal himself as close to the place as possible, for the birds will soon return, not, however, flying directly to the place, but almost parallel with the shore line. If nothing unusual is noticed, upon their next return they will perch upon the shelf, though a few may repeat the trip. In this way I have made them repeat the journey several times simply by showing myself a little. Some would perch and watch, while other species would gradually gather around, and in their comical way wonder about the strange object moving between the rocks.

This species is much the noisiest of the auklets. While hunting for their nests among the loose rocks on Walrus Island we frequently heard a variety of loud, weird cries coming from the innermost recesses of the rocks below us, which we concluded were traceable to these birds. Mr. Palmer (1899) describes a similar experience as follows:

When disturbed they utter a honk-like sound—impossible to describe on paper; but it is when quarreling among the rocks that the climax is reached. While stepping one day from rock to rock, under one of the cliffs, I was startled by suddenly hearing the most unearthly sounds issuing from among the rocks at my feet. I was soon satisfied that several foxes were quarreling over some prey, but was rather taken aback when soon after several of these birds emerged and flew off.

Mr. Nelson (1887) says that "they continually uttered a chirping note." Mr. Turner (1886) refers to its note as "a peculiar grunt of two or three syllables"; and Mr. Elliott (1880) says "the note of the 'canooskie,' while mating, is a loud, clanging, honk-like sound; at all other seasons they are as silent as the grave."

For the Aleut natives this and other auklets furnish an abundant and a welcome food supply; they are usually fat and their flesh is very palatable, as they are not fish eaters. The natives make a regular business of catching them in large numbers, as they fly over their breeding grounds. Armed with a large dip net the native hunter conceals himself behind some rock where the birds are accustomed to fly low; the net lies flat on the ground until the birds are close at hand, when it is quickly and skillfully swung up at just the right moment and, before they have time to dodge it, several birds are caught.

Winter.—The crested auklets move off of their breeding grounds when the young are able to fly in September, but they spend the winter in the vicinity of the Aleutian Islands and on the North Pacific Ocean. They probably winter as far north as they can find open water among the ice and do not wander as far south as the paroquet aukets.

DISTRIBUTION.

Breeding range.—Coast and islands of Bering Sea and North Pacific. From Kodiak Island westward throughout the Aleutian Islands and the Commander Islands to the Kurile Islands. Northward throughout Bering Sea to the Diomede Islands.

Winter range.—Bering Sea and the North Pacific in the vicinity of the Aleutian and Shumagin Islands and from the Commander Islands to the Kuriles and Japan (two records). Occasionally north to the Pribilof Islands.

Spring migration.—Has been taken at Nushagak April 22. Arrives in the Pribilof Islands early in May, sometimes as early as March 12, and has been seen in numbers off St. Matthew Island, May 25.

Fall migration.—Birds have been recorded from the Diomedes as late as September 10; near St. Michael, October 13; and Cape Iksurin, Siberia, September 26 to 28.

Casual records.—It is supposed that a specimen was taken at Chatham, Massachusetts, in the winter of 1884–85, but the evidence is not conclusive. The occurrence of this bird or the paroquet auklet in Sweden has already been mentioned under *Phaleris psittacula.* Records from Sitka are questionable. Occasionally in Arctic Ocean (Kotzebue Sound, Point Barrow, Herald and Wrangel Islands.)

Egg dates.—Northern Bering Sea: 2 records, July 20 and August 26. Pribilof Islands, 2 records, June 18 and July 7. Aleutian Islands: 1 record, July 1.

HABITS.

This was one of the few birds of the Aleutian Islands which we failed to secure on our expedition to this interesting region in 1911. We had it constantly in mind and looked for it among all the islands we visited throughout the whole length of the chain, but we did not even see a specimen to recognize it. It is said to breed about the base of Korovinski Volcano on Atkha Island. I made an unsuccessful attempt to reach this mountain on foot, but lost my way among the snow banks and fogs of the rugged peaks. We passed near it in the ship, but the beautiful, snow-capped cone was barely visible in the thick, drifting fog which concealed the coast and we were unable to land. Perhaps it is not strange that we overlooked it, for Doctor Stejneger (1885) says:

Notwithstanding the fact that the birds are rather common, it must be considered good luck to meet them and get opportunity of observing them, for they are rather shy and live quite retired in their deep holes.

Nesting.—We are indebted to Dr. Leonhard Stejneger (1885) for nearly all we know about the life history of this curious and obscure species, the rarest and the least known of the auklets. He says of its breeding habits:

This little auk, certainly the prettiest species of the whole family, has apparently the center of its distribution on the islands visited by me. On Bering Island it is rather rare, however, though it breeds in the crevices of the outlying islet Arij Kamen, in a precipice near the fishing place Saranna, and probably in several places on the southern part of the island, for instance, at Kikij Mys. Copper Island, with its steep rocky shores, is the favorite home of this bird, however. It may be found breeding all around the coast where suitable holes and crevices occur. I know of nesting places near the main village, at Karabelnij, and on Tschornij Mys. At the latter place it occupied holes in the basaltic cliff alongside those of *Oceanodroma furcata*, the latter inhabiting the deeper ones. It could be told at once by the peculiar smell emanating from the caverns of the latter bird, which species was to be found inside.

They are early breeders, in that respect being considerably ahead of their allies, for instance, *Lunda cirrhata*, so early in fact, that no eggs could be procured in the latter part of June, when I had the opportunity to go in search of them. The nests at that time already contained young ones. These remain in the nest until full fledged. A specimen having left the nest only a few days previous, was taken alive on board the steamer when at anchor at Glinka, Copper Island, July 18. This bird was found early in the morning, concealed in a fold of one of the sails, the inexperienced youth having probably mistaken it for the crevice of a rock. This would indicate that they pass the nights in holes as long as they stay near land.

Eggs.—The only eggs of this species that I have ever seen or heard of are two in the collection of Mr. Charles E. Doe, of Providence, Rhode Island.   One of these appears to be authentic; it came through Ward's Natural Science Establishment and was obtained by Professor Ward on his visit to Japan.   It was collected in the Kurile Islands, where this species is known to breed, but no further data came with it.   The egg is " ovate " in shape, dull white in color, smooth and lusterless.   It measures 48 by 33.5 millimeters.

Plumage.—Doctor Stejneger (1885) has made a careful study of the development of the plumages and the molts of this species based upon the 23 specimens he collected, " consisting of birds in all ages and nearly at all seasons," and " made on the fresh birds before and during skinning."   I quote from his conclusions as follows:

When the young leaves the egg, in the latter part of June, it is covered by a dense down, dark fuliginous above, lighter and more grayish on the abdomen. Another downy young was collected July 12; it is half fledged, the new plumage, on the whole, like that of the adults, being only a little lighter underneath, nearly pure white on the abdomen, but before long this light, or rather pure color, darkens, as in the young *Lunda cirrhata*, and a young killed only six days later, but fully fledged and without any trace of down left, is undistinguishable from the old ones as far as the general coloration of the plumage is concerned; the loral tuft, with its malar and superciliary branches, and the postocular stripe are indicated by light grayish feathers.

In this plumage the young remain until about the end of December, for No. 92962, shot on the 3d of January, is nearly identical with the last-mentioned young bird, with the exception of the bill, which is more vividly colored, and the general aspect of the plumage, which seems fresher and of a more slate-colored hue, owing to the fact that the feathers are new, many being still in their sheaths.   But on the same date I obtained five other specimens which show all the intermediate grades between this and the fully developed plumage with the long and rich crests, as exhibited by No. 92960, which was shot five days previous, and No. 92961, collected on the 30th of December.   The wing feathers are yet in pretty good condition, and are not molted now.   Alongside with the development of the new contour feathers and the ornamental plumes goes the increasing intensity and purity of the colors of the bill, the nasal shield of which, however, is still dusky.   During the following months the bill assumes still more vivid colors, the tip becomes nearly pure white, the middle scarlet, and the nasal shield finally, when the birds, just before the breeding season, appear at the rookeries, turns into a fine carmine, as shown by No. 92972, a female shot May 6, 1883.   But while in this specimen the bill shows its highest perfection, the plumage already bears evidence to the commencing decay caused by the wear of the feathers while inhabiting the deep nest holes in the crevices of the rocks, and the abrasion is particularly visible on the wing coverts, which were not shed when the other feathers of the body were molted, viz, late in winter, the middle row being light brownish gray, as are also the exposed parts of the inner primaries.   Also the ornamental plumes are on the decline, and the frontal crest is already thinned out considerably, consisting in the specimen in question of only four plumes, while some birds in " full dress " may be found having as many as a dozen.   During the incubation the plumage becomes gradually more dilapidated, and when the young are out, the parents—at other seasons so graceful and beautiful—present a rather miserable aspect, the white plumes on the head being soiled and glued together, and all the wing feathers faded into a dirty gray, with the vanes disconnected and the edges ragged. All the birds taken on the nest, July 21, were in that deplorable condition, only that the wings were spotted with slaty black as the new coverts made their appearance now, the middle row being complete already. Also the four or five inner primaries were shed, and the new ones, in different stages of development—the three innermost full grown—contrasted favorably against the faded-out remnants of the old ones. The tail feathers are still unshed, but their condition plainly shows that they will be molted before long. The ornamental feathers are worn down, the crests are thin, and many of the long plumes have already disappeared. These specimens prove beyond a possibility of doubt that the remiges and rectrices are molted toward the end of the breeding season, and that the process commences with the inner primaries. But not only are the wing feathers shed now, but also the contour feathers; all over the body protrude now the bluish sheaths containing the new feathers, which in some places have already burst through the tips. The postnuptial molt, therefore, is a complete one. At this time the brightness of the bill has likewise faded away, the white tip gets bluish, and the basal parts darken. The upper layers of the horny covering scale off, but I feel satisfied that a regular shedding of the basal parts, such as in the *Fraterculeæ*, does not take place.

The complete postnuptial molt in adults seems to take place in July and August, so that by September or earlier both old and young birds have assumed the adult winter plumage and become indistinguishable. Young birds in their first winter plumage, which is worn for only about six months, show signs of developing white plumes on the sides of the head, but they have no frontal crests. In the adult winter plumage, which is practically only a fall plumage, both the plumes and the crests are present, but are not so highly developed as in the spring. The prenuptial molt during the winter and spring is incomplete and the curious nuptial adornments which it produces soon wear away.

Food.—Judging from Doctor Stejneger's (1885) records of the stomach contents of specimens examined, I should say that the principal food of the whiskered auklet is gammarids, with which many of the stomachs or crops were filled; other amphipods were also found and a few decapods and gastropods. Some of these animals are probably found swimming on or near the surface of the sea, and others must be sought for on or about sunken ledges.

Winter.—Of the migrations and winter habits of the auklets we know very little; probably they move out to sea and roam over the open ocean. Doctor Stejneger (1885) writes:

When the breeding season is over, they, like all the allied forms, retire to the open ocean, part of them at least, going to more southerly latitudes to winter. That many stay in the neighborhood of the islands is evident from the fact that I obtained numerous specimens at Bering Island in December and January. A single female came near the coast on December 14, 1882, and was shot; but from the 29th of the same month until January 5, 1883, a few could be met with every day. They could then be seen in small societies of two to four, swimming along the rocky shores, alternately diving for food, which chiefly consisted of gammarids. When diving they raised themselves a little on the water and then made a sudden jump downward The weather was not stormy, but we had during that week a very cold spell. Later in January they became scarce, but a few specimens were secured, the last one on January 30. They appeared again at their breeding places during the first days of May.

DISTRIBUTION.

Breeding range.—From the Commander Islands to Kamtschatka and Japan. Occurrence in the Aleutian Islands probably rare or local, as far east as Unalaska.

Winter range.—Presumably some winter on the North Pacific south of their summer home, but many remain near their breeding grounds throughout the year.

Spring migration.—Birds arrive at the nesting grounds early in May.

Fall migration.—There is a specimen in the United States National Museum from Akutan Island (eastern Aleutians) taken September 10, and Stejneger took birds on the Commander Islands up to January 30.

Casual records.—Recorded by Schlegel from Sitka, but this record is believed to be erroneous.

ÆTHIA PUSILLA (Pallas).

LEAST AUKLET.

HABITS.

I first met this diminutive sea bird, the smallest of the Alcidae, in 1911 while passing through Unimak Pass, the main entrance into Bering Sea, where a few small flocks were seen among the thousands of puffins, murres, and other auklets scattered over the smooth surface of the water. But it was not until we reached Kiska Island, in the Aleutian chain, that I began to realize its abundance and learn something of its habits. One smooth, foggy afternoon Mr. R. H. Beck and I took a small skiff and rowed out of the harbor to collect sea birds. Large flocks of harlequin ducks, scoters, and Pacific eiders flew past us along the rocky shore; numerous pigeon guillemots skimmed along the surface ahead of us, and several pelagic cormorants flew out from the cliffs to meet us, circling about our boat to satisfy their curiosity. But we left them all behind us as the rocky shores faded out of sight in the fog, and we found ourselves at sea among the auklets. Immense flocks of those curious little birds surrounded us on all sides, countless thousands of them, sitting in dense masses on the water, disappearing beneath the surface as if by magic, and as suddenly reappearing or swirling about us in great swarms, reminding us more of bees than of birds, as their chunky little bodies bounded along over the waves, their small wings vibrating at high speed. They would rise readily from the surface and would dive like lightning, so quickly that we could not see how it was done; but we could frequently see them swimming under water, using their wings. When one or more of their number were shot, others would come and alight near them, showing a sympathetic interest between what were perhaps mated pairs.

Spring.—The " choochkies," as they are called by the natives, begin to arrive to their breeding grounds in hundreds about the 1st of May, increasing to thousands during that month and reaching the height of their abundance early in June, when they swarm in millions about the rocky beaches of the Pribilof Islands, outnumbering any other species in Bering Sea. It is difficult for one who has not seen them to appreciate their abundance and one is not likely to overestimate their numbers. One of their greatest breeding grounds is on the Diomede Islands, in Bering Straits, which Mr. E. W. Nelson (1887) has thus aptly described:

As we lay at anchor close under the Big Diomede the cliffs arose almost sheer for hundreds of feet. Gazing up toward one of these banks we could see the air filled with minute black specks, which seemed to be floating by in an endless stream. The roar from the rush of waves against the base of the cliffs was deadened by the strange humming chorus of faint cries from myriads of small throats, and as we landed, a glance upward showed the island standing out in bold, jagged relief against the sky and surrounded by such inconceivable numbers of flying birds that it could only be likened to a vast beehive, with the swarm of bees hovering about it. The mazy flight of the birds had the effect several times of making me dizzy as I watched them. Breeding there were several species of auks and guillemots. Our first visit was made about the middle of July, and most of the birds, including the present species, had fresh eggs.

We found them in the greatest abundance about the Pribilof Islands early in July. As we approached St. Paul Island in a dense fog we ran into great rafts of them sitting on the smooth water and they were constantly flying about us in immense flocks. Their constant twittering sounded like the distant peeping of myriads of hylas in early spring or like a great flock of peep in full cry. When we landed on one of the stony beaches where they were breeding the effect was marvelous, as they suddenly appeared from beneath the great piles of loose rocks in inconceivable numbers, like a swarm of mosquitoes rising from a marsh, whirling about us in a great bewildering cloud and flying out to sea.

Nesting.—On Walrus Island we found the least auklets breeding in smaller numbers on July 7, 1911, where they were nesting in remote crevices under the loose, rounded granite bowlders, which the action of the sea had piled up on the high beaches. Nesting with them were large numbers of paroquet and crested auklets and a few tufted puffins. Here the nests were easily found, as the rocks were not large and we could readily move them; nearly every suitable crevice seemed to be occupied. Doubtless hundreds, and perhaps thousands, of auklets must have been nesting here, for as we walked among the loose bowlders we could hear a constant sound of many voices beneath us, twittering, cackling, squealing notes, and a variety of weird calls, as the frightened birds sought shelter in the darkest crevices or scurried out under our feet and flew away. The eggs were laid on the bare rocks or on beds of small stones, with no attempt at nest building.

The eggs of the least auklet are not always laid in such accessible locations. The birds often breed on rocky shores where the rocks or bowlders are too large to move and where the eggs are far beyond reach; such was the case at Kiska Island, where droppings or feathers indicated an entrance to a nesting cavity, safe against intrusion. On St. Paul Island and on St. Matthew Island we found them nesting in the deep crevices in the solid rocky cliffs, where their eggs were entirely inaccessible. In such places one might work for hours within a few feet of countless nesting birds and be unable to secure a single egg, hence the scarcity of auklets' eggs in collections.

Eggs.—The breeding season of the least auklet usually begins in June, though fresh eggs have been taken as early as May 28, 1890, but it does not reach its height until the latter part of the month and many of the eggs are not laid until July; although most of the young are hatched during July, there are plenty of fresh eggs up to at least the middle of the month. The eggs are always a pure white, with a smooth but lusterless surface; they are "ovate" in shape, sometimes rounded at both ends, but more often more or less pointed at the small end. The measurements of 57 eggs, in the United States National Museum collection, average 39.5 by 28.5 millimeters; the eggs showing the four extremes measure **43** by 28.5, 40 by **33.5, 33.5** by 29, and 40 by **27** millimeters.

Plumages.—The young, when first hatched, are covered with a thick coat of down, "fuscous" to "clove brown" above and "hair brown" to "light drab" below; these colors become paler as the bird grows older. The wings begin to sprout when the young bird is about half grown, in August; and the white feathers begin to appear on the under parts at about this time. By the end of August the young bird is fully grown and fully fledged, the last of the down disappearing on the neck, rump, and crissum. This, the first winter plumage, is slaty black above, including the wings, chin, lores, and cheek, the scapulars pale gray and pure white below. The young bird in winter is darker above than the adult and lacks the white frontal plumes. This plumage is worn all through the winter and often through the first nuptial season, though some mottling is acquired on the breast during the spring and summer. In their first summer plumage young birds closely resemble adults, but the bills are smaller, lacking the knob, and the frontal plumes are usually lacking or very small. Young birds probably do not breed until their second nuptial season. At the first postnuptial molt, which is complete and is prolonged through August and September, young birds become indistinguishable from adults.

The adult winter plumage resembles the first winter plumage in being black above and pure white below, but the black of the upper parts is not so intense, the sides of the head and neck are " plumbeous " or " cinereous," and the bill is larger, with signs of the nuptial knob; the white frontal plumes are usually present in winter adults and are often more pronounced than in spring. A partial prenuptial molt in the spring produces the nuptial plumage with the mottled under parts.

Food.—The food of the least auklet consists mainly of amphipods and small crustaceans which it obtains by diving. Among the Aleutian Islands, I have seen them feeding a few hundred yards off shore but often they fly way out to sea to feed. Considering that the average depth of Bering Sea in the vicinity of the Pribilof Islands is from 30 to 50 fathoms, it hardly seems possible that these little birds can dive to such great depths to obtain their food on the bottom. It would seem as if they must obtain most of their food near the surface or in shallower water.

Behavior.—The natives on St. George Island capture large numbers of least auklets for food. During the late evening hours, from 7 to 10 o'clock, when the birds are returning to their breeding grounds in vast numbers after spending the day at sea, it is an easy matter for the expert natives to catch them in nets. This custom has been well described by Mr. William Palmer (1899) as follows:

On this vast breeding range of this species, on the 28th of May, I accompanied a native for the purpose of getting a few specimens for myself, while he desired a meal. With a large long-handled dip net I crouched behind one of the numerous large moss and grass-bedecked rocks which so liberally covered the ground. As the birds fly low and in a nearly straight line and have great difficulty—in fact, they have little necessity—in making a sudden curve to avoid an object, it was only necessary when a flock was seen approaching to raise the net directly in their path. If the distance and their velocity had been well calculated several birds would be unable to swerve off in time and in consequence would be engulfed in the net. A quick bringing of the net to the ground would then complete the capture. A half hour's work resulted in my securing some 20 specimens, but the Aleut close by had ten times as many.

Winter.—Very little seems to be known about the migrations and winter range of the least auklet. Doctor Stejneger (1885) found them wintering in the vicinity of the Commander Islands; he writes:

It was on December 1, 1882, that a specimen was brought me from Ladiginsk, on Bering Island. It was in full winter plumage, entirely white beneath, without knob, and with only a few traces of white feathers on the face. A few days before the end of the year several birds came near the shore, where they now could be seen to swim in small troops, or more frequently by twos and threes, parallel to the coast about a hundred yards offshore, according to the depth, usually in 3-fathom water, where they dived with great expertness for amphipods, which at that time seemed to be their chief or only food. When diving they lifted themselves up a little and went down with a quick jump. We were having a severe spell of cold when they made their appearance, and when it was over they disappeared again, none being seen after the 5th of January. They evidently winter on the open ocean somewhere about the islands.

DISTRIBUTION.

Breeding range.—Coasts and islands of Bering Sea. From the Aleutian Islands north to the Diomede Islands. Also said to breed on Kodiak Island.

Winter range.—North Pacific Ocean from the Aleutian and Commander Islands southward to Japan and Washington (Puget Sound rarely).

Spring migration.—At the Pribilof Islands the first birds were seen at sea March 26, but none came on land until April 25. In Unimak Pass they were found in numbers May 1.

Fall migration.—August 16 the birds began to leave the breeding grounds in the Pribilof Islands and the last was seen August 28. Stragglers have been taken in the vicinity so late as December 6. The last was noted at Cape Iksurin, Siberia, September 26, and in Akutan Pass, Aleutian Islands, October 6.

Casual records.—A single bird was taken, August 30, at Point Barrow, by McIlhenny; and Nelson saw two birds 30 miles north of Cape Lisburne, August 15. One was found on a lake near Kotzebue Sound in January, 1886.

Egg dates.—Pribilof Islands: 5 records, June 8 to July 7; 3 records, June 19 to 24. Diomede Islands: 3 records, June 12, July 18, and August 26.

SYNTHLIBORAMPHUS ANTIQUUS (Gmelin).

ANCIENT MURRELET.

HABITS.

In the large deep-water bays of the Aleutian Islands, protected from the furious storms of Bering Sea by towering cliffs and lofty snow-laden mountains which rise abruptly from the shores, these curious and daintly little sea birds find congenial summer homes on tranquil inland seas. Here we never failed to find them, in every harbor we visited in June, floating quietly in little parties of from four to six birds on the smooth waters of sheltered bays and often close to the shores. Although at other seasons this species frequents the open sea and is generally seen on migrations farther from land than others of its tribe, in the summer it seems to love to frequent protected harbors where it can find deep water, leaving its winter companions, the auklets, far outside.

Spring.—Mr. Harry S. Swarth (1911) noted many ancient murrelets migrating along the southern Alaska coast between May 19 and June 7, 1909. He says:

On June 7, while crossing Clarence Straits, between Prince of Wales and Duke Islands, more were observed than at any other place, but as soon as the sheltered waters about the latter island were reached they were no longer to be seen. The preference evinced for the open sea was very marked, and not a single individual was seen at any time in the sheltered waters of the inner passages.

Nesting.—The ancient murrelets arrive on their breeding grounds about the first of June, but do not mate or begin breeding immediately. We saw them swimming about in small flocks, apparently unmated, up to June 20, though the first eggs were seen at Atka Island on June 13. Mr. Chase Littlejohn, who spent the spring and summer of 1894 on different islands south of the Alaska Peninsula, furnished Major Bendire (1895) with some very full and interesting notes on the breeding habits of this species on Sanak Island. I can not do better than quote practically all he has to say on the subject, as follows:

By June 2 their nesting grounds were reached, but no birds were to be found, and to one unacquainted with their habits there was no sign of their having yet arrived. Nevertheless, we land, pitch our tent, and wait until the close of that long twilight which is only found in the far North, and just as it merges into night we see a batlike form flit by, and presently from somewhere in the gloom comes an abrupt and startling *kroo-kroo-coo*, which is at once answered with a like call, or with a nerve-destroying *kwee-ke-ke-ke*, in a very high, shrill key, the call note of Leach's petrel (*Oceanodroma leucorhoa*). Presently we hear a whir of wings in different directions, then more voices, pitched in various keys, and before we are scarcely aware of it, both heaven and earth seem to vibrate with rumbling noises and whir of wings.

As we step out of our tent, perfectly astonished at this sudden change, and move to the foot of a small knoll near by, listening to this violent outburst of noices, a muffled sound comes right from under our feet. We stoop and discover a small burrow in the earth, and from it come the cooing love notes of a petrel, *k-r-r-r, k-r-r-r*, and this is its home. Just from a somewhat larger burrow, only a few feet to our right, comes another sound, and moving cautiously in this direction we listen to the love notes of Cassin's auklet, which reminds one of the sounds produced by a squeaky bucksaw while passing through a hard knot, somewhat like *kwee-kew, kwee-kew*, which, fortunately, lasts only for three or four hours each night. These noises, coming as they do from hundreds of auklets and thousands of petrels, become almost distracting and banish sleep most effectually for the first few nights on the island.

These, then, are some of our murrelets' neighbors; but where is he? We listen in vain for some note of his, but hear none. As we walk on a little distance among the tall grass of last year's growth we notice a small dark object flapping about, and after a short chase we manage to capture it and discover our "old man," but fail to locate his nest, one of the main objects of our long and tedious voyage, and we did not succeed in finding one containing eggs until the 11th of June. This was principally because they had not commenced to lay sooner, and partly, also, because we did not then look in the places—under rank matted grass—which are mostly preferred by this murrelet for nesting sites.

We remained on this desolate, wind-swept island from May 29 until June 12. Our days were spent in hunting, preparing skins and eggs, but time passed slowly. At first we looked forward to night in order to renew our acquaintance with our feathered neighbors, but after losing about a week's sleep, owing to their squeaking, I, at least, felt like choking the whole lot; and as if not satisfied with the constant babble of their neighbors, the murrelets took especial delight in alighting at the foot of our A-shaped tent, toenailing it up to the ridgepole, resting there a moment, and then sliding down on the other side. This exercise seems to amuse them, and it certainly did us, until the novelty wore off, as it was not conducive to a restful sleep, and finally, tiring of this, and finding but few murrelets' eggs, we broke camp and started for the mainland, and did not return to the island again until June 23.

In a short time after the first birds arrive on their breeding grounds, and before one has time to realize it, the entire surface of certain favorite islands is literally alive with murrelets and auklets, in the proportion of about two of the latter to one of the former, as well as of both Leach's and fork-tailed petrels (*Oceanodroma furcata*), the first greatly outnumbering the last. When one walks obout at this time, the murrelets and auklets become frightened, running, flopping, and flying about in such numbers that one has to be careful where he steps, lest they be crushed under food. If it is windy—and it usually is—they are on the wing at once as soon as disturbed, and quickly out of sight, but when a calm prevails they have to flop to the side of a steep bank where they can jump off, and thereby gain sufficient headway to keep on the wing, and then in their frantic efforts to be off, they become bewildered and are just as apt to fly in one's face, or against the cliffs, as anywhere; although they usually strike with great force when fairly started, I have never seen one killed or even stunned. They no sooner touch the earth, than they are flopping off again at a great rate.

It is a difficult matter to calculate the numbers that visit this small island annually, but they certainly number several thousands and if left unmolested by man the island would soon become too small to accommodate their natural increase, but such is by no means the case. The native Aleuts know, almost to a day, when the first ones will arrive, and are there to meet them, invading the island armed with stout clubs, and every bird, auklet or murrelet, that is overtaken is promptly clubbed to death and thrown into a sack carried for this purpose. At each of these raids hundreds of these birds are killed, and as they are made frequently and throughout the entire season, it is astonishing that any remain. But this is not all; as soon as day dawns, the entire crew sets out to make a systematic search for eggs, which are well flavored and good eating, each one striving to get more than his mates; and as it makes no difference to a native whether they are fresh or on the point of hatching, everything goes. Fortunately it is impossible to find all the nests, or kill all the birds, so enough remain to stock the island again another season.

By no means every island in this vicinity is occupied by murrelets. Within 400 yards of the one of which I write is another of about the same size and topography, but strange to say, no murrelets are found on it, although there are two or three small colonies of auklets, the remainder of the island being given over to Leach's petrels. Again, on two other small islands, also near together, each containing about a couple of acres, and in every way alike, one is given over entirely to auklets, while on the other the murrelets have almost complete control. These facts cause me to believe that the birds always return to the island on which they have been reared.

On June 23 our party returned to the island on which we first landed, and found to our great satisfaction that the murrelets' eggs were more plentiful than on our former visit, and a few of them were taken. We also soon discovered that they were not especially particular in the selection of a nesting site. An abandoned burrow of Cassin's auklet, a dark crevice in cliffs, under large broken rocks which had fallen from the latter, or under large tussocks of rank grass, with which the higher portion of the island was covered, would answer equally well. Under these almost solid bunches (the grass remaining from several previous years), the murrelets would force their way, leaving only a slight hole in the mass, which usually was very hard to detect. After once gaining an entrance into this matted vegetation and working their way in for 2 or 3 feet, a shallow cavity about 5 inches in diameter and 2 or 3 inches deep, was scratched out and this was nicely lined with blades of dry grass of last year's growth, carried in from the outside, making a very neat and snug home, in which the two beautiful eggs comprising a set, were deposited. Some of their nests were found fully 200 yards from the water. In the other situations mentioned little and often no nest is made, and the eggs are deposited on the bare rocks, in the soft sand, or on the wet, muddy soil. I even took several sets on the bare ice at the bottom of some auklet's burrow, the ground being still frozen, immediately beneath the grass and moss on July 3, when I left the island.

The setting bird will sometimes leave the nest when danger threatens, but it will frequently allow itself to be taken from the eggs, and when brought to light it will screech, scratch, and bite with vigor. When released they can not fly unless thrown into the air, and will then often fall back to earth. One evening, just at dusk, I was crouched in the grass waiting for a shot at a Peale's falcon (*Falco peregrinus pealei*), who made regular trips to the island to prey on the auklets and murrelets, when I heard a very low but rather shrill whistle. Turning my attention to the spot from which it seemed to come, I listened; presently I heard it again, but was still unable to locate the bird, which I afterwards found to be a murrelet. Subsequent observations proved that this was a call note uttered just about the time the setting bird expected the return of its mate, and was evidently uttered to attract his or her attention, for as far as my observations went, they, like the auklets, exchange places nightly, and while one attends to the home cares, the other is usually a number of miles out at sea on the feeding grounds. This call note is the only one I could attribute to this species while on land, and so ventriloquial are their powers, that in only two instances did I succeed in locating the nest from the sound. While out at sea, the ancient murrelet utters a peculiar piping whistle entirely different from the one uttered while on the nest.

Two eggs are laid to a set, the second is deposited after an interval of two or three days, and frequently three or four days elapse before incubation begins. Occasionally two birds will occupy the same nest; at least I have found three and four eggs in one, and I have also found one in the nest of a red-breasted merganser (*Merganser serrator*). During the day, while the breeding season is on, a very few birds may be seen near land, but offshore they will be met with in small flocks of from 6 to 8, and occasionally a flock of 100 or more can be seen.

Eggs.—The eggs of the ancient murrelet are quite unique and entirely unlike the eggs of any of the other Alcidae. Major Bendire (1895) has described them very well as follows:

In shape they vary from elliptical ovate to elongate and cylindrical ovate, the elongated ovates predominating. Their shell is fine grained, moderately strong, although rather thin, and it shows little or no gloss. They are rather difficult to describe accurately, their ground color being variable and of subtle tints not readily expressed on paper, ranging from a bluish milky white through the different shades of cream color, vinaceous, olive, and salmon buffs to a rich vinaceous cinnamon and ecru-drab color. They are generally moderately well flecked, blotched, or spotted with small irregular shaped markings of different shades of brown, fawn, and Isabella color, mixed with more subdued shades of ecru drab, lavender, and lilac gray. The markings are distributed over the entire surface, and are usually heaviest about the larger end of the egg but never so profuse as to hide the ground color. In an occasional specimen, they show a tendency to run into irregular and mostly longitudinal lines or tracings; in others these markings are more bold, coarse, and fewer in numbers, and a single specimen before me now shows comparatively few and rather faint markings.

The measurements of 51 eggs, in the United States National Museum collection, average 61.1 by 38.6 millimeters; the eggs showing the fourth extremes measure **64.3** by 40.3, 60.5 by **42, 57.5** by 36.5, and 57.8 by **35.7** millimeters.

Young.—About the period of incubation and development of the young, Mr. Littlejohn says:

I left the rookery on July 3, and was therefore unable to determine the period of incubation, or the time the young remain in the nest, but in former years off the coast of some of the Kuril Islands, I have seen numbers of old birds accompanied by half grown young, still unable to fly, about the middle of September, sometimes 400 or 500 miles from land, thus proving that they must leave their breeding grounds when still very small. At that age, the young, like the old, are great divers, and no matter how long the parent remained below, or how far she dived, the young would always break water at the same time and in the same place, just at the old bird's tail. During the winter they scatter and can be found in small numbers most anywhere about or between the islands, and at this time they also associate with the crested and least auklets (*Simorhynchus cristatellus* and *S. pusillus*) and the marbled murrelet (*Brachyramphus marmoratus.*)

On Forrester Island this species evidently nests earlier than on Sanak Island, for Prof. Harold Heath (1915) found newly hatched chicks as early as May 29, 1913, and they " were very abundant during the second week in June." He has given us the following interesting account of the early departure of the young, which is certainly a striking performance:

The journey of the young to the sea is one of the most interesting sights on the island, and by the aid of a lantern was witnessed on several occasions. The pilgrimage is made during the night within a day or two after hatching, and is evidently initiated by one or both of the parents who take up a position on the sea not far from the shore. Here, about midnight, they commence a chorus of calls resembling the chirp of an English sparrow with the tremulo stop open, and in response the young beautiful, black-and-white creatures, as active as young quails, soon pour in a living flood down the hillsides. Falling over roots, scrambling through the brush, or sprawling headlong over the rocks, they race at a surprising rate of speed drawn by the all-compelling instinct to reach the sea. They may be temporarily attracted by the lantern's light, and flutter aimlessly about one's feet; but sooner or later they heed the calls and once more plunge down the slopes. Almost every night during these migrations the surf was pounding violently on the rocky beaches, and many times one could see the young swept off the cliffs, and after struggling a moment in the waves they disappeared from sight and seemed doomed to destruction.

To test the correctness of this observation a young murrelet, which came down the slopes early one evening, was liberated on the beach close to the dashing surf. Without a moment's hesitation, and without the stimulus of a parent's call, it plunged boldly into the water, poised a moment on the summit of a great foam-crested wave, and dived with surprising speed and accuracy to reappear 10 seconds later as many feet at sea. A momentary appearance, another dive and still another carried it beyond the swirl of the surf, and, swimming rapidly and paddling across patches of kelp, always in a bee line, it soon disappeared from view.

Plumages.—In the downy young the upper parts are of jet black, including the back, wings, crown, and sides of the head to a point below the eye; there is a whitish auricular patch in the black area back of the ear; the occiput and the whole dorsal region seems to be clouded with bluish gray, due to a subterminal portion of each filament being so colored; the under parts are pure white, slightly tinged with yellowish.

I have not been able to find any specimens showing the changes from the downy young to the first winter plumage, but the young bird in the fall has the throat mostly or wholly white, though in some cases there is more or less dusky on the chin; there are no white plumes on the head, neck, or shoulders, which are characteristic of the adult; the bill of the young bird is dusky and smaller than that of the adult. During the late winter or early spring a partial molt takes place, producing the black throat of the first nuptial plumage and making old and young birds practically indistinguishable.

The adult has a partial prenuptial molt in the late winter or early spring, involving mainly the head and neck and a complete postnuptial molt late in the summer producing the adult winter plumage. The adult in the fall has a more or less whitish bill and usually retains the black throat, more or less mixed with white; it also generally has some of the white plumes on the head, neck, or shoulders, which are sometimes quite conspicuous, but not so highly developed as in the spring; these are entirely absent in the young bird. These adornments are probably most highly developed in the oldest birds. The name " old man " and the Russian name " Starik," which means old man, as well as the scientific names *antiquus* and *senicula*, are supposed to have been derived from the fancied resemblance of these white plumes to the snowy locks of old age.

Food.—The food of the ancient murrelet consists of various kinds of small marine invertebrates, which it obtains mainly by diving, although much of its food must be obtained on or near the surface, for it spends much of its lifetime on the open ocean, where the water is from one to two thousand fathoms deep. Most of the murrelets and auklets have similar feeding habits and probably find an abundant supply of small invertebrates swimming a few feet or perhaps a few fathoms below the surface of the warm water of the North Pacific. Mr. Littlejohn gives the following account of its peculiar feeding habits while following a vessel:

We were about 180 miles east by south from Unga (a small island south of Sand Point on the Alaska Peninsula, in about latitude 55°, longitude 160°) when this hardy bird was first seen. They were usually in twos and threes and scattered among large flocks of crested auklets (*Simorhynchus cristatellus*). One would think at first they were amusing themselves by flying a short distance ahead of the ship, dropping into the water and swimming in, so as to be near the bow as the vessel passed, thus diving beneath the hull and coming up again just under the stern. After they had dropped astern a few hundred feet they took wing and repeated this maneuver with unvarying precision throughout the entire day. By close watching I found that it was not for pleasure they did this, but that they were feeding on small invertebrates, such as are found on ships' bottoms. At such times they are very unwary and can be easily taken with a dip net alongside of the vessel, as can also the crested auklet, the latter on the wing while flying in circles about the vessel. From the time the first were seen until land was sighted there were always some about, but as we neared the land or got on soundings they became more plentiful and did not follow the ship any farther, owing, most likely, to food becoming more abundant.

Behavior.—The flight of the ancient murrelet is swift and direct, usually close to the surface of the water, and not usually much prolonged. Its migrations are not extended and are usually performed in a leisurely manner, with frequent stops as it gradually drifts northward. I have never seen this species make a long flight; it rises readily from the surface, skims away close to the water for a short distance, and soon drops in again. It is a rapid swimmer and makes a very neat appearance in the water; the striking color contrasts in its plumage, the blue-gray back, the black throat, the white head plumes, and the white bill are all very conspicuous and good field marks. We usually saw them in small parties of from four to six birds, swimming in a straight line, one ahead of another. They seldom attempted to escape by flying, but preferred to swim away, making very good speed with little apparent effort or with very little disturbance of the smooth water; if too hard pressed they dove quickly, one at a time, or occasionally all together; they did not remain under water very long or swim very far away, appearing suddenly on the surface at no great distance without causing a ripple. The dive is made with a forward semicircular plunge; the bird often leaves the water entirely, sometimes leaping above the surface as much as 6 inches, and plunges down into the water head first, making a clean, smooth dive. While swimming under water it uses its wings freely. Mr. Swarth (1911) noted this habit and recorded his observation as follows:

On June 7, while we were passing through numerous large flocks, the sea was unusually clear and smooth, and by standing in the bow of the launch, I had frequent opportunity to observe how the murrelets used their wings under the water. When diving they make a sudden flirt of the wings that can be seen at quite a distance, but it was not until several individuals had passed close under the boat that I could see, as was plainly apparent, that they had used their wings continually. They were literally flying under the water, but the manus was held about parallel with the body, and not outstretched, as when going through the air.

Where these murrelets breed in large numbers they are severely persecuted by the natives who visit the breeding colonies regularly to gather eggs or to kill the birds for food, for both are excellent eating and much in demand. Fortunately much of the region where they breed, particularly in the Aleutian Islands, is uninhabited. The Peale's falcon seems to be one of their worst enemies. Mr. Littlejohn gives the following interesting account of its hunting methods:

Great numbers of these birds are taken by Peale's falcon, who seem to be one of their principal enemies next to man. As I have already stated, the murrelets are mainly found at some distance from land during the day, and here, too, this falcon pursues them, watching for a chance to seize any murrelet he succeeds in driving from the water. After having secured its prey, the falcon circles about for a short time and then partakes of its meal. To do this he hovers, remaining almost stationary for several minutes at the time; in the meantime the prey is raised well up to the beak with both feet, and promptly devoured. When the murrelets return to the land at nightfall, the falcon is there also to meet them, and soon again secures his nightly repast.

The only note which I have ever heard from this species is a shrill, faint, whistling call note. Mr. Littlejohn describes their call note on the breeding grounds as " a very low but rather shrill whistle," and he says that " while out at sea, the ancient murrelet utters a peculiar piping whistle, entirely different from the one uttered while on the nest." Mr. E. W. Nelson (1887) says " They were in pairs, and not shy. When one was shot the survivor would fly about in a circle, frequently alighting in the water and uttering a low, plaintive whistle."

Winter.—The fall migration consists of a general offshore movement and a gradual southward drift, off the coast, as far south as southern California. The ancient murrelet spends the winter on the open ocean, northward nearly to the Aleutian and Commander Islands, associating with the various species of auklets and other sea birds, where an abundant food supply is to be found in the warm waters of the Japan Current, drifting eastward across the North Pacific Ocean and southward along the coast of North America.

Prof. Leverett M. Loomis (1896) thus describes the behavior of this species off the coast of California in winter:

About 500 yards from the surf, a belt of drift kelp, extending from the Seaside Laboratory around Point Pinos, had gained an anchorage on the rocky bottom. The narrow strip between this breakwater and the beach was the favorite resort of ancient murrelets except on the rare days when there was a north wind, which invariably drove the bird life of the bay away from the exposed south shore. A good many were also found near the surf in the little coves in the direction of Monterey and some were seen several miles out from the land. In the sheltered places they chiefly frequented food appeared to be abundant. They were great divers and swimmers under water, and voracious in their pursuit of small fry, occasionally driving the fish to the surface in the eagerness of the chase. Often not a murrelet would be in sight for some time. Then a pair or a small company (the largest one observed numbered nine individuals) would suddenly appear from the depths. Unlike the marbled murrelets, they did not generally seek safety in flight when pursued. Neither did they dive as soon or remain as long under water when keeping out of the way of the boat. If a white cap developed near them they would always escape from it by diving. Although over a hundred were taken in the narrow belt near the surf, they were more numerous there toward the last than at the outset, new birds apparently coming in to take the places of those that had been shot.

DISTRIBUTION.

Breeding range.—Coasts and islands of the North Pacific. From the Queen Charlotte Islands, southeastern Alaska (St. Lazaria and Forrester Islands) westward to Kodiak Island, the Aleutian Islands, Commander Islands, Kamtschatka, Kurile Islands, and northern Japan.

Winter range.—Southward from the Aleutian and Commander Islands to British Columbia (Vancouver Island), Washington (Strait of Juan de Fuca and Olympia), Oregon (Netarts Bay), and California (San Francisco Bay, Monterey Bay, Santa Barbara Islands, and Pacific Beach, San Diego County), and on the Asiatic coast to Japan (Hakodadi and Yokohama).

Spring migration.—The latest date of occurrence in California is apparently April 25 (Pacific Beach); at Point Pinos, where the bird is common, none were seen later than March 22. They have

been reported from southeastern Alaska; Ketchikan, May 16; How-
kan, April 12; Warren Channel, May 19.

Fall migration.—They have been recorded from the Pribilof
Islands as late as November 7, the Aleutian Islands (Krenitzin
Islands) August 14, and Prince William Sound region August 11.
A bird taken August 9 on Puget Sound, Washington, was an early
migrant. The earliest arrivals on the Californian coast, at Point
Pinos, were seen October 21 and at Monterey September 2, and they
are stated to reach Japan (Yezzo) in October.

Casual records.—A single specimen was taken on Lake Koshkonong, Wisconsin, in October; one at Toronto, Ontario, November
18; and one on the Canadian side of Lake Erie November 15. Has
been recorded from the Pribilof Islands (St. George).

Egg dates.—Sanak Island, Alaska: 12 records, June 11 to July 28;
6 records, June 25 to 30. Southern Alaska; 7 records, May 1 to
July 16; 4 records, May 20 to June 11. Queen Charlotte Islands:
2 records, April 20 and June 10.

BRACHYRAMPHUS MARMORATUS (Gmelin).

MARBLED MURRELET.

HABITS.

While cruising northward through the picturesque inside passages which extend from Puget Sound to Alaska, where the heavily
timbered hills rise abruptly from the water, range after range up
to the snow-capped mountain tops, and where frequent waterfalls
come tumbling down over the cliffs into the placid waters of the
bays and channels, we frequently saw these little sea birds skimming
over the surface of the water. This is their chosen summer home,
for, unlike the other murrelets and auklets, they seem to prefer
these sheltered waters to the open sea. They were always shy and
generally flew away so far in advance of the ship that it required
sharp eyes to see them, but occasionally when surprised near at
hand they were forced to escape by diving. Near Ketchikan we
collected a few by chasing them in a skiff, but this required considerable chasing, for they were always on the alert. If we chanced
to get near them they would dive like a flash, but at a greater distance they would jump into the air and fly away with a burst of
speed. We had the best success in drifting upon them with the
tide, or down wind, while they were fishing in the tide rips, and
taking a long shot at them as they rose.

Nesting.—Somewhere in this general region are their breeding
grounds, but we did not succeed in finding them, nor have any
other ornithologists, several of whom have spent considerable time
in the search. I have even offered substantial rewards to natives

who thought they could find their nests, but in vain. The nesting of the marbled murrelet is one of the unsolved mysteries in American ornithology. This is rather remarkable, too, because it is really an abundant bird in a fairly accessible region. Mr. George G. Cantwell (1898) took a nearly perfect specimen of an egg from the oviduct of a bird shot in the Prince of Wales Archipelago on May 23, 1897, which is now in the United States National Museum collection. He writes:

A careful watch failed to reveal any nesting sites, and on inquiring of the Indians about it they told me that they had always supposed the bird to breed high up on the mountains in hollow trees. One old fellow declared he had found the young in such places. As I had previously noticed the birds flying about high overhead at dusk I resolved to look into the matter and spent many hours searching for them in the woods, but without success.

It seems hardly likely that these birds should nest in hollow trees, but there is some evidence to indicate that they breed somewhere in the mountains, perhaps in holes or crevices in the rocks or under large stones. Dr. Joseph Grinnell (1897b) says that the Indians hear them " at night passing high over the mountains and islands." And Mr. W. L. Dawson (1909) writes:

At Glacier, on the North Fork of the Nooksack River, and near the foot of Mount Baker, having risen before daybreak for an early bird walk, on the morning of May 11, 1905, I heard voices from an invisible party of marbled murrelets high in the air as they proceeded down the valley as though to repair to the sea for the day's fishing.

Eggs.—The egg, referred to above as taken from the oviduct of a bird by Mr. Cantwell, is apparently the only positively identified egg of this species in existence. It is " cylindrical ovate " in shape. The ground color is " pale chalcedony yellow "; it is uniformly, but not thickly spotted with small spots of very dark " blackish brown " or nearly black. It is too badly broken to be measured accurately. There are two eggs in the United States National Museum, collected by Ferd. Bischoff at Sitka, Alaska, in June 1866, which are supposed to be eggs of the marbled murrelet. Major Bendire was evidently in doubt about the authenticity of these eggs, but they are much smaller than any of our large series of ancient murrelets' eggs and different in shape; they closely resemble certain eggs of Xantus's murrelet, which might be expected in such a closely related species. In shape they are elongate ovate. In one the ground color is " pinkish buff," which is heavily blotched, splashed and clouded about both ends with " cinnamon brown " and some darker shades. In the other the ground color is " light buff," which is more evenly covered with small spots of drab and dark browns, also splashed and washed about both ends with " snuff brown " and lighter shades of brown. These two eggs measure 54 by 36 and 54 by 36.2 millimeters and thus fall well within the limits of the measurements of the eggs of both *hypoleucus* and *craveri*.

There is an egg in the collection of Mr. Charles E. Doe which is said to be of this species and it looks as if it might be correctly identified. It was taken by Mr. A. H. Dunham, of Nome, Alaska, on June 10, 1904. The egg was found on rocky land above the Iron River about 70 miles north of Nome; the parent birds were also taken. In general appearance it much resembles the egg taken by Mr. Cantwell. In shape it is " elliptical ovate." The color is " massicot yellow " and it is uniformly, but not thickly, covered with small spots of " bone brown " and " deep quaker drab." It measures 60.5 by 37.5 millimeters.

Plumages.—Even less is known about the downy young; for, so far as I know, no specimen has ever been taken. In the juvenal plumage the young bird is pure, clear, " blackish brown " above, except for the white on the scapulars, and the under parts are finely barred with dusky. The dusky barring on the under parts disappears during the fall and winter; usually by the end of November the under parts are pure white, as in the adult, but sometimes traces of the barring remain until February. Young birds can hardly be distinguished from adults during the first winter, but they have blacker backs, without so much plumbeous. This first winter plumage is worn without much change throughout the first spring or until the first postnuptial molt, when young birds become indistinguishable from adults in the winter plumage.

Adults have two conspicuous seasonal molts producing strikingly different plumages. The prenuptial molt, which includes everything but the wings and tail, sometimes begins early in February, but more often not until March or April; it is often well along in May before the beautiful, marbled plumage of the spring adult is completed. The postnuptial molt is complete. It occurs mainly in September and October, but it is often prolonged into November; during this molt the heavier, dark, crescentic markings on the under parts, which are the last of the spring plumage to disappear, will serve to distinguish adults from young birds. By the latter part of November, at the latest, adults are in their full winter plumage and can be distinguished from young birds by having pure white under parts and more plumbeous on the upper parts.

Food.—The food of the marbled murrelet seems to consist largely of fish which it obtains by diving in the tide rips and other places where it can find small fry swimming in schools. Doctor Grinnell (1910) writes:

At the head of Cordova Bay a dozen or so were observed; one shot, disgorged fishes 3 inches in length.

At Montague, Dixon records rowing within 10 yards of a marbled murrelet that appeared to have a school of small fish completely at its mercy. The fishes were in a mass about as large as a bushel basket near the surface of the water. The bird kept diving down, back and across, with the result that the fishes acted as though thoroughly frightened; at least they made no attempt to scatter or to seek safety in the depths.

The same writer (1897b) says:

Small fish caught by diving seemed to be the standard article of food, but dissection of the stomachs also showed remains of some small mollusks. A shoal of candle-fish was sure to have among its followers, besides a cloud of Pacific kittiwakes, several of the murrelets.

Behavior.—The flight of this species is very swift, direct, and strong, usually close to the water when on its feeding grounds, but at a great height in the air when flying inland. Its wings are small but very stiff and powerful, and they vibrate very rapidly. Like most of the Alcidae it is equipped with wings as small as it can use to propel it through the air and as large as it can use to advantage under water; they are a compromise between the requirements of the two media, but enable it to actually fly, and swiftly too, in either. The marbled murrelet rises quickly and easily from the surface of smooth water and dashes away, gaining full speed very quickly. Doctor Grinnell (1897b) estimated the speed as " not less than 100 miles an hour," and says:

The murrelets have a peculiar habit when rising from the surface of the water of falling back and touching the water two or three times in rapid succession before gaining full headway. These same birds have another strange habit of flying at great heights over the ocean and even across large islands. They become active and fly in this manner at dusk, and may be seen leaving the water in pairs, and starting upward uttering their wild, weird cries.

The marbled murrelet dives so quickly that it is almost impossible to see how it is done and under water it uses both wings and feet to produce its rapid locomotion. Doctor Grinnell (1897b) made some interesting observations on a wounded bird at close range, of which he writes:

The feet seemed not of very great aid in diving, except at change of direction, when they were moved in alternate rhythm. The wings gave regular strokes, about two beats in three seconds. To my wonder most of the diving horizontally was performed with the belly upward and back downward; that is, in a reverse position to that during flight through air. I do not think this was an exceptional case on account of the disablement of the bird, and on second thought it does not seem strange.

The reason for this is obvious when we realize that the buoyancy of the bird's body tends to bring it to the surface and that it can not fly downward in the water except by exerting its force in a direction exactly opposite to that required to rise in the air.

Winter.—The winter range of the marbled murrelet extends from its breeding grounds in Washington all along the coast to southern

California. It is particularly abundant in winter about Puget Sound and the straits and channels around Vancouver Island. Mr. Dawson (1909) has sketched a vivid picture of it in its winter home, from which I quote as follows:

To be sure it is a bit chilly out and there are spiteful dabs of rain between whiles, but the forward deck is clear, for the helpless ones are crowded in the cabin. We may have the bow to ourselves and what a glorious company of sights and sounds there are about us. Every blue-gray wave has 'a voice, and the blue-gray wind tries every tone with its deft fingers. But there are those who enjoy the conflict of the storm even more than we. Above the whining of the waters and the crashing of the prow come shrill exultant cries, *Meer-meer-meer-meer.* The murrelets are in their element, and they shriek to each other across the dancing waters like Tritons at play. Perhaps association will partly account for it, but somehow the note of the marbled murrelet seems of itself to suggest piping gales and rugged cliffs beset by pounding surf. It is the articulate cry of the sea in a royal mood.

DISTRIBUTION.

Breeding range.—Coasts and islands of the North Pacific. From the eastern Aleutian Islands (Unalaska Island) along the coast of southern Alaska (Kodiak Island, Prince Williams Sound, and Sitkan district) and south along the coast of British Columbia (Queen Charlotte Islands, and Vancouver Island) to northwestern Washington (Puget Sound region). This is the summer distribution and the species is assumed to breed within this range. Probably Bering Sea should be included, but records are not conclusive. Dunham reports eggs take near Nome, Alaska. Also said to breed in the Kurile Islands.

Winter range.—Southward from British Columbia (Burrard Inlet, Departure Bay, and Barkley Sound) and Washington (Puget Sound) to California (San Francisco Bay, Santa Cruz, Monterey Bay, and Santa Barbara).

Spring migration.—Birds were noted at Point Pinos, California, flying northward, late in February and through March, the last seen April 2. In southeastern Alaska one was shot on Frederick Sound, April 10, and several were seen April 17 at Admiralty Island.

Fall migration.—A bird was taken near Nushagak (north of the Alaska Peninsula) on September 5, and several supposed to be marbled murrelets seen on Kanatak Bay as late as October 13. In the Prince William Sound region the last specimen was taken August 13, while they remained common on Baranof Island, Sitkan district, until August 27. One was taken in Sitka Bay, October 2. Off Point Pinos, California, the first migrants were taken June 22, 1907 (adult) and June 29, 1907 (immature). In 1894 they first appeared early in July. At Santa Barbara a bird was found dead July 30.

Casual records.—Koren saw a pair and shot one at Idlidlja Island, near Koliutschin Bay, northeastern Siberia.

Egg dates.—Howcan, Alaska; 1 record, May 23. Near Nome, Alaska: 1 record, June 10.

BRACHYRAMPHUS BREVIROSTRIS (Vigors).

KITTLITZ'S MURRELET.

HABITS.

Until within recent years this murrelet has always been considered a very rare bird in American waters. Mr. E. W. Nelson (1887) secured the " first example of this rare bird known to exist in any American museum—in Unalaska Harbor the last of May, 1877. The birds were in company with *S. antiquus* and *B. marmoratus*, and, like the latter, were not shy. Their habits appeared to be the same, all feeding upon small crustacea. These three species kept about the outer bays all the last half of May, but about the first of June became scarce, as they sought their breeding places. Since my capture Mr. Turner has taken another specimen in the Aleutian Islands, and the species may be found more common there when the islands have been more thoroughly explored." Mr. Turner's (1886) bird was taken in the same region on April 24, 1879, and he " observed several of these birds to the westward of Unalashka Island. They were not rare on Amchitka Island and in the neighborhood of the Old Harbor, on Atkha Island." These birds were probably migrants from a winter home somewhere on the Asiatic side of the Pacific Ocean to their breeding grounds on the south side of the Alaska Peninsula. We spent the whole month of June, in 1911, cruising the whole length of the Aleutian chain and visiting many of the islands, without seeing a single Kittlitz's murrelet, or anything that looked like one, though we were constantly on the lookout for them.

The Alexander Alaska Expedition of 1907 deserves the credit for discovering the center of abundance of this species (which can now no longer be considered very rare) in Glacier Bay and vicinity. Dr. Joseph Grinnell (1909) quotes Mr. Dixon's notes, as follows:

We saw at least 500 of these gray murrelets in one flock. They were feeding in the channels among the numerous islands that lie near the mouth of the bay. Their principal diet was a slippery, sluglike animal about an inch long. A number of immature birds were seen, but they formed only a small proportion of the whole. These murrelets get off the water far more rapidly than do the marbled murrelets. They seem to come up flying. Their flight is much swifter than the other murrelets and they were much wilder. A large flock started by us and we began shooting. Sometimes we would drop a bird and all the rest of the flock would settle right down, so that we thought we had killed the whole bunch until we came to pick them up.

Nesting.—For what we know about the breeding habits of Kittlitz's murrelet we are indebted to Col. John E. Thayer (1914), who has what are probably the only authentic eggs of this rare species in existence. The eggs were collected by Mr. Frank E. Kleinschmidt in May and June, 1913, in the vicinity of Pavloff Bay, which " is near the west end and on the south side of the Alaska Peninsula, a little northwest of the Shumagin Islands." He publishes Mr. Kleinschmidt's notes in full, from which I quote the following:

Eight years ago when I shot my first Kittlitz murrelet in the ice pack of Bering Sea, an Eskimo, looking at the bird, said, " Him lay egg way up in snow on mountain." I ridiculed the idea then of this bird laying its egg in the snow far from the sea on the mountain side, but, keeping a constant lookout, expected to find its breeding place on the rocky islands of Alaska or Siberia, perhaps in company with the auks and murres. Now, however, I found the Eskimo's words corroborated and the murrelet's solitary egg laid in just such a strange place as he described. I inclose a photograph marking the spot where I found it, and this egg also.

During my recent expedition I spent the time between the first and middle of May cruising in Chatham Strait, Icy Strait, and Glacier Bay. Among other specimens we collected quite a few marbled murrelets and also several Kittlitz murrelets. It was the height of the breeding season of these two species, for we found in every specimen fully or partly formed eggs, most of which, however, were broken in the collecting. However, I preserved, of the Kittlitz murrelet, one fully formed and colored egg, besides several broken ones.

On June 5, while lying at anchor off Pavloff Bay, Alaska Peninsula, a trapper and miner came aboard, who saw me preparing skins of the Kittlitz and marbled murrelets. He recognized the Kittlitz immediately, and said it was strange that a water bird should lay its egg far inland, high on the mountain sides, in the snow. Upon closer questioning he said he meant that the egg was laid, not on the snow, but far above timber line on the mountain, in bare spots, amid the snow. In the 16 years he had been there he had found but two eggs, but he remembered well the eggs and bird. I had him describe the egg carefully before I showed him the one I possessed, and it tallied with his description.

On June 6 I was hunting brown bear for the Carnegie Museum, in company with this man, and while crossing a high divide, a Kittlitz murrelet flew past us. " There is your bird," called the trapper immediately; " it has a nest here somewhere." On June 10 I saw with my glasses a she-bear and two cubs far up in the snow of Mount Pavloff. To reach them I had to climb several miles inside the snow line, with only here and there a few bare spots to give me a much-desired walking ground, when close to my feet rose a Kittlitz murrelet. There on the bare lava, without even the pretension of a hollow, lay a single egg.

Eggs.—Colonel Thayer (1914) describes the eggs as follows:

The egg found on the ground, on the side of Pavloff Mountain, June 10, 1913, has a ground color of olive lake, dotted all over with different-sized markings of dark and light brown. It measures, in inches, 2.29 by 1.40. The other egg, taken from the oviduct of a bird May 29, 1913, is perfectly formed, and was evidently about to be laid. Its ground color is yellow glaucous, with dark-brown spots over the whole egg. The measurements are 2.46 by 1.45. The second egg taken from a bird's oviduct was so broken that it could not be measured, but color and markings are the same as in the one last described. I have both the females from which these eggs were taken.

Plumage.—The downy young still remains unknown, and the sequence of plumages to maturity is not fully demonstrated by specimens, but from what we have seen it is fair to assume that the changes are similar to those of the closely related marbled murrelet.

The adult has two·seasonal molts similar to those of the preceding species. I have not seen enough specimens to work out the dates of the molts satisfactorily. Mr. Turner's bird, collected April 24, is still in full winter plumage, and so is a specimen in the United States National Museum, taken April 3, but possibly these may be young birds. The complete molt in the late summer or early fall produces a winter plumage entirely unlike the nuptial plumage and much like the winter plumage of the marbled murrelet; Kittlitz's murrelet in this plumage may, however, be distinguished by its much smaller and shorter bill and by having much more white on the sides of the head and neck, which includes the lores, extends above the eyes, and forms a broad collar nearly around the neck, interrupted by only a narrow, median, dusky band. The prenuptial molt apparently involves all of the contour feathers, the scapulars, and perhaps some of the wing coverts. This produces the beautifully mottled nuptial plumage, which is worn through the spring and summer. Nearly all of the specimens in collections are in this plumage.

Food.—The two statements included in the above quotations tell all that we know about the food of this species. Mr. Nelson (1887) remarked that it appeared to be " feeding upon small crustacea." Doctor Grinnell (1909), in Mr. Dixon's notes, states that the " principal diet was a slippery, slug-like animal about an inch long."

Winter.—Regarding the fall migration and the winter home of Kittlitz's murrelet very little is known. It certainly does not migrate south along the American coast. The indications are that it is a bird of Asiatic origin, which has extended its summer range northward to the Arctic coast of Siberia and eastward through the Aleutian Islands to its Alaskan breeding range. If such is the case, it probably returns to spend the winter in the region from which it emanated, perhaps somewhere between the Commander Islands and the coast of Japan.

DISTRIBUTION.

Breeding range.—Presumably from the Aleutian Islands (Atkha, Amchitka, and Unalaska) east along the southern Alaskan coast to Glacier Bay. Has been taken in the Kurile Islands in summer and several specimens at Indian Point, Siberia. Records of the marbled murrelet from Plover Bay and other points on the Siberian coast may refer to this species. Thayer and Bangs record *brevirostris* from the Arctic coast of Siberia west to Cape Yakan, where they were seen until September 8. One was taken at Cape Lisburne, Alaska, in May, 1885. The only authentic eggs known were taken at Pavloff Bay, on the Alaskan Peninsula.

Winter range.—Mainly along the Asiatic coast, from Kamtschatka to Kurile Islands.

Egg dates.—Pavloff Mountain, Alaska: 2 records, May 29 and June 10.

BRACHYRAMPHUS HYPOLEUCUS Xantus.

XANTUS'S MURRELET.

HABITS.

This white-breasted murrelet is now well known as a fairly common bird about the rocky islands from southern California along the west coast of Lower California at least as far as Magdalena Bay. Its discoverer, Mr. Xantus, found it as far south as Cape San Lucas in 1859 and Mr. J. G. Cooper found it breeding as far north as Santa Barbara Island in 1863. Mr. A. B. Howell has sent me the following notes on its present distribution in southern California:

This species was discovered breeding on Los Coronados Islands, Mexico, by A. van Rossem April 7, 1908. A few years ago they were very rare in this locality, but at present are almost abundant. Their case is somewhat similar on Santa Barbara and Anacapa Islands, California, for at the latter place during May, 1913, Mr. van Rossem found them to be fairly common. Hence it would seem that the species is increasing in numbers at the northern end of its range. The presence of foxes on the larger islands of southern California precludes them from breeding on these, but I believe that they may breed on whatever islets near them offer suitable conditions.

Los Coronados Islands, one of the principal breeding places of Xantus's murrelet, are briefly described by Mr. Howard W. Wright (1909), as follows:

These islands are located about 15 miles south of San Diego. There are three main islands: North, Middle, and South. Their names indicate their position. They are very high and rugged, the highest being 672 feet and about a mile long. The only good harbor, and that only suitable for small craft, is the little bay on the northeast side of South Island in which we anchored. There is no water on these islands. Consequently, there is little vegetation—cactus and ice plant being the most abundant, though there was some kind of a scraggly bush scattered throughout.

Nesting.—Mr. Howell's notes refer to the nesting habits of the species on these islands as follows:

Hypoleueus begins to lay about the middle of March, and I have found well-incubated eggs as late as July 11, so it would seem that two sets each year is the rule. The favorite nesting site is a cranny among loose bowlders, but nearly as frequently one finds them back under a rock where it was necessary for them to scratch away a little of the loose dirt in order to gain entrance. Dark pockets of caves are also used, and I have even found them in slight hollows made by the birds themselves beneath dense bushes on the hillsides, but I have never known a bird of this species to occupy a burrow in soft ground. One egg is nearly as often found as two, but this is frequently addled, and I believe that the larger number constitutes the normal set. Nests are located from a couple of feet above high-water mark to the very tops of the islands. No material is used in construction, and a surprising number of eggs are cracked by the sharp rocks with which they come in contact.

Mr. Henry B. Kaeding (1905) reports this species as—

fairly common on and about Todos Santos, San Martin, San Geronimo, and San Benitos Islands, breeding most accessibly on San Benitos, where, in addition to nesting in the crannies in the cliffs, the nest is often placed under the foliage of the maguey (*Agave shawi*), on the sandy slopes facing the sea. The eggs, taken March 27, were slightly incubated.

Xantus's murrelet is credited with raising two broods in a season. Mr. Howell (1910) says:

From my observations, it seems to be beyond doubt that these birds nest twice during the year, once toward the last of March, as has been proved time and again, and once more during the middle of June; for I found fully as many of their eggs at this latter date as did Mr. P. I. Osburn earlier in the season. Mr. Osburn has done considerable collecting here within the last few years, and spent four days with me during June. I have even taken half-incubated eggs from under the sitting bird as late as July 11, and it seems hardly likely that one nesting could straggle along continuously from March until July. And besides, no ornithologist has ever taken eggs of this species in May, as far as I can find out, and there are plenty of them who have visited the islands in that month in order to collect eggs of the other kinds of birds that are found nesting here.

Eggs.—Either one or two eggs constitutes a full set. In sets of two the eggs are often very different in color, suggesting the possibility that they may have been laid by two birds. Often one of the two eggs is infertile. Mr. Howell says that 48 hours elapse between the laying of the two eggs. The eggs are subject to great variations in color and markings. Mr. Howell has handled a large series of these eggs and writes to me that—

None of our sea birds except the murre exhibits as much variation in their eggs as does *hypoleucus*. Those even of the same set run from an almost solid dark chocolate to a plain sky blue with a very few spots, but the majority have a sea green or drab ground color with a great variety of brown and lavender cloudings, spots, and blotches. It is but rarely that both eggs of a set are of the chocolate type.

Three eggs in the Thayer colection are elliptical ovate in shape, smooth and somewhat glossy. One is "pale pinkish buff," finely spotted over the entire surface and heavily blotched about the larger end with various shades of "sepia" and other dark browns, with numerous underlying spots of lilac and light drab. Another is light "buffy brown," very finely sprinkled and conspicuously scrawled with the above colors. Still another is "wood brown," finely sprinkled with reddish-brown dots which are thickly concentrated into a dense ring of dark brown and reddish brown dots near the large end. The measurements of 152 eggs, furnished by Mr. Howell, vary in length from 58.5 to 49, in breadth from 38.3 to 33, and average 53.5 by 36 millimeters.

The period of incubation does not seem to be known, but this duty is evidently performed by both sexes. Mr. Howell (1910) says:

The old birds not engaged in incubation spend the entire day at sea and are not to be seen near the islands. These return after dark, when their mates leave for the feeding grounds, and in their turns, reseek the burrows just before the first gray lights of morning.

Young.—When first hatched the young murrelet remains in the nesting site for perhaps two or three days, never more than four days, according to several good observers. As soon as the young bird is strong enough, perhaps soon after its down is thoroughly dry, it is conducted by its parents to the water and led away to sea. It seems remarkable that such tender young can stand the buffeting that they must endure in a rough sea and many of them must lose their lives in finding their way through the breakers which surround their rocky birthplace, but perhaps they are safer at sea than on land. Mr. Howell writes me, on this subject, as follows:

When the eggs are once pipped they show amazing vitality. A set that was rescued by A. van Rossem and me after having been deserted by the parents among the cold rocks for 36 hours hatched out two lusty youngsters and these we succeeded in keeping alive for several days on a diet of hardboiled egg. When we substituted bits of fish for this, one died. The other crawled out of the tent, tumbled down a cliff, and when discovered, was making his way out to sea with all speed. They are surely made for swimming for the tarsus when one day old is equal to that of the adults. When in the downy stage they present the most attractive appearance of any bird that I know and are truly full of life, hopping up and down and flapping their little wings from pure joy of life. Upon being placed in the water at the age of two days they at once made themselves thoroughly at home. They can then swim as fast as a man usually walks and dive at the slightest suspicion of danger, swimming for several yards beneath the surface. A large fish rose to one of them twice and the little fellow cleverly dodged him. No one as far as I know has ever taken a young *hypoleucus* on land that was more than a few days old. Twelve that I kept under observation were taken out to sea before they were 4 days old. H. Wright shot a downy young beside an adult several miles from land, and others have observed them. How they reach the water is a question, for a murrelet's bill is not made to carry anything so bulky and they could not be carried on the old bird's back. Many must fall a prey to large fish during the first couple of weeks of their life and many more die of exposure during heavy winds. Their down, although very dense, soon becomes water-soaked and it seems that their only salvation would be to climb upon their parent's back and dry themselves in the sun.

Plumages.—The downy young murrelet is thickly and warmly clad in soft down of fine texture, which is particularly dense on the lower parts, so that it is well equipped for swimming at an early age. The upper parts are "sooty black," blacker on the head and more sooty on the back; this color extends down on the sides of the head to include the lores and a space below the eyes; it also includes the sides of the neck and the flanks. There is a small white spot above and another below the eye. The under parts are pure white from the chin to the belly and grayish white posteriorly.

I have never seen any specimens showing the change from the downy young to the first winter plumage, nor have I been able to detect any difference between young birds during their first winter and adults, except that young birds have slightly smaller bills and a more blackish cast to the dorsal plumage. It has been suggested by several writers that the dusky mottling of the under wing coverts, which is the principal character of Craveri's murrelet, is a sign of immaturity; I have not examined enough material to decide the matter definitely, but am inclined to think that the young of both species will be found to have more dusy in the under wing coverts than old birds; this need not necessarily affect, however, the validity of *Brachyramphus craveri* as a species.

The seasonal plumage changes of Xantus's murrelet are not conspicuous. A complete postnuptial molt occurs in August and probably there is an incomplete prenuptial molt late in the winter. Mr. Adriaan van Rossem (1915) has made some study of the plumages of this and the next species, which has thrown some light on the subject.

He has illustrated his paper with a good photograph showing the seasonal changes in adults of the present species.

Food.—Mr. Howell contributes the following notes on the food and habits of this murrelet:

It has been stated that the species vomits a thin yellow oil when handled, after the manner of the petrels, but from a hundred or more birds which I have had in the hand not one has shown any inclination to do this, nor has their stomach contained any oily substance, but only a clotted greenish slime and very little of that. This was no doubt some kind of sea vegetation mixed with saliva. They must dive for their food, and I believe that a very small proportion of their fare, if any, consists of fish, for their throats are not capable of enough expansion to indicate that they are fish eaters. Probably they are partial to all forms of small crustacea and minute forms of sea life which are so plentiful among the weeds and rocks.

Behavior.—In flight the wing beats are very rapid, almost a buzz, and they are capable of great speed. When attacked by a duck hawk while flying they will suffer themselves to be caught rather than take to the water. Shortly after dark large numbers of the birds make their way into the coves and shallow water near the islands. From then until dawn they can be heard giving their characteristic cry, which can best be described as a shrill slow twitter, about four notes to the second. At night, especially when hunting a nesting site, they are sometimes attracted by a light on shore. Doubtless they make several trips to the burrows throughout the night. During the day they keep well out to sea and are usually to be found in pairs or family parties. When pressed too closely they rise to the wind and fly into the distance, but refuse to dive unless wounded.

Mr. L. M. Huey writes me that—

The murrelet has a few chattering notes when changing shifts on the eggs, as one near my bed this season was watched two days; the other bird would appear just after dark with a whirring of wings and a little chatter, and this same performance would take place just before dawn. They apparently do not fly all the way from the feeding grounds as a call, I am sure to be made by these birds, is heard constantly after dark very near the islands, a sort of rolling whistle, very shrill and clear.

Fall.—The fall migration is not well marked and is but little more than a wandering away from the breeding grounds, both northward and southward, to spend the winter over a wider range, the limits of which are not well known. The species has been taken as far north as Monterey and as far south as Cape San Lucas.

DISTRIBUTION.

Breeding range.—From the islands off the coast of southern California (Santa Barbara and Anacapa Islands) southward on islands along the Lower California coast (Los Coronados, Todos Santos, San Martin, San Geronimo, and San Benitos Islands) as far as Magdalena Bay. Although the type came from Cape San Lucas, the species does not appear to breed there nor has it been recently observed in that locality.

Winter range.—The species is largely resident throughout its range, but there appears to be a northward movement after the breeding season. At Point Pinos, California, they winter; arriving July 29 and remaining until February 25; a single pair seen April 25.

Egg dates.—Coronados Islands: 41 records, March 30 to July 6; 21 records, May 27 to June 17. Santa Barbara Islands: 6 records, May 12 to June 15; 3 records, May 25 to 29. San Benitos Islands: 4 records, March 10, 28, and 30 and July 27.

BRACHYRAMPHUS CRAVERI (Salvadori).

CRAVERI'S MURRELET.

HABITS.

The murrelets of the Cape San Lucas region so closely resemble those found breeding farther north on the Pacific coast of Lower California that much doubt has been expressed as to the validity of this species, and many theories have been advanced as to the true relationship of *Brachyramphus hypoleucus* and *B. craveri*. Without attempting to rehearse the history of the discussion or to enter into details I will merely say that it seems to have been firmly established that the two forms are distinct; certainly they are at least subspecifically separable, and perhaps we are fully justified in regarding them, as we now do, as distinct species. Mr. William Brewster

(1902a) has made the matter quite clear in the published results of his study of his large series of specimens from the Cape region. Mr. Adriaan van Rossem (1915) has thrown considerable light on the subject in his excellent paper on birds collected near Los Coronados Islands.

Nesting.—The first account we have of the breeding habits of Craveri's murrelet was published by Dr. Thomas H. Streets (1877). He found it breeding in Isla Raza, in the Gulf of California, in April, 1875. He writes:

It was breeding in holes in the rocks, amid the innumerable gathering of *Larus heermanni*, already noticed. Eggs two, taken from a crevice of a rock at arm's length. These eggs resemble those of the tern, though rather elliptical ovoid in shape. They differ from each other decidedly in the ground color as well as in the markings. The darkest one is brownish drab, with nearly half of the surface (on the larger end) heavily and confluently blotched with reddish brown and dark brown, with a few neutral-tint shell markings interspersed. The rest of the egg is sparsely sprinkled with smaller and more distinct markings of the same color. The ground of the other egg is clay colored, or very pale stone gray, with markings of the same colors as before, but less heavy, more distinct, and smaller. There is the same aggregation of spots about the larger end, but not so fully carried out, and the rest of the surface is more thickly and uniformly flecked than the same portion is on the other egg. The darker egg measured 2.95 by 1.40; the other 1.95 by 1.35.

Col. John E. Thayer (1909) published a letter from Mr. Wilmot W. Brown, jr., giving an interesting account of the nesting and other habits of this species, from which I quote, as follows:

The object of the expedition to the islands was to make a search for the eggs of *Brachyramphus craveri*, the Craveri murrelet. I am pleased to write you that I took over 40 eggs of this species on a rock that lies about 2 miles from San Jose Island. I also took a series of 35 skins. We found the murrelets nesting in the crevices among the rocks of the bluff. The nest in all instances was a slight depression in the earth at the end of the crevice and generally contained two eggs, but some nests only contained one. The young take to the sea two days after being hatched. Twenty-two days is the period of incubation. The males help in the act of incubation, many males being taken on the eggs in the day time.

Behavior.—In the early morning hours, particularly about an hour before dawn, there was much activity among the murrelets, they at this time being seen in pairs chasing each other, and making much noise among the rocks. Our tent was at the foot of the bluff and it was impossible to sleep, the murrelets made so much noise; for when they fly there is a loud whirring sound. Toward the end of our stay they learned that the walls of our tent were soft and seemed to take delight in butting into it in their amorous frolics. One pair in the excitement must have hit its head onward, for they dropped to the ground with a thud and fluttered together under the side of the tent into my bed, where I was trying to sleep. I caught them by throwing my blanket over them. This is the first collecting I have ever done in bed. They proved to be male and female. In the daytime I did not observe any in the waters around the island. They seem to feed far out to sea, for with the exception of the setting birds in the crevices, I did not see any in the vicinity of the islands in the daytime. But in the early hours of the morning the rocks of the bluff seemed alive with them; they all disappeared on the approach of dawn. This species has three distinct notes, the one of displeasure being very harsh. According to Mr. Brewster's book, it seems only one set of eggs of this species has been taken and that was on the island of Raza in 1875, and was taken by Doctor Streets. The island of Raza is over 300 miles north of San Jose Island.

His letter is dated March 10, a few days after returning from the islands.

Eggs.—The eggs referred to above, now in the Thayer Museum, form a beautiful series and show interesting variations. They are "elliptical ovate" in shape, smooth, and somewhat glossy. In a general way they closely resemble the eggs of Xantus's murrelet. The ground color varies from "Sayal brown" or "snuff brown" to "light pinkish brown," "ivory yellow," or various pale shades of olive or buff which are almost white. The markings are very variable also; some eggs are finely and evenly sprinkled with small spots or dots over the whole surface, and in others these markings are gathered in a ring about the larger end; some are heavily spotted or blotched irregularly or in a wreath about the larger end; the markings are in various shades of brown, mostly the darker shades, with underlying spots or blotches of various shades of lilac or drab. The measurements of 34 eggs, in various collections, average 52.3 by 34.9 millimeters; the eggs showing the four extremes measure **55** by 34.5, 53 by **37, 48.5** by 35, and 54.5 by **32.5** millimeters.

Plumages.—The newly hatched downy young has never been described and, so far as I can learn, no such specimen exists in any collection. Mr. Brewster (1902a) has carefully described the development of the plumage of the young bird, as follows:

Two of Mr. Frazar's specimens, both taken on the same date (March 1), are young, about one-half grown and still clothed, for the most part, in down. This, over the upper parts, is seal brown, slightly redder as well as paler than in adult birds and with fine transverse markings of whitish besprinkling the back and rump, but not the crown nor the wings. The throat is grayish, the abdomen white. On the jugulum and breast the down has been replaced by true feathers, those of the second stage of plumage and everywhere silky white save on the sides of the breast, where they are flecked with minute spots of blackish. The sides of the body with the under as well as the upper surfaces of the wings are covered with down of nearly the same shade of brown as that of the crown and back, but there are also a few budding wing coverts, as well as quills, the expanding tips of which are decidedly darker in color.

Other specimens in my series illustrate practically every stage through which the young pass in arriving at maturity. They show that the natal down is shed first on the breast, next on the throat and abdomen, next on the wings, next on the back, next on the chin, next on the center of the crown, next on the forehead, last of all on the occiput and sides of the crown. With the disappearance of the last shreds of down the bird completes what I suppose must be called its first winter plumage, although this in specimens which, like mine, were hatched and reared in January and February is really assumed in early spring. After perfecting this plumage the young can be distinguished from their parents only by their shorter and weaker bills, by the darker (nearly dead black) coloring of their upper parts, and by the presence of numerous fine but rather conspicuous blackish spots or bars on the tips of the feathers of the sides of the breast and body.

The sequence of plumages to maturity and the seasonal molts of adults are undoubtedly similar to those of the closely related Xantus's murrelet. It probably does not differ materially in habits from its northern relative. Its northward migration after the breeding season must be more pronounced, however, if we are to refer to this species the well-marked specimens taken by Mr. Adriaan van Rossem (1915) near Los Coronados Islands.

DISTRIBUTION.

Breeding range.—Islands in the Gulf of California. From Cape San Lucas, San Francisco Island, San Jose Island, Ildefonso Island, north to Isla Raza.

Winter range.—Probably near the breeding grounds, but some, at least, "winter" on the Pacific side of Lower California north to Natividad and Los Coronados Islands. As this species breeds in February, the word "winter" is hardly an appropriate term to designate its range during the nonbreeding season.

Egg dates.—Lower California, Cape Region: 22 records, February 6 to April 12; 11 records, February 14 to 24.

CEPPHUS GRYLLE (Linnaeus).

BLACK GUILLEMOT.

HABITS.

The picturesque coast of Maine is deeply cut by numerous rockbound bays and harbors, protected by rugged promontories, and dotted with many attractive islands, where forests of pointed firs and spruces grow almost down to the water's edge. It well deserves its popularity, for I can not imagine a more delightful coast for a summer cruise. Not the least of its attractions is this beautiful little "sea pigeon," so common about all the rocky islands and harbors, where it skims away in front of us in a wide circle, flying close to the water, with its trim, little, black body swiftly propelled by the rapid movements of its wings, the white wing patches flashing in the sunlight and the bright red feet showing behind. It is interesting to watch it as it rises from the water ahead of the boat, flying forward at first until well ahead of us, then swinging in a long curve to one side, and finally dropping into the water again far astern; every bird seems to fly in exactly the same course, almost never flying straight away to one side, as other birds do. It is a handsome bird when held in the hand; its compact form, its velvet black plumage, glistening with a greenish luster, and its brilliant red feet and mouth make a rich and pleasing combination.

Spring.—As the black guillemot does not wander far from its breeding range in winter, it has not far to go in the spring, but it usually withdraws from the Massachusetts coast during the first two weeks in April. Probably the birds which winter here breed on the coast of Maine, and a general northward movement occurs all through its range. On May 22 and 23, 1909, while cruising along the north shore of the Gulf of St. Lawrence, we saw a number of these birds, which were evidently migrating, for fewer birds were seen here on our return in June.

Courtship.—Mr. John Walpole-Bond (1914) describes the courtship of the black guillemot as follows:

A pair engaged in amorous antics is a pleasing sight. The male, recognizable by reason of his brighter plumage—there being no difference in the color of the two sexes—swims furiously after his ladylove, at times even literally running along the water in his ardor. He fails to catch her. Presently he tries fresh tactics. Waiting till she is up and floating, he hovers momentarily in the air above her, intending to drop suddenly on her back. Clumsy fellow that he is, he misses his mark, and once again she alludes his advances. So the chase continues until at length her swain's repeated gallantries win the day.

Nesting.—Its nest building consists in finding a suitable crevice, the more remote the better, under loose rocks or bowlders on a beach above high-water mark or in some rocky cliff, where it is reasonably safe from the attacks of all its enemies except man, and where even he finds the labor of procuring the eggs rather more than they are worth, though they are excellent eating. Often the eggs are laid on the bare ground or rock, but more often on rough beds of pebbles, broken stones, or shells, which must be cold and uncomfortable nests for the downy young.

The largest and most interesting colony that I have ever seen was on Seal Island, 25 miles off the southern coast of Nova Scotia. Here, on the ocean side of the sea-girt isle, where great masses of water-worn bowlders are piled along the shore, the accumulated results of the many furious winter storms which sweep across the Atlantic, where the ocean swell rises and falls on the outer rocks and the flying spray of drifting fogs keep the beaches moist and cool, the black guillemots find a congenial summer home. During my pleasant visit with Mr. John Crowell, the lighthouse keeper and owner of this attractive island, I spent portions of two days, July 3 and 4, 1904, studying these birds. Mr. Crowell and his family are appreciative bird lovers and they guard with jealous care the " sea widgeons," as they call them, whose breeding grounds are but a short distance from the house; consequently the birds are tamer and more friendly than I have ever seen them elsewhere. After considerable hard work, crawling over, under, and around the piled-up bowlders, sometimes almost standing on our heads, we succeeded in finding about half a dozen nests, aided by the droppings and feathers in the pathways leading to them; by rolling away some of the smaller rocks we were able to photograph the eggs on their crude beds of small stones or on the bare rocks. There were two eggs in each nest and apparently few, if any, young had yet hatched. Most of the birds were very tame, sitting quietly on their egg while we were at work, until fully exposed to view, when they would crawl away out of sight; but sometimes they scrambled out under our feet and flew out to sea. I spent an interesting afternoon, partially hidden among the rocks, watching and photographing them. They all flew off into the water and swam away at first, but I concealed myself near one of their favorite roosting rocks, where they were accustomed to sit and sun themselves, and waited patiently for their return. There was quite a flock of them on the water just beyond the breakers, where I could plainly see them swimming about, dipping their bills into the water occasionally, diving, preening their feathers, or rising at intervals to shake the water from their wings. As their confidence returned they worked in gradually toward the rocks, riding buoyantly over the breakers or diving through them, until one venturesome fellow flew up on to a rock only 15 feet away and stared at me. His soft, shrill whistle gave assurance to his companions that I was harmless and one by one they flew up to join him until I had four of them just where I wanted to photograph them. One or two settled down to rest in a sitting posture; others walked about in a semierect attitude, their little red legs being just long enough to keep their spiny tails clear of the rock; others were more restless, coming and going all the time, with their feet widespread in flight and held straight out behind. It was an unusually good opportunity to photograph this species and I regret exceedingly that nearly all of the plates were lost in some unaccountable way.

Although the above-described nesting sites may be considered as typical of the species or as generally preferred by it, the black guillemot often nests in entirely different situations. Audubon (1840) describes a perilous attempt of one of the sailors to secure the eggs of this bird by swinging on a long rope over the face of a rocky cliff, several hundred feet above the sea, in the Magdalen Islands, and I have seen them there myself nesting in the fissures, deep crevices, and caves of the soft red sandstone cliffs, where their nests were practically inaccessible. On the south coast of Labrador we found a few pairs breeding on Esquimo Island, where we saw them flying into and out of crevices in the perpendicular cliffs of limestone rock 30 or 40 feet high, as we walked along the stony beach below. Black guillemots were not common on this coast, probably on account of the scarcity of suitable nesting sites.

On the northeast coast of Labrador, in the summer of 1912, we found this species evenly distributed and one of the commonest of the sea birds, as far north as Nain. Mandt's guillemot is said to breed in the northern portion of the coast also, but all that we shot proved to be *Cepphus grylle*. They breed mostly on the outer islands, which are bare and rocky, laying their eggs in remote cavities under the numerous piles of broken rocks or in crevices in the rocky cliffs which are often inaccessible. Their eggs are persistently collected for food all summer and it is a wonder that they are not entirely exterminated. We found plenty of eggs which were nearly fresh as late as the first week in August. We saw no young birds anywhere, and probably only these birds that had selected inaccessible locations had succeeded in hatching any eggs.

Eggs.—The black guillemot lays almost invariably two eggs, though occasionally one egg constitutes a full set; where more than two eggs are found in a nest, as some writers have reported, these are probably the product of more than one female. The eggs are handsome and boldly marked. The ground color is dull white, often with a faint bluish or greenish tinge, sometimes "cream color," or "cream buff." Some eggs are fairly well covered with small spots, but usually the markings are grouped about the larger end, often forming a ring, in large irregular blotches of dark shades of brown, varying from "clove brown" to "sepia." One particularly handsome egg in my series is heavily blotched with "cinnamon," overlaid with "chocolate," on a cream-colored ground, with numerous faint spots of "lilac gray." Most eggs are more or less spotted and some are quite heavily blotched with "lavender" or "lilac gray" of various shades. They vary in shape from "ovate" to "elliptical ovate." The measurements of 54 eggs, in the United States National Museum collection, average 59.5 by 40 millimeters; the eggs showing the four extremes measure **65.5** by 42, 62.5 by **43, 55** by 42, and 60.5 by **38** millimeters.

Young.—Incubation lasts for about 21 days and is shared by both sexes. The young remain in the nest, or in the crevices among the rocks near it, for a long time and are fed by their parents until they are fully fledged or nearly so and ready to learn to fly. The principal food of the young seems to be rock eels, small fish, and other soft-bodied sea animals which their parents find among the seaweed and rocks at low tide or obtain by diving.

Plumages.—The young when first hatched are covered with thick down which is uniform sooty blackish above, and paler or more grayish below. They remain hidden among the rocks until the juvenal plumage is acquired in August; this is sooty black above and white below heavily mottled with dusky on the sides, less heavily on the belly and breast, and only very finely spotted on the throat and chin. The white wing patches are much concealed by the broad dusky tips of the feathers. The juvenal plumage is soon replaced by the first winter plumage, which is similar to the adult winter plumage but with less white and more dusky; there is much more dusky on the head, and the white wing patches are broken by black-tipped feathers; this plumage is worn all winter, but is molted wholly or partly into the black plumage during the first spring. I believe that young birds molt later in the spring than adults and that the molt is often less complete than in adults, producing a variety of mottled black and white plumages. The change into the adult winter begins in August but is not completed until October or later; winter adults may be distinguished from young birds by the greater proportion of white, particularly on the head, and by the pure white wing patches. The spring molt, which includes all but the wings and tail, is considerably prolonged or varies greatly in date with different individuals. Some birds acquire their full summer plumage as early as the 1st of February, but I have seen birds during the first week in May in practically full winter plumage, and have birds in my collection in various stages of molt taken as late as June 18.

Food.—On the coast of Maine the black guillemot feeds largely on rock eels (*Gunellus gunnellus*), small fish which can be found at low tide under loose stones. It also eats small mussels and other small mollusks, which it obtains by diving and swallows whole, sea insects, marine worms, shrimps, small crabs, and other small crustaceans, which swim on or near the surface. Small fish are frequently included in its diet. Mr. Lucien M. Turner, in his unpublished notes on the birds of Ungava, says:

The food of the birds is essentially marine, consisting of all manner of smaller crustacea. Several stomachs were opened and found to contain recently swallowed specimens of *Mysis mixta* only; no other food being apparent. Other stomachs contained only a semiviscid fluid of reddish, amber color, such as might result from the digestion of such food as that just mentioned.

Behavior.—The only note that I have heard this species utter is a faint, shrill, piping whistle which is apparently used as a call rather than an alarm note. When disturbed on its nest it emits a hissing note of protests. It is usually silent, however.

Its flight is strong, swift, and direct, with rapid wing strokes, usually close to the water. In diving it flops under the surface with open wings, using them regularly in subaqueous flight. Dr. Charles W. Townsend writes to me:

The habit possessed by the black guillemot of dabbling with its bill at the water may have arisen in attempts to obtain food or to sip the water, but it has apparently degenerated into a nervous trick devoid of useful purpose, like the tail wagging of pipits and other birds. When disturbed by the approach of a boat, black guillemots often dab frequently at the water as if in nervous trepidation before taking flight. In rising from the water the feet are used as an aid, and strike back the water one after the other alternately. Black guillemots often chase one another in play or in passion, and make the water boil as they dodge in and out above and below the surface with much flapping of wings and spreading of tails as they thrust with their pointed bills.

Winter.—As soon as the young are able to fly, the black guillemots desert their breeding grounds and frequent during the winter the rocky shores of the north Atlantic coasts from Greenland to Long Island, though they are rare south of Cape Cod. They are very shy at this season and are usually scattered about in small parties or pairs, playing in the surf off the rocky beaches or even well out at sea.

DISTRIBUTION.

Breeding range.—Coasts of northeastern North America and northwestern Europe. From Maine (Matinicus Rock, eastward), New Brunswick (Grand Manan), and Nova Scotia (Seal Island) north to Labrador and southern Greenland (Holsteinborg, probably rarely to Disco Bay). Also from Iceland, the Faroe Islands, Orkneys, Shetlands, and some of the Hebrides, northern Scotland, Ireland, and Wales (formerly) east to Scandinavia and the White Sea. South to Denmark.

Winter range.—Slightly south of its summer home. Many remain as far north as southwestern Greenland (Ivigtut) and few pass south of Massachusetts. There is one record for Connecticut, one definite and several indefinite records from Long Island, and it has been supposed to occur on the Delaware River several times, but there is apparently but one recent definite record. It is also said to have been taken in Lancaster and Perry Counties, Pennsylvania, and once on Lake Ontario, New York. A bird taken at Toronto, Ontario, may be *mandti*. In Europe as far north as Norway and south rarely to northern France.

Spring migration.—Birds wintering on the Massachusetts coast pass northward in April (April 11 to 19); occasionally individuals linger till May.

Fall migration.—Fall migrants arrive on the Massachusetts coast early in November (November 5); rarely as early as September.

Egg dates.—Maine: 25 records, June 12 to July 16; 13 records, June 18 to 30. Bay of Fundy and Nova Scotia: 25 records, June 11 to July 6; 13 records, June 20 to 28. Gulf of St. Lawrence: 13 records, June 8 to July 15; 7 records, June 15 to 25. Great Britain: 11 records, May 23 to June 17; 6 records, June 5 to 11. Labrador, east coast: 7 records, July 1 to August 2; 4 records, July 12 to 17.

CEPPHUS MANDTI (Mandt).

MANDT'S GUILLEMOT.

HABITS.

The northern "sea pigeon" is essentially a bird of the Arctic Ocean, though it also breeds in portions of Hudson Bay and the North Atlantic, where it can find practically Arctic conditions in summer. It has been seen as far north as 84° in summer, and apparently pushes northwards in the spring as fast and as far as the leads open in the ice.

Mr. W. Elmer Ekblaw writes to me as follows:

If any water bird in the Smith Sound region merits the adjective ubiquitous, the guillemot certainly does. Throughout the entire extent of the northwest Greenland coast and along the shores of Ellesmereland this active, pigeon-like bird is found throughout the open season; in the open water of the sound it finds sustenance even in the dark of winter. There is no fjord so deep that the guillemot does not enter into its head; there is no promontory so stormy or so steep that the guillemot does not frequent it. As there is hardly a rock ledge on land that does not form the home or hunting ground of the snow bunting so along the coast there is no ledge or cliff that does not afford a home and nesting site to one or many guillemots.

This species has been said to breed in northern Labrador, and perhaps it may do so in the vicinity of Cape Chidley, but all the birds that we collected as far north as Nain proved to be *Cepphus grylle.* Mr. Lucien M. Turner did not find it breeding in Hudson Strait and saw only occasional pairs or solitary individuals. According to Rev. C. W. G. Eifrig (1905), the Canadian *Neptune* Expedition found this species "at Cape Fullerton, where they are common summer and winter, as also throughout Hudson Bay and northward; some were seen at North Devon."

Nesting.—Mr. Ekblaw describes the nesting habits of Mandt's guillemot quite fully, as follows:

The birds begin mating about the 1st of June; the first eggs are laid about the 10th or 15th of June, though some pairs begin more than a month later. The mating act takes place on the edge of the ice along the leads of the open water, or on the small pans of ice floating about. The mating antics suggest those of domestic ducks. It is not so gregarious in nesting time as are the kittiwakes, the murres, or the fulmars; single pairs not infrequently are the sole occupants of a ledge or cliff, but generally they have considerable company of their own species. It does not avoid the proximity of other birds, nor does it seek their company. It nests in crevices and joint fissures in the rocks rather than on ledges, and this choice of nesting place determines the assemblage of its own kind and other species with which it may be found. If the crevices be numerous, and near good feeding grounds, many guillemots may be associated; if ledges suitable to the nesting of other species are found about the crevices, then usually the company is mixed; or if the right kind of talus slope be near, the dovekie may nest beside or above it. Because it thus frequents the crevices and deep niches in the rocks rather than the ledges, it is not so readily detected at home, and one comparing the relative numbers of the birds of various species frequenting a nesting place would be sure to consider the guillemots much fewer in number than they really are; though on the edge of the ice, in the leads, or on the open sea, he would realize his error.

In a few localities, such as the southeast corner of Saunders Island, the bird colony is composed almost wholly of the guillemot, and may be very large. At this place, in a sharp reentrant in the cliff face, the rocks are evidently much transected by numerous crevices which furnish good nesting places near good feeding grounds. Here whole bevies of guillemots fly in and out, and about, in the nesting season, like bees hived in trees; but instead of a steady hum, there comes from the place the intermittent nervous, shrill, whistle much like a squeal, that one learns to know so well along the Northland coasts. Similar, almost pure colonies, of guillemots are found at Crystal Palace Cliffs, at Cape Parry, at Cape Atholl, and other places. Usually the guillemot nests lower on the cliffs than do the other birds with which it is sometimes found, but in these pure colonies it may nest far up, even to the tops of the highest cliffs.

The nest is usually placed on a pile of broken débris well back in the crevices, or on a shelf that seems safe. Rarely are the eggs so near the opening that one can reach them without a " spoon " mounted on a rather long handle. The eggs are generally two in number, but occasionally the Eskimo find three in a clutch. The eggs do not exhibit such variations as do the eggs of *Uria lomvia lomvia*, different clutches being uniformly similar, though on some the blotching is denser or more confluent, than on others.

Eggs.—Mandt's guillemot lays ordinarily two eggs, occasionally only one and, according to some writers, rarely three; probably sets of three are accidental and the result of more than one bird's laying. The nesting habits and the eggs do not differ essentially from those of the black guillemot. I have never been able to detect any distinguishing characters in such eggs as I have examined, except that the ground color is usually more greenish or bluish white; so rather than attempt to describe them, I will refer the reader to my description of the eggs of the foregoing species. The measurements of 53 eggs in various collections, average 59.6 by 39.5; the eggs showing the four extremes measure **64.3** by 40.8, 62 by **42, 53.5** by 38.5, and 55.6 by **37.6** millimeters.

Young.—Regarding the young, Mr. Ekblaw writes:

The young of this species develop rather slowly even for an altricial bird in this latitude, more slowly than do those of the other northern species. Since the birds apparently do not need to migrate south but require only open water for their winter home, this slowness of development probably does not endanger the birds. The young are fed constantly, both old birds having a part in the feeding. Sea food is all the young get; almost exclusively their diet is made up of shrimps, with which the water teems, though I have also found in their crops the gastropod, that looks so much like the ordinary land snail, and of which the eider is so fond. The young call insistently for food from their emergence from the shell in their dark, dusky-brown down to their first dip into the sea in their nice light suits of feathers to begin to learn to find for themselves. They get into the water immediately from the nest and do not return. They are attended by the parent bird for some time after. They do not frequent the shore closely but stay fairly well out at sea, usually near to some iceberg or ice pan, where the food is apparently more abundant, or where perhaps the water is quieter, at least on the lee side, or perhaps both. The young birds can not, or at least do not, remain submerged so long when diving at alarm.

Plumages.—Ridgway's Manual (1887) gives the description of the downy young as " uniform sooty blackish, paler and more grayish below." On account of the late dates at which the young are hatched, they are often not fully fledged and ready to leave the nests until September 1 or later. According to Messrs. Thayer and Bangs (1914), Mr. John Koren visited a breeding place of this species at Cape Kibera Island, east Siberia, August 30–31, 1912, " at which time all of the young birds were still in the nests. On September 10 of the previous year, however, there were no guillemots to be seen at this same place, both young and adults evidently having left by that date. At Cape Irkaipig, September 6, 1911, a few birds were observed still feeding their young on the bluffs."

The juvenal and first winter plumages are apparently the same as in *Cepphus grylle.* Dr. Witmer Stone (1900) publishes the following note on a series of birds from Point Barrow:

Eight young (birds of the year), September 23, January 11 (2), February 6, March 10, March 24, March 28, March 30, exhibit much variation in the amount of black on the head and black spots on wing coverts. All have narrow black tips to white feathers of the abdomen. None of these birds show any trace of the spring molt, which was well under way in the adults at the time that most of these were taken.

Probably young birds do not acquire the full black nuptial plumage until the second spring, but at the first postnuptial moult they assume the adult winter plumage. Young birds are always darker or show more black mottling during the fall and winter than adults. They also have the mottled speculum.

Adults have a prenuptial molt which is nearly complete, involving everything but the wings, which begins in March. They have a complete postnuptial molt, beginning about the middle of August and lasting a month or more; during this molt the wing feathers are shed almost simultaneously, rendering the bird flightless. The adult winter plumage is similar to that of *Cepphus grylle,* but it is much whiter. Adult Mandt's guillemots can always be distinguished from black guillemots by the white bases of the greater wing coverts and by the slenderer bills; in young birds this distinction is not so well marked, but young Mandt's guillemots have much less dusky at the bases of these feathers than young black guillemots, where it occupies not only the basal half of each feather but the whole of the inner web nearly or quite to the tip.

Food.—The food of Mandt's guillemot seems to consist mainly of small fishes, crustaceans, and other soft-bodied sea animals.

Behavior.—Mr. Ekblaw contributes the following notes on the habits of this species:

When resting idle and unalarmed on the water, it floats high so that much white of its under parts shows, but when alarmed or ready for a dive it sinks itself and rides low, only its black head and back showing. From this low position it dives most easily, like a flash, and with but very little commotion. It dives readily and fast, using its wings to help its feet in propelling itself; it dives so quickly at gunfire that it seems often to evade the shot fired at it from a distance, in this respect resembling the murre, which seems even quicker, however. While swimming about it has the peculiar habit of nervously moving its head backward and forward. It is less shy than most other sea birds, both on the cliffs and in the leads or pools, or on the open sea, apparently trusting and unafraid, undisturbed by the proximity of man. This apparent confidence is quite different from the shyness of the guillemot farther south in Danish Greenland where it is practicaly unapproachable.

A flock of guillemots contentedly feeding in a pool or lead is a pleasant sight; sometimes they dive as individuals, sometimes as a flock. When satisfied with food, or when tired of the water, they crawl out on the edge of the ice to bask or sleep, often in dense flocks. Once when in need of dinner, I shot 11 birds from one such flock, with a 12-gauge shotgun, No. 6 shot.

When resting on the ice, the guillemot is likely to take flight if suddenly startled, but if more gradually alarmed, it prefers to take to the water to dive. Either from the edge of the ice or in the water, one bird more shy takes the lead in diving, then a few follow, and in a moment the whole flock, leaving trails of bubbles behind. They soon come to the surface, but if the source of their alarm has come nearer them, they dive again at once, remaining submerged for a longer time. It can stay under the water for some little time, either when frightened or feeding—up to a minute and a quarter. Even when injured it dives deep and fast. I once wounded two by shot, that almost escaped, with one wing on either broken, by diving beneath a heavy, deep iceberg or floe and coming up on the side away from me. When repeatedly frightened it can not continue submerging itself and finally takes flight.

Rising against the wind, the guillemot takes to its wings rather quickly and easily; but with the wind, or when there is no wind at all, it has considerable difficulty. Under either of these conditions the bird must make a determined effort; it flutters along the surface partly flying, partly paddling with its little red feet, to develop enough initial velocity to raise it, often for long distances before it trusts to its wings alone. Once in the air, it sways from side to side as it rises, resembling a quail or partridge. Its flight is exceedingly rapid, yet it can turn most abruptly in flight, and likewise most abruptly check its flight— apparently by assuming a sudden vertical position of the body—to drop hoveringly into the water, in a manner quite different from its usual " shoot-the-chute " slide into a pool, like a ship slipping uncontrolled into the sea from her ways. Often the bird stoops so sharply from considerable heights that it drops like a meteor; the noise a flock of such dropping birds makes is like that of a little hurricane.

Winter.—The Eskimo told me that about the Cary Islands, where the water is usually open all the year round, large numbers of the guillemot spend the winter; and when the sea is open throughout the winter even farther north in Smith Sound proper, between Cape Sabine and Lyttleton Island, the guillemot frequents it and thrives. On January 25, 1914, one of our Eskimo saw two Mandt's guillemots in open water along the edge of the ice north of Sunrise Point, and south of Cape Olsen; the same day, another of our Eskimo saw a flock in a small tidal pool beside a grounded iceberg between Lyttleton Island and Cape Hatherton, and Mr. MacMillan heard them whistling off Sunrise Point. Returning from Cape Sabine to Cairn Point in mid-February, 1914, I saw many guillemots in the open water along the edge of the young ice. On March 1, 1914, Doctor Hunt, the surgeon of our party, shot 19, all in winter plumage, in open leads off the mouth of Foulke Fjord, where many flocks of them were feeding.

The fall migration of this species is not very extensive, so far as it is known, for it can be driven from its summer home only when the ocean is solidly frozen. Probably most of the Greenland birds are forced out to winter on the open ocean or around the edges of the ice packs. The birds which breed north of Hudson Bay probably do not migrate through Hudson Strait, but winter in the southern part of Hudson Bay or in James Bay, which is almost always more or less open; the occasional freezing of this bay may account for the accidental occurrence of this species in Ontario. Mandt's guillemot winters in Bering Strait, but does not seem to wander south of Norton Sound, Alaska.

Cepphus mandti will probably prove to be a subspecies of *Cepphus grylle*. Numerous specimens of intermediate birds are to be found in collections, which are either intergrades or hybrids. Two summer birds from the Gulf of St. Lawrence, which I have seen, show the intermediate characters.

DISTRIBUTION.

Breeding range.—Coasts and islands of the Arctic Ocean. From northern Greenland (Cape Union, Thank God Harbor, Bessells Bay, and Cape Lieber south to about Disco Bay), Spitzbergen, Franz Josef Land, Nova Zembla, the northern Siberian coast to Herald and Wrangel Islands, the vicinity of Point Barrow, Alaska, and islands north of Hudson Bay. South along the west coast of Ungava into James Bay. Birds have been recorded as far north as latitude 84°. Nonbreeding birds may occasionally be found in Bering Sea and on the coast of Labrador (Cape Whittle, June 24), but breeding records from these localities need confirmation. Has been taken at Gaspe, Quebec, June 10.

Winter range.—As far north as open water can be found, south to Bering Strait (rarely Norton Sound) and Hudson Strait. Many doubtless winter in Hudson Bay and James Bay, occasionally reaching Lake Ontario, and some probably occur on the Labrador coast at this season.

Spring migration.—Arrive in northern Greenland; Bowdoin Bay, May 8 (not common until late June) ; Thank God Harbor, February 28 and during March; Cape Sabine, first seen March 15; northeastern Greenland, latitude 80° 10′, June 10.

Fall migration.—In northern Greenland last seen at Floeberg Beach, latitude 82° 27′, August 29; at Port Foulke, September 1;

Bowdoin Bay, September 6; and eastern Greenland, latitude 78° 20′, September 3.

Egg dates.—Hudson Bay: 6 records, June 10 and 21, July 6, 7, 10, and 24. Cumberland Gulf: 2 records, June 28 and July 2. Greenland: 1 record, July 4.

CEPPHUS COLUMBA (Pallas).

PIGEON GUILLEMOT.

HABITS.

From the painted caves of the Santa Barbara Islands northward to the bold rocky islands of northern Bering Sea we found the pigeon guillemot, the Pacific coast representative of our familiar "sea pigeon," everywhere common in the vicinity of rocky shores or high precipitous cliffs, where it finds congenial summer homes. South of the Aleutian Islands and the Alaska Peninsula it is present throughout the year, but there is a decided migratory movement north of this line and probably a less noticeable migration throughout its range.

Spring.—From its winter wanderings, at sea or along the coast, it returns in early spring to its breeding grounds. In the Commander Islands, according to Stejneger (1885), this occurs as early as the middle of March, and farther north as soon as open water can be found. On their arrival at their breeding grounds the birds congreate about their favorite nesting sites, but are in no hurry to begin laying. Egg laying does not begin on the California coast much before the middle of May, and in the Aleutian Islands not before the middle or last of June. During the mating season the males indulge in many little squabbles and even vigorous combats. Dawson (1909) describes the encounter as follows:

A cockfight between rival suitors is apt to be quite a spirited affair. As they face each other upon the surface of the water, the combatants hold their tails, inconspicuous at other times, bolt upright; and this, with their open mandibles disclosing a bright-red mouth and throat, gives the birds a somewhat formidable appearance. The actual scrimmage, however, is likely to take place beneath the water rather than upon it; and the onlooker has no means of guessing the battle's progress till the weaker bird bursts from the water like a flying fish, and so by change of scene gains a momentary advantage of his pursuer or owns defeat outright.

Nesting.—In the precipitous rocky cliffs of the Santa Barbara Islands are numerous large, deep caverns, worn away by the action of the waves, which have for unknown ages been pounding at the foundations of these solid walls of rock and carved them into fantastic shapes. At high tide or in rough weather most of them are inaccessible, but under favorable circumstances some of them can be explored in a boat or even on foot in safety. In the "painted caves" of Santa Cruz Island, one of the scenic spots of this region, we could row our boat far into the innermost recesses of picturesque winding channels and lofty, vaulted caverns of rock. A few cormorants were disturbed near the entrance and numerous pigeon guillemots darted past us from within, as the reports of our guns frightened them from their nests in the darkest corners. We were surprised to see also a number of house finches flitting about the high shelves and pinnacles of rock in the largest chambers, where they probably had nests within the reach of daylight. In such situations the guillemots lay their eggs in various nooks and crannies about the walls and roofs of the caves, in cavities under loose rocks, in open situations on flat rocks or shelves, or even on the sandy floor of the cave, if beyond the reach of daylight and water; as they seem to find security in darkness, these caverns offer many suitable nesting sites.

Much has been written about the nesting habits of the pigeon guillemot on the Farallone Islands, but the following extracts from Mr. Chester Barlow's (1894) writings will suffice to give an idea of its normal nesting habits here and elsewhere:

The "sea pigeons," or pigeon guillemots, are among the most interesting of the birds. They are lovers of the sea and prefer the rocks near the surf, when not incubating their eggs. We were fortunate in discovering a rookery of these birds, and had it not been late for fresh eggs, a splendid series could have been secured. The hill, at the summit of which is the lighthouse, is very steep, and the cliffs at the top are more or less honeycombed with burrows in which the puffins and auklets nest. Farther down is a stretch of loose, shifting chips of rock, while near the bottom are numerous bowlders, some of gigantic proportions, under and between which are cavities in which the guillemots nest. As one approaches this rookery many of the birds are seen sitting upright, softly "whistling," but upon close approach those on the rocks take wing, while their mates flutter from among the rocks and join them. Then, by a careful search of promising-looking cavities, one may secure a nice series.

No nest is constructed in which to deposit the eggs, but almost invariably the eggs repose upon a collection of small granite chips or pebbles gathered by the birds. Both birds assist at incubation, and I have a male bird taken with a set of two eggs. The rookery described is not near the ocean, but many of the guillemots nest in holes in the cliffs above the sea. At any time groups of birds may be seen gathered on the rocks near the surf. I have noticed young ones so close to the water that the spent force of a "roller" would almost wash them away.

Mr. Milton S. Ray (1904) says of this species on the Farallones:

These birds became more abundant every day during our stay, but they did not begin to lay until the end of the first week in June. We found well-incubated single eggs as well as pairs; hence incubation must really have begun, although the majority of all the eggs we found were fresh. The nests, merely pebble-lined slight hollows, were located under projecting ledges, bowlders, or in spaces between piles of rocks, where they could be seen, not infrequently, from above. I also noticed a number of pairs nesting under the wooden platform that overhangs the rocks at North Landing. It is usually several days after laying the first egg before the bird lays the second.

In the Puget Sound region the pigeon guillemot has frequently been found nesting in high cliffs or clay banks, sometimes 200 feet above the sea, where it excavates its own burrows. Dawson (1909) writes:

In excavating a tunnel in a claybank the bird uses beak and claws and is forced at the outset to maintain herself in midair, a task which, by reason of her shortened wings, she accomplishes with no little exertion and infinitely less grace than that, say, displayed by a bank swallow. Not infrequently the bird encounters a bowlder a few inches in, and then the task is all to do over again. If, however, excavation has progressed sufficiently, the tunnel is continued at right angles. These tunnels are driven at any height which pleases the pigeon's fancy, and most of them are accessible only by rope, although Mr. Bowles records an instance near Tacoma of a tunnel which was placed only 2 feet above the beach line. Incubation lasts a little over three weeks, and eggs are oftener hatched after the 10th of July than before that date. The same burrows, if undisturbed, are used year after year.

Throughout the whole length of the Aleutian chain the pigeon guillemot was one of the common birds, sitting in little groups on the kelp-fringed rocks about the harbors or flying out around us in circles to satisfy its curiosity. We found it nesting during the latter half of June under the piles of loose rocks and bowlders along the shores, at the bases of rocky cliffs, as well as in the crevices in the rocks above. Farther north, on the rugged headlands of St. Matthew and Hall Islands, we saw a few pigeon guillemots flying out from the crevices in the lofty cliffs or sitting in little groups on the ledges among the puffins, auklets, and fulmars. They were undoubtedly nesting here in the inaccessible crevices in the rocks, where the nests of all these species were beyond our reach.

Some observers state that the guillemot gathers small stones to line its nest, but this hardly seems likely; perhaps it may prefer to select hollows in which such small stones have accumulated, but it frequently lays its eggs on the bare rock or ground or in whatever débris it happens to find in a suitable cavity. It may scrape together into a pile what material is available within easy reach, but I doubt if it actually brings in any new material. The pigeon guillemot regularly lays two eggs; generally several days intervene between the laying of the first and second eggs, during which time incubation is going on.

Eggs.—The eggs of the pigeon guillemot closely resemble those of the black guillemot, but they average slightly larger and are usually more heavily and more handsomely marked. The shape varies from pointed ovate to elongate ovate. The ground color varies from "pale glaucous green" to greenish white, bluish white, or pure

white. The eggs are usually heavily spotted or boldly blotched with
the darkest shades of brown or black; also with underlying spots
and blotches of variout shades of drab, gray, lilac, or lavender, producing very pretty effects; many eggs are less boldly marked or
even finely speckled. The measurements of 51 eggs in the United
States National Museum average 60.5 by 41 millimeters; the eggs
showing the four extremes measure **68.5** by 41, 64 by **43.5, 57** by
39.5, and 60 by **38.5** millimeters.

Young.—Mr. W. Otto Emerson, in his notes sent to Major Bendire, gives the period of incubation as 21 days and says that both
sexes incubate by turns, both of which statements are corroborated
by others. He also says that the young are fed principally on small
fish and do not leave the nesting site for the water until they are
fully fledged. After the first few days the young become very
lively; they dislike daylight and, if exposed to it, will run away
and hide in the remotest crevices; it is very difficult to catch them,
much more so to photograph them, among the loose rocks where
they live until big enough to fly. It is well that they are so secre-
tive in their habits, for they have many enemies and protection is
much needed at this critical time for the survival of the species.

Plumages.—The young guillemot is hatched with a complete covering of soft, thick down, " fuscous black " above, shading into
" clove brown " below. Late in July or early in August the juvenal
plumage begins to appear on the sides of the breast. The juvenal
plumage is similar to the corresponding plumage in the black guillemot, but it is usually more dusky both above and below, the dusky
markings on the breast sometimes predominating. This plumage is
worn through September, when a partial and gradual molt produces the first winter plumage. Young birds in winter are darker
than adults, especially on the upper parts, which are almost wholly
" fuscous black " without any white edgings; the throat and breast
are mottled with dusky. A partial prenuptial molt in young birds
takes place during March, April, and May, at which the black first
nuptial plumage is partially acquired; but young birds may still
be recognized by the wings, in which the white patches are mottled
with black and which are not molted until the following summer.
Beginning about the middle of August, a complete postnuptial molt
occurs, and by the last of September, when the young bird is between
14 and 15 months old, the adult winter plumage is acquired and
old and young birds become indistinguishable.

The adult winter plumage differs from the first winter in being
almost wholly white below and in having the scapulars broadly
edged with white, the feathers of the back narrowly edged with
white and the pure white wing patches. Adults have a prenuptial
molt involving all the contour feathers, at which the black plumage

is acquired; this molt is very much prolonged or variable, beginning often in February, sometimes in January, and lasting well into June. I have in my collection birds in full nuptial plumage, taken as early as May 2, and birds still showing many white feathers, taken as late as June 15. The postnuptial molt in adults is complete; it begins before the middle of August and is usually completed during September.

Food.—The food of the pigeon guillemot seems to consist of small fish, mollusks, crustacea, and other marine animals which it obtains by diving as well as on the surface. Doctor Grinnell (1910) speaks of seeing one flying about its nesting site, " with a long yellow marine worm hanging from her bill."

Behavior.—In flight or on the water the pigeon guillemot closely resembles the black guillemot, the only distinguishing mark being the black wedge in the white wing patch, which is not very conspicuous at a distance. It flies swiftly and strongly, usually close to the water, and seems to prefer to fly out and around an approaching boat in a circle. It is a good diver and " flies " under water, using only its wings for propulsion, with its conspicuous red feet held straight out behind, probably to help it in steering. It swims buoyantly and gracefully, frequently with its head below the surface, as if feeding or looking for food. It congregates in small parties on the low rocks near the shore, to bask in the sun or to rest, where it stands nearly upright with its tail resting on the rock or sits upon its breast in a more restful attitude. Its feet are strong enough for it to stand upon and it can walk about quite freely.

The only notes which I have heard it utter are a faint, shrill, whistling call note and a hissing note of angry protest when disturbed on its nest. Nelson (1887) says:

Their common note is a low piping whistle, and Dr. Bean heard them uttering calls like the chipping of a sparrow.

The pigeon guillemot is associated on its breeding grounds with a great variety of other species, practically all of the seabirds of the Pacific coast, among which it seems to be always a peaceful and harmless neighbor. It never seems to disturb the eggs or young of other species. Its own eggs and young are usually too well concealed in the crevices among the rocks for the gulls to find them. According to Prof. Harold Heath (1915), these birds suffer greatly from the depredations of the northwestern crow, on Forrester Island, Alaska, for he observed that—

Out of six pairs only one succeeded in hatching a brood, and cracked and punctured shells indicated the culprit. The natives report that the fish crow destroys the eggs of every species of birds where nests are exposed, and they declare it to be fully as great a pest as the eagle.

Fall.—The fall migration, which is nothing more than a withdrawal of the species from the northern portion of its breeding range, occurs late in the fall, with the closing in of the ice. Nelson (1887) says that, "when hunting far out at sea the Eskimo of Norton Sound find them late in November about the holes in the ice." South of the Aleutian Islands the species is present throughout the winter, but apparently less numerous than in summer because individuals are more widely scattered on the open sea; they are much shyer and are clad in their inconspicuous winter coat of gray and white. Probably many of them spend the winter way off on the open ocean.

DISTRIBUTION.

Breeding range.—Coasts and islands of the North Pacific Ocean and Bering Sea. From California (Santa Barbara Islands and Farallones), Oregon (Three Arch Rocks), Washington (Puget Sound region), and British Columbia (Vancouver Island and Queen Charlotte Islands) along the coast of southern Alaska and throughout the Aleutian Islands; northward along the coast and islands of Bering Sea to Bering Strait; and from the Kurile Islands and the Commander Islands northward along the Siberian coast to East Cape and Koliutschin Bay. Perhaps rarely north to Cape Lisburne, Alaska.

Winter range.—From the Aleutian Islands and the Pribilof Islands southward to California (San Clemente Island) and northern Japan.

Spring migration.—Migration in spring is limited to the return of the birds to their breeding places from the near-by sea. In Norton Sound, Alaska, this takes place from the last of March to the first of April, if open spaces occur in the sea ice. First arrivals at the Commander Islands were noted March 14.

Fall migration.—They desert the breeding localities as soon as the young are raised and resort to the ocean in the vicinity. About Norton Sound they sometimes occur as late as November.

Egg dates.—Farallone Islands: 63 records, May 3 to July 9; 32 records, June 1 to 26. British Columbia and Washington: 21 records, May 9 to July 13; 11 records, June 12 to 23. Santa Barbara Islands: 16 records, May 15 to July 18; 8 records, June 6 to 23. Southern Alaska: 7 records, June 15 to July 5; 4 records, June 18

URIA TROILLE TROILLE (Linnæus).

MURRE.

HABITS.

As we approached Bird Rock on June 23, 1904, the setting sun shone full upon the tall, red sandstone cliffs, roughly sculptured by the elements into broad shelves, narrow ledges, and deep crevices, which offered lodging room for countless sea fowl, domiciled in their summer homes to rear their young. Most conspicuous, at a distance, were the broad white bands of nesting gannets on the wider ledges; hovering above and about the rock was a restless cloud of snowy kittiwakes, while a steady stream of birds from the varied throng flowed constantly around it. Between the bands of gannets we could see, as we drew near, row upon row of smaller, black birds standing in seried ranks, shoulder to shoulder, on the narrow ledges scattered over the face of the cliff. These were the murres and the Brünnich's murres standing on or near their eggs in their customary attitude, facing the cliff and with their backs to the sea; the report of a gun brought a sudden change, as they faced about showing their white breasts and began pouring off the rock in hundreds to circle about it in a bewildering maze, or plunging downwards to the sea to settle in the water and watch proceedings.

Bird Rock is now the main stronghold of this and several other species south of the coast of Labrador, where once these seabirds bred in such profusion. The following quotation from Audubon's (1840) graphic pen will give some idea of the abundance of this species there in his time:

Not far from Great Macatina Harbor lie the Murre Rocks, consisting of several low islands, destitute of vegetation, and not rising high from the waters. There thousands of guillemots annually assemble in the beginning of May to deposit each its single egg and raise its young. As you approach these islands the air becomes darkened with the multitudes of birds that fly about; every square foot of the ground seems to be occupied by a guillemot planted erect, as it were, on the granite rock, but carefully warming its cherished egg. All look toward the south, and if you are fronting them, the snowy white of their bodies produces a very remarkable effect, for the birds at some distance look as if they were destitute of head, so much does that part assimilate with the dark hue of the rocks on which they stand. On the other hand, if you approach them in the rear, the isle appears as if covered with a black pall.

On one occasion, whilst at anchor at Great Macatina, one of our boats was sent for eggs. The sailors had 8 miles to pull before reaching the Murre Islands, and yet ere many hours had elapsed the boat was again alongside, loaded to a few inches of the gunwale with 2,500 eggs. Many of them, however, being addled, were thrown overboard. The order given to the tars had been to bring only a few dozens, but, as they said, they had forgotten.

Mr. William Brewster (1883), when he visited this region in 1881, found the murres still breeding on Parroquet Island near Mingan, of which he writes:

When we first saw the place the water was covered with murres, and hundreds were sitting on their eggs along the ledges of the western end of the island. But a week later, when we landed there, the colony had been practically annihilated by Indians, and the few birds remaining were so shy that I could not get near any of them. All that I saw, however, seemed to belong to the present species.

In 1861 Verrill found murres breeding in large numbers at the eastern end of Anticosti; but we saw none there, although razor-billed auks were numerous at Wreck Bay.

In 1884 Mr. M. Abbott Frazar (1887) spent the summer in the vicinity of Cape Whittle on this coast and reported the murre as "very common, but rapidly diminishing." Doctor Townsend and I made a 250-mile trip along the south east of Labrador in 1909, cruising much of the time in a small boat among the islands, but we saw only nine murres, although we were constantly on the lookout for them. All the men with whom we talked, along the coast as far east as Natashquan, told us that no murres bred there now. At Parroquet Island we did not even see any. The nine birds which we saw near Agwanus may have been migrants or stragglers from Bird Rock. Farther east, near Cape Whittle, a few colonies still remain; Doctor Charles W. Townsend in his explorations along this coast in 1915 found two breeding colonies of about a thousand pairs each.

On the north coast of Labrador the story is similar; where the murre was once common or abundant it is now very rare or has entirely disappeared. Mr. H. B. Bigelow (1902), writing of his trip to this coast in 1900, says:

We found the murres fairly common to Hamilton Inlet, north of which we saw very few. A large colony was reported to us, however, at Eclipse Harbor. Probably no bird has suffered more from the depredations of the eggers than this, which is in merely a remnant of its former numbers.

Doctors Townsend and Allen (1907) reported that in 1906 they "saw but very few murres on the Labrador coast, namely, 1 near Hawkes Harbor on July 16 and 10 near Indian Tickle on July 17." On my two-months' trip "down" the coast in 1912 I saw only one murre north of the Straits of Belle Isle and found no evidence of recent breeding colonies; there were some eggs in Reverend W. W. Perretts's collection taken many years ago near Nain.

I saw no signs of murre colonies on the west or north coasts of Newfoundland, but was told that they were still to be found on the south coast.

Courtship.—Audubon (1840) has given us the following account of the courtship of the murre:

The guillemots pair during their migrations—many of them at least do so. While on my way toward Labrador they were constantly within sight, gambolling over the surface of the water, the males courting the females, and the latter receiving the caresses of their mates. These would at times rise erect in the sea, swell their throats, and emit a hoarse puffing guttural note, to which the females at once responded, with numerous noddings to their beaux. Then the pair would rise, take a round in the air, re-alight, and seal the conjugal compact; after which they flew or swam together for the season, and so closely that among multitudes on the wing or on the waves one might easily distinguish a mated pair.

Nesting.—The Bird Rock colonies have been so often described that any lengthy account of them would be unnecessary repetition. At the time of our visit, June 23 to 25, 1904, the total population of the rock was estimated as about 10,000 birds. We thought that the common murres ranked about fifth in numerical strength, although not far behind the Brünnich's murres in this respect. I estimated that the common murres numbered about 1,400. The murres and Brünnich's murres were nesting in mixed colonies, arranged in long rows along the narrower ledges, such as were not available for gannets. The eggs were generally inaccessible, except with the aid of a rope, and were mostly on the lower or middle sections of the cliffs, but there were some which we could reach by going down the ladders and climbing around on the broader ledges. Here the eggs were laid on the bare rock or on the loose soil accumulated by disintegrating rock; they were laid in rows, about as close as the birds could sit, and usually with the smaller end pointing outward. Nearly every one who has written about the eggs of the murres has called attention to their pyriform shape, which is supposed to cause them to roll in a circle, when disturbed, instead of rolling off the ledges; but anyone who has had much experience in murre rookeries knows that any sudden disturbance, which frightens the birds off their nests, generally results in a shower of eggs, showing that this theory does not always work out in practice.

On the flat rocky islands off the south coast of Labrador the murres evidently nested in compact open colonies, as is often the case with the California murres. Such colonies were much more easily robbed of their eggs than the cliff colonies, which would account for their rapid extermination. Dr. Townsend writes me, in regard to one of the islands he visited near Cape Whittle:

On one of these, Outer Island, off Coacoacho Bay, besides the nests of some 600 pairs of double-crested cormorants, were about a thousand eggs of murres. The combined colony of these two species was crowded together on about an acre of the summit of the small rocky island. The large nests of the double-crested cormorant occupied every available site, and the eggs of the murres were thickly scattered between the nests. This was on July 14, and nearly all of the cormorant eggs had hatched and the young in various stages were clamoring for food. None of the murres' eggs had hatched, some were fresh, but the majority were considerably incubated. As we landed on the island most of the adult cormorants took to flight but the murres allowed a close approach, and, as we walked among them, they shuffled out of the way, walking almost erect and moving their small wings like arms. Every now and then they would fall over on their bellies, and they often launched themselves headlong over the rocks in their efforts to take to wing. Everything was daubed with excrement, the nests, rocks, and eggs. Most of the murres' eggs were so covered with the filth that their beautiful markings could not be seen, and the birds themselves had sadly soiled their white breasts. I counted a hundred eggs in the space 10 feet square.

Eggs.—The murre lays a single egg, which varies in shape from " ovate pyriform " to "elliptical ovate " or " elongate ovate," with a decided tendency toward the more pointed form. The shell is thick, rather rough, and without luster; the egg is very tough and fortunately not easily broken, as it receives very rough usage. The eggs are not distinguishable from those of the other American species of *Uria*, and they are subject to almost endless variations in color and markings. The ground color shows a great variety of light blues, light greens, and intermediate shades, with all the paler tints down to pure white; these blue and green eggs are the commonest types; the less common types vary from " vinaceous tawny," " pinkish buff," or "cream buff " down to white. Some eggs, particularly the palest types, are entirely spotless, but the great majority of them are more or less heavily and conspicuously marked in an endless variety of patterns, finely speckled, deeply clouded and washed, heavily and boldly blotched or beautifully scrawled in fantastic patterns of two or three colors. Most of the markings are in the darkest shades of brown or sooty black, but some are in the brighter or lighter shades, such as " bay," " chestnut," " burnt umber," or " sepia." Many eggs show lines and scrawls of olive shades, light browns, drab, lilac, or lavender. The eggs are usually handsome, and a large series of them makes a striking display. The measurements of 64 eggs in the United States National Museum average 81 by 50.5 millimeters; the eggs showing the four extremes measure **89** by 50.5, 84 by **54.5,** and **66** by **44** millimeters.

The period of incubation is given as from four weeks to one month. Both sexes assist in this duty and the male usually stands beside the female while she is incubating, except when he finds it necessary to go to sea for food. The incubating bird sits horizontally upon the egg, as other birds do, and not standing up straddling it, as some writers have stated. The following quotation from Yarrell (1871) is interesting:

It may be accepted as a fact that each bird recognizes its own egg, for Messrs. Theodore Walker and G. Maclachlan marked a number of birds on the ledges at Barra Head by splashing red paint over them, and the same individuals were found at their accustomed post day after day. Mr. Seebohm says that, at Flamborough, Lowney the veteran cliff climber is of opinion that if the egg is taken the same bird will lay a second about nine days later, and this agrees with the experience of Mr. Maclachlan; but if the second egg is taken the bird lays no more that season. If undisturbed, the same birds return year by year to the same ledge and deposit their egg in the same spot, but if the eggs are taken the birds will shift their ground; it may be only to the next ledge. It is also pretty well established that the same bird lays a similar egg year after year.

Young.—The young are fed by both parents, at first on semi-digested food, but later on small fishes and other marine animals.

When about 5 or 6 weeks old, long before they are grown or fully fledged, they are able to take to the water and they often do so, either accidentally or because forced off the ledges by their parents. Because of this habit the breeding rookeries are deserted by both old and young birds much earlier than would be expected and long before the other species that breed with them have left. During the last week in July, 1915, I visited Bird Rock to study and collect the young of the various species to be found breeding there, but was disappointed to find that many, perhaps most, of the common murres had left. There were quite a number of very small downy young which were still unable to move about much and a few of the larger young, about half grown and wearing their soft, juvenal plumage; these half-grown birds were very lively and very noisy; evidently they had about reached the stage where they are ready to leave and probably many of them had already left. I estimated that there were not over one-quarter as many murres on the rock as I saw on my previous visit, but this apparently striking reduction in numbers was probably partially due to the fact that so many had already left.

Various writers have stated that the young birds are transported to the water on the backs of their parents or that the old bird carries the young one in its bill, seizing it by the neck or the wing. Both of these methods seem improbable, and I can not find an authentic account of anyone who has seen it done. Where it is possible to do so, the young birds probably scramble or climb down to the water's edge; but where they breed on steep cliffs overhanging the water, the following method, described by Gätke (1895), is probably the one usually employed; he writes:

In Heligoland this descent of the young birds from the cliff to the sea is accomplished in the following manner: On very fine calm evenings at the end of June or the beginning of July one may hear soon after sunset, from a distance of more than a mile, the confused noise of a thousand voices, the calls of the parent birds, *arr-r-r-r—orr-r-r-r—errr-r-r-r*, and mingled with these the countless tiny voices of their young offspring on the face of the cliff, *irrr-r-r-idd—irrr-r-r-idd*, uttered in timid and anxious accents. The old birds swim about quite close to the foot of the cliff, and the tone of their incessant calls has in it something really persuasive and reasoning, as though they were saying in their language, " Now, do come down, don't be afraid, it is not so hard as it looks," whilst the little timorous voices from above seem to reply quite distinctly, " I can not, I am so afraid, it is so dreadfully high." Nevertheless, in its distress, the little chick tries to get as near as possible to the mother waiting for it below, and keeps tripping about on the outermost ledge of rock, often of no more than a finger's breadth, until it ends by slipping off, and, turning two or three somersaults, lands with a faint splash on the surface of the water; both parents at once take charge of it between them, and swim off with it toward the open sea.

Plumages.—When first hatched the young murre is covered with short down which varies from " bone brown " to " hair brown " above, almost black on the head and neck, except that the throat is mottled with white; the under parts are white; the head and neck are sparsely covered with long, hairlike filaments, grayish white or buffy white in color, giving the bird a coarse, hairy appearance. The juvenal plumage is acquired when the young bird is about half grown and is not very different, except in texture, from the first winter plumage, dark " seal brown " above, including the sides of the head and neck, the throat mottled with dusky and whitish and the under parts white; there are no white tips on the secondaries in this plumage and the bill is very small. This first plumage is replaced, by the end of September, by the first winter plumage, which is similar to the adult winter plumage. Young birds may be recognized, however, by their smaller and lighter colored bills, by their mottled throats, and by having less white on the sides of the head and neck. A partial molt takes place in the spring, at which a plumage similar to the adult nuptial plumage is assumed; but young birds are still recognizable by their bills until after the postnuptial molt, when the adult plumage is assumed.

Adults have a complete postnuptial molt beginning sometimes in August but often not until September; I have seen birds beginning to molt as early as August 2 and others which had not started to molt on September 11; I have also seen birds in full spring plumage in December. Adults in winter can be recognized by having larger and blacker bills, white throats, and more white on the sides of the head and neck than in young birds, although the latter character is not very well marked. The adult winter plumage is worn for a short time only, as the prenuptial molt sometimes begins as early as November and is often completed in December. In studying large series of California murres I have been puzzled to decide whether certain fall specimens were molting into or out of the winter plumage, and I am led to infer that the birds are in nearly continual molt throughout the fall, and that many individuals never acquire the full winter plumage, as the two molts may overlap. Probably most of the birds in winter plumages in collections are young birds, as the prenuptial molt in young birds does not occur until spring.

Before leaving the subject of plumages we might consider briefly the status of the ringed murre (*Uria ringvia*), which now seems to be regarded as a plumage phase of the common species. The evidence is puzzling and far from conclusive, though most of it seems to indicate that the ringed murre, with its conspicuous white spectacles, is a distinct species. Macgillivray (1852) treats it as a doubtful species under the name *Uria lacrymans*, but says that, in searching his collections, he finds " only one specimen, which, however, is very interesting, it being a young bird in its first winter plumage, thus proving that the ring is not peculiar to old birds, as had been supposed."

Mr. William Brewster (1883), Dr. Louis B. Bishop (1889), and Mr. C. J. Maynard (1896) all reported this bird in mated pairs on Bird Rock, and suggested that it be entitled to specific rank. On my visit to Bird Rock in 1915, 11 ringed murres were noted in a group by themselves. Doctor Townsend, the same season, saw about 15 together in one place, on the south coast of Labrador, all belonging to this form. Mr. Brewster added the following comment:

> If, as has been so generally maintained, it is simply an exceptional or dichromatic condition of *L. troile*, it is difficult to account for the fact that two or three ringed individuals had selected mates of their own style among so many thousands of the common kind, for it is well known that with other birds addicted to dichromatism or great variability, the different varieties are quite as apt to be found paired with their opposite extremes as with individuals of similar coloring.

Mr. William Palmer (1890) noticed in a specimen of this form, collected at Bird Rock, that its feet " were much smaller and less strongly colored " than those of the common murre. And finally no such phase occurs in the California murre, the Pacific subspecies.

On the other hand, Mr. Howard Saunders, in editing Yarrell's British Birds (1871), states that, on the Farne Islands, he " observed several birds with well-developed eye rings and streaks, sitting on their eggs, whilst others exhibited gradations from the above to the usual furrow, with only a few white feathers at its junction with the eye." Dr. Charles W. Townsend (1907) quotes Mr. S. H. C. Müller as saying that it " is certainly only a variety of *Uria troile*. I have been an eyewitness that a ringed and a common guillemot have paired themselves together and, besides, have seen a *ringvia* feed a young one which a *troile* had under its wing." With the above evidence before him I shall let the reader bring in his own verdict.

Food.—The food of the murre consists largely of lant, capelin, and other small fishes or the fry of larger species, which it pursues and catches under water. Morris (1903) quotes the following account, to show the apparent intelligence displayed by the murre in the pursuit of its prey:

> Mr. Couch observes of the guillemot, in his Illustrations of Instinct, " I have watched with much interest the proceedings of this bird when capturing the stragglers of a school of young mullets, and the admirable skill with which their dispersion was prevented until a full meal had been secured. It is the nature of this bird, as well as of most of those birds which habitually dive to take their prey, to perform all their evolutions under water with the aid of their wings; but instead of dashing at once into the midst of the terrified group of small fry, by which only a few would be captured, it passes round and round

them, and so drives them into a heap, and thus has an opportunity of snatching here one and there another, as it finds it convenient to swallow them, and if any one pushes out to escape, it falls the first prey of the devourer."

The murre also feeds on shrimps and other crustaceans, marine insects, and other soft-bodied animals which it finds in the sea. Morris (1903) says that it feeds " on sprats, young herrings, anchovies, sardines, and other fish, mollusca, testacea, and sea insects."

Behavior.—The murre's flight is swift, direct, strong, and protracted, accomplished by steady, rapid wing beats. When traveling long distances it flies in flocks high in the air, but when moving about near its feeding or breeding grounds it flies close to the water with frequent turnings from side to side. It is so heavy bodied and small winged that it can not rise off the water without pattering along the surface. In flying from a cliff, it glides rapidly downward at a steep angle, sweeping in a long curve outward and into a level course. Its momentum is so great in proportion to its wing area that, in alighting on a ledge, it has to approach it in a long upward curve and check its speed by flattening its body, spreading its feet and " back peddling " vigorously with its wings; even then it alights far from gracefully. I found that with practice, one could learn to distinguish the common murre in flight from either the razor-billed auk or the Brünnich's murre, even at a considerable distance. The razorbill is the shortest and most compact; the common murre is the longest and slenderest and the Brünnich's murre is intermediate between the other two in that respect. The common murre usually carries its head and neck well stretched out and somewhat below the level of its body, whereas Brünnich's carries its shorter neck nearly straight and the razorbill still more so.

In diving the murre flops under with its wings half spread, using both wings and feet, or perhaps only the wings, in the rapid subaqueous flight necessary to capture the small fish on which it feeds. Mr. Edmund Selous (1905) writes:

Whilst watching the guillemots (common murres) on the ledges, one of them flew down into the sea, just below, which was like a great, clear basin, and thus gave me the first opportunity I have yet had of seeing a guillemot under water. It progressed, like the razorbill and puffin, by repeated strokes of its wings, which were not, however, outspread as in flight, but held as they are when closed, parallel, that is to say, roughly speaking, with the sides, from which they were moved outward, and then back with a flap-like motion, as though attached to them all along. Thus the flight through the water is managed in a very different way from the flight through the air.

Although much of the murre's food is obtainable near the surface or at moderate depths, it must occasionally dive to considerable depths, for Mr. J. H. Gurney (1913) states that Mr. William Leckie has " seen guillemots brought up in nets which were set at a depth of 120 feet"; again he says "we are told of guillemots being often taken in cod nets in Loch Striven at a depth of 180 feet."

The vocal powers of the murre are decidedly limited. The only note I have heard it utter on its breeding grounds is a soft, purring sound suggested by its name. This seems to be given in a conversational tone, as a means of friendly communication. This characteristic purring sound is constantly heard throughout the breeding season on Bird Rock and it is often accompanied by the ludicrous bowing performance which looks like a courtship salute but probably has no such significance, as it is seen quite as often late in the season as earlier; probably it is a sign of nervousness or agitation. While several birds are crowded together on a narrow ledge one begins by swinging the head and neck rapidly downward in a graceful curve until the bill almost touches the rock, one after another the others follow suit until all have taken part in the curious salute, uttering their soft notes simultaneously.

Murres might be considered the doves among sea birds, for they are the gentlest and most harmless of all. They live in densely packed colonies of their own, and closely related species in perfect harmony with them; and they are often intimately associated with gulls, cormorants, and other species, occupying the same ledges within a few feet, or even a few inches, of their neighbors, with whom they seldom quarrel, and against whom they are almost never the aggressors. On the other hand, they are often the patient, innocent sufferers from the depredations of their many enemies, chiefly the larger gulls, which rob them of their eggs and young. The Kittiwakes, I believe, never trouble them. Their worst enemies are, of course, human beings, who have for generations killed them in enormous numbers and robbed them of their eggs unmercifully, as indicated above, until they have been practically extirpated in their former strongholds on the Labrador coasts.

Fall.—The murres leave their breeding grounds as soon as the young are able to swim and before the young can fly they begin swimming away from the cliffs. The migration consists mainly of a gradual movement out onto the open sea where the birds spend the winter and this may not be at any great distance from the breeding grounds except where ice forces them to travel farther. The common murre seems to have been abundant on the New England coast in winter in Audubon's time, but within recent years it has become very rare, probably on account of its practical extermination on the Labrador coast. There has not been such a marked decrease in the numbers of Brünnich's murre, which still breeds abundantly in Greenland and the far north.

DISTRIBUTION.

Breeding range.—Coasts and islands of the North Atlantic. From the Gulf of St. Lawrence (Bird Rock and islands along north shore) and Newfoundland, northward along the Labrador coast to southern Greenland. Also from Portugal (Berlenger Islands) and western France, northward through the British Isles to the Faroe Islands, Iceland, and Norway (Varanger Fiord).

Winter range.—From Labrador (Hamilton Inlet), Nova Scotia, and New Brunswick to coast of Maine, rarely to Massachusetts (one specimen in Boston Society of National History. All other recent records refer to Brünnich's murre with little doubt). The Rhode Island record is considered very doubtful and all from south of New England can not be verified, but probably refer to *lomvia*. In Europe from the British Isles south to the west coast of Morocco; occasional in the Mediterranean Sea (Malta) and recorded from the Canary Islands.

Casual records.—Recorded from York Factory, Hudson Bay, by Swainson and Richardson, and taken by Bell in Hudson Bay in 1885.

Egg dates.—Gulf of St. Lawrence: 35 records, May 20 to July 25; 18 records, June 18 to July 1. Great Britain: 20 records, May 10 to June 19; 10 records, June 5 to 13. Newfoundland: 3 records, June 14 and 20 and July 3.

URIA TROILLE CALIFORNICA (H. Bryant).

CALIFORNIA MURRE.

HABITS.

The Pacific coast subspecies of the common murre differs but slightly in appearance or in habits from its relative of the Atlantic Ocean; it is somewhat larger and its bill is a little different in shape and relative dimensions; its life history is so similar that I shall not attempt to repeat what I have said about the foregoing bird, but shall endeavor to give what additional information we have relating to the California murre and describe a few of its most striking breeding colonies. Whereas the Atlantic murre is now confined, in the breeding season, to a few restricted localities on the American side of the ocean, the California murre is very widely distributed all along the Pacific coast, breeding in nearly all suitable localities, from the Santa Barbara Islands, off southern California, to the Pribilof and other islands in Bering Sea. Moreover, the common murre is comparatively rare as an American bird, whereas the California murre is excessively abundant throughout most of its range.

The name, California murre, at once suggests the Farallone Islands, one of the largest and certainly the most famous of the breeding

resorts of this species.   These islands are far too well known and
have been too often written up to require any elaborate description
here.   But, for the benefit of those of us who have never been there,
I am tempted to quote the following short historical and descriptive
note by Mr. W. Otto Emerson (1904) :

From the old Spanish chronicles we learn of the discovery of the Farallone
Islands in 1543 by Ferrelo.   It was Sir Francis Drake, however, who gave us
the first particular description of the " Island of St. James," as they were then
known (1579).   Drake, it seems, landed to replenish his larder with seal meat.
Doubtless he laid in a stock of eggs, for a man is never too old a boy to collect
eggs where they may be had for the taking.   In 1775 Bodega and Maurelle, on
their way up the northwest coast, named the islands " Los Farallones de los
Frayles," in honor of the monks who had discovered San Francisco Bay in
1769, the same year that the Franciscans founded their first mission in Alta
California, at San Diego.   The first settlers on the islands, we know, were Rus-
sians from the North, who came with Aleuts to fish and seal hunt.   There
remain to-day, on the southeastern part of the island, the well-preserved stone
walls of their low huts, but the date of their occupancy is unknown.

The islands are formed of crystalline granite, a ridge rising many hundred
feet above the ocean floor.   Sugar Loaf Rock in Fishermans Bay is an
exception, being a conglomerate of coarse gravel standing isolated 185 feet
above sea level.   South Farallone Island is the largest of the group.   At
water line the rocks are of a blackish brown where the surf beats, and then
above high water mark change to a yellow or light grayish tone over all the
island, where not occupied by the roosting or nesting areas of the sea fowl
or changed by the presence of introduced plants.   The granite readily yields
to a pick and offers a firm footing but is rather hard on shoe leather.   Shore
lines are all cut up into great channel-like troughs, with arched grottos running far into the rock and filled with gorgeously tinted marine life.   There
are natural bridges, pot holes, and shelving ledges of all descriptions.

Mr. Walter E. Bryant (1888) says that the California murres
" begin to arrive on the island in myriad numbers by the first of
April.   Their arrival usually occurs at night, when great numbers
come suddenly, and perhaps leave the next day; especially are they
likely to leave soon after coming—and before mating—if a storm
occurs, returning, of course, later."

Nesting.—Mr. Milton S. Ray (1904) gives a very good account
of the main breeding colonies on the Farallones as follows:

The largest rookeries on the main island are in Great Murre Cave and at
Tower Point, on East End, on the rocky shelves and terraces below Main Top
Peak, and on the dizzy sides, from sea to summit, of the Great Arch, the
natural bridge par excellence, on West End.   The birds also breed abundantly
all along the ridge and in the numberless grottoes along the seashore, while
the surrounding islets are covered with them in countless thousands.   Great
Murre Cave, which runs in from the ocean on Shulbrick Point, with its vast
bird population, is a wonder to behold.   All ledges and projections, as well
as the cave floor, were murre covered, and on our approach the great colony
became a scene of animation, with a vast nodding of dusky heads and a
ringing concert of gurgling cries.   The birds, at first in tens and then in

twenties, flew out, or by sprawling and flapping over the rocks and into the foaming surf, thus gained the open sea. Some were terribly thrown about in the breakers but apparently received little injury. On our entrance the main body took flight, with a mighty roar of wings, and so close did they fill the cave that it behooved us to get behind bowlders to prevent being struck by them. Many birds still remained in the cave, retreating deep into the branching recesses or, sheeplike, huddled into the corners, where they could be picked up by the hand. The multitudes which took wing would wait, scattered over the water about a quarter of a mile from shore, until the commotion was over and would then come trooping back to the cave.

Messrs. Finley and Bohlman in various illustrated articles and lectures have made famous the great breeding colonies of California murres on the Three Arch Rocks, off the coast of Oregon. In these wonderful rookeries the population is fully as dense as on the Farallones, though fewer naturalists have seen them. Mr. Finley (1905) has given us an interesting account of the behavior of the murres in their efforts to find their own eggs, as follows:

When a murre arrived from the fishing grounds, he lit on the outer edge of the table, where he looked about after two or three elaborate bows. Then, like a man in a Fourth of July crowd, he looked for an opening in the dense front ranks. Seeing none, he boldly squeezed in, pushing and shoving to right and left. The neighbors resented such behavior and pecked at the new arrival with their long, sharp bills, but on he pressed, amid much opposition and complaint, until he reached his wife. They changed places, and he took up his vigil on the egg. The wife, upon leaving the rookery, instead of taking flight from where she stood, went through the former proceeding, although in reverse order, much to the disgust of the neighbors. They made a vigorous protest, and sped the departing sister with a fusillade of blows, until she arrived at the edge of the ledge, where she dropped off into space. Others were coming and going and kept up an interesting performance for the onlooker from above.

Then we went down and scared all the birds from the ledge and watched them return. Almost before we got back into position the first one pitched awkwardly in and lit on the edge. She sat for a little bit clucking and craning her neck. Then she hobbled up the rock past two eggs, bowing and looking around. On she went in her straddling gait, stopping and cocking her head on one side till I saw her pass eight or nine eggs. Finally she poked an egg gently with her bill, looked it over, and tucked it under her leg. By that time the ledge was half full of birds, all cackling, pecking at each other, and shuffling about looking among the eggs. It took almost half an hour for life in the colony to drop back to its normal stage.

My own experience with the nesting habits of the California murre was gained on the bird islands of Bering Sea. Among the vast hordes of Pallas's murres, which we found breeding on the rocky pinnacles of Bogoslof Island on July 4, 1911, we saw a few scattering pairs of California murres and on the flat top of the high, rounded cliff at the west end of the island, the sides of which were covered with Pallas's murres, we found several small compact colonies of California murres sitting on their eggs in close bunches of 15 or 20 pairs. No other breeding colonies were found among the Aleutian

Islands, but we found plenty of murres, mostly of this species, on the perpendicular cliffs at the north end of St. Matthew Island. Although the murre colonies at Bogoslof Island were the most extensive I had ever seen and probably included the greatest number of birds, they were totally eclipsed in density by the wonderful colonies on Walrus Island. This is a most remarkable little island, an ornithological wonderland, where 10 species of sea birds breed in countless multitudes, far surpassing anything I have ever seen. The California murres rank first in numbers, literally covering the low cliffs and rocky shores all around the island, as well as large spaces on top of it, with dense masses of birds sitting remarkably closely. They were exceedingly tame or stupid and would allow a near approach; but if hard pressed, they would rise on their toes and waddle off, flapping their wings rapidly. The clatter of many hundred pairs of wings increasing to a deafening roar, they would pour off in streams, stumbling over each other as they scrambled down to the water, pattering over its surface to join the distant rafts of murres on the water or diving straight downward and flying away rapidly below the surface. Among the many thousands of California murres with which the island was mainly populated we noticed a few of the thick-billed Pallas's murres, which could be easily recognized by their blacker heads and stockier build. The relative abundance and distribution of these two species on this island seems to change from time to time, for Dr. F. A. Lucas (1901) writes:

Mr. William Palmer notes that at the time of his visit in 1890 these birds were mostly on the western side, while on the east and south were the legions of the California murre (*Uria troile californica*), but no such striking peculiarity of distribution was noticed by our party, nor were the California murres much in evidence.

Eggs.—The description already written of the eggs of the common murre will do equally well for the eggs of this subspecies for there is no constant difference between the two, except a slight average difference in size. Both are subject to almost endless variations in ground color and pattern of markings. Mr. W. L. Dawson (1909) says on this subject:

It would appear highly probable that this variety is introduced by nature to facilitate recognition on the part of the birds, whose property might otherwise become hopelessly confused or lost. Certainly no two adjacent eggs are exactly alike, and the differences are usually so striking that a birdless ledge looks like an oölogical bouquet. These differences, moreover, are probably constant as between given birds. At least we found by experiment in 1907 that if a handsomely marked egg were removed, another of the same type might be expected in its place from one to three weeks later.

The measurements of 74 eggs, in the United States National Museum collection average 82.2 by 50.2 millimeters; the eggs showing the

four extremes measure **90** by 52, 84 by **54,** and **69.5** by **42.5** millimeters.

Young.—This species has been reported as raising two broods in a
season, but this is undoubtedly an error due to the prolonged breeding season on account of frequent robbing. Mr. W. Otto Emerson
gives the period of incubation, in which both sexes share, as 28 days.
The young remain on the ledges where they are hatched until about
half grown and are, at least partially, fledged in their soft juvenal
plumage, but they are induced by their parents to take to the water
long before they can fly. Mr. Finley (1905) gives the following
graphic account of the behavior of the young murres and their
brooding parents:

Where it was a little noisy during the days of incubation, it was the triple
extract of bedlam turned loose when the murres had young. We tried the
same experiment of scaring the birds from the ledge and watched their return.
The young kept up a constant squealing from the time the old birds left; a
noise that had the penetration of an equal number of young pigs that had just
been roped and gunney sacked. When the first old hen returned and lit on the
edge, she bowed elaborately and started calling in cries that sounded, at times,
just like the bass voice of a man and varied all the way up to the cackling of
an old chicken. After sitting there for five minutes, she straddled up a few
steps and started in from the beginning again. Some of the young came waddling down to meet their parents, calling all the time in piercing screams.
One crawled hurriedly down to get under the old murre's wing, but she gave
him a jab that knocked him clear off his feet, and sent him looking for his
real mamma. She looked at two more that sat squealing, but passed them by
and knocked another one sprawling out of her way. At last a chick came up
that seemed to qualify, for she let him crawl under her wing. The same thing
seemed to be going on in every part of the ledge; I didn't see an old bird that
accepted a chick until after calling and looking around for from 5 to 20 minutes.
If the difference in size, shape, and color helps the murre to recognize her own
egg, then the great variation in pitch, volume, and tone of the voice surely
helps her to know her own child among so many others.

As soon as the young murre reaches the water it swims away with
its parents, often to a long distance from its birthplace. Prof.
Leverett M. Loomis (1895) says that at Monterey—

young birds, unable to fly and under the care of adults, appeared early in
August, probably from a rookery somewhere in the vicinity of Point Santa Cruz.
These young birds were expert divers. When an adult and its charge were
approached the young bird would dive first. If the two became separated the
old one would call loudly and as soon as the young responded the old bird
would dive, coming to the surface at the spot where the young one had taken
refuge.

Mr. Andrew Halkett (1898) saw a murre "one day when hundreds of miles from land, on the surface of the waves with her
brood, which consisted of a single young one."

Plumages.—I have been puzzled to find any constant characters by
which the downy young of the two species of murres could be distinguished and between the two subspecies of each there is probably

no constant difference.   There is much individual variation in the young of all four.   I have had so much difficulty myself in identifying young murres, in the rookeries where both species breed, that I have learned to look with suspicion on all specimens in collections, which may not have been correctly identified.   Mr. William Palmer (1899), however, says:

The downy young of *californica* would seem to differ from *arra* in the dry skin by being of a paler color, and by having the upper edge of the white of the under parts blending into the dark neck color, instead of being bluntly and sharply separated, as in *arra*.   The first feathering to appear on the young bird is on the wings and scapulars, along the sides of the breast and across the lower neck.   Soon the down begins to drop off between the nostrils and the eyes and around the mouth and the base of the lower mandible, and as the birds get older the new feathering extends across the back, up the sides of the neck, and all over the under parts up to the bill.   At the same time the feathering extends around the eyes and bill and running well back of the eyes, so that the only remains of the downy plumage is on the top of the head, extending down the back of the neck almost to the scapulars, scattering down the back, and extensive about the rump, where it is still attached to the tips of the new feathering beneath.

The sequence of plumages to maturity and the seasonal molts and plumages are of course similar to those of the common murre; in fact the greater part of what I have learned about the plumage changes of the species has come from a study of the large series of specimens which have been collected on the California coast.

Behavior.—In its feeding habits, flight, swimming and diving habits the California murre does not differ from its Atlantic relative to any extent.   Mr. Dawson (1909) says that its " notes consist chiefly of a mumbled and apologetic *ow ow*, or a louder *arry* of protest; but occasionally the birds explode in stentorous *kerawks*, absurdly out of character with their mild eyes."

On their breeding grounds the poor murres have many enemies, among which the large gulls are the most formidable, next to man. Any of the larger species of gulls which happen to be breeding near the murres love to feed on the eggs and young of the latter, but the western gulls on the Farrallone Islands are apparently the boldest and most successful robbers.   Mr. Ray (1904) writes:

From my own observations I do not think that in a battle royal the gull with its hooked bill has any advantage over the murre with its stiletto-like weapon, but succeeds in its high-handed robbery by better control of wing and foot and overwhelming numbers.   The gulls swoop down when the murres have been flushed from their eggs and secure the booty, or a number by harassing a single bird simultaneously from all sides finally start the egg a rolling.   It is amusing to see a bob-tailed, erect, soldier-like murre with an egg between its legs and a single swaggering gull endeavoring to secure it.   Every time the gull cranes its neck forward for the egg the murre also bends with a vicious snap of its bill, which the gull is wise to dodge; and thus the birds will keep salaaming, like two polite Japanese, until another gull comes to aid its fellow or, unaided, the bird gives up the attempt. The cave colonies are the only ones where the murres are secure from persecution by these bird pirates.

Mr. Bryant (1888) mentions two other enemies of the murres on Farallones, as follows:

The young sea lions have a great fondness for murre's eggs, and as soon as they are large enough to know what an egg is, and once get the taste of them, they become another factor in the destruction of eggs. Mr. Emerson has seen young sea lions with their muzzles slobbered with egg. The old sea lions do not trouble the rookeries, but spend their time ashore basking about the water's edge. The island mule has also found that eggs make an agreeable variation to his diet. He hunts nests very assiduously, growing fat and sleek in the breeding season.

The chief cause of egg destruction on the Farallones has been the depredations of the professional eggers; the results of their work in the past have been astounding, but fortunately for the murres this has long ago been stopped. Mr. Bryant (1888) says:

Between 1850 and 1856 there was reported to have been brought to San Francisco between three and four millions of eggs. For the last few years the number of eggs marketed has averaged from 180,000 to 228,000. In 1886 two men who were left on Sugar Loaf collected 108,000 eggs.

The eggs were considered a delicacy and sold in the markets at from 12 to 20 cents a dozen. The wholesale destruction of eggs reduced the numbers of the murres to such an extent that the attention of the Lighthouse Board was called to the matter in 1897, and they put a stop to the traffic, leaving the murres to contend with only their natural enemies. The methods employed by the eggers have been fully described by Mr. Bryant (1888) from which I quote the following:

Before proceeding further it will be well to notice closely the men who engage in this nest robbing extraordinary, and the methods they employ. The eggers are Italians and Greeks, usually those who have been engaged in fishing about the islands. The first party to take possession each year manages to hold their position against all comers and to even defy the United States authorities to remove them. Being trespassers, they have, on more than one occasion, been taken away, but only to return the following year. This season the party secreted themselves in Murre Cave while the revenue cutter *Corwin* hovered about the island for hours. Living in caves or tents improvised from old sails and spars their requirements of life are few. A cotton flour sack (100-pound size) is made into an egg shirt by cutting out a hole in the bottom for the head and one on each side for arm holes; a gathering string is passed around the mouth of the sack which, when it is put on, is drawn tightly about the waist; a slit down the front of the shirt from the neck makes an opening for stowing the eggs, while a padding of Farallon weed inside on the bottom forms a cushion for them.

When sending the eggs to San Francisco they are simply tumbled into the fishing boat; many are thereby dented or slightly cracked, but they are seldom broken enough to injure their market value. At San Francisco they are boxed and taken to market.

Fall.—Mr. Bryant (1888) says that the murres begin to leave the Farallones "about the middle of September; by the first of October they have all left the island but can be seen upon the water." Mr. Loomis (1895) noted a decided migration of this species at Monterey, on August 17 and 18, 1894; on the 17th he noted that—

Many were on the water, but the greater number were pursuing their way south. One flock of migrants had 30 in it. Migration in the California murre was greater on the 18th than upon any previous day of the season. Not only did they appear in quicker succession, but large wedge-shaped flocks were numerous. A good many companies were on the water, but these were insignificant in numbers compared with those winging their way southward.

Winter.—The California murres spend the winter in large numbers off the coast of California and many of them return to the Farallone Islands or their vicinity in December, although perhaps these are birds from farther north. There is a specimen in the United States National Museum collected at the Pribilof Islands on January 29, 1874, which shows that at least a few birds winter as far north as Bering Sea.

DISTRIBUTION.

Breeding range.—Coast and islands of the North Pacific and Bering Sea. From California (San Miguel Island, Farallones, and one or two points on the coast), Oregon (Three Arch Rocks), Washington (coast islands), British Columbia and coast of southern Alaska (Forrester Island and St. Lazaria Island) westward throughout the Aleutian Islands and Commander Islands to Kamtschatka. In Bering Sea it breeds north to the Pribilofs and on St. Matthew Island. Herald Island and Wrangel Island records apparently refer to *arra*.

Winter range.—Throughout the North Pacific from the Aleutian and Commander Islands to California (Newport Beach, Orange County). One taken at the Pribilof Islands January 29 and others seen February 4.

Spring migration.—Arrive at the Farallone Islands April 1.

Fall migration.—Birds leave their breeding places on the Farallones from September 15 to October, and migrants passed Monterey commonly August 17 and 18.

Egg dates.—Farallone Islands: 110 records, March 6 to July 25; 55 records, June 13 to July 4. Bering Sea: 6 records, July 3 to 22; 3 records, July 7 to 18. Southern Alaska: 3 records, June 20, July 10 and 12. Santa Barbara Islands: 3 records, June 5, 6, and 15.

URIA LOMVIA LOMVIA (Linnaeus).

BRÜNNICH'S MURRE.

HABITS.

All along the bold rocky shores of the Atlantic Ocean, from the Gulf of St. Lawrence northward to Greenland and Ellesmere Land, the thick-billed guillemot, as it was formerly called, or the Brunnich's murre, as the eastern race of this species is now called, is one of the commonest sea birds, a characteristic bird of the rough, cold, northern ocean, following the first advance of spring among the breaking fields of ice to its summer breeding grounds on the rugged cliffs of our Arctic coasts.

Spring.—Although it pushes northward as early as it can find open water, its breeding season does not begin, even in the southern portion of its range, until the middle of June or later. When we visited Bird Rock, in the Gulf of St. Lawrence, which is near the southern limit of its breeding range, on June 24, 1904, the breeding season was well under way, but all the eggs examined were fresh or nearly so. The lighthouse keeper and his family welcome the return of the birds to the rock, after their long and lonesome winter, as a sign of coming spring and the opening of navigation. A few of the birds also serve as a welcome addition to their table, for they are fairly good eating where other fresh meat can not be obtained. The Bird Rock colony was estimated to contain at that time about 10,000 birds, made up of gannets, kittiwakes, razor-billed auks, Brünnich's murres, murres, and puffins, their relative abundance being about in the order named. The two species of murres occupied the narrower ledges, which were not wide enough for the gannets, and were scattered all over the perpendicular sides of the red sandstone rock, both species being more or less intermingled and living in perfect harmony. On the south coast of Labrador west of Natashquan, where the murres were once so abundant, we found in 1909 only a few scattering birds and no breeding colonies. In 1884 Mr. William Brewster found a large colony of murres at the Parroquet Islands off Mingan, but at the present day not a murre is to be found breeding along the Labrador coast to the west of Mingan. Many years of persistent egging by Indians, fishermen, and professional eggers have practically exterminated them.

Mr. Lucien M. Turner found this species breeding abundantly on the Atlantic coast of Labrador in 1882, notably on the outlying islands of Hamilton Inlet, Davis Inlet, Cape Mugford, and Cape Chidley. He says in his unpublished notes:

Wherever these murres are found during the summer months there they breed. They select the high cliffs on which suitable ledges project. No attempt is made to construct a nest for in all the instances which have come under my observation the egg, sometimes two, are deposited on the bare rock. If the vicinity is one affording an abundance of food, many thousands of these birds resort to a single cliff to breed and often the eggs are so close together that one can scarcely step without touching two or more eggs.

Since that time great changes have taken place, for in 1912 I cruised the whole length of this coast, as far north as Cape Mugford, **and saw only one solitary Brünnich's murre.**

Courtship.—Mr. W. Elmer Ekblaw contributes the following interesting notes on the courtship of this species:

The birds begin mating about the last week in May, the birds in their best years being probably the first to begin. The mating season is at its height, however, about the fifteenth or twentieth of June. Mating takes place both on the ice and on the ledges of the cliff. Their courting and nuptial struggles are grotesque. The male is very aggressive and persistent, the female apparently most indifferent to all the male's blandishments or reluctant to assume the task of incubation and brooding. Sometimes she so effectively resists the attentions of the male by pecking and striking him that he gives up in despair and neglects her. Then she usually squats seductively before him. The sexual act seems to be of great interest to the birds upon the same and neighboring ledges, for they crane their necks to watch it, and chatter volubly, as if commenting caustically upon such open and flagrant misconduct, even at home. Often a pair, in their nuptial struggles on the cliff, tumble precipitately off like balls of black-and-white yarn. The male does not for a moment release his hold upon the female's crest, apparently determined to do or die, even though both he and she be dashed to death upon the ice or rocks below. But always, just as an awful bump seems inevitable, they separate, flying congenially out across the ice or over the open sea.

Nesting.—Mr. J. D. Figgins has sent me the following notes on the breeding habits of this species in Greenland:

Brünnich's murre nests on bare ledges of vertical cliffs (Parker Snow Bay and Saunders Island, Greenland) from near the water to about 200 feet above. The first eggs are laid about June 25. Because of excessive crowding of the narrow ledges and a lack of nest material, many eggs are lost. Fresh eggs were found about August 1, but there is no evidence of there being a second laying other than because of breakage. In other words, I saw no evidence of rearing a second young. Both males and females were on the cliffs but in what proportion I am unable to say, but because of the absence of the birds, except in the immediate vicinity of the rookery, it may be presumed that they remain with the females during the season. The exception to this is in the instances where the young are on the water. Small young are often seen on the water at some distance from the rookery, always accompanied by the female only. As young of considerable size were numerous on the cliffs during August, it was believed those seen on the water had been dislodged rather than through intent of leaving the ledges.

As there is no attempt at nest building, eggs being deposited on the bare rock, many are lost through the continual cumbersome movements of the birds. Quarrels or unusual sounds often create local panics among the adults and when they leave the ledges a shower of eggs and often small young are precipitated to the water below. Gregarious in the extreme during the breeding season, Brünnich's murres mass upon certain ledges, although equally suitable localities adjoin. There was no evidence of mating performances. Scolding was continuous.

Mr. Ekblaw has sent me the following account of the Saunders Island colony:

To attempt to paint an adequate picture of the rookery on Saunders Island would almost be futile; to succeed in doing so, would be to convict one's self of wild exaggeration. Literally millions of the birds make the west end of the island their home, and with them are associated hundreds of glaucous gulls and guillemots and thousands of kittiwakes and fulmars; every niche, every ledge, furnishes nesting places; I believe the number of birds on the cliffs is limited only by the number of possible nesting or perching places. The ledges formed by the harder, projecting strata are covered with birds; by the files of birds ranged upon them, one may trace the ledges with one's eyes as far as one can see. When the rock back of the narrow ledge is dark brown or chocolate brown, the white underparts of the perched birds form a line that is so distinctly visible that it seems like a band of white marble, between the black bands of the darker portions of the birds. Little niches or grottoes in the cliffs exhibit a salt-and-pepper admixture of white and black. Joint fissures, filled by débris or scree, form high columns of similar admixture. The noise on the cliffs is appalling; it sounds like a colossal poultry exhibit, or a combination of this with a similar crow rookery.

The cliffs resemble nothing so much as a mountain-sized beehive, with the bees swarming. When a gun is fired near, the cliffs become a pandemonium of startled cries and shrieks and screams, and a chaos of frightened forms dashing downward and outward like a storm cloud, over the ice. The report of the gun but reaches the cliffs, when the birds all leave with a rush of wings that sounds for all the world like a tornado, so tumultuous is it. In a few moments the birds return, to fly back and forth until their alarm is abated. They assemble again in long rows, tier upon tier, crowded so close together that it must be a tax upon their voluble good natures and alcidine tempers, to allow yet one more to alight in accordance with the saying "Always room for one more." As it is, there seems to be but little argument over the crowding, though occasionally there are contests for the more desirable places, and some particularly aggressive bird coming in tired from the sea, pushes some more passive one off his ledge. Occasionally, too, a pair get into a real bill-to-bill fight, and tumble off the cliff, hanging on to each other for dear life, down upon the icefoot, or into the sea. In the latter case, the fight usually continues fiercely for some time, and then suddenly, as if by agreement, it seems, they mutually abandon the contest and swim apart, preening themselves and smoothing their ruffled feelings and feathers.

The millions of birds fringing the ledges of these cliffs leave them for periods of several days in the early part of the season, but when the brooding season begins they sally out in the morning in long lines and files to the open water where they feed, to return to the cliffs in the evening. Though large numbers are constantly coming and going throughout the 24-hour day, the greatest exodus is at about 6 or 7 o'clock in the morning. Upon alighting on the ledges when they return, the birds face toward the cliff, give their wings a flutter or two, shake out their feathers vigorously, and preen them carefully. After a glance or two around to see which of their neighbors are at home and a friendly exchange of greetings with those nearest them, they face about and make a careful and critical examination of the prospect.

The Brünnich's murre, like its relative the common murre, makes no attempt at nest building. Its single egg is laid on a bare open ledge of rock, generally on some perpendicular and inaccessible cliff facing the sea, where its pyriform, pointed shape causes it to roll in a circle instead of rolling off the rock. The endless variety of color patterns in the eggs evidently assists the parent bird in finding its own egg among thousands of others in the colony. I have frequently seen a murre, on its arrival in a colony, waddle about among the eggs looking them over and even poking them about with its bill until the right one was found. Sometimes a mistake is made and the rightful owner finds a stranger sitting on its egg, which leads to a little squabble. That both sexes incubate I have proven by finding both males and females with bare abdominal spaces. The incubating bird sits in a horizontal position and does not " straddle " its single egg in an upright position, as has been stated; while one of a pair is incubating the other frequently stands beside it.

Eggs.—The eggs of this species show such striking and endless variations in color patterns that any attempt to describe them can not but fail to convey an adequate idea of what a large series of these beautiful eggs will show. The prevailing ground color is bluish green or greenish blue, varying from pale bluish white to deep " Nile blue " or from pale greenish white to " glaucous green," pale " beryl green " or " malachite green "; pale shades of " apple green " or " oil green " are rarely found; sometimes the ground color is pure white, varying to " cream buff " or " olive buff." Absolutely spotless eggs of the lighter shades are occasionally found. Many eggs are more or less covered with small spots of various shades of dark brown and a few show underlying blotches of lilac or " ecru drab "; many are beautifully or fantastically scrawled with irregular markings of " ecru drab," " wood brown," " raw umber," " sepia," or " clove brown." But the prevailing types are more or less heavily blotched, spotted or scrawled with course markings of the last two shades. These blotches are often confluent in rings about the larger end of the egg. Some particularly handsome specimens are heavily clouded with lilac and light brown, overlaid with blotches of darker browns. They vary greatly in shape but are generally pyriform and elongated. The measurements of 41 eggs, in various collections average 80 by 50 millimeters; the eggs showing the four extremes measure **87.5** by **53.5** and **67.5** by **43** millimeters.

Young.—After a period of incubation lasting about 28 days the young murre is hatched in a weak and helpless condition. It is brooded and fed by its parents until it gains sufficient strength to move about, but it grows rapidly and soon becomes very lively. While in the helpless downy stage it makes a very shrill, but faint peeping noise; but when about half grown and clothed in its soft, juvenal plumage it can stand erect and walk or run about on the ledges, uttering its loud, shrill, emphatic cries, which sound to me like the syllables " beat it, beat it, beat it." The cliffs fairly resound with the cries of the young at this season, the last week of July or first week of August on Bird Rock; it is the most critical period in their lives, for then it is that their parents are persuading them or forcing them to leave the cliffs, long before they can fly, and to take their chances on the watery deep. After making the perilous descent from the cliff the youngster is conducted by one or both of its fond parents out onto the open sea, often far from land, where it is well cared for until it learns to shift for itself. The young murres with their parents leave Bird Rock so early in the season, long before the other seabirds have left, that a visitor to the rock in August would get the impression that very few of this species had bred there.

Plumages.—When first hatched the young Brünnich's murre is covered with a short, thick coat of soft down, which varies from "blackish brown" or almost black to "clove brown," "benzo brown," or "snuff brown" on the upper parts, shading off to "mouse gray" on the throat and sides; there is a broad, median whitish streak on the breast and belly, but nothing like the extensive white under parts of the downy young *Uria troille;* the head and neck are variegated or mottled with many long, whitish or pale buffy filaments, which are soon shed. Mr. William Palmer (1899) has given a full and accurate description of the development of the downy young of the Pallas's murre showing what becomes of these filaments. A soft juvenal plumage is worn until the young murre is nearly grown, when it is replaced by the first winter plumage. This differs from the adult plumage in being lighter brown on the back; the white of the throat is usually more mottled with dusky, but there are no constant plumage characters that I can find by which old and young birds can be distinguished in the fall. The bill of the young bird, however, is decidedly smaller and weaker than that of the adult. At the first prenuptial molt, which occurs late in the winter or early in the spring, young birds become indistinguishable from adults.

Adults have a complete postnuptial molt beginning in August but often prolonged until late in the fall, by which the partially white throat of the winter plumage is acquired; the white of the throat is usually much more extensive and less mottled with dusky in old birds than in young. This plumage is apparently not worn for a long time in old birds and is replaced by a partial molt into the nuptial plumage during the winter, though the material available does not show this very clearly.

Food.—The food of Brünnich's murre consists mainly of small fish, crustaceans, and mollusks, which it obtains at sea both on the surface and by diving, at which it is an adept. Mr. J. D. Figgins writes to me that "their food consists largely of marine insects and salmon-colored ovate eggs, or larvae, not determined."

Behavior.—Its flight in the air is strong, swift, and direct, with steady, rapid wing motion; its heavier, shorter build helps the practiced eye to distinguish it from *Uria troille;* and from *Alca torda* it can be distinguished by the short neck and long tail of the latter bird. When launching into the air off a cliff or when rising from the ground or water, in which it experiences considerable difficulty in calm weather, the body plumage is very much flattened, producing an aeroplane effect; it does the same thing when about to alight, checking its motion by spreading its body against the air with widely extended feet and rapidly "back peddling" with its wings. It is a good swimmer and an expert diver. When swimming below the surface it uses its wings to good advantage and makes rapid progress.

Mr. Turner says of its vocal performances:

The note of this species is at times peculiarly hoarse and guttural and at other times it makes a note impossible to imitate when it thrusts its beak into the water. Another sound uttered is exactly like the bleating of a sheep and also scarcely distinguishable from one of the sounds made by the fur seal *Callorhinus ursinus.*

It is usually a silent bird, but has a soft purring note suggested by its name; I have also heard it utter a loud croaking note when on the wing.

Winter.—Although the Brünnich's murre often spends the winter as far north as it can find open water there is a general southward movement of the species. It frequently remains all winter in Hudson Bay during favorable seasons; it winters regularly in the Gulf of St. Lawrence and on the coast of Maine from November to March; it occurs more or less regularly off the coast of Massachusetts in winter and as a straggler to Long Island, and even to North and South Carolina. The erratic wanderings of this species in winter have furnished material for a large number of interesting records, along the Atlantic coast and, strangely enough, well into the interior, chiefly in the vicinity of the Great Lakes, as far west as Michigan and Indiana. Rather than attempt to give these records or even outline the unusual migration, I would refer the reader to an excellent paper on the subject read by Mr. J. H. Fleming, of Toronto, at the International Ornithological Congress in 1905. The conclusion to be drawn from a study of these wanderings, for a period of 15 years from 1890 to 1905, over a wide inland area far remote from the normal haunts of this maritime species, is that its winter feeding grounds in the southern portions of Hudson Bay became so thoroughly blocked with drift ice, and frozen over, that the birds were forced to migrate in search of food and many of them perished in a fruitless effort to find it.

DISTRIBUTION.

Breeding range.—Coasts and islands of the North Atlantic and Arctic Oceans. From the Gulf of St. Lawrence (Bird Rock), Newfoundland and Labrador northward to northern Greenland (Bowdoin Bay, Smith Sound, Cape Sabine to 81° and 82°), North Devon,

Ellesmere Land, Prince Regent Inlet (Port Bowen), and presumably Hudson Bay. It was stated by the late Manly Hardy to have nested on an island in Penobscot Bay 50 years ago (about 1847) and a bird and egg were taken. Stone refers 17 specimens from Point Barrow, Alaska, to this form. In Europe breeds from Jan Mayen, Iceland, Spitzbergen, Franz Josef Land, and Nova Zembla to the Siberian coast (eastern limits not determined) and Bennett Islands, 76° 39′ N.

Winter range.—From Southern Greenland and Hudson Bay south to Maine. Irregular, but at times common, from Massachusetts, southward, New York (Long Island), New Jersey, and Delaware to South Carolina (Anderson). Occasionally common on the Great Lakes, straggling to northern Ohio (many taken 1896), Indiana (December, 1896), and central Iowa (two specimens). In Europe winters farther north, rarely south of Norway, Great Britain, and the North Sea.

Spring migration.—Said to arrive at Franz Josef Land as early as March 9; at Prince Regent Inlet, west of Baffin Land, early in June. Northern Greenland, Cape York, May 10; Saunders Island, May 20; Cape Sabine, June 11.

Fall migration.—Birds leave their nesting grounds by early September. The last seen in northeastern Greenland, latitude 74°, August 1. Migration in the eastern United States usually occurs in December and through the Great Lake region during November or early December; Ontario, Ottawa, November 25 to December 8.

Egg dates.—Bird Rock, Gulf of St. Lawrence: 16 records, June 5 to July 25; 8 records, June 18 to 26. Greenland: 8 records June 10 to July 18; 4 records July 3 to 12. Eastern Labrador: 4 records, June 10, July 1, 2, and 11.

URIA LOMVIA ARRA (Pallas).

PALLAS'S MURRE.

HABITS.

The western form of *Uria lomvia* known as Pallas's murre (*Uria lomvia arra*) is decidedly larger than the eastern or Atlantic form; the bill is larger and more slender and the white of the maxillary tomium is duller or more grayish. The "crowbill," as it is called by the sailors, is the most important, probably the most numerous, and certainly the most generally distributed of the birds of Bering Sea. To the natives it is most valuable as an egg bird, for its eggs are large, palatable, abundant, and easily obtained; its flesh is also desirable as food. While cruising about the Aleutian and Pribilof Islands, in the extensive fogs which prevail there almost constantly in summer, we found the murres very useful in helping us to locate certain islands which they frequent as breeding grounds; murres are constantly flying to and from such islands in their search for feeding grounds, and their unerring sense of direction leads them with certainty through the densest fog. Twice we passed near the dangerous volcanic rocks of Bogoslof and could not have located it except by noting the direction in which the murres were flying. They must fly long distances for food, for anywhere within a hundred miles of their breeding resorts they were frequently in sight.

Spring.—The Pallas's murres arrive on their breeding grounds in Bering Sea early in the season, following the leads in the ice, as it breaks up in the spring, and reaching their northern summer homes in the vicinity of Bering Strait before the end of May. They do not begin to lay before the middle of June, and fresh eggs may be found all through July or even into August.

Nesting.—The largest breeding colony of Pallas's murres, probably the largest breeding colony of any kind, that I have ever seen was on the most famous volcanic island of Bering Sea, Bogoslof Island, about 70 miles northwest of Unalaska. Considering the wonderful volcanic performances of this interesting island, it is surprising that the murres still resort to it as a breeding ground, for at each of its frequent eruptions many thousands of these poor birds have been killed; but still the " foolish guillemots," as they have well been called, return to it again the next season. The violent eruptions of the summer of 1910 threw up enough material to join together the three little islands forming the Bogoslof group. In 1911 the volcano had subsided and the towering peaks of Castle Rock, from 200 to 300 feet high, were literally covered with nesting murres. I could hardly hazard a guess as to how many hundred thousand murres were breeding on this and on other portions of the island. On the steep sides of the rocky peaks every available ledge, shelf, or cavity was occupied by murres, sitting as close as they could, in long rows on the narrow ledges and in dense masses on the flat places and on the sloping piles of volcanic dust, sand, and loose rocks below the cliffs. As we walked up these slopes the murres began pouring off the rocks above us, sweeping down by us in steady streams, stumbling, scrambling, and bounding along over the rocks and stones, in their frantic efforts to get awing, a ludicrous performance; and down with them came a shower of eggs, dislodged in their haste, rolling or bounding along to smash on the first rock they struck. Plenty of birds still remained in the rookeries, however, and if we kept still the others would soon return after circling about us in a bewildering cloud. They were very tame as a rule and, if approached cautiously, could almost be caught by hand; we had no difficulty in knocking them over with sticks. When undisturbed they usually sat facing the cliff, but when alarmed they would turn quickly about showing a row of white breasts. Occasionally, without any apparent cause and even when we were a long way off, a cloud of birds would leave the rookery, circle around the rocks several times in a steady stream and then quietly settle down again. They became more restless toward night and indulged in these spasmodic flights more frequently, as the population of the colony was increased by the incoming birds. From about 5 o'clock until sunset birds were constantly coming in from their feeding grounds at sea, sometimes in regular formations, straight lines or V-shaped flocks, but more often in loose straggling masses or small bunches.

The Pallas's murres do not differ materially from their eastern relatives in their breeding habits, in the development of the young, or in subsequent plumage changes. They mingle freely and live in harmony with the California murres. On Bogoslof Island we found a few scattering pairs and several small compact colonies of California murres among them. Both species breed on Walrus Island in the Pribilof group; at the time of our visit there were very few Pallas's murres on this island, but at other times the reverse has been the case.

Eggs.—The eggs are indistinguishable from those of the Brünnich's murre, though they average a trifle larger. The measurements of 79 eggs in the United States National Museum collection average 82 by 51.5 millimeters; the eggs showing the four extremes measure **91** by **55.5, 73** by 48, and 79 by **47** millimeters.

Young.—Mr. William Palmer (1899) thus describes their method of feeding their young:

> Like probably all their congeners the small young are fed by disgorged crustaceans, but I know that the larger young and even quite small individuals are fed upon whole fish. On August 4 I collected a young murre and also a small fish, a tufted blenny, *Bryostemma polyactocephalus* (No. 43005, U.S.N.M.) lying at its side. I had previously witnessed the feeding of several others. With the breast to the rock the mother lands, and bending her head downward to her young utters a harsh, croaking sound. The youngster raises its head and, taking the fish from its parent's bill by the tail, works it sideways in its own bill, until it gets the head in its mouth, when the fish rapidly disappears. If the young has had enough, the fish is laid at its side until needed. The fish is carried by the parent with the head partly down its throat, the tail sticking out from between the mandibles.

Behavior.—In their rookeries they live peaceably, as a rule, with only occasional little squabbles, but we once saw a most exciting fight between two birds in the air, a vigorous struggle, so absorbing that they paid no attention to us and fell to the water near our boat, where they continued the battle, both on the surface and below it, with bills, claws, and wings, making the water fly for several minutes, until one had enough and flew away with the other in hot pursuit. The presence of dead birds about the rookeries indicates that deadly combats may sometimes occur.

Winter.—During mild winters the Pallas's murres often spend the winter not far from their summer homes in the southern portion of Bering Sea, but they ordinarily winter about the Aleutian Islands, where the water is usually open, or on the North Pacific Ocean. It is interesting to note in this connection that, whereas the Brünnich's murre winters much farther south than the common murre on the Atlantic coast, the Pallas's murre winters much farther north and apparently not far from its breeding range.

DISTRIBUTION.

Breeding range.—Coasts and islands of the North Pacific, Bering Sea, and western Arctic Ocean. From Kodiak, the Aleutian and the Commander Islands northward throughout Bering Sea; and in the Arctic Ocean from Wrangel and Herald Islands, and Koliutschin Island, Siberia, to Kotzebue Sound and Cape Lisburne, Alaska. Recorded in summer from Kamtschatka, Kurile Islands, and Japan (Yezzo), where they probably breed.

Winter range.—The open sea about the Aleutian and the Commander Islands, and probably along part of the coast of southern Alaska to Seymour Narrows and to southern Japan. In favorable seasons birds occur north to the Pribilof Islands.

Spring migration.—Birds arrive on their breeding grounds, Bogoslof Island, April 26; Pribilof Islands, April 1 (first taken); St. Michael, last of May (sometimes earlier); Kotzebue Sound, Chamisso Island, June 6; Point Hope, April 14 (earliest).

Fall migration.—Birds leave their nesting places in Bering Sea, beginning in August, but the colonies are not deserted until the middle of September or later.

Egg dates.—Bering Sea Islands: 25 records, June 2 to September 1; 13 records, June 18 to July 12. North of Bering Strait: 7 records, July 3 to August 8; 4 records, July 6 to August 1. South of Alaska Peninsula: 6 records. June 10 to 26; 3 records, June 18 to 24.

ALCA TORDA Linnaeus.

RAZOR-BILLED AUK.

HABITS.

Far off to the southward of Grand Manan Island an outlying group of rocky islands, the Murre Ledges, mark the entrance to the Bay of Fundy. The outermost and southernmost of these is known as Yellow Ledge; it is a low, flat rocky island, about half an acre in extent at high tide, and is covered with a mass of loose rocks and bowlders. Here on June 17, 1891, I first made the acquaintance of the razor-billed auk in what was then the most southern outpost of its breeding range, from which it has since retreated. As we approached the ledge, after a five-hours' sail from Grand Manan, several eiders flew off and a cloud of herring gulls arose; and, never having seen at that time any of the great breeding grounds of the Alcidae, we were particularly interested to see a number of black birds, with white breasts, standing on the rock, which we knew were razor-billed auks. As they began flying off their numbers were increased by others scrambling out from the rocks, until we estimated that at least a hundred had left the island; when we landed not one was to be found, but when we concealed ourselves among the rocks they began flying back over the ledge singly or in small flocks. We lost no time in hunting for their eggs, some of which were in plain sight under the rocks; all of them were in sheltered places and most of them were so well hidden in remote and dark crevices under the large, loose rocks, that after two or three hours of hard work, crawling into all sorts of holes and crevices, and feeling for the eggs with a long-handled net, we succeeded in collecting only 37 eggs. The eggs were laid on the bare rock, a single egg in each case. This was an interesting experience for us at the time, as every new experience is, but it is also worth mentioning here as a record of conditions that have passed; the breeding grounds of our larger, wilder, and shyer birds are gradually becoming more and more restricted through persecution and with the advance of civilization. The razor-billed auk undoubtedly once bred still farther south, or west, along the coast of Maine; Knight (1908) says "there is a dimly verified statement that some 50 years ago or more it nested as far south as the Cranberry Islands." It is said to have bred near Grand Manan as recently as 1897, six years after my visit.

But the story of its decrease does not end here; it has been sadly depleted in numbers much farther north. On Funk Island, off the coast of Newfoundland, the razor-billed auk, together with several other species of sea birds, once bred abundantly, but frequent and persistent raids, at which the birds were killed for their feathers or for bait and their eggs gathered in large numbers for food, finally reduced these populous colonies to a pitiful remnant. Mr. William Palmer (1890), who visited Funk Island in 1887, writes of it as follows:

It is easy to imagine what must have been the abundance of these birds in former years on this lonely, almost inaccessible ocean island. Great auks, murres, razorbills, puffins, Arctic terns, gannets, and perhaps other species undoubtedly swarmed, each species having its own nesting ground, and never molested except by an occasional visit from the now extinct Newfoundland red man; but now, since the white fisherman began to plunder this, to them, food and feather giving rock, how changed: To-day, but for the Arctic terns (which are useless for food or feathers) and the puffins (which are in most cases impossible to dig out), the island may be said to be deserted by birds. Only bones of the great auk, a few murres, still fewer razorbills, and a few birds of other species are all that now breed on the island. Sixteen barrels of murre and razorbill eggs have been known to be gathered at one time, and taken to St. John's. On July 23 and 24, aside from those of the Arctic tern, we did not see a dozen eggs.

Even in Audubon's time the destruction of this species had already begun on the south coast of Labrador and it has continued ever since. Mr. W. A. Stearns (1883) speaks of it as abundant on this coast up to 1882. Mr. M. A. Frazar (1887) found this species still " common everywhere " in the vicinity of Cape Whittle in 1884; " owing to its habit of breeding in less frequented places and concealing its eggs in cracks and crevices among the rocks," it had not béen so much disturbed as the murres and was surviving better. But when Doctor Townsend and I visited this region, in 1909, and spent nearly a month cruising all along the coast as far east as Natashquan, we saw in all less than 50 razor-billed auks; a few pairs, seen near Bald Island on June 8 and 9, were apparently courting and preparing to breed, but no eggs were found.

Although razor-billed auks formerly bred abundantly along the north coast of Labrador, they seem to have disappeared even more completely from that region. Mr. Lucien M. Turner, in his unpublished notes, says:

The razorbill is very abundant along the Labrador coast; although, at the season (June 24 to July 26) I was there they appeared to be more plentiful north of Eskimo Bay or Hamilton Inlet. Off Davis Inlet and Nakvak they were very common and long streams of these birds could be distinguished flying far from land and invariably headed to the northward. While passing some of the rugged islets and points I often saw these birds sitting on the rocks or in proximity to them. They appeared to be more wary while on the wing than when sitting on the land or water. They associate quite freely with *Fratercula* and an occasional *Larus*. They seem to be on most intimate terms with the species of *Uria*, with which it agrees so closely in habits.

Mr. Henry B. Bigelow (1902) found them still " abundant all along the coast " in 1900. Doctors Townsend and Allen (1907), who explored the coast as far north as Nain in 1906, say of this species:

Between Battle Harbor and Nain Fiord north we saw about 84 razor-billed auks, and about 47 on our return south. We saw about 25 flying around an island between Holton and Cape Harrison, and about 40 near a high rocky island a little south of Nain. The " thousands " of bygone years are no more.

Although I spent the greater part of the summer in 1912, from July 5 to August 25, on the northeast coast of Labrador, cruising in a small power boat among the islands much of the time, as far north as Cape Mugford, I failed to see a razor-billed auk north of the Straits of Belle Isle. As I kept a sharp lookout for birds of all kinds, I was forced to the conclusion that the large breeding colonies of the Alcidae had been nearly, if not quite, annihilated on "the Labrador."

A few pairs of razor-billed auks may still breed on some of the islands off the southern coast of Labrador or perhaps in the extreme north of Labrador there may be some small colonies, but the only colony of any size still remaining is on that impregnable sea birds' stronghold, Bird Rock; on this famous crag, much of which is inaccessible, the sea birds are well protected by nature and by man; here they will probably make their last stand or perhaps, let us hope, be perpetuated for future generations within easy reach of civilization.

Nesting.—When we visited Bird Rock in 1904 we estimated that the total population was about 10,000 birds, of which about 1,800 were razor-billed auks; the auks apparently outnumbered either one species of murre, but not the two species combined, and were exceeded in abundance only by the gannets and the kittiwakes. The strongholds of the auks were mainly on the upper ledges, near the top of the rock, where they had crawled into every available crevice or cavity and under every overhanging rock to lay their single eggs. Occasionally a razorbill's egg could be found on the open ledges with the murres, or in the entrance to a puffin burrow, but, as a rule, they were more or less concealed or under cover. The razorbills were the tamest, the least suspicious, and the most sociable, or perhaps, I should say inquisitive, of all the birds on the rock; I need only sit still for a few moments in the vicinity of their nests, when they would begin to gather on all the surrounding rocks in small parties, eyeing me with curiosity, waddling awkwardly about and making a faint guttural sound. They certainly looked very attractive in their sleek coats of dark seal brown and pure white breasts; occasionally one would open its mouth, showing the rich yellow interior, a marked color contrast which adds brilliancy to its courtship display. I noticed that whereas both the auks and murres usually sit in an upright position, while perched on the ledges, they assume the normal horizontal position, as other birds do, while incubating on their eggs; moreover, there is a bare space in the center of the breast of an incubating bird in which the egg is held horizontally and lengthwise. Although the egg is often laid on a bed of small stones, I doubt if the stones are ever placed there for that purpose by the birds, as more often the egg is laid on the bare rough rock without any attempt at nest building.

Audubon (1840) found these auks, on the south coast of Labrador, breeding in deep and narrow fissures in the rocks.

One place in particular was full of birds; it was an horizontal fissure, about 2 feet in height, and 30 or 40 yards in depth. We crawled slowly into it, and as the birds affrighted flew hurriedly past us by hundreds, many of their eggs were smashed.

He says further:

> When the auks deposit their eggs along with the guillemots, which they some-
> times do, they drop them in spots from which the water can escape without
> injuring them; but when they breed in deep fissures, which is more frequently
> the case, many of them lie close together, and the eggs are deposited on small
> beds of pebbles or broken stones raised a couple of inches or more, to let the
> water pass beneath them. Call this instinct if you will; I really do not much
> care, but you must permit me to admire the wonderful arrangements of that
> nature from which they have received so much useful knowledge. When they
> lay their eggs in such an horizontal cavern as that which I have mentioned
> above, you find them scattered at the distance of a few inches from each other;
> and there, as well as in the fissures, they sit flat upon them like ducks, for
> example, whereas on an exposed rock, each bird stands almost upright upon
> its egg. Another thing quite as curious which I observed is, that while in
> exposed situations the auk seldom lays more than one egg, yet in places of
> greater security I have, in many instances, found two under a single bird. This
> may, perhaps, astonish you, but I really can not help it.

Eggs.—The razor-billed auk never attempts to raise more than
one young bird in a season and never lays but a single egg, I believe,
unless the first one is taken, when, of course, it will keep on laying.
Two eggs have frequently been found together and are probably
in such cases incubated by a single bird, but I believe that, in such
cases, the two eggs have been accidentally rolled together or have
been laid by two birds. Some specimens of the eggs closely resemble certain types of eggs of the murres, but they can usually be
easily recognized. They are less pointed, as a rule, and are never
really pyriform. In shape they vary from " elliptical ovate " to
" elongate ovate." They also never show the deep blue colors of
the murres' eggs. The ground color varies from " pinkish buff " to
" ivory yellow " or " Marguerite yellow " in some specimens, but more
often it is a very pale bluish white or greenish white and often dull
pure white. The markings are variable in size, shape, density,
and arrangement; sometimes the egg is fairly evenly covered with
small spots and sometimes it is boldly blotched and scrawled;
frequently the markings are confluent in a ring around the larger
end. The colors in the markings are only the darker shades of
brown, from " warm sepia " or " bone brown " to black; frequently
there are inconspicuous, underlying spots of various shades of
lavender, lilac, or gray. The texture of the shell is coarse, thick, and
lusterless. The measurements of 80 eggs in the United States National Museum average 75.9 by 47.9 millimeters; the eggs showing
the four extremes measure **83.5** by 48, 78.5 by **51.5, 69** by 48.5, and
75 by **42** millimeters.

Young.—The period of incubation is about 30 days and both
sexes incubate. Audubon (1840) says that the young have " a lisp-
ing note " and are " fed freely on shrimps and small bits of fish, the
food with which their parents supply them. They were very friendly

toward each other, differing greatly in this respect from the young puffins, which were continually quarreling. They stood almost upright." The young remain on the cliffs where they were hatched and are fed by their parents until they are about half grown and still unable to fly. The old birds then persuade, induce, or even force them to fly or throw themselves down to the sea, an operation which requires considerable urging on the part of the parents and often results fatally for the young birds, in case they happen to fall on the rocks. Yarrell (1871) quotes from an interesting account given by Mr. Theodore Walker, who has seen this performance in the Hebrides:

The habits of the razorbill and guillemot are very similar; they both take about three weeks and four days from the time they are hatched until they leave the islands. When once they are enticed down they do not return to the rocks; not being full-fledged they could not very well fly up. They generally fly down to the sea before sunrise. I have seen scores fly down to the sea on a fine morning. At the time they leave they are not' full-fledged, only the wing and tail being feathered; the neck and line of the spine from the wing to the tail is still downy. I observed one razorbill enticing her young one to follow her down to the sea. I do not think it got any food that day, as it ran about from one bird to another, crying all day and all night; until nearly day-light it was still crying, but by the time I put out the light it was nowhere to be seen; doubtless the mother had returned about that time and enticed it off with food. Sometimes when the young one is obstinate, the mother will take it by the back of the neck and fly down to the sea. It is great fun watching the old bird teaching the young one to dive; the mother takes it by the neck and dives with it; up comes the young one again, only to get another dose; but the young bird can not remain so long under water as the mother, and it often dodges her by diving for an instant. The young birds remain in the sea for one or two days, when they all prepare to leave, the old birds getting restless and taking short flights. One can generally tell the night before they leave, as they make such a noise; should the wind be favorable they take their departure before sunrise in small strings.

Plumages.—The downy young is covered with soft thick down, "blackish-brown" basally above, clear "bone brown" on the rump, and paler buffy on the breast; the longer filaments on the upper parts are paler at the tips, grayish white or buffy on the back becoming more rufous on the crown; the colors fade, as the chick grows, and the light, downy tips, which give the youngest birds a decidedly hoary appearance and conceal the darker plumage under them, wear away or drop off, exposing the dark, "brownish black" juvenal plumage of the upper parts. Macgillivray (1852) gives an excellent account of the progress toward maturity which I quote, in part, as follows:

When about a fortnight old the covering is not down, properly so called, but a downy plumage, composed of regularly formed, downy, oblong, very soft, weak feathers, with disunited downy filaments; those on the head and neck extremely soft, on the lower parts a little firmer, and on the upper somewhat more so. There are regular primary and secondary quills, as well as tail feathers, but all of looser texture than afterwards. The head, throat, hind neck, and the rest of the upper parts, are brownish black, the throat paler, with many whitish filaments. The white lines from the bill to the eye are distinct, but the secondary quills have no white at the end. The feathers at the lower part of the tibia are dusky.

Gradually these first feathers are substituted by others of a firmer texture. Greenish-black quills, coverts, and tail feathers sprout forth; the secondaries terminally margined with pure white. The other parts are then invested with the new feathers: The cheeks and throat now become white; so that in this stage the colouring resembles that of the adult in winter, whereas formerly it resembled that of the bird in summer. The bill gradually elongates, assumes a darker tint, and assumes some slight appearance of rugae; and the feet also become darker.

On the head, neck, and lower parts the feathers are again changed, and at length, by the end of September, the bird has acquired its full winter plumage.

In the first winter plumage, which is acquired as explained above, young birds closely resemble the adults, so far as their plumage is concerned, though the colors of the upper parts are duller and paler, with more white or gray about the head and neck; but the bills are very much smaller and entirely different in shape, more pointed and lacking the grooves. A partial prenuptial molt occurs in the spring, involving chiefly the head and neck, at which the nuptial plumage of the adult is assumed, but the bill still remains small and only partially grooved. The postnuptial molt in August is complete and young birds then assume the adult winter plumage, at an age of 14 months.

The adult winter plumage is similar to the first winter, but it is darker and clearer above and the white throat is more distinctly outlined; the bill is about the same as in the spring adult, but the white stripes in the grooves are less distinct. The adult has a partial prenuptial molt in the spring, involving at least the head and neck and a complete postnuptial molt. The time at which the prenuptial molt takes place seems to be very variable; I have seen birds molting as early as December and as late as May, but probably both of these extremes are unusual. The postnuptial molt seems to be accomplished in August and September.

Food.—Audubon (1840) says:

The food of the razor-billed auk consists of shrimps, various other marine animals and small fishes, as well as roe.

It obtains much of its food, such as small herring and surface swimming crustacea and other marine life, on or near the surface, by swimming about on the ocean, often many miles from land, and dipping its head under occasionally. But it must also be capable of diving to great depths to obtain the various small mollusks on which it feeds.

Behavior.—While on Bird Rock, where I could easily compare all three species in flight, I learned to recognize the two murres and the razorbills by their shapes and attitudes on the wing. The razorbill is the shortest and most thick set of the three; it holds itself very compactly, with the head well drawn in and the bill pointing straight forward; the head, body, and tail are all in a straight line. The common murre on the other hand, carries its long neck and head outstretched, but dropped somewhat below the level of the body. The Brünnich's murre is intermediate between the two, in this respect. All three of these species sway from side to side in flight, showing white breasts and black backs alternately. Their flight is swift and direct, accomplished by very rapid wing strokes. Doctor Townsend (1907) has noted that, as the razorbills " fly away, they show white on either side of a black median line, while the puffin shows a continuous black back." Morris (1903) gives, a quotation from Meyer, regarding their behavior while migrating, as follows:

During these migrations an interesting circumstance may be observed, namely, that when the several divisions or groups of a flock descend upon the sea to rest themselves, the parties that are behind alight some distance in advance of those that first settled, so that when the first-arrived parties have recruited their strength and taken wing again, the later-arrived groups having alighted so much in advance, have had time to rest themselves also, and are prepared in their turn to follow in the train of their former leaders as soon as these have passed over.

The razor-billed auk swims lightly and swiftly on the surface, with its head retracted and its tail pointed upward. It dives quickly and strongly, partially opening its wings as it plunges forward and downward. Like all of the Alcidae, it uses its wings freely in " flying " under water, making great speed with the wings only half extended. Mr. Edmund Selous (1905), who has had excellent opportunities for studying this, says:

Razorbills also dive briskly, opening the wings * * * One remarks then that the wings are moved both together—flapped or beaten—so that the bird really flies through the water. In flight, however, they are spread straight out without a bend in them, whereas here they are all the while flexed at the joint, wing raised from and brought downward again toward the sides in the same position in which they repose against them when closed.

It can dive to great depths, swim for long distances, and remain under water for a long time.

The vocal performances of the razor-billed auk are not elaborate. On its breeding grounds it indulges in occasional hoarse guttural notes or low croaking sounds, which are not audible at any considerable distance. During its courtship, which has apparently never been described, it may have a more varied or interesting vocabulary. Morris (1903) says " the note is likened to the syllables ' arr ' and 'odd,' also to ' hurr-ray.' "

Although the razor-billed auk is said to be of a quarrelsome disposition, I saw no evidence of it on Bird Rock, where it associates
on friendly terms with the murres and puffins, sitting in little mixed
groups close together on their favorite rocks.   It has few enemies,
though it is preyed upon by the large falcons to some extent.   Its
habit of nesting in inaccessible crevices on high cliffs has protected
its eggs from the gulls and has saved it from total extermination by
egg hunters.   Its eggs were gathered in large quantities, with the
eggs of the murres, when it was abundant, but now the eggs of the
razorbill are too scarce and too hard to get to make it pay to collect
them.   Nuttall (1834) refers to this as follows:

Its flesh is quite palatable, although very dark, and much eaten by the Green-
landers, according to Cranz, forming their chief subsistence during the months
of February and March.   These birds are killed with missiles, chased, and
driven ashore in canoes, or taken in nets made of split whalebone.   Their skins
are also used for clothing.   The eggs are everywhere accounted a delicacy,
and the feathers of the breast are extremely fine, warm, and elastic.   For the
sake of this handful of feathers, according to Audubon, thousands of these
birds are killed in Labrador, and their bodies strewed on the shore.

Winter.—The razor-billed auk is a hardy bird, pushing north
through the ice in early spring and being driven south again only
by the advent of cold weather.   Late in the fall large numbers are
seen migrating around Nova Scotia to their winter haunts on the
New England coasts, following in the wake of the last of the flight
of scoters and brant.   They fly well off shore as a rule and spend
most of their time on the open sea; consequently they are seldom
seen and they are probably more abundant than we realize.   Long
Island probably marks about the southern limit of the normal winter
range of this species, where it is known as the " sea crow."   Dr.
William C. Braislin (1907) says that they—

occur on the beach chiefly by reason of their being driven in by winds and surf.
It is doubtful whether even a few survive this experience.   They do not will-
ingly approach the sands in mild weather and in the fury of a gale, exhausted
with their struggles and beaten by the surf, they probably nearly all succumb.

DISTRIBUTION.

Breeding range.—Coasts and islands of the north Atlantic and
Arctic Oceans.   From New Brunswick (Grand Manan), Gulf of St.
Lawrence (Bird Rock), and Newfoundland, and north along the Labrador coast to Greenland (west coast to Tasiusak).   Also from Iceland, Faroe Islands, and British Isles (south to Channel Islands);
east to coast of Norway and Lapland.   Recorded as far north as
Mallemukfjeldet, northeast Greenland, latitude 81° 12', but not
breeding.   May possibly have bred in Maine many years ago.

Winter range.—South along the Atlantic coasts. From southern Labrador, New Brunswick (Grand Manan), and Ontario (Toronto, Hamilton and western Lake Ontario) south to New York (Long Island) and New Jersey. Rarely or casually to Virginia (Cobbs Island and Smiths Island) and North Carolina (Lookout Cove). No records for Great Lakes west of Lake Ontario. Michigan records discredited. In Europe from the British Isles and Baltic Sea south to the Mediterranean Sea and the Azores and Canary Islands; east to the Adriatic Sea.

Spring migration.—Northward along the coast in March and April. New York: Long Island, March 5. Rhode Island: Newport, April 10 (latest). Massachusetts: Marthas Vineyard, May 12 (latest). Nova Scotia: Cape Sable, May 4. Arrive on breeding grounds, Gulf of St. Lawrence, about April 15.

Fall migration.—Southward along the coast during November (perhaps earlier). Massachusetts: November 1. New York: Long Island, November 14. New Jersey: Delaware River, November. Virginia: Norfolk, October 15.

Egg dates.—Gulf of St. Lawrence: 76 records, June 10 to July 25; 38 records, June 21 to July 4. Great Britain: 24 records, May 17, to June 30; 12 records, May 28, to June 5. Ungava: 2 records, June 13, to July 1. Bay of Fundy: 2 records, June 11, to 17.

PLAUTUS IMPENNIS (Linnaeus).

GREAT AUK.

HABITS.

Contributed by Charles Wendell Townsend.

The great auk is extinct. So thoroughly and suddenly did its extinction come about that at one time the bird was considered to be a myth, yet a comparatively few years ago it existed in great numbers. The date of its final taking off, the cause of its disappearance, former abundance, distribution, and habits are all matters of exceeding interest, about which much has been culled by diligent searchers from various historical and traditional sources as well as from investigation of the remains of these birds found at their breeding places and in shell heaps. To Alfred Newton, J. Steenstrup, Symington Grieve, and Frederic A. Lucas we owe most of our knowledge of this interesting bird, and their writings will be freely drawn upon in the present epitome.

Nuttall (1834) forcibly illustrates the erroneous opinions that existed and still exists in the popular mind as to the range of this bird. He says:

The great auk, or northern penguin, inhabits the highest latitudes of the globe, dwelling by choice and instinct amidst the horrors of a region covered with eternal ice. Here it is commonly found upon the floating masses of the gelid ocean, far from land, to which alone it resorts in the season of procreation.

This is far from being the case, for it is doubtful whether the great auk ever extended its range north of the Arctic Circle and its remains have been found in shell heaps as far south as the Bay of Biscay on the eastern side of the Atlantic and Florida on the western side. The only record of this bird north of the Arctic Circle, namely, at Disco, in Greenland, is considered by Newton of very doubtful value.

The positively known breeding places of the great auk are quickly enumerated. The chief of these on the American side of the Atlantic was Funk Island, a rocky island 32 miles off Fogo on the northeastern side of Newfoundland. It is possible that the bird also bred at Penguin Islands on the south coast, and Penguin Islands near Cape Freel. The latter islands were visited in 1887 by Lucas (1887), but he found no evidence of such former occupation. He says:

> There can be little doubt that the extent of the breeding range of the great auk has been, as a rule, much overestimated, and the writer's own belief is that, like the gannet, the garefowl was confined to a very few localities.

The Bird Rocks in the Bay of St. Lawrence, Cape Breton, and the Virgin Rocks, southeast of Newfoundland, are all more or less doubtful former breeding sites. The records of its occurrence in Greenland are very few and all doubtful. Capt. George Cartwright, that acute observer and recorder, who frequented the Labrador coast from 1770 to 1786, was familiar with the bird and has written a classic account of its status on Funk Island, but never mentions any breeding place on the Labrador coast. I believe that he would have described it if any such existed to the south of Hamilton Inlet.

The fact that Gosnold found great auks at Cape Cod in the spring and summer of 1602, and that Joselyn says one was taken at Black Point, near Portland, Maine, in the spring, has been used as an argument in favor of former breeding places at Cape Cod and elsewhere along the New England coast. Hardy says that the shell heaps along this coast were made almost entirely in summer, and, as these contained great auk remains, therefore this bird probably bred at Cape Cod and elsewhere. The conclusion, however, is not warranted, for there are many species of sea birds at the present day that summer far south of their breeding grounds, owing either to sterility or immaturity. Also many sea birds that breed in the north tarry along the coast until June and are back again in July.

Catesby (1771) gives a list of " European water fowls which I have observed to be also inhabitants of America, which, though they abide the winter in Carolina, most of them return north in the spring to breed." In this list " penguin " is included. As has been already stated, bones of the great auk have occurred in shell heaps as far south as Florida. At Ormond, on the Halifax River in Florida, two left humeri of this species were found. In the shell heaps of the Massachusetts coast the bones of the great auk have several times been found, at Marblehead, Ipswich, and Plum Island. I have myself found them at Mount Desert Island, Maine.

On the eastern side of the Atlantic one comes first to Iceland, which was probably the last stronghold of this bird. Here are to be found numerous rocky islands or skerries where the great auk undoubtedly bred. Several of these bear the name of the extinct bird, and are called Geirfuglasker. Eldey, or Fire Island, where the last birds were taken, is one of a chain of volcanic Bird Islands (*Fuglasker*) lying off Cape Reykjanes, the southwestern point of Iceland. At a few places in the British Isles remains of this bird have been found and there are historic references to their occurrence at St. Kilda, the Hebrides, Orkney, Shetland, and Faroe Islands and at Waterford and Belfast, Ireland. At the Scottish Islands they probably bred. In the shell heaps or kitchen middens of Denmark remains of this bird have been found, and there are traditions of its existence in this region. There is some evidence of its occurrence on the coast of Norway and it probably migrated all along the European coast as far as the Bay of Biscay. The last of these birds, two individuals, were taken alive on June 3, 1844, at Eldey, a skerry or rocky islet off the southwest point of Iceland. Their viscera are now preserved in the Royal University Museum, Copenhagen, but it is not known what became of the skins and bones. The narrative by Grieve (1885) of this capture is of such a tragically historic character, it is quoted here:

As the men clambered up they saw two garefowls sitting among numberless other rock-birds (*Uria troile* and *Alca torda*), and at once gave chase. The garefowls showed not the slightest disposition to repel the invaders, but immediately ran along under the high cliff, their heads erect, their little wings somewhat extended. They uttered no cry of alarm, and moved, with their short steps, about as quickly as a man could walk. Jon (Brandsson) with outstretched arms, drove one into a corner, where he soon had it fast. Siguror (Islefsson) and Ketil pursued the second, and the former seized it close to the edge of the rock here risen to a precipice some fathoms high, the water being directly below it. Ketil (Ketilsm) then returned to the sloping shelf whence the birds had started, and saw an egg lying on the lava slab, which he knew to be a garefowl's. Whether there was not another egg is uncertain. All this took place in much less time than it takes to tell it.

This date, June 3, 1844, is probably the last authentic date. A live bird was said to have been seen on the Newfoundland Banks in December, 1852, and a dead one to have been picked up in Trinity Bay, Newfoundland, in 1853, but these records are considered of doubtful authenticity by Grieve (1885).

The fundamental cause of the extinction of the great auk was the systematic onslaught made for various reasons by so-called civilized man. Breeding on remote islands, the bird had little to fear from savages and other mammalian enemies. Although it could not fly, it could easily take care of itself in the water.

By most of the men of those days when the great auk flourished the idea of its extinction would have been flouted, and, even if they could have realized it, they would not have viewed the death of a species in the same manner as do the more enlightened of the human race at the present day. Richard Whitbourne (1622) wrote:

God made the innocencie of so poor a creature to become such an admirable instrument for the sustentation of man.

The reasons for the slaughter of this bird were primarily for food, later for bait, for its fat and its feathers, and last of all, when it was doomed to extinction, the finishing blow was put by collectors. Sir Richard Bonnycastle in his " Newfoundland in 1842 " says:

In winter many of the arctic ice birds frequent the coast, but the large auk or penguin (*Alca impennis*), which, not 50 years ago, was a sure sea mark in the edge of and inside the banks, has totally disappeared, from the ruthless trade in the eggs and skin.

Cartwright (1792) in his journal under date of July 5, 1785, prophesies the speedy extermination of the great auk. He says:

A boat came in from Funk Island laden with birds, chiefly penguins. Funk Island is a small flat island rock about 20 leagues east of the island of Fogo, in the latitude of 50° north. Innumerable flocks of sea fowl breed upon it every summer, which are of great service to the poor inhabitants of Fogo, who make voyages there to load with birds and eggs. When the water is smooth. they make their shallop fast to the shore, lay their gangboards from the gunwale of the boat to the rocks, and then drive as many penguins on board as she will hold; for, the wings of those birds being remarkably short, they can not fly, but it has been customary of late years for several crews of men to live all summer on that island for the sole purpose of killing birds for the sake of their feathers; the destruction which they have made is incredible. If a stop is not soon put to that practice, the whole breed will be diminished to almost nothing, particularly the penguins; for this is now the only island they have left to breed upon; all others lying so near to the shores of New-foundland, they are continually robbed. The birds which the people bring from thence they salt and eat, in lieu of salted pork.

The following note by J. A. Allen (1876) describes more in detail the horrible slaughter for the feathers:

Mr. Michael Carrol, of Bonavista, Newfoundland, has recently given me the following very interesting facts respecting the extermination of the great auk (*Alca impennis*) at the Funk Islands. In early life he was often a visitor to these islands, and a witness of what he here describes. He says these birds were formerly very numerous on the Funk Islands, and 45 to 50 years ago were hunted for their feathers, soon after which time they were wholly exterminated. As the auks could not fly, the fishermen would surround them in small boats and drive them ashore into pounds previously constructed of stones. The birds were then easily killed, and their feathers removed by immersing the birds in scalding water, which was ready at hand in large kettles set for this purpose. The bodies were used as fuel for boiling the water.

The remains of the huts and pounds are still on the island, but the birds are no more! The quantity of great auk's bones and even of mummified remains found on Funk Island by Lucas and others all testify to the destruction that went on there.

It would seem as if nature herself wished to help in the destruction of this bird, for, in 1830, a submarine eruption took place off Reykjanes, Iceland, during which a skerry frequented by great auks sank under water.

As in the case of many species that have become extinct, men at the time have not realized the fact. Thus, in 1848, Hugh Strickland makes no mention of the great auk in a paper on species recently extinct. Yarrell in 1842 speaks of it as "a very rare British bird," but no hint is given of its probable fate. When the fact of its extreme rarity was discovered, it was believed that it had merely retreated into the more inaccessible northern regions and Arctic expeditions were requested to search for it.

Nesting.—As has been pointed out by Lucas (1887) the gregarious habits of the great auk and its predilection for certain breeding places has been an important factor in its extermination. He goes on to say that there were apparently plenty of suitable breeding grounds for the great auk in Maine and Labrador, and had the bird bred in small colonies at localities scattered along this wide expanse of territory, it would have been in existence to-day. The habits of the great auk are largely matters of history to be gathered from old writers. It bred in colonies on rocky islands as has already been shown; and possibly, although not probably, on sandy shores. No nest was built, and the single egg was laid on the bare rock or the accumulation of guano. Pennant (1765) says:

If the egg is taken away it will not lay another that season * * * It lays its egg close to the sea mark, being incapable, by reason of the shortness of its wings, to mount higher.

The later statement is not entirely correct for the bird as at Funk Island, already described often nested a considerable distance from the water.

Eggs.—[Author's note: The series of 10 eggs of this extinct bird in the Thayer Museum is probably the finest series of these rare eggs in existence in any one collection. In shape they are nearly "ovate pyriform" and suggest in general appearance large murre's eggs. The shell is thick, tough and roughly granulated. The ground color is dull, dirty white or even yellowish white in one. This yellowish egg is covered quite uniformly with fine scrawls or irregular lines of pale gray or drab. The other eggs are more conspicuously and unevenly scrawled or blotched, chiefly about the larger end with black or very dark brown, sometimes with lighter brown, drab or gray.

The measurements of 40 eggs, obtained from the Thayer collection and through the kindness of Rev. F. C. R. Jourdain, average 123.7 by 75.5 millimeters; the eggs showing the four extremes measure **140** by 70, 126.5 by **83.5, 111** by 72, and 116 by **69** millimeters.]

Behavior.—Contemporaneous writers, especially some of the older ones, show considerable imagination in their description of this bird and its habits, but many of their accounts are evidently truthful and are of great interest. A number of these are quoted here as a contribution to the life history of this extinct bird.

The following description is by M. Martin (1753), who lived for three weeks on St. Kilda in June, 1697:

The sea fowl are first gairfowl, being the stateliest as well as the largest sort, and above the size of a solan goose, of a black color, red about the eyes, a large spot under each, a long broad bill; it stands stately, its whole body erected, its wings short, flies not at all; lays its egg upon the bare rock, which if taken away, she lays no more for that year; she is whole footed, and has the hatching spot upon her breast, i. e., a bare spot from which the feathers have fallen off with the heat in hatching; its egg is twice as big as that of a solan goose, and is variously spotted, black, green, and dark; it comes without regard to any wind, appears the first of May, and goes away about the middle of June.

Cartwright (1792) under date of August 5, 1771, wrote in his journal:

During a calm in the afternoon Shuglawina went off in his kyack in pursuit of a penguin; he presently came within a proper distance of the bird, and stuck his dart into it; but, as the weapon did not enter a mortal part, the penguin swam and dived so well that he would have lost both the bird and the dart had he not driven it near enough the vessel for me to shoot it.

Plumages.—On the 18th of August, 1821 (or 1822), a great auk was captured near the Island of Glass or Scalpa (one of the Hebrides). A description of this bird by Fleming (1824), who was present at the time, throws light on the change from nuptial to winter plumage of the species. He says:

A few white feathers were at this time making their appearance in the sides of its neck and throat, which increased considerable during the following week, and left no room to doubt, that, like its congeners, the blackness of the throat feathers of summer is exchanged for white during the winter season.

Food.—As to its food, according to Grieve (1885), Fabricius said:

The great auk fed on *Cottus scorpius*, or the bullhead, and *Cyclopterus lumpus*, or the lump fish, and other fishes of the same size.

It is said that one was caught about 1812 near Papa Westray, Orkney, on the open sea by some fishermen, who enticed it to the side of the boat by holding out a few fish, and then striking it with an oar. Another bird was caught in a similar manner at the entrance to Waterford Harbor in May, 1834. They were also caught by baited lines on the Newfoundland banks. The bird caught at Waterford partook greedily of potatoes and milk. It "stood very erect, and frequently stroked its head with its foot, especially when any favorite food was permitted. When in Mr. Gough's possession it was chiefly fed on fish, of which fresh-water species (trout, etc.) were preferred to sea fish. They were swallowed entire. It was rather fierce."

Behavior.—It was a common saying among mariners that this bird never strayed away from soundings, but the fact that individuals were from time to time found on the coast of the British Islands in the nineteenth century at the time that they did not breed at any point nearer than Iceland, it is evident they must have wandered over deep water. That they were capable of making long journeys is shown by their remains in regions so remote from their breeding haunts as Florida. Professor Newton (1861), writing on Mr. J. Wolley's "Researches in Iceland" respecting the garefowl, says:

They swam with their heads much lifted up, but their necks drawn in; they never tried to flap along the water, but dived as soon as alarmed. On the rocks they sat more upright than either guillemots or razorbills, and their station was further removed from the sea. They were easily frightened by noise, but not by what they saw. They sometimes uttered a few low croaks. They have never been known to defend their eggs, but would bite fiercely if they had the chance when caught. They walk or run with little short steps and go straight like a man. One has been known to drop down some two fathoms off the rock into the water. Finally, I may add that the color of the inside of their mouths is said to have been yellow, as in the allied species.

This last fact would give us a hint as to their courtship, and suggest that they opened wide their mouths for display during this performance.

Like all the Alcidae it used its wings in swimming under water, and, as large wings are an impediment in subaqueous flight, these parts had become reduced so much in size that although they were ideal for use under the water, they were useless in the air. In these respects the bird resembled closely the Penguin of the Southern seas. The rapidity with which it swam above and under water may be judged from the fact that "one chased by Mr. Bullock among the Northern Isles, left a six-oared boat far behind." Circumstantial evidence of the use of its wings under water is presented by Fleming (1824), who says it dives and swims under water, "even with a long cord attached to its foot, with incredible swiftness."

Audubon (1840) says:

The only authentic account of the occurrence of this bird on our coast that I possess was obtained from Mr. Henry Havell, brother of my engraver, who, when on his passage from New York to England, hooked a great auk on the banks of Newfoundland, in extremely boisterous weather. On being hauled on board, it was left at liberty on the deck. It walked very awkwardly, often tumbling over, bit everyone within reach of its powerful bill, and refused food of all kinds. After continuing several days on board, it was restored to its proper element.

Of the voice of this extinct bird we have but scanty record. Some of the older writers speak of a croak. Dr. Fleming, as quoted by Grieve (1885), said:

When fed in confinement it holds up its head, expressing its anxiety by shaking its head and neck and uttering a gurgling noise.

Grieve (1885) listed 79 or 81 skins of the great auk, 2 or 3 physiological preparations, 10 skeletons, 121 or 131 birds represented by detached bones and 68 or 70 eggs still in existence. The numbers of these have slightly increased, especially in the list of detached bones, which would bring the number of individuals up to many thousands. The value of the skins and of the eggs has increased many fold and has reached fabulous sums.

DISTRIBUTION.

Breeding range.—Formerly coasts and islands of the North Atlantic. The best-known breeding place was Funk Island, Newfoundland. It also bred on the Faroes and on islands off the southwest coast of Iceland, where the last pair of birds were taken alive in June, 1844. Although recorded from Greenland (Disco Island), it is now considered doubtful if the species bred north of the Arctic Circle. A cast was found in a loam deposit in southern Sweden that agrees with the egg of this species and this probably marks the eastern limit of its range.

Winter range.—Probably south along the coast from Newfoundland and Cape Breton to Maine and Massachusetts, casually to South Carolina and Florida; and from Denmark to France and northern Spain. One was found dead in Norway in the winter of 1838.

ALLE ALLE (Linnaeus).

DOVEKIE.

HABITS.

Although not so strictly confined to the Arctic Ocean in winter as Ross's gull there is no more characteristic bird of the Arctic regions than the "little auk," which swarms as abundantly, on the Atlantic side of this continent, as the various auklets do in Bering Sea. It winters much farther south than the little auklets, but it returns to its summer home at remarkably early dates, as soon as it can push northward into the forbidden regions of ice and snow, a hardy little

Arctic explorer that loves those inhospitable shores. It penetrates as far north as 82° and has been found breeding up to the seventy-eighth parallel of latitude, probably farther north than any other species regularly breeds.

Spring.—Mr. William Eagle Clarke (1898), writing of the migration of this species on Franz Josef Land, says:

It arrived at Frederick Jackson Island in 1896 on the 25th of February, as related by Doctor Nansen. On the 10th of March Doctor Nansen mentions that "millions" were seen flying up the sound at 6 a. m., and "when we went out at 2 in the afternoon there was an unceasing passage of flock after flock out to sea, and this continued until late in the afternoon." On the 17th of March they were in plenty at the Gully Rocks, and, as far as could be seen they were all in full summer plumage. They continually occupied and deserted their breeding-cliffs during April, May, and early June. After the 10th of June the little auks were seen on the rocks every day during our stay. They bred in the cliffs, at both east and west ends, at Cape Flora in great numbers, though most plentifully in the Gully Rocks.

The approach of the Arctic spring and the arrival of the birds is well portrayed by Dr. I. I. Hayes (1867) as follows:

The snow had mainly disappeared from the valley, and, although no flowers had yet appeared, the early vegetation was covering the banks with green, and the feeble growths opened their little leaves almost under the very snow, and stood alive and fresh in the frozen turf, looking as glad of the spring as their more ambitious cousins of the warm south. Gushing rivulets and fantastic waterfalls mingled their pleasant music with the ceaseless hum of birds, myriads of which sat upon the rocks of the hillside, or were perched upon the cliffs, or sailed through the air in swarms so thick that they seemed like a cloud passing before the sun. These birds were the hitherto mentioned little auk, and are a waterfowl not larger than a quail. The swift flutter of their wings and their constant cry filled the air with a roar like that of a storm advancing among the forest trees. The valley was glowing with the sunlight of the early morning, which streamed in over the glacier, and robed hill, mountain, and plain in brightness.

Nearly all Arctic explorers have referred to the astonishing abundance of the little "rotche," as this species is called, on its breeding grounds. The following two quotations by Morris (1903) will serve as illustrations:

Captain Beechey says:

They are so numerous that we have often seen an uninterrupted line of them extending full halfway over the bay, or to a distance of more than 3 miles. This column, on the average, might have been about 6 yards broad and as many deep. There must have been nearly four millions of birds on the wing at one time.

Meyer writes:

The incredible numbers of this species that have been seen by voyagers, on the surface of the northern seas, are very remarkable; it is said that they cover the surface of the water, and the floating masses of ice as far as the eye can discern, and when they take flight they actually darken the sky.

Nesting.—Mr. W. Elmer Ekblaw contributes the following excellent account of the nesting habits of the dovekie:

The nesting sites are determined probably by several factors, perhaps of equal significance. These sites are always along cliffs with rather steep talus slopes, of rather large fragments, among which the birds can find entrances, and cavities well enough within shelter to be safe from winds and weather and predatory animals. In suitable talus slopes its nests extend from near the high tide water mark to the top of the slope, in every possible place. Because of the slow disintegration of the rocks, as compared with the breaking off of the fragments from the cliffs, the talus slopes are piles of coarse rocks with cavities, passages, crevices, and tunnels everywhere among them. In these cavities and passages at various distances from the outside, according to the convenience and safety of the place, the nests are placed. Frequently a mat of grass grows over the surface of the rocks, but since it is only a superficial mat, and as long as openings are left for the ingress of the birds, this does not detract in the least from the desirability of the site. Along Foulke Fjord, on the cliffs south of Cape Alexander, and near Sonntag Bay I have found thousands nesting on what was apparently only a grass slope with an occasional projecting rock, but examination revealed the fact that it was only a concealed talus slope after all. Where the breaking down of the cliff above, or where there is considerable rolling of the surface rocks, the grass does not form, though upon the margins of the talus tongues, and in a semicircle about their terminations when they do not reach the sea the grass mat encroaches. In a few cases the grass mat has so deeply covered the talus that the auklets have abandoned it, because they could not enter. Not only in the talus piles does the dovekie nest, but also in crevices—almost without exception in horizontal crevices—it makes its home as well; but this only when talus slopes near at hand have nests too, for this little bird is most socially inclined, nesting, feeding, swimming, flying, and migrating in great gregarious flocks.

It builds no nest. Its one egg, or rarely two, is laid on a rock or shelf in a passageway or cavity, usually in a niche along, or at the end of, a passageway. This rock, after many generations of auks have nested there, is covered with more or less damp dung, upon which the egg or eggs are laid. Several nests may be very close together, or considerable interval may occur between a nest and its neighbor. The entrance to a nest is usually marked by a white patch on the rock, where more than the usual amount of dung is deposited, for whenever one of the old birds alights at the entrance, he, or she, almost invariably defecates. The earliest eggs are laid in the last week of June, but it is during the first week of July that laying is at its height, at Etah. In the last week in June the Eskimo women begin gathering the eggs, but they are not so plentiful as they become a week later. Each female lays one egg and this is the usual number. Rarely two eggs are laid, and in four cases of this that I saw the eggs were slightly smaller than the normal egg.

Eggs.—The single egg is "ovate" or pointed ovate in shape. Its shell is smooth but without luster. All the eggs that I have seen are plain bluish white and immaculate; I have never seen any of the alleged spotted eggs of this species. The measurements of 44 eggs, in various collections, average 48.2 by 33 millimeters; the eggs showing the four extremes measure 51 by 34, 49 by 35.5, 45 by 33, and 46 by 32 millimeters.

Mr. Ekblaw says:

The eggs are quite uniform in size, and also in color. Most of them are a pale blue, the blue being but a tinge. From this pale blue type they vary in both directions slightly, to quite white and to pale robin-egg blues. However, most of the eggs are a typical pale-blue color. Though not a precocial bird the dovekie lays an abnormally large egg, so large, in fact, in proportion to the size of the bird that the mother could with difficulty and little success keep more than one egg warm. The shell of the egg is so thick that the inside must be cooled slowly when the old birds leave the nest. I can not state that the male takes part in the incubation, but I have seen whichever bird it is that is not on the eggs, come to the entrance of the nest and enter with his pouch distended with food, in the same manner as it is later when the young are being fed, so I presume that the food is for the incubating bird, male or female. The eggs do not always mature. I have found many that had spoiled and not hatched. Some of these were probably old eggs of former years, but about 1 egg in 10 was spoiled.

Young.—The young begin hatching about the middle of July, and from then almost until the last week in August some are being hatched, though the most of them hatch about the middle of August, or a little before. They at once become voraciously hungry, and tax the energies of both parents to satisfy them, even though the day be 24 hours light. The young birds, as soon as they hear any noise outside the entrance, set up an impatient shrill chirping, which continues until the old bird feeds them by disgorging into their bills the contents of its well-filled pouch. The consoling, soothing murmur of the old bird to the young, and the satisfied chirping of the young shows how solicitous the one is, and how grateful the other. The birds of adjacent nests often leave and arrive together; when they come with a great rush of wings, they usually alight together in a group on some prominent large rock near their nests, and then after a survey of the vicinity, hop or fly to their respective entrances. Before leaving, they gather together similarly.

The first birds come off the nest about the middle of August, and the last not until the last of the month, so that the latest departures from the nesting sites are those retarded by their belated young. Thus after the great number are gone south, a few still remain a few days—these belated young and their parents. On August 24, 1915, when I went up on the slopes along the fjord to collect young and old birds for the winter's food, the birds had already begun leaving, so that the number was noticeably diminished. The departure continued constantly through the day, great flocks rising over the south cliffs and passing out of sight southward. The following day the most of those remaining left, and this was the day of the greatest exodus. On the 25th we found most of the young gone, though a number remained, and of these several had not yet developed the wing feathers needed for their flight, and could not leave for at least a week or 10 days yet. Many of the young were leaving the nest. Apparently when they are sufficiently developed they emerge from their nest and impelled by an instinctive impulse essay the first flight; I could not see that any coaxing was resorted to by the older birds. The young bird waddled awkwardly about the rocks, watched not only by his own parents but by all the old birds as well. From time to time he would stretch and flap his wings, and then finally when those about him rose in flight he, too, took to his wings. He quickly fell behind the most; but at least one, sometimes two, old birds stuck by him. His flight was awkward, and he could easily be distinguished in his erratic course, from the old birds. Some of the weaker ones returned soon to the rocks or sank to the water to rest, but the stronger apparently sailed away out of sight.

Plumages.—Ridgway (1887) describes the downy young as " uniform sooty slate color, paler or more grayish below." The juvenal plumage soon appears and is practically complete before the young bird leaves the nest, the last of the down disappearing on the chest, belly, and rump. Strangely enough, the juvenal plumage is similar, in color pattern, to the nuptial plumage and entirely unlike that of the first winter; the entire head, neck, and throat are " clove brown;" the upper parts are similar, but blacker, and the lower parts are white. Within a few weeks, before the end of September, the young bird prepares for its fall migration by a complete molt of the body plumage, producting the first winter plumage, much thicker and of firmer texture. This plumage is very much like the adult winter plumage, but the upper parts are duller and browner, and the bill is smaller and weaker. At the first prenuptial molt young birds become practically indistinguishable from adults.

Adults have a partial prenuptial molt late in the winter or very early in the spring and a complete postnuptial molt in August and September. The clear, glossy black back is characteristic of the winter adult.

Food.—Mr. Ekblaw writes to me:

The food of the young dovekies is largely made up of the so-called " shrimps " (*Schizopoda-Myris?*) so numerous in Arctic waters, and the so-called " blackberries," the little black " arthropods " that are numerous in the water too. I think it is this latter food that gives rise to the pink and lavender dung of the dovekie. The intervals at which the young are fed varies, but they are usually measured by hours, though when food does come it is in quantity.

The food of the adult bird is probably the same as that of the young while in their summer home. This food it obtains in the sea, usually most easily, apparently in certain currents, or about headlands, ice pans, or icebergs. Before the nesting period begins, the bird spends long periods in the water offshore. It travels considerable distances after food, those at Etah going at least as far as Cairn Point and Force Bay to the northward.

Audubon (1840) found in the stomachs of dovekies " shrimps and other crustacea and particles of seaweed." Nuttall (1834) mentions marine insects and a small species of crab as included in their food. According to Yarrell (1871), Major Feilden's notes state:

During the breeding season the pouch-like enlargement of the cheeks give them a singular appearance. The contents of the cheeks is a reddish-colored substance, which on closer examination is found to consist of immense numbers of minute crustacea. The adaptation of the mouth in this species as a receptacle for the food required for their young does not appear to have attracted much attention among naturalists; and yet a little consideration would have shown that some such arrangement must be required. With fish feeders, such as *Alca*, *Uria*, and *Fratercula*, no difficulty arises in transporting food to their young; but in the case of *Mergulus alle*, which, I believe, subsists entirely on minute crustacea, the bill is manifestly incapable of conveying the requisite amount of food, especially as very often the breeding places of the little auk are found inland, at considerable distances from the sea.

Mr. William Brewster (1906) writes that the stomachs of several killed on Fresh Pond, Cambridge, Massachusetts, were " filled with the remains of young alewives," which abounded in the pond.

Behavior.—Mr. Ekblaw says of the behavior of the dovekie:

Like the murre and the guillemot, the dovekie floats either high or low in the water, and dives more easily from the lower position. They dive very quickly, and remain submerged for some little time. Observations of approximately 761 birds in 51 groups gave an average of 33 seconds for submergence, when frightened by the approach of the steamer off Cape Walsingham, August 11, 1913. The maximum time of submergence was 68 seconds. The dovekie, like the murre and guillemot, uses his wings as well as his feet in diving, veritably flying through the water. On the dive it tips down as it goes under, just like a " bobber " on a country boy's fish line, and then starts down at an angle of from 45° to 60°, only its little white tail visible, like a white bubble sinking fast into the depths.

The flight of the auklet suggests in the wing movements, at least, that of the chimney swifts. It is a good strong flier when the expanse of wing surface in respect to the weight of the bird is considered, but it does not fly nearly so swiftly as the guillemot or murre, and in direct flight can not escape from its enemies, the great burgomaster gull or the gyrfalcon. I have several times seen the burgomaster gull far behind a flock of dovekies start in pursuit, and though the little birds exerted themselves to the utmost to escape, the big gull in a few movements overtook them, scattering them. The victim he singled out then found his only hope of escaping in dodging his pursuer and taking refuge in the water or among rocks. Likewise I have seen guillemots take wing with the dovekies and soon distance them. The dovekie has a habit of stooping from a considerable height at a very steep gradient, like a hawk stooping to his prey, and at this time, the descent is meteoric in noise and speed. At such a time, if one happens to be standing at the base of its descent or near it, he receives an impression of great speed, undoubtedly more or less correct, for the impetus of their rapid descent must give a high velocity. On straight flying, however, the flight is not out of the ordinary—quite what one would expect from a bird with such relation of weight to wing expanse.

Morris (1903) says, of its vocal powers:

The note of this interesting little bird is a pretty chirrup or pipe, partly plaintive and partly lively; it resembles the syllables " try " and " eye " frequently repeated, especially when engaged with the nest.

The note has also been likened to the syllables " al-le."

The important place which the dovekie fills in maintaining the balance of life in the far north is well shown in the following observations by Mr. Ekblaw:

The dovekie is preeminently a social bird. Its vast colonies on these northwest Greenland shores form one of the most striking features of the coast and play an important part in the ecology and human economy of the region. They furnish the food for the many foxes of this region; without these birds the foxes would be so few that the natives could not secure adequate clothing, and these " Arctic Highlanders " could not have persisted here as the most northern people of the world. No trading station would have been established by the Danes; one of the chief incentives to some of Peary's and other expeditions of the coast would have been missing. The grass slopes about the rookeries, the luxuriant herbage being due to their dung, support the largest numbers of hare and ptarmigan, and probably afforded the richest pastures for the caribou before the introduction of firearms effected their extermination from some of the areas along the coast. The burgomaster gull and the gyrfalcon feed upon the dovekie throughout the summer and rear their young upon them too. The fox, burgomaster gull, and gyrfalcon are the chief natural enemies of the dovekie; in additon, the Eskimo, the raven, and perhaps some of the water animals prey upon the birdlets; the whitewhale, so the Eskimo say, catches and eats many.

The fox preys not only upon the bird but upon the eggs as well. Through the nesting season and while the young are growing the foxes frequent the talus slopes, gorging themselves and laying in their winter stores. Lurking behind a rock until a flock alights near and then rushing upon the birds, stealthily creeping upon a flock and pouncing upon them, or crawling into the holes after them—in one way or another the fox gets all he wants. And the auklets recognize him as an enemy, for at his approach, if they detect him, they are off in confusion and haste.

The most terrible and persistent of the dovekie's enemies is the burgomaster gull, for the only refuge from him is a hole in the rocks. Even the swift gyrfalcon that pursues them relentlessly in the air is not so inexorable, for from him they can escape in the water. When a burgomaster singles out a dovekie as his prey the only hope for the auklet is to escape into a hole in the rocks, or by a quick dash into a flock succeed in diverting the pursuit to some other luckless dovekie. The burgomaster displays much agility and skill in following up the evolutions of the frightened dovekie, and often catches him on the wing. When the dovekie dives into the water the burgomaster hovers over him like an aeroplane over a submarine, following his underwater course, and the moment he comes up striking at him to force him under without a chance for rest or breath, repeating this until the little fellow is exhaused, when his big tormentor seizes him and makes a meal of him in a single gulp. The dovekies live in deadly terror of the gull and gyrfalcon, and whenever one of these big birds sails along the cliffs it is the signal for a panic-stricken flight of the dovekies. The raven is not so feared because not so greedy, and because he likes a varied diet, and does not bother them so much. Teedly-ingwah, a reliable Eskimo, says he has seen white whales catch many dovekies and eat them, and that he has found the whole birds in the stomachs of the whale.

The importance of the dovekie as a food bird to the Eskimos of northern Greenland is well illustrated by the following quotation from Mr. Figgins's (1899) notes:

To me the dovekie was the most interesting as well as the most numerous bird observed, and it is surprising that they survive the persecution to which they are subjected. During years when game is scarce, the natives depend almost entirely on the dovekie for food, and they are caught by the thousands and stored in great piles for winter use. Without the dovekie the little tribe of north Greenland Eskimos would long since have perished of hunger. The ground about their villages is thickly strewn with the bones of the dovekie, giving abundant proof of the millions which have been devoured. When on the water they are entirely safe from the natives, but seem to be very stupid when on land and are then easily captured with nets. When one alights on a rock it is immediately joined by others, until there is a struggling mass, as if it were the only rock in the neighborhood on which to alight. At such times they are easily approached and the quick use of a net or a well-directed stone usually results in the destruction of a number.

Again (1902) he says:

Dovekies display great curiosity, and if the hunter sits quietly in full view he will soon have an audience of them near him, all bent on occupying one rock, regardless of its size or of their numbers. A compact flock of birds soon results, and a well-directed stone thrown into their midst does great execution. Stones may be thrown a number of times at the same flock before they decide to adjourn.

Dr. Hayes (1867) gives us the following graphic account of how he accompanied an Eskimo on an auk-catching expedition in Greenland:

The birds were more noisy than usual, for they had just returned in immense swarms from the sea, where they had been getting their breakfast. Kalutunah carried a small net, made of light strings of sealskin knitted together very ingeniously. The staff by which it was held was about 10 feet long. After clambering over the rough, sharp stones, we arrived at length about halfway up to the base of the cliffs, where Kalutunah crouched behind a rock and invited me to follow his example. I observed that the birds were nearly all in flight, and were, with rare exceptions, the males. The length of the slope on which they were congregated was about a mile, and a constant stream of birds was rushing over it, but a few feet above the stones, and, after making in their rapid flight the whole length of the hill, they returned higher in the air, performing over and over again the complete circuit. Occasionally a few hundreds or thousands of them would drop down, as if following some leader, and in an instant the rocks for a space of several rods would swarm all over with them, their black backs and pure white breasts speckling the hill very prettily.

While I was watching these movements with much interest my companion was intent only upon business, and warned me to lie lower, as the birds saw me and were flying too high overhead. Having at length got myself stowed away to the satisfaction of my savage companion, the sport began. The birds were beginning again to whirl their flight closer to our heads—so close, indeed, did they come that it seemed almost as if I could catch them with my cap. Presently I observed by companion preparing himself as a flock of unusual thickness was approaching, and in a moment up went the net; a half dozen birds flew bang into it, and, stunned with the blow, they could not flutter out before Kalutunah had slipped the staff quickly through his hands and seized the net. With his left hand he now pressed down the birds, while with the right he drew them out one by one, and for want of a third hand he used his teeth to crush their heads. The wings were then locked across each other to keep them from fluttering away, and with an air of triumph the old fellow looked around at me, spat the blood and feathers from his mouth, and went on with the sport, tossing up his net and hauling it in with much rapidity, until he had caught about a hundred birds; when my curiosity being amply satisfied, we returned to camp and made a hearty meal out of the game which we had bagged in this novel and unsportsman-like manner. While an immense stew was preparing, Kalutunah amused himself with tearing off the birds' skins and consuming the raw flesh while it was yet warm.

Winter.—Although large numbers of dovekies migrate as far south as the coasts of New England a great many spend the winter near the edge of the Arctic ice pack, off the coasts of Labrador and Newfoundland, on the Atlantic Ocean, and even in southern Greenland. They leave their northernmost breeding grounds about the first or second week in September and work slowly southward as cold weather advances, reaching the New England coast in November. They are generally common and sometimes abundant on the Maine coast in winter, but south of the neighborhood of Massachusetts Bay they are rare, or irregular in appearance. While with us in winter they ordinarily spend their time out on the open sea, several miles from land, skimming over the tops of the waves or swimming about singly or in little groups; they are more often seen in the vicinity of sunken ledges or about little rocky islets than off the sandy shores of Cape Cod. In stormy weather they are often driven in near the beaches or even into harbors, creeks, and rivers. There are numerous instances on record where these little sea birds have been driven far inland and have perished from hunger and exhaustion. Mr. William Brewster (1906) relates his recollections of a memorable flight of this kind "which inundated eastern Massachusetts on November 15, 1871," which probably "comprised nearly, if not quite all, the birds which were living at that time off our coast."

On the date just named a violent easterly storm, accompanied by torrents of rain and an exceptionally high tide, forced multitudes of dovekies to seek refuge in the fresh-water ponds and rivers near the coast, and many birds were picked up in an exhausted condition in fields, meadows, barnyards, and even in our city streets. Within the area to which this paper relates they appeared in the greatest numbers in Charles River between Cambridge and Waltham, in the Mystic Ponds, and in Fresh Pond. The sheet of water last named was visited by hundreds, which came in singly or by twos and threes, and occasionally in flocks of from 10 or a dozen to 30 or 40 individuals each. The larger flocks often rose and left the pond, when disturbed, but the single birds, although somewhat restless, were absurdly tame. Some of them were taken alive, others killed with oars, and very many shot by collectors or sportsmen, 50 or more being captured in all.

DISTRIBUTION.

Breeding range.—Coasts and islands of the north Atlantic and Arctic Oceans. Baffin Land, Ellesmere Land, northern Greenland (Disco Island, Cape York, and Kane Basin), northern Iceland (Isle of Grimsey), Spitzbergen, Franz Josef Land, and Nova Zembla. Often ranges north in summer to latitude 81° or 82°. Has been recorded in July in 77° north, 151 east (near Bennett Islands), near

Melville Island in August, and two birds seen near Wainwright Inlet, Alaska, August 10, 1914.

Winter range.—From southern Greenland (Ivigtut and Arsuk) south along the coast to New York (Long Island), rarely to New Jersey (Cape May, Egg Harbor, Delaware River), Virginia (Chincoteague Bay, Cobbs Island, Smiths Island), North Carolina (Currituck Sound, Roanoke Island), and South Carolina (Beaufort). Also from the British Isles and the North Sea south along the coasts of Holland, France, and Spain to the Azores, Canary, and Madeira Islands.

Spring migration.—Birds leave the coast of Maine about March 15. Massachusetts: May 1 (latest). Rhode Island: April 27 (latest). New York: Long Island, in April (latest May 29). An unusually late record is Vermont: Bennington, May 31. Grand Manan: May 4. Latitude 48° 20′ north, longitude 46° 30′ west: May 22. They arrive in Greenland: Davis Strait, May 20; Baffin Bay, May 18 (rarely in April); Bowdoin Bay, May 8; Smith Sound, May 26; Spitzbergen, March 28; Franz Josef Land, February 25.

Fall migration.—Probably starts in July in Greenland: Davis Strait, common in July; Foulke Fiord, last, September 3; Cape Parry, last, September 11; Bowdoin Bay, last, September 6; northeastern Greenland, latitude 75°, August 2 (latest). Labrador: Cape Harrison, September 18. Anticosti Island, Gulf of St. Lawrence, in September. Birds reach New England usually in November. Early dates are: Maine coast, July 15. Massachusetts: Cape Cod, September 10; Nantucket, October 11. Connecticut: September, 1874. New York: Long Island, August.

Casual records.—Wisconsin: Point Washington, January 11. Michigan: Detroit River, November 30. Bermuda Island, January 28. The two Ontario records prove to refer to specimens of the ancient murrelet.

Egg dates.—Greenland: 19 records, June 7 to July 28; 10 records, June 16 to July 12. Iceland: 4 records, June 3, 8, and 28, and July 12.

REFERENCES TO BIBLIOGRAPHY.

ABBOTT, CLINTON GILBERT.
  1907—Summer Bird Life of the Newark, New Jersey, Marshes. The Auk, vol. 24, p. 1.
ALLEN, ARTHUR AUGUSTUS.
  1914—At Home with a Hell-Diver. Bird Lore, vol. 16, p. 248.
ALLEN, JOEL ASAPH.
  1876—The extinction of the Great Auk at the Funk Islands. American Naturalist, vol. 10, p. 48.
  1905—Report on the Birds Collected in Northeastern Siberia by the Jesup North Pacific Expedition. Bulletin of the American Museum of Natural History, vol. 21, p. 219.
ANTHONY, ALFRED WEBSTER.
  1896—Grebe Notes. The Nidologist, vol. 3, p. 71.
AUDUBON, JOHN JAMES.
  1840–1844—The Birds of America.
AUDUBON, MARIA REBECCA.
  1897—Audubon and his Journals.
BAILEY, VERNON.
  1902—Notes in "Handbook of Birds of the Western United States," by Florence Merriam Bailey.
BARLOW, CHESTER.
  1894—An Ornithological Paradise. The Museum, vol. 1, p. 37.
  1894a—A Few Notes on the Tufted Puffin. The Oologist, vol. 11, p. 353.
BARNES, R. MAGOON.
  1897—The Circling Loon. The Osprey, vol. 1, p. 77.
BECK, ROLLO HOWARD.
  1910—Water Birds of the Vicinity of Point Pinos, California. Proceedings of the California Academy of Sciences, ser. 4, vol. 3, p. 57.
BEEBE, CHARLES WILLIAM.
  1907—Notes on the Early Life of Loon Chicks. The Auk, vol. 24, p. 34.
BENDIRE, CHARLES EMIL.
  1895—Notes on the Ancient Murrelet, by Chase Littlejohn, with Annotations. The Auk, vol. 12, p. 270.
BENT, ARTHUR CLEVELAND.
  1913—Notes from Labrador. Bird Lore, vol. 15, p. 11.
BIGELOW, HENRY BRYANT.
  1902—Birds of the Northeastern Coast of Labrador. The Auk, vol. 19, p. 24.
BISHOP, LOUIS BENNETT.
  1889—Notes on the Birds of the Magdalen Islands. The Auk, vol. 6, p. 144.
BOND, JOHN A. WALPOLE.
  1914—Field Studies of Some Rarer British Birds.
BORASTON, JOHN MACLAIR.
  1905—Birds by Land and Sea.

BOWLES, JOHN HOOPER.
　　1908—Tapeworm Epidemic among Washington Seabirds.　The Condor, vol.
　　　　11, p. 33.

BRAISLIN, WILLIAM COUGHLIN.
　　1907—A List of the Birds of Long Island, New York.　Abstract of the
　　　　Proceedings of the Linnaean Society of New York, for the year
　　　　ending March, 1907.

BRETHERTON, BERNARD J.
　　1896—Kadiak Island.　A Contribution to the Avifauna of Alaska.　The
　　　　Oregon Naturalist, vol. 3, p. 45.

BREWSTER, WILLIAM.
　　1883—Notes on the Birds Observed during a Summer Cruise in the Gulf
　　　　of St. Lawrence.　Proceedings of the Boston Society of Natural
　　　　History, vol. 22, p. 364.
　　1902a—Birds of the Cape Region of Lower California.　Bulletin of the
　　　　Museum of Comparative Zoology at Harvard College, vol. 41, No. 1.
　　1906—The Birds of the Cambridge Region of Massachusetts.　Memoirs of
　　　　the Nuttall Ornithological Club, No. 4.

BROOKS, ALLAN.
　　1903—Notes on the Birds of the Cariboo District, British Columbia.　The
　　　　Auk, vol. 20, p. 277.

BRYANT, WALTER E.
　　1888—Birds and Eggs from the Farallone Islands.　Proceedings of the
　　　　California Academy of Sciences,　ser. 2, vol. 1, p. 25.

CAHN, ALVIN R.
　　1912—The Freezing of Cayuga Lake in its Relation to Bird Life.　The
　　　　Auk, vol. 29, p. 437.

CANTWELL, GEORGE G.
　　1898—Notes on the Egg of the Marbled Murrelet.　The Auk, vol. 15, p. 49.

CARTWRIGHT, GEORGE,
　　1792—A Journal of Transactions and Events during a Residence of nearly
　　　　Sixteen Years on the Coast of Labrador.

CATESBY, MARK.
　　1771—The Natural History of Carolina, Florida, and the Bahama Islands.

CHAPMAN, FRANK MICHLER.
　　1899a—Report of Birds Received Through the Peary Expeditions to Green-
　　　　land.　Bulletin of the American Museum of Natural History, vol.
　　　　12, p. 219.
　　1899b—Description of Two New Subspecies of Colymbus dominicus Linn.
　　　　Bulletin of the American Museum of Natural History, vol. 12,
　　　　p. 255.
　　1908—Camps and Cruises of an Ornithologist.
　　1912—Handbook of Birds of Eastern North America.

CLARKE, WILLIAM EAGLE.
　　1898—On the Avifauna of Franz Josef-Land.　The Ibis, ser. 7, vol. 4, p. 249.

COLLETT, ROBERT.
　　1894—On the Occurrence of Colymbus adamsi in Norway.　The Ibis, ser. 6,
　　　　vol. 6, p. 269.

COUES, ELLIOTT.
　　1861—Notes on the Ornithology of Labrador.　Proceedings of the Philadel-
　　　　phia Academy of Natural Sciences, 1861, p. 215.
　　1877—Birds of the North-West.
　　1903—Key to North American Birds, Fifth Edition.

CULVER, DELOS E.
    1914—Concealing Postures of Grebes. The Auk, vol. 31, p. 395.
CURRIER, EDMONDE SAMUEL.
    1904—Summer Birds of the Leech Lake Region, Minnesota. The Auk, vol. 21, p. 29.
DAWSON, WILLIAM LEON.
    1908—The New Reserves on the Washington Coast. The Condor, vol. 10, p. 45.
    1908a—The Bird Colonies of the Olympiades. The Auk, vol. 25, p. 153.
    1909—The Birds of Washington.
    1911—Another Fortnight on the Farallones. The Condor, vol. 13, p. 171.
DIXON, JOSEPH.
    1916—Migration of the Yellow-billed Loon. The Auk, vol. 33, p. 370.
DUTCHER, WILLIAM.
    1904—Report of the A. O. U. Committee on the Protection of North American Birds, for the Year 1903. The Auk, vol. 21, p. 97.
EATON, ELON HOWARD.
    1910—Birds of New York.
EIFRIG, CHARLES WILLIAM GUSTAVE.
    1905—Ornithological Results of the Canadian *Neptune* Expedition to Hudson Bay and Northward. The Auk, vol. 22, p. 233.
ELLIOTT, HENRY WOOD.
    1880—Report on the Seal Islands of Alaska.
EMERSON, W. OTTO.
    1904—The Farallone Islands Revisited, 1887–1903. The Condor, vol. 6, p. 61.
FIGGINS, JESSE DADE.
    1899—Notes in " Report on Birds Received Through the Peary Expeditions to Greenland," by Frank M. Chapman. Bulletin of the American Museum of Natural History, vol. 12, p. 219.
    1902—Some Food Birds of the Eskimos of Northwestern Greenland. Abstract of the Proceedings of the Linnaean Society of New York, for the Year ending March 11, 1902, p. 61.
FINLEY, WILLIAM LOVELL.
    1905—Among the Seabirds off the Oregon Coast. The Condor, vol. 7, pp. 119 and 161.
    1907a—The Grebes of Southern Oregon. The Condor, vol. 9, p. 97.
FLEMING, JOHN.
    1824—Gleanings of Natural History Gathered on the Coast of Scotland during a Voyage in 1821. Edinburgh Philosophical Journal, vol. 10, p. 94.
FRAZAR, MARTIN ABBOTT.
    1887—An Ornithologist's Summer in Labrador. Ornithologist and Oologist, vol. 12, p. 1.
GANONG, WILLIAM FRANCIS.
    1890—Do Young Loons eat Fresh-water Clams? The Auk, vol. 13, p. 77.
GÄTKE HEINRICH.
    1895—Heligoland as an Ornithological Observatory.
GOSS, BENJAMIN FRANKLIN.
    1883—Breeding Habits of the Carolina and American Eared Grebes. Ornithologist and Oologist, vol. 8, p. 1.
GOSS, NATHANIEL STICKNEY.
    1889—Additions to the Catalogue of the Birds of Kansas, with Notes in Regard to their Habits. The Auk, vol. 6, p. 122.

GOSSE, PHILIP HENRY.
    1847—The Birds of Jamaica.
GRIEVE, SYMINGTON.
    1885—The Great Auk, or Garefowl.
GRINNELL, JOSEPH.
    1897a—Report on the Birds Recorded during a Visit to the Islands of
          Santa Barbara, San Nicolas and San Clemente, in the Spring of
          1897. Pasadena Academy of Sciences, Publication, No. 1.
    1897b—Notes on the Marbled Murrelet. The Osprey, vol. 1, p. 115.
    1899—The Rhinoceros Auklet at Catalina Island. Bulletin of the Cooper
          Ornithological Club, vol. 1, p. 17.
    1900—Birds of the Kotzebue Sound Region. Pacific Coast Avifauna, No. 1.
    1909—Birds and Mammals of the 1907 Alexander Expedition to South-
          eastern Alaska. University of California Publications in Zoology,
          vol. 5, p. 171.
    1910—Birds of the 1908 Alexander Alaska Expedition. University of
          California Publications in Zoology, vol. 5, p. 361.
GURNEY, JOHN HENRY.
    1913—The Gannet.
HALKETT, ANDREW.
    1898—An Ottawa Naturalists' Journey Westward. The Ottawa Naturalist,
          vol. 12, p. 81.
HATCH, PHILO LOUIS.
    1892—Notes on the Birds of Minnesota.
HAYES, ISAAC ISRAEL.
    1867—The Open Polar Sea.
HEATH, HAROLD.
    1915—Birds Observed on Forrester Island, Alaska, during the Summer of
          1913. The Condor, vol. 17, p. 20.
HERSEY, F. SEYMOUR.
    1917—The Status of the Black-throated Loon (Gavia arctica) as a North
          American Bird. The Auk, vol. 34, p. 283.
HOWELL, ALFRED BRAZIER.
    1910—Notes from Los Coronados Islands. The Condor, vol. 12, p. 184.
JONES, LYNDS.
    1908—June with the Birds of the Washington Coast. The Wilson Bulletin,
          vol. 10, pp. 19, 57, and 189, and vol. 21, p. 3.
    1909—The Birds of Cedar Point and Vicinity. The Wilson Bulletin, No.
          67, vol. 21, p. 55.
KAEDING, HENRY B.
    1905—Birds from the West Coast of Lower California and adjacent Islands.
          The Condor, vol. 7, p. 105.
KEELER, CHARLES AUGUSTUS.
    1892—On the Natural History of the Farallone Islands. Zoe, vol. 3, p. 144.
KNIGHT, ORA WILLIS.
    1908—The Birds of Maine.
LINTON, C. B.
    1908—Notes from Santa Cruz Island. The Condor, vol. 10, p. 124.
LOOMIS, LEVERETT MILLS.
    1895—California Water Birds, No. 1. Proceedings of the California
          Academy of Sciences, ser. 2, vol. 5, p. 177.
    1896—California Water Birds No. 2. Proceedings of the California
          Academy of Sciences, ser. 2, vol. 6, p. 1.

LUCAS, FREDERIC AUGUSTUS.
1890—The Expedition to Funk Island with Observations upon the History and Anatomy of the Great Auk. Smithsonian Institution. Report of the National Museum for the Year ending June 30, 1888.
1901—Walrus Island, a Bird Metropolis of Bering Sea. Bird Lore, vol. 3, p. 45.

MCATEE, WALDO LEE and BEAL, F. E. L.
1912—Some Common Game, Aquatic and Rapacious Birds in Relation to Man. U. S. Department of Agriculture, Farmers' Bulletin 497.

MCILWRAITH, THOMAS.
1894—The Birds of Ontario.

MACFARLANE, RODERICK.
1891—Notes on and List of Birds and Eggs Collected in Arctic America, 1861–1866. Proceedings of the United States National Museum, vol. 14, p. 412.
1908—List of Birds and Eggs Observed and Collected in the North-West Territories of Canada, between 1880 and 1894. " Through the Mackenzie Basin," by Charles Mair.

MACGILLIVRAY, WILLIAM.
1837–1852—A History of British Birds.

MACOUN, JOHN.
1909—Catalogue of Canadian Birds. Second Edition.

MARTIN, MARTIN.
1753—A Voyage to St. Kilda.

MAYNARD, CHARLES JOHNSON.
1896—The Birds of Eastern North America.

MORRIS, F. O.
1903—A History of British Birds. Fifth edition.

MURDOCH, JOHN.
1885—Report of the International Polar Expedition to Point Barrow, Alaska. Part 4. Natural History, p. 91.

NELSON, EDWARD WILLIAM.
1887—Report upon Natural History Collections made in Alaska.

NEWTON, ALFRED.
1861—Abstract of Mr. J. Wolley's Reasearches in Iceland respecting the Gare-fowl or Great Auk (*Alca impennis* Linn.) Ibis, vol. 3, p. 374.
1865—The Gare-fowl and its Historians. Natural History Review, p. 467.

NUTTALL, THOMAS.
1834—A Manual of the Ornithology of the United States and Canada. Water Birds.

OSGOOD, WILFRED HUDSON.
1904—A Biological Reconnaissance of the Base of the Alaska Peninsula. North American Fauna, No. 24.

PALMER, WILLIAM.
1890—Notes on the Birds Observed during the Cruise of the United States Fish Commission Schooner *Grampus* in the Summer of 1887. Proceedings of the United States National Museum, vol. 13, p. 249.
1899—The Avifauna of the Pribilof Islands. The Fur-Seals and Fur-Seal Islands of the North Pacific Ocean. Part 3, p. 355.

PENNANT, THOMAS.
1776—British Zoology, vol. 2.

PREBLE, EDWARD ALEXANDER.
    1908—A Biological Investigation of the Athabaska-Mackenzie Region.
        North American Fauna, No. 27.
QUILLIN, ROY W. and HOLLEMAN, RIDLEY.
    1916—The San Domingo Grebe in Bexar County, Texas. The Condor, vol.
        18, p. 221.
RAINE, WALTER.
    1893—Bird-nesting in Northwest Canada. The Nidiologist, vol. 1, pp. 67,
        84, 102, 117, and 130; vol. 2, pp. 9, 19, and 36. 1894.
RAY, MILTON SMITH.
    1904—A Fortnight on the Farallones. The Auk, vol. 21, p. 425.
RIDGWAY, ROBERT.
    1887—A Manual of North American Birds.
ROBERTS, THOMAS SADLER.
    1900—An Account of the Nesting Habits of Franklin's Rosy Gull (*Larus
        franklinii*), as Observed at Heron Lake in Southern Minnesota.
        The Auk, vol. 17, p. 272.
ROBERTSON, HOWARD.
    1903—Cassin Auklet, Ptychoramphus aleuticus. The Condor, vol. 5, p. 96.
ROCKWELL, ROBERT BLANCHARD.
    1910—Nesting Notes on the American Eared Grebe and Pied-billed Grebe.
        The Condor, vol. 12, p. 188.
ROSSAM, ADRIAAN VAN.
    1915—Notes on Murrelets and Petrels. The Condor, vol. 17, p. 74.
SARUDNY, N. A.
    1912—Urinator arcticus suschkini. Messager Ornithologique, vol. 3, p. 111.
SELBY, PRIDEAUX JOHN.
    1833—Illustrations of British Ornithology.
SELOUS, EDMUND.
    1905—The Bird Watcher in the Shetlands.
SILLOWAY, PERLEY MILTON.
    1902—The Holboell Grebe in Montana. The Condor, vol. 4, p. 128.
SIM, ROBERT J.
    1904—Notes on the Holboell Grebe. The Wilson Bulletin, vol. 16, p. 67,
        No. 48.
STEARNS, WINFRED A.
    1883—Notes on the Natural History of Labrador. Proceedings of the
        United States National Museum, vol. 6, p. 111.
STEJNEGER, LEONHARD.
    1885—Results of Ornithological Explorations in the Commander Islands
        and in Kamtschatka. Bulletin of the United States National
        Museum, No. 29.
STEPHENS, FRANK.
    1893—Notes on Cassin's Auklet. The Auk, vol. 10, p. 298.
STONE, WITMER.
    1900—Report on the Birds and Mammals obtained by the McIlhenny
        Expedition to Point Barrow, Alaska. Proceedings of the Acad-
        emy of Natural Sciences of Philadelphia, 1900, p. 4.
STREETS, THOMAS HALE.
    1877—Contributions to the Natural History of the Hawaiian and Fanning
        Islands and Lower California. Bulletin of the United States
        National Museum, No. 7.
SUCKLEY, GEORGE (COOPER, JAMES GRAHAM).
    1860—The Natural History of Washington Territory and Oregon.

SWARTH, HARRY SCHELWALDT.
    1911—Birds and Mammals of the 1909 Alexander Alaska Expedition.
        University of California Publications in Zoology, vol. 7, p. 9.
THAYER, JOHN ELIOT.
    1909—Two letters from W. W. Brown, Jr., published in The Condor, vol. 11,
        p. 142.
    1914—Nesting of the Kittlitz Murrelet. The Condor, vol. 16, p. 117.
THAYER, JOHN E., and BANGS, OUTRAM.
    1914—Notes on the Birds and Mammals of the Arctic Coast of East
        Siberia. Birds. Proceedings of the New England Zoological
        Club, vol. 5, p. 1.
TOWNSEND, CHARLES HASKINS.
    1908—Observations on a Tame Loon. Bird Lore, vol. 10, p. 171.
    1913—The Crested Auklet. The National Association of Audubon So-
        cieties, Educational Leaflet, No. 65. Bird Lore, vol. 15, p. 133.
TOWNSEND, CHARLES WENDELL.
    1905—The Birds of Essex County, Massachusetts. Memoirs of the Nuttall
        Ornithological Club. No. 3.
    1909—The Use of the Wings and Feet by Diving Birds. The Auk, vol. 26,
        p. 234.
TOWNSEND, CHARLES WENDELL, and ALLEN, GLOVER M.
    1907—Birds of Labrador. Proceedings of the Boston Society of Natural
        History, vol. 33, No. 7, p. 277.
TURNER, LUCIEN MCSHAN.
    1886—Contributions to the Natural History of Alaska.
WARREN, BENJAMIN HARRY.
    1890—Report on the Birds of Pennsylvania.
WAYNE, ARTHUR TREZEVANT.
    1910—Birds of South Carolina. Contributions from the Charleston Mu-
        seum, I.
WHITBOURNE, RICHARD.
    1622—A discourse and discovery of Newfoundland.
WRIGHT, HOWARD W.
    1909—An Ornithological Trip to Los Coronados Islands, Mexico. The
        Condor, vol. 11, p. 96.
YARRELL, WILLIAM.
    1871—History of British Birds, Fourth Edition, 1871–85. Revised and
        enlarged by Alfred Newton and Howard Saunders.

EXPLANATION OF PLATES 44-55

The eggs illustrated were selected from the collection of the United States National Museum, except as otherwise indicated. After the Museum catalogue number of each specimen is given the name of the collector, the locality, and the date as far as known.

PLATE 44.

1. Western grebe, 21563, Fort Klamath, Oregon, May 28, 1883, C. E. Bendire.
2. Mexican grebe, 24917, Brownsville, Texas, July 28, 1891, F. B. Armstrong.
3. Holbœll's grebe, 6774, Porcupine River, Alaska, R. Kennicott.
4. Eared grebe, 33251, Stinking Lake, New Mexico, July 30, 1913, Stokley Ligon.
5. Pied-billed grebe, 27434, Brownsville, Texas, August 25, 1891, F. B. Armstrong.
6. Tufted puffin, 28483, Lapush, Washington, June 21, 1897, R. T. Young.
7. Horned grebe, 6737, Porcupine River, Alaska, R. Kennicott.
8. Horned puffin, 16730, Saint George Island, Alaska, July 12, 1873, H. W. Elliott.

PLATE 45.

1. Loon, 12951, Saint Croix River, Maine, G. A. Boardman.
2. Black-throated loon, 2633, Europe, H. Drouet (dealer).
3. Pacific loon, 9658, Anderson River, Mackenzie, June 29, 1869, R. MacFarlane.

PLATE 46.

1. Yellow-billed loon, A. C. Bent collection, Point Hope, Alaska, June 22, 1916, Rev. A. R. Hoare.
2. Red-throated loon, 19046, Greenland, Governor Fencker.
3. Red-throated loon, 12621, Anderson River, Mackenzie, R. MacFarlane.

PLATE 47.

1. Cassin's auklet, 22163, Kodiak Island, Alaska, May 28, 1884, W. J. Fisher.
2. Paroquet auklet, 22157, Kodiak Island, Alaska, June 19, 1884, W. J. Fisher.
3. Crested auklet, 21431, Saint Michael, Alaska, 1884, E. W. Nelson.
4. Least auklet, 24077, Saint Paul Island, Alaska, June 5, 1890, Wm. Palmer.
5. Puffin, 19052, Greenland, July 23, 1879, Governor Fencker.
6. Whiskered auklet, C. E. Doe collection, Kurile Islands (see page 126).
7. Large-billed puffin, 18480, Greenland, June, 1881, Governor Fencker.

PLATE 48.

1. Ancient murrelet, 25093, Sanak Island, Alaska, Chase Littlejohn.
2. Ancient murrelet, 22154, Kodiak Island, Alaska, June 1, 1884, W. J. Fisher.
3. Rhinoceros auklet, 27633, Smith's Island, Washington, April 22, 1895, G. W. Dennison.
4. Rhinoceros auklet, 27649, Whitby Island, Washington, April 25, 1895, G. W. Dennison.
5. Marbled murrelet, 28473, Howcan, Alaska, May 22, 1897, G. G. Cantwell.

PLATE 49.

1. Craveri's murrelet, 17272, Isla Raza, Gulf of California, T. H. Streets.
2. Craveri's murrelet, 17272, same data.
3. Kittlitz's murrelet, J. E. Thayer collection, Pavlof Mountain, Alaska, June 10, 1913, F. E. Kleinschmidt.
4. Dovekie, 19053, Greenland, July 23, 1879, Governor Fencker.
5. Xantus's murrelet, 28128, Los Coronados Islands, Mexico, May 11, 1895, A. W Anthony.
6. Xantus's murrelet, 33226, Los Coronados Islands, Mexico, April 3, 1912, C. S. Thompson.

PLATE 50.

1. Black guillemot, 2518, Bay of Fundy, New Brunswick, 1859, Dr. Henry Bryant.
2. Black guillemot, 9799, Bay of Fundy, New Brunswick, Dr. Henry Bryant.
3. Pigeon guillemot, 27472, Smith's Island, Puget Sound, Washington, May 9, 1894, G. W. Dennison.
4. Pigeon guillemot, 18711, Kodiak Island, Alaska, June, 1882, W. J. Fisher.
5. Mandt's guillemot, 31556, Whale River, Ungava, A. A. Chesterfield.

PLATE 51.

1. Murre, 27587, Cape Whittle, Labrador, June 19, 1884, M. A. Frazar.
2. Murre, 27589, Cape Whittle, Labrador, July 18, 1884, M. A. Frazar.
3. California murre, 26459, Farallone Islands, California, June 17, 1885, A. M. Ingersoll.

PLATE 52.

1. California murre, 21450, Saint Michael, Alaska, August 3, 1880, E. W. Nelson.
2. California murre, 2117, Farallone Islands, California, California Society of Natural History.
3. California murre, 2117, same data.

PLATE 53.

1. Brünnich's murre, 19049, Greenland, 1884, Governor Fencker.
2. Pallas's murre, 24072, Walrus Island, Alaska, June 13, 1890, William Palmer.
3. Brünnich's murre, 19049, Greenland, 1884, Governor Fencker.

PLATE 54.

1. Pallas's murre, 16718, Saint George Island, Alaska, July 1, 1873, H. W. Elliott.
2. Pallas's murre, 16719, Saint George Island, Alaska, June 27, 1873, H. W. Elliott.
3. Pallas's murre, 18703, Lemida Island, Alaska, June, 1882, W. J. Fisher.

PLATE 55.

1. Razor-billed auk, 24425, Cape Whittle, Labrador, July 12, 1884, M. A. Frazar.
2. Razor-billed auk, 27601, Cape Whittle, Labrador, July 17, 1884, M. A. Frazar.
3. Razor-billed auk, 27604, Cape Whittle, Labrador, July 20, 1884, M. A. Frazar.
4. Razor-billed auk, 27596, Cape Whittle, Labrador, July 3, 1884, M. A. Frazar.

INDEX.

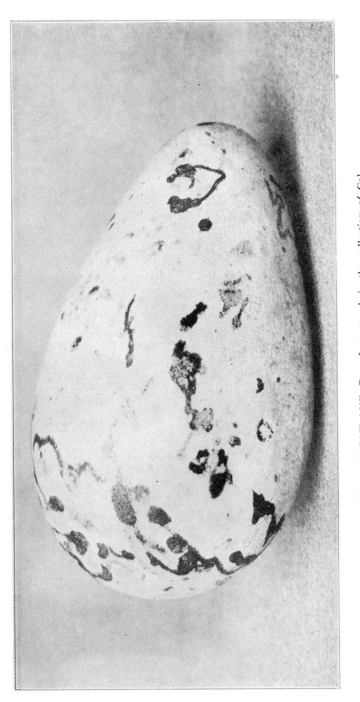

PLATE 1. GREAT AUK. Egg of great auk in the collection of Col. John E. Thayer, Lancaster, Massachusetts, formerly in the collection of Sir William Milner, Nunappleton, Yorkshire, England, and purchased by him in 1847 from M. Perrot, a dealer in Paris, photo presented by Col. J. E. Thayer.

PLATE 2. WESTERN GREBE. *Upper:* Nesting site of western grebe near Crane Lake, Saskatchewan, June 8, 1905, referred to on page 3. *Lower:* Nest and eggs in the above locality.

PLATE 3. WESTERN GREBE. *Upper:* Nest and large set of eggs of western grebe, referred to on page 5. *Lower:* Young western grebe recently hatched, photo presented by Mr. William L. Finley.

PLATE 4. HOLBŒLL'S GREBE. *Upper:* Nesting site of Holbœll's grebe, Lake Winnipegosis, Manitoba, June 11, 1913, referred to on page 10. *Lower:* Nest and eggs in the above locality.

PLATE 5. HOLBŒLL'S GREBE. *Upper:* Nest and eggs of Holbœll's grebe, Lake Winnipegosis, Manitoba. *Lower:* Holbœll's grebe on its nest, photo purchased from Mr. S. S. S. Stansell.

PLATE 6. HORNED GREBE. *Upper:* Nesting site of the horned grebe, Crane Lake, Saskatchewan, June 7, 1905. *Lower:* Another nest in the same locality. Both referred to on page 21.

PLATE 7. HORNED GREBE. *Upper:* Distant view of horned grebe's nest, eggs covered, Magdalen Islands, June 22, 1904, referred to on page 21. *Lower:* Horned grebe on its nest, courtesy of Bird-Lore.

PLATE 8. EARED GREBE. *Upper:* Nesting colony of eared grebes, Dry Lake, North Dakota, June 26, 1901, photo presented by Mr. Herbert K. Job. *Lower:* Nest and eggs of eared grebe in Franklin Gull colony, Lake of the Narrows, Saskatchewan, June 12, 1905, referred to on page 29.

PLATE 9. PIED-BILLED GREBE. *Upper:* Nest and eggs of pied-billed
grebe, June 8, 1901, referred to on page 40. *Lower:* Another nest, eggs
covered, same locality and date.

PLATE 10. PIED-BILLED GREBE. *Upper:* Pied-billed grebe on its nest, photo presented by Mr. Francis Harper. *Lower:* Young pied-billed grebes just hatched, photo presented by Mr. Robert B. Rockwell.

PLATE 11. LOON. *Upper:* Nest and eggs of loon, June 7, 1913, from negative taken by Mr. Herbert K. Job for the author. *Lower:* Nest and eggs of loon, June 23, 1912, referred to on page 49.

PLATE 12. LOON. *Upper:* Loon on its nest, courtesy of Bird-Lore. *Lower:* Young loon swimming among lily pads, photo purchased from Mr. S. S. S. Stansell.

PLATE 13. YELLOW-BILLED LOON. *Upper:* Nest and eggs of yellow-billed loon, referred to on page 61. *Lower:* More distant view of the same nest. Both from negatives taken by Rev. A. R. Hoare for the author.

PLATE 14. PACIFIC LOON. *Upper:* Nesting site of Pacific loon, referred to on page 68. *Lower:* Nest and eggs of Pacific loon, July 4, 1914. Photos presented by Mr. Winthrop S. Brooks.

PLATE 15. RED-THROATED LOON. *Upper:* Nest and egg of red-throated loon, June 20, 1915, from negative taken by Mr. F. Seymour Hersey for the author. *Lower:* Nest and eggs of red-throated loon, June 27, 1916, from negative taken by Mr. T. L. Richardson for the author.

PLATE 16. RED-THROATED LOON. *Upper:* Nest and eggs of red-throated loon. *Lower:* Nearer view of same nest. Photos presented by Mr. Donald B. MacMillan, courtesy of the American Museum of Natural History.

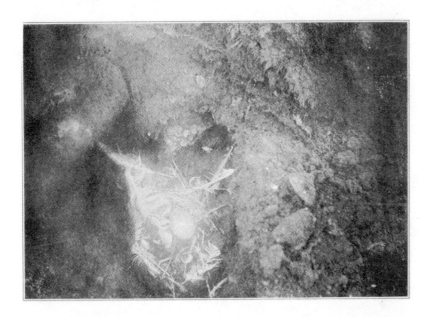

PLATE 17. TUFTED PUFFIN. *Upper:* Burrow of tufted puffin, opened to show nest and egg, July 7, 1911, referred to on page 83. *Lower:* Entrance to burrow of tufted puffin, July 4, 1911, referred to on page 83.

PLATE 18. TUFTED PUFFIN. *Upper:* Breeding colony of tufted puffin, referred to on page 84, photo presented by Mr. William L. Dawson. *Lower:* Young tufted puffin, recently hatched, photo presented by Mr. William L. Finley.

PLATE 19. PUFFIN. *Upper:* Breeding colony of puffins, referred to on page 89, photo presented by Mr. F. A. Brown. *Lower:* Puffins on the top of Bird Rock, near their nesting burrows, July 25, 1915.

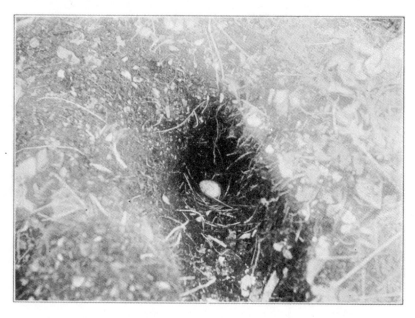

PLATE 20. PUFFIN. *Upper:* Entrance to burrow of puffin, June 9, 1909, referred to on page 91. *Lower:* Same burrow opened to show nest and egg.

PLATE 21. HORNED PUFFIN. *Upper:* Nesting site of horned puffin, June 9, 1915, near St. Michael, Alaska, from negative taken by Mr. F. Seymour Hersey for the author. *Lower:* Another view of the same colony.

PLATE 22. RHINOCEROS AUKLET. *Upper:* Nesting site of rhinoceros auklet, referred to on page 104. Lower: Nesting burrow in same colony, opened to show nest and egg. Photos presented by Mr. William L. Dawson.

PLATE 23. RHINOCEROS AUKLET. Entrance to burrow of rhinoceros auklet, photo presented by Mr. William L. Dawson.

PLATE 24. CASSIN'S AUKLET. *Upper:* Entrance to burrow of Cassin's auklet, 'photo presented by Mr. William L. Dawson. *Lower:* Burrow of Cassin's auklet opened to show bird and egg, photo presented by Mr. George Willett.

PLATE 25. *Upper:* AUKLETS. Nesting site of paroquet, crested and least auklets, July 7, 1911, referred to on pages 117, 121, and 129. *Lower:* PAROQUET AUKLET. Nest and egg of paroquet auklet in above locality.

PLATE 26. *Upper:* CRESTED AUKLET. Nest and egg of crested auklet, July 7, 1911, referred to on page 121. *Lower:* LEAST AUKLET.
Nest and egg of least auklet, July 7, 1911, referred to on page 129.

PLATE 27. LEAST AUKLET. Nesting colony of least auklets, photo presented by Mr. Charles H. Townsend, locality referred to on page 129.

PLATE 28. XANTUS'S MURRELET. Xantus's murrelet on its nest, photo presented by Mr. Donald R. Dickey.

PLATE 29. XANTUS'S MURRELET. *Upper:* Young Xantus's murrelet, recently hatched. *Lower:* Nest and eggs of Xantus's murrelet. Photos presented by Mr. Donald R. Dickey.

PLATE 30. BLACK GUILLEMOT. *Upper:* Nesting site of black guillemot, July 3, 1904, referred to on page 157. *Lower:* Young black guillemots, nearly ready to leave the nest, photo presented by Mr. Herbert K. Job.

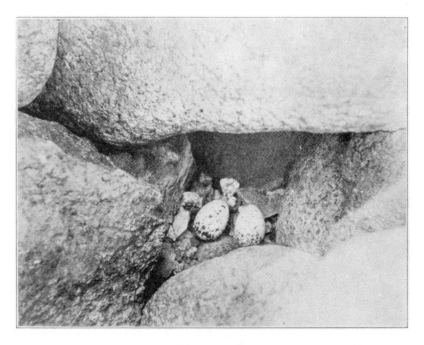

PLATE 31. BLACK GUILLEMOT. *Upper:* Nest and eggs of black guillemot, July 3, 1904, referred to on page 158. *Lower:* Nearer view of same nest.

PLATE 32. PIGEON GUILLEMOT. *Upper:* Nesting site of pigeon guillemot. *Lower:* Nest and eggs of same in same locality. Photos presented by Mr. William L. Dawson.

PLATE 33. MURRE. *Upper:* Breeding colony of murres, June 24, 1904, referred to on page 175. *Lower:* Eggs in colony shown above.

PLATE 34. MURRE. *Upper:* Breeding colony of murres and double-crested cormorants, referred to on page 175, photo presented by Dr. Charles W. Townsend. *Lower:* Young murre, nearly ready to leave the cliffs, July 24, 1915, referred to on page 177.

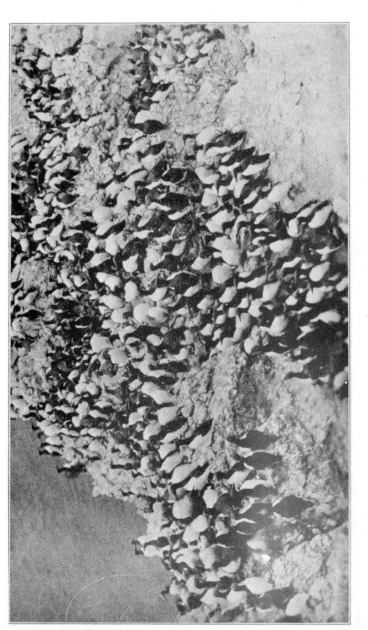

PLATE 35. CALIFORNIA MURRE. Breeding colony of California murres, referred to on page 184, photo presented by Mr. William L. Finley.

PLATE 36. CALIFORNIA MURRE. *Upper:* Breeding colony of California murres, July 7, 1911, referred to on page 185. *Lower:* Part of same colony.

PLATE 37. CALIFORNIA MURRE. Young California murres, photo presented by Mr. William L. Finley.

PLATE 38. BRÜNNICH'S MURRE. *Upper:* Brünnich's murres on their eggs, June 25, 1904, from negative taken by Mr. Herbert K. Job for the author. *Lower:* Eggs of Brünnich's murre, photo presented by Mr. Herbert K. Job.

PLATE 39. PALLAS'S MURRE. *Upper:* Breeding colony of Pallas's
murres, July 4, 1911, referred to on page 197. *Lower:* Eggs in above
colony.

PLATE 40. PALLAS'S MURRE. *Upper:* Pair of Pallas's murres and their egg, July 4, 1911. *Lower:* Group of nesting Pallas's murres, July 4, 1911.

PLATE 41. RAZOR-BILLED AUK. *Upper:* Breeding colony of razor-billed auks, June 25, 1904, referred to on page 202. *Lower:* Egg of same in above locality, photo presented by Mr. Herbert K. Job.

PLATE 42. DOVEKIE. *Upper:* Flock of dovekies on water. *Lower:* Flock of dovekies on rocks. Photos presented by Mr. Donald B. Mac-Millan, courtesy of the American Museum of Natural History.

PLATE 43. DOVEKIE. *Upper:* Young dovekie, half-fledged. *Lower:* Dovekies flying over their nesting sites. Photos presented by Mr. Donald B. MacMillan, courtesy of the American Museum of Natural History.

PLATE 44. 1, Western Grebe; 2, Mexican Grebe; 3, Holbœll's Grebe; 4, Eared Grebe; 5, Pied-billed Grebe; 6, Tufted Puffin; 7, Horned Grebe; 8, Horned Puffin. For description, see page 233.

PLATE 45. 1, Loon; 2, Black-throated Loon; 3, Pacific Loon. For description, see page 233.

PLATE 46. 1, Yellow-billed Loon; 2 and 3, Red-throated Loon. For
description, see page 233.

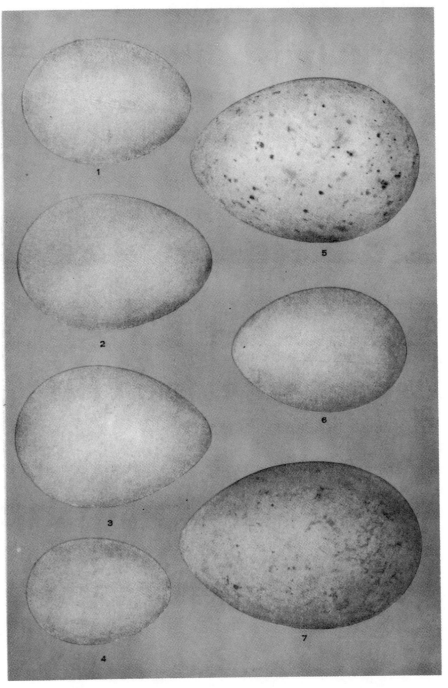

PLATE 47. 1, Cassin's Auklet; 2, Paroquet Auklet; 3, Crested Auklet;
4, Least Auklet; 5, Puffin; 6, Whiskered Auklet; 7, Large-billed Puffin.
For description, see page 233.

PLATE 48. 1 and 2, Ancient Murrelet; 3 and 4, Rhinoceros Auklet;
5, Marbled Murrelet. For description, see page 233.

PLATE 49. 1 and 2, Craveri's Murrelet; 3, Kittlitz's Murrelet; 4, Dovekie; 5 and 6, Xantus's Murrelet. For description, see page 234.

PLATE 50. 1 and 2, Black Guillemot; 3 and 4, Pigeon Guillemot; 5, Mandt's Guillemot. For description, see page 234.

PLATE 51. 1 and 2, Murre; 3, California Murre. For description, see page 234.

PLATE 52. California Murre. For description, see page 234.

PLATE 53. 1 and 3, Brunnich's Murre; 2, Pallas's Murre. For description, see page 234.

PLATE 54. Pallas's Murre. For description, see page 234.

PLATE 55. Razor-billed Auk. For description, see page 234.

A CATALOG OF SELECTED DOVER BOOKS IN ALL FIELDS OF INTEREST

CONCERNING THE SPIRITUAL IN ART, Wassily Kandinsky. Pioneering work by father of abstract art. Thoughts on color theory, nature of art. Analysis of earlier masters. 12 illustrations. 80pp. of text. 5⅜ × 8½. 23411-8 Pa. $2.50

LEONARDO ON THE HUMAN BODY, Leonardo da Vinci. More than 1200 of Leonardo's anatomical drawings on 215 plates. Leonardo's text, which accompanies the drawings, has been translated into English. 506pp. 8⅜ × 11¾. 24483-0 Pa. $10.95

GOBLIN MARKET, Christina Rossetti. Best-known work by poet comparable to Emily Dickinson, Alfred Tennyson. With 46 delightfully grotesque illustrations by Laurence Housman. 64pp. 4 × 6¾. 24516-0 Pa. $2.50

THE HEART OF THOREAU'S JOURNALS, edited by Odell Shepard. Selections from *Journal*, ranging over full gamut of interests. 228pp. 5⅜ × 8½. 20741-2 Pa. $4.50

MR. LINCOLN'S CAMERA MAN: MATHEW B. BRADY, Roy Meredith. Over 300 Brady photos reproduced directly from original negatives, photos. Lively commentary. 368pp. 8⅜ × 11¼. 23021-X Pa. $14.95

PHOTOGRAPHIC VIEWS OF SHERMAN'S CAMPAIGN, George N. Barnard. Reprint of landmark 1866 volume with 61 plates: battlefield of New Hope Church, the Etawah Bridge, the capture of Atlanta, etc. 80pp. 9 × 12. 23445-2 Pa. $6.00

A SHORT HISTORY OF ANATOMY AND PHYSIOLOGY FROM THE GREEKS TO HARVEY, Dr. Charles Singer. Thoroughly engrossing nontechnical survey. 270 illustrations. 211pp. 5⅜ × 8½. 20389-1 Pa. $4.95

REDOUTE ROSES IRON-ON TRANSFER PATTERNS, Barbara Christopher. Redouté was botanical painter to the Empress Josephine; transfer his famous roses onto fabric with these 24 transfer patterns. 80pp. 8¼ × 10⅞. 24292-7 Pa. $3.50

THE FIVE BOOKS OF ARCHITECTURE, Sebastiano Serlio. Architectural milestone, first (1611) English translation of Renaissance classic. Unabridged reproduction of original edition includes over 300 woodcut illustrations. 416pp. 9⅜ × 12¼. 24349-4 Pa. $14.95

CARLSON'S GUIDE TO LANDSCAPE PAINTING, John F. Carlson. Authoritative, comprehensive guide covers, every aspect of landscape painting. 34 reproductions of paintings by author; 58 explanatory diagrams. 144pp. 8⅜ × 11. 22927-0 Pa. $5.95

101 PUZZLES IN THOUGHT AND LOGIC, C.R. Wylie, Jr. Solve murders, robberies, see which fishermen are liars—purely by reasoning! 107pp. 5⅜ × 8½. 20367-0 Pa. $2.00

TEST YOUR LOGIC, George J. Summers. 50 more truly new puzzles with new turns of thought, new subtleties of inference. 100pp. 5⅜ × 8½. 22877-0 Pa. $2.25

THE MURDER BOOK OF J.G. REEDER, Edgar Wallace. Eight suspenseful stories by bestselling mystery writer of 20s and 30s. Features the donnish Mr. J.G. Reeder of Public Prosecutor's Office. 128pp. 5⅜ × 8½. (Available in U.S. only)
24374-5 Pa. $3.50

ANNE ORR'S CHARTED DESIGNS, Anne Orr. Best designs by premier needlework designer, all on charts: flowers, borders, birds, children, alphabets, etc. Over 100 charts, 10 in color. Total of 40pp. 8¼ × 11. 23704-4 Pa. $2.50

BASIC CONSTRUCTION TECHNIQUES FOR HOUSES AND SMALL BUILDINGS SIMPLY EXPLAINED, U.S. Bureau of Naval Personnel. Grading, masonry, woodworking, floor and wall framing, roof framing, plastering, tile setting, much more. Over 675 illustrations. 568pp. 6½ × 9¼. 20242-9 Pa. $8.95

MATISSE LINE DRAWINGS AND PRINTS, Henri Matisse. Representative collection of female nudes, faces, still lifes, experimental works, etc., from 1898 to 1948. 50 illustrations. 48pp. 8⅜ × 11¼. 23877-6 Pa. $2.50

HOW TO PLAY THE CHESS OPENINGS, Eugene Znosko-Borovsky. Clear, profound examinations of just what each opening is intended to do and how opponent can counter. Many sample games. 147pp. 5⅜ × 8½. 22795-2 Pa. $2.95

DUPLICATE BRIDGE, Alfred Sheinwold. Clear, thorough, easily followed account: rules, etiquette, scoring, strategy, bidding; Goren's point-count system, Blackwood and Gerber conventions, etc. 158pp. 5⅜ × 8½. 22741-3 Pa. $3.00

SARGENT PORTRAIT DRAWINGS, J.S. Sargent. Collection of 42 portraits reveals technical skill and intuitive eye of noted American portrait painter, John Singer Sargent. 48pp. 8¼ × 11⅛. 24524-1 Pa. $2.95

ENTERTAINING SCIENCE EXPERIMENTS WITH EVERYDAY OBJECTS, Martin Gardner. Over 100 experiments for youngsters. Will amuse, astonish, teach, and entertain. Over 100 illustrations. 127pp. 5⅜ × 8½. 24201-3 Pa. $2.50

TEDDY BEAR PAPER DOLLS IN FULL COLOR: A Family of Four Bears and Their Costumes, Crystal Collins. A family of four Teddy Bear paper dolls and nearly 60 cut-out costumes. Full color, printed one side only. 32pp. 9¼ × 12¼.
24550-0 Pa. $3.50

NEW CALLIGRAPHIC ORNAMENTS AND FLOURISHES, Arthur Baker. Unusual, multi-useable material: arrows, pointing hands, brackets and frames, ovals, swirls, birds, etc. Nearly 700 illustrations. 80pp. 8⅜ × 11¼.
24095-9 Pa. $3.75

DINOSAUR DIORAMAS TO CUT & ASSEMBLE, M. Kalmenoff. Two complete three-dimensional scenes in full color, with 31 cut-out animals and plants. Excellent educational toy for youngsters. Instructions; 2 assembly diagrams. 32pp. 9¼ × 12¼. 24541-1 Pa. $4.50

SILHOUETTES: A PICTORIAL ARCHIVE OF VARIED ILLUSTRATIONS, edited by Carol Belanger Grafton. Over 600 silhouettes from the 18th to 20th centuries. Profiles and full figures of men, women, children, birds, animals, groups and scenes, nature, ships, an alphabet. 144pp. 8⅜ × 11¼. 23781-8 Pa. $4.95

YUCATAN BEFORE AND AFTER THE CONQUEST, Diego de Landa. Only significant account of Yucatan written in the early post-Conquest era. Translated by William Gates. Over 120 illustrations. 162pp. 5⅜ × 8½.　　23622-6 Pa. $3.50

ORNATE PICTORIAL CALLIGRAPHY, E.A. Lupfer. Complete instructions, over 150 examples help you create magnificent "flourishes" from which beautiful animals and objects gracefully emerge. 8⅛ × 11.　　21957-7 Pa. $2.95

DOLLY DINGLE PAPER DOLLS, Grace Drayton. Cute chubby children by same artist who did Campbell Kids. Rare plates from 1910s. 30 paper dolls and over 100 outfits reproduced in full color. 32pp. 9¼ × 12¼.　　23711-7 Pa. $3.50

CURIOUS GEORGE PAPER DOLLS IN FULL COLOR, H. A. Rey, Kathy Allert. Naughty little monkey-hero of children's books in two doll figures, plus 48 full-color costumes: pirate, Indian chief, fireman, more. 32pp. 9¼ × 12¼.
　　24386-9 Pa. $3.50

GERMAN: HOW TO SPEAK AND WRITE IT, Joseph Rosenberg. Like *French, How to Speak and Write It.* Very rich modern course, with a wealth of pictorial material. 330 illustrations. 384pp. 5⅜ × 8½. (USUKO)　　20271-2 Pa. $4.75

CATS AND KITTENS: 24 Ready-to-Mail Color Photo Postcards, D. Holby. Handsome collection; feline in a variety of adorable poses. Identifications. 12pp. on postcard stock. 8¼ × 11.　　24469-5 Pa. $2.95

MARILYN MONROE PAPER DOLLS, Tom Tierney. 31 full-color designs on heavy stock, from *The Asphalt Jungle, Gentlemen Prefer Blondes,* 22 others.1 doll. 16 plates. 32pp. 9⅜ × 12¼.　　23769-9 Pa. $3.50

FUNDAMENTALS OF LAYOUT, F.H. Wills. All phases of layout design discussed and illustrated in 121 illustrations. Indispensable as student's text or handbook for professional. 124pp. 8⅛.× 11.　　21279-3 Pa. $4.50

FANTASTIC SUPER STICKERS, Ed Sibbett, Jr. 75 colorful pressure-sensitive stickers. Peel off and place for a touch of pizzazz: clowns, penguins, teddy bears, etc. Full color. 16pp. 8¼ × 11.　　24471-7 Pa. $2.95

LABELS FOR ALL OCCASIONS, Ed Sibbett, Jr. 6 labels each of 16 different designs—baroque, art nouveau, art deco, Pennsylvania Dutch, etc.—in full color. 24pp. 8¼ × 11.　　23688-9 Pa. $2.95

HOW TO CALCULATE QUICKLY: RAPID METHODS IN BASIC MATHE-MATICS, Henry Sticker. Addition, subtraction, multiplication, division, checks, etc. More than 8000 problems, solutions. 185pp. 5 × 7¼.　　20295-X Pa. $2.95

THE CAT COLORING BOOK, Karen Baldauski. Handsome, realistic renderings of 40 splendid felines, from American shorthair to exotic types. 44 plates. Captions. 48pp. 8¼ × 11.　　24011-8 Pa. $2.25

THE TALE OF PETER RABBIT, Beatrix Potter. The inimitable Peter's terrifying adventure in Mr. McGregor's garden, with all 27 wonderful, full-color Potter illustrations. 55pp. 4¼ × 5½. (Available in U.S. only)　　22827-4 Pa. $1.75

BASIC ELECTRICITY, U.S. Bureau of Naval Personnel. Batteries, circuits, conductors, AC and DC, inductance and capacitance, generators, motors, trans-formers, amplifiers, etc. 349 illustrations. 448pp. 6½ × 9¼.　　20973-3 Pa. $7.95

THE BOOK OF WOOD CARVING, Charles Marshall Sayers. Still finest book for beginning student. Fundamentals, technique; gives 34 designs, over 34 projects for panels, bookends, mirrors, etc. 33 photos. 118pp. 7¾ × 10⅝. 23654-4 Pa. $3.95

CARVING COUNTRY CHARACTERS, Bill Higginbotham. Expert advice for beginning, advanced carvers on materials, techniques for creating 18 projects—mirthful panorama of American characters. 105 illustrations. 80pp. 8⅜ × 11. 24135-1 Pa. $2.50

300 ART NOUVEAU DESIGNS AND MOTIFS IN FULL COLOR, C.B. Grafton. 44 full-page plates display swirling lines and muted colors typical of Art Nouveau. Borders, frames, panels, cartouches, dingbats, etc. 48pp. 9⅜ × 12¼. 24354-0 Pa. $6.95

SELF-WORKING CARD TRICKS, Karl Fulves. Editor of *Pallbearer* offers 72 tricks that work automatically through nature of card deck. No sleight of hand needed. Often spectacular. 42 illustrations. 113pp. 5⅜ × 8½. 23334-0 Pa. $3.50

CUT AND ASSEMBLE A WESTERN FRONTIER TOWN, Edmund V. Gillon, Jr. Ten authentic full-color buildings on heavy cardboard stock in H-O scale. Sheriff's Office and Jail, Saloon, Wells Fargo, Opera House, others. 48pp. 9¼ × 12¼. 23736-2 Pa. $3.95

CUT AND ASSEMBLE AN EARLY NEW ENGLAND VILLAGE, Edmund V. Gillon, Jr. Printed in full color on heavy cardboard stock. 12 authentic buildings in H-O scale: Adams home in Quincy, Mass., Oliver Wight house in Sturbridge, smithy, store, church, others. 48pp. 9¼ × 12¼. 23536-X Pa. $4.95

THE TALE OF TWO BAD MICE, Beatrix Potter. Tom Thumb and Hunca Munca squeeze out of their hole and go exploring. 27 full-color Potter illustrations. 59pp. 4¼ × 5½. (Available in U.S. only) 23065-1 Pa. $1.75

CARVING FIGURE CARICATURES IN THE OZARK STYLE, Harold L. Enlow. Instructions and illustrations for ten delightful projects, plus general carving instructions. 22 drawings and 47 photographs altogether. 39pp. 8⅜ × 11. 23151-8 Pa. $2.50

A TREASURY OF FLOWER DESIGNS FOR ARTISTS, EMBROIDERERS AND CRAFTSMEN, Susan Gaber. 100 garden favorites lushly rendered by artist for artists, craftsmen, needleworkers. Many form frames, borders. 80pp. 8¼ × 11. 24096-7 Pa. $3.50

CUT & ASSEMBLE A TOY THEATER/THE NUTCRACKER BALLET, Tom Tierney. Model of a complete, full-color production of Tchaikovsky's classic. 6 backdrops, dozens of characters, familiar dance sequences. 32pp. 9⅜ × 12¼. 24194-7 Pa. $4.50

ANIMALS: 1,419 COPYRIGHT-FREE ILLUSTRATIONS OF MAMMALS, BIRDS, FISH, INSECTS, ETC., edited by Jim Harter. Clear wood engravings present, in extremely lifelike poses, over 1,000 species of animals. 284pp. 9 × 12. 23766-4 Pa. $9.95

MORE HAND SHADOWS, Henry Bursill. For those at their 'finger ends," 16 more effects—Shakespeare, a hare, a squirrel, Mr. Punch, and twelve more—each explained by a full-page illustration. Considerable period charm. 30pp. 6½ × 9¼. 21384-6 Pa. $1.95

TOLL HOUSE TRIED AND TRUE RECIPES, Ruth Graves Wakefield. Popovers, veal and ham loaf, baked beans, much more from the famous Mass. restaurant. Nearly 700 recipes. 376pp. 5⅜ × 8½. 23560-2 Pa. $4.95

FAVORITE CHRISTMAS CAROLS, selected and arranged by Charles J.F. Cofone. Title, music, first verse and refrain of 34 traditional carols in handsome calligraphy; also subsequent verses and other information in type. 79pp. 8⅜ × 11. 20445-6 Pa. $3.50

CAMERA WORK: A PICTORIAL GUIDE, Alfred Stieglitz. All 559 illustrations from most important periodical in history of art photography. Reduced in size but still clear, in strict chronological order, with complete captions. 176pp. 8⅜ × 11¼. 23591-2 Pa. $6.95

FAVORITE SONGS OF THE NINETIES, edited by Robert Fremont. 88 favorites: "Ta-Ra-Ra-Boom-De-Aye," "The Band Played On," "Bird in a Gilded Cage," etc. 401pp. 9 × 12. 21536-9 Pa. $12.95

STRING FIGURES AND HOW TO MAKE THEM, Caroline F. Jayne. Fullest, clearest instructions on string figures from around world: Eskimo, Navajo, Lapp, Europe, more. Cat's cradle, moving spear, lightning, stars. 950 illustrations. 407pp. 5⅜ × 8½. 20152-X Pa. $5.95

LIFE IN ANCIENT EGYPT, Adolf Erman. Detailed older account, with much not in more recent books: domestic life, religion, magic, medicine, commerce, and whatever else needed for complete picture. Many illustrations. 597pp. 5⅜ × 8½. 22632-8 Pa. $7.95

ANCIENT EGYPT: ITS CULTURE AND HISTORY, J.E. Manchip White. From pre-dynastics through Ptolemies: society, history, political structure, religion, daily life, literature, cultural heritage. 48 plates. 217pp. 5⅜ × 8½. (EBE) 22548-8 Pa. $4.95

KEPT IN THE DARK, Anthony Trollope. Unusual short novel about Victorian morality and abnormal psychology by the great English author. Probably the first American publication. Frontispiece by Sir John Millais. 92pp. 6½ × 9¼. 23609-9 Pa. $2.95

MAN AND WIFE, Wilkie Collins. Nineteenth-century master launches an attack on out-moded Scottish marital laws and Victorian cult of athleticism. Artfully plotted. 35 illustrations. 239pp. 6⅛ × 9¼. 24451-2 Pa. $5.95

RELATIVITY AND COMMON SENSE, Herman Bondi. Radically reoriented presentation of Einstein's Special Theory and one of most valuable popular accounts available. 60 illustrations. 177pp. 5⅜ × 8. (EUK) 24021-5 Pa. $3.95

THE EGYPTIAN BOOK OF THE DEAD, E.A. Wallis Budge. Complete reproduction of Ani's papyrus, finest ever found. Full hieroglyphic text, interlinear transliteration, word-for-word translation, smooth translation. 533pp. 6½ × 9¼. (USO) 21866-X Pa. $8.95

COUNTRY AND SUBURBAN HOMES OF THE PRAIRIE SCHOOL PERIOD, H.V. von Holst. Over 400 photographs floor plans, elevations, detailed drawings (exteriors and interiors) for over 100 structures. Text. Important primary source. 128pp. 8⅜ × 11¼. 24373-7 Pa. $5.95

READY-TO-USE BORDERS, Ted Menten. Both traditional and unusual interchangeable borders in a tremendous array of sizes, shapes, and styles. 32 plates. 64pp. 8¼ × 11. 23782-6 Pa. $3.50

THE WHOLE CRAFT OF SPINNING, Carol Kroll. Preparing fiber, drop spindle, treadle wheel, other fibers, more. Highly creative, yet simple. 43 illustrations. 48pp. 8¼ × 11. 23968-3 Pa. $2.50

HIDDEN PICTURE PUZZLE COLORING BOOK, Anna Pomaska. 31 delightful pictures to color with dozens of objects, people and animals hidden away to find. Captions. Solutions. 48pp. 8¼ × 11. 23909-8 Pa. $2.25

QUILTING WITH STRIPS AND STRINGS, H.W. Rose. Quickest, easiest way to turn left-over fabric into handsome quilt. 46 patchwork quilts; 31 full-size templates. 48pp. 8¼ × 11. 24357-5 Pa. $3.25

NATURAL DYES AND HOME DYEING, Rita J. Adrosko. Over 135 specific recipes from historical sources for cotton, wool, other fabrics. Genuine premodern handicrafts. 12 illustrations. 160pp. 5⅜ × 8½. 22688-3 Pa. $2.95

CARVING REALISTIC BIRDS, H.D. Green. Full-sized patterns, step-by-step instructions for robins, jays, cardinals, finches, etc. 97 illustrations. 80pp. 8¼ × 11. 23484-3 Pa. $3.00

GEOMETRY, RELATIVITY AND THE FOURTH DIMENSION, Rudolf Rucker. Exposition of fourth dimension, concepts of relativity as Flatland characters continue adventures. Popular, easily followed yet accurate, profound. 141 illustrations. 133pp. 5⅜ × 8½. 23400-2 Pa. $3.00

READY-TO-USE SMALL FRAMES AND BORDERS, Carol B. Grafton. Graphic message? Frame it graphically with 373 new frames and borders in many styles: Art Nouveau, Art Deco, Op Art. 64pp. 8¼ × 11. 24375-3 Pa. $3.50

CELTIC ART: THE METHODS OF CONSTRUCTION, George Bain. Simple geometric techniques for making Celtic interlacements, spirals, Kellstype initials, animals, humans, etc. Over 500 illustrations. 160pp. 9 × 12. (Available in U.S. only) 22923-8 Pa. $6.00

THE TALE OF TOM KITTEN, Beatrix Potter. Exciting text and all 27 vivid, full-color illustrations to charming tale of naughty little Tom getting into mischief again. 58pp. 4¼ × 5½. (USO) 24502-0 Pa. $1.75

WOODEN PUZZLE TOYS, Ed Sibbett, Jr. Transfer patterns and instructions for 24 easy-to-do projects: fish, butterflies, cats, acrobats, Humpty Dumpty, 19 others. 48pp. 8¼ × 11. 23713-3 Pa. $2.50

MY FAMILY TREE WORKBOOK, Rosemary A. Chorzempa. Enjoyable, easy-to-use introduction to genealogy designed specially for children. Data pages plus text. Instructive, educational, valuable. 64pp. 8¼ × 11. 24229-3 Pa. $2.50

Prices subject to change without notice.

Available at your book dealer or write for free catalog to Dept. GI, Dover Publications, Inc., 31 East 2nd St. Mineola, N.Y. 11501. Dover publishes more than 175 books each year on science, elementary and advanced mathematics, biology, music, art, literary history, social sciences and other areas.